D1601213

LIBEL LAW
AND THE PRESS

LIBEL LAW
AND THE PRESS

Myth and Reality

Randall P. Bezanson
Gilbert Cranberg
John Soloski

THE FREE PRESS
A Division of Macmillan, Inc.
NEW YORK
Collier Macmillan Publishers
LONDON

The Free Press
A Division of Macmillan, Inc.
866 Third Avenue, New York, N. Y. 10022

Collier Macmillan Canada, Inc.

Printed in the United States of America

printing number
1   2   3   4   5   6   7   8   9   10

Library of Congress Cataloging-in-Publication Data

Bezanson, Randall P.
    Libel law and the press.

    1. Libel and slander—United States. 2. Press law—
United States.   3. Mass media—Law and legislation—
United States.   I. Cranberg, Gilbert.   II. Soloski,
John.   III. Title.
KF1266.B49   1987   346.7303′4   86–33579
ISBN 0–02–905870–8   347.30634

Contents

Acknowledgments

This book represents one part of the Iowa Libel Research Project. The objective of the larger project is to explore the feasibility of non-litigation processes through which libel disputes might be resolved. In order to do so, we had to understand the anatomy of the libel dispute from its inception to its conclusion, and the only way to do so was to collect and analyze data on actual disputes and the parties to them. This book represents a distillation of much of that data, as well as our analysis of it.

The material for this book was compiled over many months by many people. It could not have been assembled without financial support from the John and Mary R. Markle Foundation and financial as well as other help from the University of Iowa. We are indebted especially to Deborah Wadsworth, who served as program officer at the Foundation, and to Duane C. Spriestersbach, Vice-President for Research and Educational Development at the University, for helping make the assistance possible.

Libel is one of the points where law and journalism intersect. The Iowa Libel Research Project reflects the interdisciplinary character of the subject. Faculty, staff, and students from the University's College of Law and School of Journalism and Mass Communication made major contributions of time, energy, and talent to the project. Our gratitude for a variety of contributions goes to: Thomas H. Boyd, Jan Christie, Dorsey D. Ellis, Jr., Estella Vallejo Fickel, Terry Francisco, Lisa McLaughlin, George W. Oelschlaeger, Timothy J. Sear, William S. Simmer, Linda D. Smith, Kenneth Starck, Christopher D. Thomas, Alan I. Widiss, and William Zima. Our special thanks go to Diana L. DeWalle, whose administrative support and secretarial assistance were of immeasurable value. Our special thanks, also, to Mark L. Hill, whose great contributions have been felt from the outset of the Iowa Libel Research Project.

The study was conceived and organized in 1982. Data-gathering began in early 1983 and continued through 1985. The material reported herein reflects information as it was obtained from interviews and records. We have not attempted to account for later changes in such things as employment status, job titles, or news organization practices.

1

INTRODUCTION

A PERSON'S GOOD NAME is priceless. So, too, is free expression. The law of libel is the attempt to reconcile both values. In this book we will explore the anatomy of the libel system in an effort to determine whether the attempt succeeds in the context of libel suits against the media.

Libel law has had a long and tortuous history. Libel is a legal wrong, or tort, that is largely judge-made (or common law) in origin, on the basis of which persons whose reputations have been harmed by published statements about them can recover money damages. At common law, the truth or falsity of the offending statements were not, strictly speaking, decisive, as the common law action could be based on disparaging statements that were not disprovable.[1] Falsity of the damaging statement, to the extent relevant, was presumed; if truth of the statement would prevent liability, it was usually the publisher's duty to prove it.

Prior to the recently-developed constitutional privileges, the libel plaintiffs' success at common law was not dependent on any proof of fault or unreasonable publication by the publisher of the statement. If publication, defamation (reputational disparagement), and injury could be shown, the publisher was strictly liable, even if there was an honest mistake or understandable oversight. Because of the rather onerous impact of the rule of strict liability, special protection was granted to the publisher in certain settings in the form of common law privileges. These privileges generally required that, to succeed, the plaintiff had to overcome them by showing that the publisher acted out of ill will or beyond the scope of the privilege. The privileges were designed to protect expression in settings of special

1

importance, such as statements drawn from public records, opinions expressed about public issues, and confidential communications in the employment setting.[2] While many in number, the privileges were usually strictly limited in scope, and did not disguise the fundamental compensatory purposes of the libel tort. At common law, what was important was whether someone was hurt, not who they were or how or why they were hurt.

While the common law libel tort continues to exist today, it has been dramatically altered by an additional, broadly-applicable layer of privileges tied to the First Amendment. These privileges, first announced in the famous 1964 Supreme Court decision in *New York Times v. Sullivan*,[3] are based on the principle that "debate on public issues should be uninhibited, robust, and wide-open."[4] Free and uninhibited expression must extend to matters of self-government and to "issues about which information is needed or appropriate to enable the members of society to cope with the exigencies of their period."[5] In the context of libel, according to the Supreme Court, the command of free and robust expression requires a rule which protects some falsity in order to assure that truth is neither punished nor deterred. The innocent mistake, therefore, should not give rise to liability, lest publishers be inhibited from publishing facts as they know them for fear of disabling damage awards in libel suits.

This view of the First Amendment speech and press guarantees has yielded a complex set of *constitutional* privileges applicable to virtually all libel suits. In order to protect the innocent mistake from liability, a plaintiff in any libel suit against the media, or any suit that does not involve a limited circulation, special purpose publication,[6] must not only prove the common law elements of publication, defamation, and injury, but must also prove that a false statement was published negligently.[7]

A second and higher level of privilege applies if the person suing for libel is a public figure—a public office holder or private person whose public position or private activity is associated with a controversial or public issue to which the allegedly libelous statement relates.[8] Such plaintiffs must prove that the publisher (or reporter, or editor) knew that the offending statement was false and published nevertheless, or *actually* entertained serious doubts about its truth and published recklessly in light of that knowledge.[9] This privilege—called the actual malice privilege—focuses exclusively on the publisher's state of mind (what was believed about truth).

The intricacies of the complex system of constitutional negligence and actual malice privileges will be explored at various points in this book. For our present introductory purposes, two general points should be made. First, both constitutional privileges are concerned with what was known about the truth or falsity of a statement, and the decisions flowing from that knowledge, *at the time of publication*. The actual truth or falsity of the statement, and the harm it may have inflicted, are distinct issues having no necessary relevance to the privilege question.[10] Second, the privileges apply broadly to virtually all media defamation suits, requiring plaintiffs in all such cases to prove *fault* on the publisher's part. The suit based on a damaging, but faultless, libel cannot legally succeed. Put differently, because of the constitutional privileges, the central question in media libel suits is not (as at common law) whether someone was hurt, but rather who they were and how and why they were hurt.

It should be apparent from this description of today's libel law that the libel tort has experienced profound change in the past 23 years. So, too, has the reconciliation between the values of a person's good name and free expression. Our chief focus is the libel action against the media. Our method is to explore libel suits from the perspectives of the parties to the actions. Our findings will not hearten those who support current approaches to the libel problem.

We found a legal system whose underlying assumptions about libel— that libel suits provide a reasonable opportunity to repair damage to reputation, that money is necessary to undo the harm to libel victims, that the constitutional privileges protect the press—bear little relationship to the real world of plaintiffs and media defendants.

Dissatisfaction with the system increases daily. Those who bring suit confront a frustrating obstacle course, and they almost always lose. "The few plaintiffs who succeed," points out media lawyer Robert Sack, "resemble the remnants of an army platoon caught in an enemy crossfire. Their awards stand witness to their good luck, not to their virtue, their skill, or the justice of their cause. It is difficult to perceive the law of defamation, in this light, as a real 'system' for protection of reputation at all."[11]

No less unhappy are members of the press, who stand in perpetual fear of being sued. Their costs when sued frequently make it difficult to distinguish the winners from the losers. The system puts at the greatest disadvantage the least advantaged segments of the press. As Professor David Anderson of the University of Texas observed, those most heavily penalized by suits and the threat of suits "are the smaller, newer, and less conventional media voices" who, to survive, must attract attention by tackling subjects not being covered by the established media. "In short, they must take risks. On the other hand, because of their financial insecurity, a libel suit, even though ultimately unsuccessful, would probably be fatal."[12] To the extent that dread of libel litigation produces unwarranted self-censorship, society as a whole is the ultimate victim of libel law.

Given the problems with the system for resolving libel disputes, it seemed to us important to explore the feasibility of developing non-litigation alternatives. It became evident, however, that any consideration of alternatives requires a fuller understanding of the existing system. Of special importance to an understanding of the libel system are the attitudes and actions of the actors in the system. We undertook, therefore, a detailed analysis of the libel litigation process as a whole, from the appearance of the allegedly libelous story, through discussions between plaintiff and attorney, to the outcome of the case. We drew upon a broad range of sources, including libel and privacy cases decided between 1974 and 1984, interviews with libel plaintiffs, media defendants, and their lawyers, in-depth interviews at media organizations, a survey of newspapers, and information drawn from the claim files of a major media libel insurer. [13] We were interested particularly in examining why plaintiffs sue, and what, if anything, the media can do to prevent suit. We also wanted to know how plaintiffs feel about the disputed story, the media, and their experience with litigation, as well as the outlook and behavior of plaintiffs and the press.

The chapters that follow describe in depth what we did and what we found. They disclose a situation in greater disarray than had been suspected. We found:

Plaintiffs who claim primarily non-financial harm but a legal system geared to produce money damages.

Plaintiffs who experience economic hardship but a set of legal rules which permits rare and seemingly arbitrary damage awards and produces tremendous frustration.

Plaintiffs who sue to "get even" and a legal system whose rules are designed to discourage them but instead encourage them.

Plaintiffs whose complaint about the alleged libel is chiefly that it was false, and who say they sue to restore reputation by setting the record straight, but who become enmeshed in a legal process that seldom addresses the issue of falsity.

A legal process so protracted that in cases where the question of falsity is addressed the resolution comes long after the time when it can help to restore reputation.

A system that encourages litigation by those who lack any other formal response, and by those for whom the truth would be harmful knowing as they do that truth seldom is decided.

A system that puts the press on trial for the *way* it does a story instead of for the intrinsic accuracy of the story, and that makes judges the ultimate arbiters of editorial judgment and press responsibility.

Privileges intended to protect the press against money damages but which promote invasion of the newsroom even when money does not appear to be an overriding objective of most plaintiffs.

- Privileges intended to safeguard free expression, but which also threaten it by fostering suits that should not be fostered, by enforcing responsibility at the expense of freedom, and by foreclosing truth in the interests of protecting falsity.
- Plaintiffs as a group who are not especially litigious and who turn initially to the media for redress rather than to a lawyer or to the legal system, but a press both poorly organized to deal with reader complaints and predisposed to react in ways that antagonize complainants.
- Plaintiffs who overwhelmingly express interest in resolving disputes with the press by non-litigation methods but face an almost total absence of such methods.

We began our inquiry with a question: Is it possible to find a solution to libel disputes outside the legal system? The answer depends in large measure on the design of alternatives and how they would function in actual disputes diverted from the courts. No voluntary system of alternatives could work, of course, without the participation of both parties. The press almost certainly would not be willing to participate in an alternative to libel litigation if the alternative would have as an objective the award of money damages. For all of the legal system's shortcomings from the media's vantage point, it produces victory for the press at least 90 percent of the time. While the victories are costly and sometimes Pyrrhic, few if any members of the media would want to forego the protections they enjoy in court if money were at stake in an alternative procedure with a less certain outcome. The finding that many libel plaintiffs appear to be interested primarily in some form of non-monetary vindication or reputational repair has important implications for the development of non-legal dispute-resolution procedures as well as for libel law.

More important, the apparent interest by plaintiffs in having the record set straight suggests the existence of significant common ground on the divisive libel issue. The press as a whole, and the public at large, both place high value on the dissemination of accurate information and on having the record corrected when it is inaccurate. Indeed, a consensus is emerging that ways need to be found to focus on the issue of truth in libel disputes. That is also among our conclusions. These conclusions, the findings from which they are drawn, and how they were obtained, are the subject of the pages that follow.

2

WHO SUES FOR LIBEL?

PLAINTIFFS

Who are the people who sue the media for libel? Do libel plaintiffs share any characteristics, or are libel plaintiffs just a mix of people who have nothing in common other than having filed a libel suit? Is it possible to draw a picture of the typical libel plaintiff? Despite the coverage libel suits receive in the popular media and the amount of time spent discussing the problem at professional meetings, it is surprising how little we know about libel plaintiffs. To date, Marc A. Franklin's studies of libel cases represent the most thorough examination of plaintiffs, but he was limited to information about plaintiffs that was available in the reported decisions. [1]

The purpose of this chapter is to examine the people who sue for libel. A large amount of demographic data was obtained from a survey of 164 plaintiffs who sued the media for libel. [2] Additional data were obtained from: (1) an analysis of virtually all reported defamation and privacy cases decided between 1974 and 1984; (2) a survey of 61 media defendants who were sued by the libel plaintiffs we interviewed; and (3) in-depth interviews conducted at six Midwestern newspapers. In the following section, we will outline much of the basic demographic information upon which our analysis in later chapters will be built.

Demographics of Libel Plaintiffs

The lack of any systematic studies of plaintiffs involved in civil cases makes it difficult to ascertain whether libel plaintiffs differ from plaintiffs

6

involved in other types of civil cases. One study that did examine the types of plaintiffs in civil cases was undertaken by Craig Wanner, who examined the court records of 7,800 randomly-selected civil cases from courts in Baltimore, Cleveland, and Milwaukee.[3] Wanner found that organizations were plaintiffs in about half of the cases, individuals were the plaintiffs in about 40 percent, and the remaining 10 percent were brought by various government agencies. If we consider Wanner's findings to be more or less representative of civil cases in the United States,[4] we find that libel plaintiffs are very different. For libel cases decided between 1974 and 1984, individuals were the plaintiffs in 89.6 percent of all libel cases, and organizations were plaintiffs in the remainder.[5] This 9-to-1 ratio of individuals to organizations is true for libel cases involving media as well as non-media defendants.

In our survey of 164 libel plaintiffs, we found that males were the plaintiffs in 88.5 percent of the cases brought by individuals, and females were the plaintiffs in 11.5 percent of the cases. These results are nearly identical to those reported by Franklin in his study of media and non-media defendants in libel cases.[6] In contrast, Wanner found that in 3,029 civil suits brought by individuals, males were the plaintiffs in 51.4 percent of the cases and females the plaintiffs in 37 percent.[7]

The reason for the large percentage of male plaintiffs in libel suits can be explained by the types of jobs held by libel plaintiffs. Despite increases in the number of women who hold public office and who work as professionals, males dominate these fields. And, as we shall see, individuals who hold public office or who work as professionals are more likely to be the subject of news stories and are more likely to have opportunities to sue the media for libel.

Table 2–1 summarizes an array of demographic information collected from the plaintiffs interviewed. Most libel plaintiffs are between the ages of 36 and 65. We found that only about 13 percent of the plaintiffs were under 36 years of age, and about 14 percent were over 65. About three-quarters of the plaintiffs were married, 15.5 percent were single, and 7.7 percent were divorced. Nearly 54 percent are college graduates, and over a third of them have graduate or professional degrees. Over 70 percent reported that they have annual household incomes of more than $25,000, and about 39 percent reported annual incomes of more than $50,000.

Plaintiffs who sue the media for libel are long-established members of their communities. Over 78 percent of the libel plaintiffs we interviewed had lived in their communities for more than 10 years, and well over a third had lived in their communities more than 34 years. In fact, almost a third (31 percent) of the libel plaintiffs were life-long residents of their communities.

TABLE 2-1   Demographics of Libel Plaintiffs*

Age:	
35 and under	19 (13.2%)
36 to 50	61 (42.4%)
51 to 65	44 (30.6%)
Over 65	20 (13.9%)
Marital status:	
Single	22 (15.5%)
Married	109 (76.8%)
Divorced	11 (7.7%)
Education:	
High school graduate or less	33 (23.1%)
Some college	33 (23.1%)
College graduate	22 (15.4%)
Some graduate school	7 (4.9%)
Graduate or professional degree	48 (33.6%)
Household income:	
Under $15,000	17 (13.4%)
$15,000–$25,000	21 (16.5%)
$25,000–$50,000	39 (30.7%)
Over $50,000	50 (39.4%)
Length of time lived in community:	
Less than 10 years	31 (21.8%)
10–20 years	26 (18.3%)
20–34 years	34 (23.9%)
Over 34 years	51 (35.9%)

*The numbers in the table do not add to 164 because some plaintiffs declined to answer certain questions and some questions did not pertain to all plaintiffs.

We also obtained information on the extent of the plaintiffs' involvement in their communities. Over 40 percent of the plaintiffs interviewed described themselves as being highly visible in their communities, and another 36 percent said that they had above-average community visibility. [8] Only about 14 percent of the libel plaintiffs said that they had below-average community visibility. As would be expected, the high level of community visibility is related to the types of jobs the plaintiffs held at the time the alleged libel occurred. [9] The largest percentage of libel plaintiffs (29.7 percent) were working as public employees when the allegedly libelous story appeared. About 20 percent of the plaintiffs held elected office or had been candidates for office when the alleged libel occurred. Twenty-four percent of libel plaintiffs were working as professionals when the alleged libel appeared; 16.7 percent were business proprietors or managers; and 10.2 percent held white-collar positions. These and related characteristics will be explored in depth in later chapters.

Plaintiffs' Legal Status

For purposes of constitutional privilege, plaintiffs are categorized by courts into two general categories: public plaintiffs and private plaintiffs. Each of these categories, in turn, can be subdivided. The public plaintiffs consist of public officials, public figures, and public-figure corporations (or entities). Private plaintiffs consist of private individuals and private corporations (or entities).

As discussed in more depth in Chapter 6, public officials are those plaintiffs who hold public office, whose public responsibilities are related to the alleged libel, and who, by virtue of their position, will influence the resolution of public issues related to the alleged libel. Public figures are persons who, by virtue of widespread fame or notoriety or through their voluntary efforts, attempt to influence the resolution of public issues related to the subject of the alleged libel. Public-figure corporations (or entities) are those non-individual plaintiffs who satisfy the same criteria applicable to public figures. Private plaintiffs, both individual and corporate, consist of all plaintiffs not qualifying as public officials or public figures, either because they hold no office or have no general notoriety, or because the allegedly defamatory statement bears no relationship to their public office or position of public influence. Private plaintiffs must establish negligence on the part of the publisher in order to succeed in a defamation action against a media defendant.[10] In actions against non-media defendants, the constitutional rules seem to permit strict liability—recovery upon a showing of defamation and harm, in the absence of truth as a defense—although a significant number of states require a showing of negligence in these cases as well.

Libel law requires public officials and public figures to show that the information published about them was not only defamatory but also that it was published with actual malice, making the determination of a libel plaintiff's legal status a central issue in defamation cases. When we examined the main legal issues adjudicated in libel cases we found that the determination of plaintiffs' legal status was the main legal issue adjudicated in about 15 percent of the media defamation cases decided between 1974 and 1984, and was a prominent issue in another 30 percent of the cases. About 88 percent of the media defamation cases decided between 1974 and 1984 focused on constitution privilege issues related to plaintiffs' legal status.[11]

Since plaintiffs' legal status is critical in defamation cases, we were interested in exploring the demographic relationship between plaintiffs who were determined by the courts to be public officials or public figures, and private individuals. The categories of public figures and public officials are analytically similar, the issue in either case being the degree of influence the person exerts, by virtue of public office, voluntary action, or notoriety, on the discussion and resolution of a public controversy with respect to which the alleged libel was published. For both groups, the same constitutional standards of malice apply, although the two groups include very dissimilar types of individuals. [12] As Frederick Schauer notes, "Reggie Jackson, Michael Jackson, and Leonard Bernstein are constrained in bringing defamation actions by the same rules that constrain Ronald Reagan, Jesse Helms, and Harold Washington."[13] Since the analytical distinction between public officials and public figures has been eroded as a result of *Gertz v. Welch*,[14] in most of our discussions of the data we will combine public figures and public officials into one category labeled "public plaintiffs." However, we will report the data for both groups in the tables. For consistency, we will refer to private individuals as "private plaintiffs."

Public plaintiffs accounted for 56.3 percent of the libel cases involving media defendants that were decided between 1974 and 1984.[15] Private plaintiffs brought 33 percent of the libel suits against the media. Private-figure corporations were the plaintiffs in 6 percent of the cases, and public-figure corporations were the plaintiffs in 4.6 percent of the cases. Thus more than 60 percent of libel cases involving the media are brought by individuals or corporations who must prove that the material was published with actual malice.

Based on data obtained from the plaintiff interviews, public plaintiffs tend to be better educated than private plaintiffs.[16] Approximately 58 percent of the public plaintiffs are college graduates, while 43 percent of the private plaintiffs graduated from college. About 38 percent of the public plaintiffs, and 23 percent of the private individuals, have graduate or professional degrees. As one would expect, the educational level of libel plaintiffs is related to employment.[17]

Not surprisingly, plaintiffs' legal status is closely related to their employment.[18] Nearly 91 percent of the plaintiffs who were public employees were determined to be public plaintiffs by the courts, and nearly all of the plaintiffs who held elected office or who had been candidates for office were determined to be public plaintiffs. About 73 percent of libel plaintiffs who worked as professionals were determined by the courts to be public plaintiffs. The only employment categories in which plaintiffs were likely to be classified as private plaintiffs were white-collar employees and owners and managers of businesses. Sixty percent of the white-collar employees were determined to be private plaintiffs by the courts, and about 41 percent of the business owners and managers were determined to be private plaintiffs.

The high percentage of public plaintiffs in all employment categories can be explained, in part, by the fact that people who sue for libel tend to be in the public eye and likely would be subjects of stories in the media. As would be expected, public plaintiffs are very visible within their communities.[19] Forty-nine percent of them reported that they have very high community visibility, and another 38 percent said that they have above-average community visibility. Even the private plaintiffs are very visible in their communities. Twenty-seven percent of them reported that they have very high community visibility, and another 33 percent said that they have above-average community visibility. Only 23 percent of the private plaintiffs reported that they have below-average community visibility.

The high degree of community visibility of libel plaintiffs is also related to the jobs they held at the time of the alleged libel.[20] As expected, all of the plaintiffs who held elected office or who had been candidates for office at the time of the alleged libel had above-average community visibility.[21] Seventy-eight percent of the public employees had above-average community visibility, and about 74 percent of the professionals were above average in community visibility. Libel plaintiffs in business likewise were very visible. Nearly 82 percent of the business owners or managers had above-average community visibility. Although white-collar employees reported the lowest degree of community visibility, 69 percent of these plaintiffs said they had average or above-average visibility.

The high degree of community visibility exhibited by many libel plaintiffs helps to explain why they were determined to be public plaintiffs. These plaintiffs, through their own actions, have achieved considerable fame and notoriety within their communities and would be likely subjects of stories in the media. Many of the plaintiffs in all employment categories had held public office, either before or during the time the alleged libel appeared, or had been candidates for office.[22] Nearly a third of the plaintiffs who were working as professionals had held public office either before or during the time the alleged libel occurred. About a fifth (23 percent) of the white-collar employees had held public office either before or during the time of the alleged libel, and nearly a fifth of the business owners and managers reported that they had held public office either before or during the time of the alleged libel. In all, over 43 percent of the plaintiffs interviewed reported that they had held public office either before or during the time of the alleged libel or had been candidates for office when the alleged libel occurred.

However, a high degree of community visibility does not fully explain why plaintiffs are determined to be public plaintiffs. In general, there are two ways for an individual to become a public figure.[23] A plaintiff may achieve such a high degree of community visibility and fame that he will be a public figure for all purposes and contexts. However, it is more likely that a plaintiff will become a public figure by injecting himself into a particular controversy, or, by virtue of the plaintiff's public position, be drawn into a public discussion of a controversial issue. For public plaintiffs, then, it is the relationship between their public activities and the content of the alleged libel that determines their legal status.

The Content of the Alleged Libel

The only study that has systematically examined the types of charges made in the allegedly libelous stories is Franklin's study of libel suits involving media defendants.[24] Franklin examined the case decisions to determine what the media had said about the plaintiffs. He found that three types of charges predominated in 79 percent of the cases.[25] Thirty-one percent of the cases concerned charges of criminal activity, and 31 percent involved charges of the plaintiffs' moral failing. Charges of business or professional incompetence accounted for another 17 percent of the cases.[26]

In our study of defamation cases decided between 1974 and 1984, each case was classified according to the focus of the allegedly libelous statement, based on reading the case decision.[27] In half of the defamation cases between 1974 and 1984 involving either media or non-media defendants, the alleged libel focused on the plaintiffs' business or trade activities.[28] In about 17 percent of the cases, the alleged libel dealt with the plaintiffs' moral conduct, and in 28 percent of the cases the libel dealt with both the plaintiffs' business or trade activities and with their moral conduct. In the remaining 4 percent of the cases the research assistants were unable to agree on the focus of the libel. This breakdown of the content of the alleged libel is the same for media defendants and non-media defendants.[29]

Additional information about libel cases involving media defendants is provided by a comparison of the focus of the alleged libel with plaintiffs' legal status.[30] Plaintiffs who are public plaintiffs almost always sue over stories that deal with their professional or trade activities. Specifically, in 91.2 percent of the media defamation cases decided between 1974 and 1984 involving public plaintiffs, the alleged libel dealt in some way with their professional or trade activities. However, for plaintiffs who are private plaintiffs, the focus of the alleged libel was nearly evenly divided between moral conduct and professional or trade activities.

To allow for a more detailed analysis of the content of the alleged libel, we asked the plaintiffs interviewed about the content of the story that resulted in their libel suit (Table 2–2). About 44 percent of the plaintiffs said

TABLE 2–2   Focus of the Alleged Libel

Personal or private activity	15 (9.3%)
Business or professional activity	50 (30.9%)
Public or political activity	72 (44.4%)
Criminal activity	25 (15.4%)

that the alleged libel dealt with their public or political activities; 30.9 percent said the libel concerned their business or professional activities; 15.4 percent said the libel focused on their allegedly criminal activities; and 9.3 percent said the libel dealt with their personal or private activities.

Comparing the content of the alleged libel with the plaintiffs' legal status, we find that 59.3 percent of the public plaintiffs sued over stories that dealt with their public or political activities, and 25.3 percent sued over stories that dealt with their business or professional activities (Table 2–3). The trend in the data is the same for public figures and public officials. The majority of plaintiffs in both groups sued over stories that dealt with their public or political activities. Over three-quarters of public plaintiffs who held public office either before or at the time the alleged libel occurred sued over stories that dealt with their public or political activities.[31] These data are consistent with the legal theory behind the determination of legal status of libel plaintiffs. The plaintiffs who were determined to be public plaintiffs were not only highly visible within their communities, but the content of the alleged libel focused on their public activities. Private plaintiffs, on the other hand, tended to sue over stories that dealt with their alleged criminal activities (30 percent) or with their business or professional activities (26.7 percent).

Table 2–4 compares the content of the alleged libel with plaintiffs' employment. Not surprisingly, nearly 93 percent of the plaintiffs who were

TABLE 2–3   Plaintiffs' Legal Status Compared with the Focus of the Alleged Libel

	Focus of the Alleged Libel			
	Personal or private activities	*Business or professional activities*	*Public or political activities*	*Criminal activities*
Public figure	1 (2.2%)	13 (28.3%)	25 (54.3%)	7 (15.2%)
Public official	1 (2.2%)	10 (22.2%)	29 (64.4%)	5 (11.1%)
Private figure	7 (23.3%)	8 (26.7%)	6 (20.0%)	9 (30.0%)
		p. < .001		

TABLE 2–4   Plaintiffs' Employment Compared with the Focus of the Alleged Libel

	Focus of the Alleged Libel			
	Personal or private activities	Business or professional activities	Public or political activities	Criminal activities
Elected official or candidate for office	0	0	25 (92.6%)	2 (7.4%)
White-collar employee	2 (15.4%)	6 (46.2%)	2 (15.4%)	3 (23.1%)
Public employee	4 (9.8%)	6 (14.6%)	23 (56.1%)	8 (19.5%)
Business owner or manager	2 (8.7%)	14 (60.9%)	5 (21.7%)	2 (8.7%)
Professional	2 (6.1%)	12 (36.4%)	12 (36.4%)	7 (21.1%)
		$p. < .001$		

elected officials or had been candidates for office said that they sued over a story that dealt with their public or political activities. Business owners or managers and white-collar employees tended to sue over stories that focused on their business or professional activities. Public employees sued over stories that dealt with their public or political activities. Only for plaintiffs who were professionals is there a split among content categories of the alleged libel. These plaintiffs said they sued over stories that dealt with their business or professional activities (36.4 percent) or over stories that focused on their public or political activities (36.4 percent). One possible reason so many professionals sued over stories that dealt with their public or political activities is that many of them are highly visible and active in community affairs.[32] This is demonstrated by the fact that nearly a third of the professionals had held public office either before or during the time the alleged libel occurred.

The data concerning the plaintiffs' employment, their community visibility, and the focus of the alleged libel yield conclusions that both comport with our expectations and tend to confirm the operation of the constitutional privileges, which focus on the plaintiffs' involvement in public controversies rather than on their public position as such. The data show:

1. Upwards of 75 percent of all libel cases brought against the media involve stories that focus on plaintiffs' public or political activities or business or trade activities.

2. A relationship exists between the content of the alleged libel and plaintiffs' employment. Plaintiffs who hold public office sue over stories

that deal with their public or political activities, and plaintiffs who work in business sue over stories that deal with their business or professional activities. Plaintiffs who work as professionals are a mixed group, suing over stories that focus on their public or political activities or their business or professional activities.

3. The public plaintiffs have a very high degree of community visibility; 40 percent of them have held public office before or during the time the alleged libel occurred. This relationship is consistent with the legal theory underlying the public-plaintiff categories, which requires that the content of the alleged libel be related to the plaintiff's public activities. In combination with the subject matter of the alleged libel, plaintiff visibility corresponds most closely with the legal classification.

Litigation Experience

The lack of a benchmark with which to compare libel plaintiffs makes it impossible to know whether libel plaintiffs are more litigious than plaintiffs in other types of civil cases. Clearly, the types of jobs held by libel plaintiffs provide opportunities for them to be involved in law suits. For example, a large number of plaintiffs who work as professionals or as business owners or managers must have been involved in other civil cases, if for no other reason than attempting to collect delinquent bills.

About 67 percent of the libel plaintiffs interviewed had never filed a law suit prior to their libel suit.[33] And nearly three-quarters of libel plaintiffs had not filed another law suit since their libel action.[34] For 57 percent of libel plaintiffs, the libel suit was the only time they had initiated litigation (Table 2–5). Only 16.8 percent of the plaintiffs were plaintiffs in actions both before and after their libel suit. For most libel plaintiffs, the libel suit marked the only time they had sought redress in court. Less than a fifth of libel plaintiffs can be considered to be veterans of legal warfare. It is conceivable these plaintiffs also had more opportunities to be involved in civil cases.

Within the group of plaintiffs who had filed one or more civil suits, 18 of them (11 percent of the plaintiffs interviewed) had brought other libel or invasion of privacy suits against media or non-media entities. Twelve of

TABLE 2–5   Plaintiffs' Civil Litigation Experience

Only civil suit was the libel suit	85 (57.0%)
Filed one other civil suit other than the libel suit	39 (26.2%)
Filed civil suits before and after their libel suit	25 (16.8%)

these plaintiffs (7.3 percent) sued for libel at least one other time, and three (1.8 percent) sued for invasion of privacy. Three plaintiffs (1.8 percent) sued for both libel and invasion of privacy. But for 89 percent of libel plaintiffs, their libel suit was the first and only time they had sued for libel.

When we examined the libel plaintiffs who had brought other civil suits, we found that they act differently in some ways than plaintiffs whose only civil action was their libel suit. The more experienced plaintiffs tend to take matters more into their own hands and to be less dependent on an attorney for advice. Fifty-seven percent of the plaintiffs who had been involved in other civil suits contacted the media about the allegedly libelous story before they contacted an attorney. On the other hand, 53 percent of the libel plaintiffs whose only experience as a plaintiff was their libel suit initially contacted an attorney after the alleged libel appeared.

Libel plaintiffs with other litigation experience who contact the media almost never deal with the reporter who wrote the allegedly libelous story.[35] Instead, they go to the top. Forty-two percent of the libel plaintiffs who were involved in other civil suits contacted the editor or news director, 44 percent contacted the publisher or station manager, and 11 percent contacted more than one person at the media. On the other hand, 25 percent of the plaintiffs with no other litigation experience contacted the reporter who wrote the allegedly libelous story, 46 percent contacted the editor or news director, 23 percent contacted the publisher or station manager and 7 percent contacted more than one person at the media.

Forty-eight percent of the libel plaintiffs who were involved in other civil suits said that when they contacted their attorney they did so determined to sue the media for libel (Table 2–6). On the other hand, about 58 percent of libel plaintiffs who had not been plaintiffs in other civil cases contacted an attorney to obtain advice about how to deal with the alleged libel. Only about 32 percent of these libel plaintiffs had made up their

TABLE 2–6   Plaintiffs' Litigation Experience Compared with Why Plaintiffs Contacted an Attorney

	Why Did Plaintiffs Contact an Attorney?		
	To Obtain Advice	To Get a Retraction	To Sue the Media for Libel
Filed at least one other suit besides the libel suit	25 (50.0%)	1 (2.0%)	24 (48.0%)
Only civil suit was the libel suit	38 (57.6%)	7 (10.6%)	21 (31.8%)
		p. < .08	

minds to sue prior to contacting an attorney. About 47 percent of the less experienced plaintiffs said that their attorney's advice was very important in the decision to sue, and another 20 percent said that the attorney's advice was somewhat important in the decision. On the other hand, 53 percent of the libel plaintiffs who had been plaintiffs in other cases said that the attorney's advice was of little or no importance in the decision to sue for libel.

Nearly all of the plaintiffs whose only experience as plaintiffs was their libel suit were represented by attorneys on a contingency arrangement.[36] But only 68 percent of the libel plaintiffs who had been plaintiffs in other civil actions were represented by attorneys on contingency. It appears that libel plaintiffs who have brought other civil actions experience greater litigation costs than do plaintiffs whose only civil suit was the libel suit.[37] About 42 percent of the libel plaintiffs with other litigation experience paid more than $5,000 in fees and expenses for their libel action, while only 22 percent of the libel plaintiffs with no other litigation experience paid this much.[38]

None of the plaintiffs who had brought other civil suits and who contacted the media before filing their libel suit asked the media to pay money damages. Most of the plaintiffs who brought other civil suits and who contacted the media before filing their libel suit wanted the media to run a retraction or correction. Once these plaintiffs decided to sue, about 19 percent of them said they sued to win money damages, while nearly 23 percent of the less experienced plaintiffs said they sued to win money damages. And when asked if they would consider non-litigation alternatives to resolve the libel dispute, there are no differences between the more experienced plaintiffs and the less experienced ones.

Based on our data concerning experienced plaintiffs, one can conclude that they exhibit different, and largely expected, patterns of dealing with the media and consulting with counsel. The data do not support an assertion that most libel plaintiffs are litigious, or that those who have brought other civil suits exhibit unique motives. As discussed in detail in Chapters 5 and 7, the role of money as a motivating factor in libel litigation is complex and appears to predominate with a distinct minority of the plaintiffs. Of equal note, it does not appear that there is any relationship between a plaintiff's litigation experience and his suing the media for libel in order to win a large damage award.

Conclusion

Libel plaintiffs share a number of demographic characteristics that allow us to describe the typical plaintiff who sues the media as a male, between the ages of 36 and 65, who is a college graduate and likely to have a graduate or professional degree, who is financially well off, having an annual household income of over $25,000, and often over $50,000. Libel plaintiffs tend to be employed as professionals, as public employees, or to hold elected office.

For the public-plaintiff group, the content of the alleged libel relates to their public activities; they are highly visible members of their communities, and the alleged libel focuses on the activities that have made them visible. This is consistent with the legal privilege rules, which provide greatest protection for libelous statements about persons who have injected themselves into a public controversy or have been drawn into a public discussion of a controversial issue, and whose relationship to the controversy tends to influence or bear on its resolution. The strong correlations among plaintiff legal status, degree of visibility, and content of the alleged libel indicate that the courts have been consistent in applying the constitutional standards.

The most important, although obvious, conclusion reached from the data is that most libel suits result from stories that deal with a plaintiff's public activities. As is discussed in the next chapter, this suggests that for most plaintiffs the alleged libel is likely to damage their public or political reputation.

The findings about plaintiffs suggest:

1. The media should be aware that plaintiffs are not a monolithic group. Indeed, we discuss in subsequent chapters how various types of plaintiffs act. Nevertheless, the characteristics shared by many plaintiffs should help the media to better understand the types of people who sue for libel.

2. The typical plaintiff holds a position of high visibility within his community. In addition, the plaintiff's employment is often tied directly to his reputation. The ability of professionals, elected officials, or non-elected public officials to successfully pursue their careers is dependent on their public reputations. For many plaintiffs, their reputation is their most valuable asset.

3. Since most plaintiffs are financially secure, the role money plays in libel litigation may not be as clear-cut as many have assumed. In subsequent chapters, we explore the complex role that money plays in libel litigation. The idea that libel plaintiffs are after a "quick buck" needs to be re-examined. It does appear that a small percentage of plaintiffs are prone to litigate.

3

LIBEL DEFENDANTS' AND PLAINTIFFS' ACTIONS

THIS CHAPTER EXAMINES libel defendants, the content of the allegedly libelous statements, and what plaintiffs do about the alleged libel. Two main issues are examined in the second half of this chapter: (1) How did the alleged libel affect the plaintiffs?, and (2) What did the plaintiffs do after the alleged libel appeared? Data about plaintiffs' actions and attitudes were obtained from the plaintiff interviews.

THE DEFENDANT

Members of the mass media were the defendants in 75.3 percent of the reported defamation cases decided between 1974 and 1984, and non-media defendants accounted for the remaining 24.7 percent.[1] The allegedly libelous statements almost always appeared in news stories. In our study of defamation cases decided between 1974 and 1984, we found that 70.7 percent of the libel cases were the result of news stories, 4.8 percent involved entertainment and 5.9 percent involved literature.[2] In the remaining 18.6 percent of the cases, mostly involving non-media defendants, the allegedly libelous material appeared in a variety of forms, such as letters

TABLE 3–1   Where Did the Alleged Libel Appear?

Type of Defendant	Number	Percentage
Newspaper	114	69.5%
Television	26	15.9%
Periodical	18	11.0%
Radio	4	2.4%
Other	2	1.2%

and intra-company memos, but none involved publication in the media. Nearly all of the libel cases (85.1 percent) brought against the mass media were the result of news stories.

Despite being outnumbered by nearly six to one by broadcast stations, daily newspapers are the mass medium most often sued for libel. In our survey of 164 libel plaintiffs, newspapers were sued in 69.5 percent of the cases, television stations in 15.9 percent, periodicals in 11 percent, and radio stations in about 2 percent of the cases (Table 3–1). These findings are similar to those reported by Marc A. Franklin in his study of libel litigation involving media defendants. [3]

Contrary to the popular myth that libel suits are the result of hard-hitting, investigative stories that are run on front pages of newspapers under banner headlines, only about 46 percent of the libel suits concerned stories that had appeared on the front page of newspapers, 35.1 percent of the libel suits concerned stories on inside news pages, and 19.1 percent concerned material on the editorial page. [4] The front-page stories that generated libel suits were likely to be about public employees, elected officials, candidates for office, and professionals. [5] The stories on inside news pages usually dealt with business owners and managers, white-collar employees, and public employees. The material on editorial pages was most likely to involve elected officials or candidates for office.

One comparison that is noteworthy involves the content of the alleged libel and its location in the newspaper. [6] As would be expected, front-page stories that led to the filing of a libel suit usually dealt with plaintiffs' public or political activities. And the stories on the editorial page that led to a libel suit usually focused on plaintiffs' public or political activities. But stories that appeared on the inside pages of the newspaper that resulted in a libel suit usually dealt with plaintiffs' business or professional activities.

About half of the newspapers sued by the plaintiffs we studied were local papers, and less than a quarter of the newspapers sued were regional papers, circulating in a number of counties.[7] Only about 25 percent of the newspapers sued for libel can be considered to have wide circulation areas: about 19 percent of the papers had state-wide circulations, about 2 percent circulated in more than one state, and 4.5 percent had nation-wide circulations. When the defendant was a broadcaster, 96 percent of the libel cases involved programs that appeared during prime time.[8] Since 92 percent of the libel suits filed against broadcasters involved news stories, it appears that most libel suits involving broadcasters resulted from stories on news programs.

How Libel Affected Plaintiffs

There are three interrelated variables that will be discussed in this section: (1) What did the media say about the plaintiffs in the alleged libel?; (2) How did plaintiffs perceive the harm caused by the alleged libel?; and (3) What was it about the alleged libel that most upset the plaintiffs?

The plaintiffs interviewed were asked an open-ended question about what upset them most about the alleged libel (Table 3–2). Over 65 percent of the plaintiffs we interviewed said that what upset them most about the alleged libel was that it was false. Twenty percent of the plaintiffs cited the alleged libel's impact on their business or professional reputation, nearly 7 percent cited its impact on their personal reputation, and about 4 percent said that the alleged libel violated their privacy.

Plaintiffs were then asked an open-ended question about how they believed the alleged libel had harmed them. Those who responded were divided fairly evenly over the types of harm they felt had been caused by the alleged libel (Table 3–3). About 27 percent of the plaintiffs said the alleged libel caused them emotional harm. Another 21.9 percent said the

TABLE 3–2   What Upset Plaintiffs Most About the Alleged Libel

What Upset Plaintiff	Number	Percentage
Story was false	106	65.4%
Violated privacy	7	4.3%
Damaged personal reputation	11	6.8%
Damaged business or professional reputation	33	20.4%
Other	5	3.1%

TABLE 3–3   How Were the Plaintiffs Harmed by the Alleged Libel?

How Plaintiff Harmed	Number	Percentage
Suffered emotional harm	42	27.1%
Suffered emotional and financial harm	34	21.9%
Suffered financial harm	22	14.2%
Damaged business or professional reputation	34	21.9%
Damaged political status	23	14.8%

alleged libel caused them emotional and financial harm. Twenty-two percent said the alleged libel damaged their business or professional reputation, and 14.8 percent said the alleged libel damaged their political status. About 14 percent of the plaintiffs said the alleged libel caused them financial harm.

Table 3–4 compares plaintiffs' employment with the type of harm caused by the alleged libel. Nearly half of the plaintiffs who were elected officials or candidates for office reported that the alleged libel damaged their political status. Over 63 percent of the plaintiffs who were business owners or managers said the alleged libel caused them financial harm or emotional and financial harm. Almost half of the plaintiffs who were employed in white-collar positions said the alleged libel damaged their business or professional reputation. Twenty-five percent of the plaintiffs who were professionals said the alleged libel damaged their business or pofessional reputation. Over 56 percent of the professionals said the alleged libel caused them emotional harm or caused emotional and financial harm. About a quarter of the plaintiffs who were public employees said that the alleged libel damaged their business or professional reputation, and 35.9 percent of these plaintiffs said the alleged libel caused them emotional harm.

As would be expected, there is a relationship between the focus of the alleged libel and the harm caused to the plaintiffs.[9] When the alleged libel focused on plaintiffs' business or professional activities, plaintiffs reported that the alleged libel caused them some financial harm. When the alleged libel dealt with the plaintiffs' public or political activities, they reported that the alleged libel damaged their political status or caused them emotional harm. And when the alleged libel focused on plaintiffs' personal or private activities or on their allegedly criminal activities, they said the alleged libel caused them emotional harm.

TABLE 3–4 How Plaintiffs Were Harmed by the Alleged Libel Compared with Plaintiffs' Employment

	How did Alleged Libel Harm the Plaintiffs?				
	Emotional Harm	Emotional and Financial Harm	Financial Harm	Business or Professional Reputation Damaged	Political Status Damaged
Elected official or candidate for office	5 (18.5%)	5 (18.5%)	2 (7.4%)	2 (7.4%)	13 (48.1%)
White-collar employee	3 (27.3%)	1 (9.1%)	2 (18.2%)	5 (45.5%)	0
Public employee	14 (35.9%)	9 (23.1%)	1 (2.6%)	10 (25.6%)	5 (12.8%)
Business owner or manager	2 (9.1%)	7 (31.8%)	7 (31.8%)	4 (18.2%)	2 (9.1%)
Professional	10 (31.3%)	8 (25.0%)	4 (12.5%)	8 (25.0%)	2 (6.3%)

$p. < .001$

23

The data indicate that there is a relationship between the focus of the alleged libel, the harm caused by the alleged libel, and plaintiffs' employment. Libel plaintiffs who were public employees tended to sue over stories that focused on their public or political activities and they reported that the alleged libel damaged their political status or caused them emotional harm. Plaintiffs who were business owners or managers usually sued over stories that dealt with their business or professional activities and said that the alleged libel caused them financial and emotional harm. Since white-collar employees receive a salary and will not necessarily suffer a direct financial loss because of the alleged libel, they said the alleged libel damaged their business or professional reputation. Plaintiffs who were elected officials or candidates for office said that the alleged libel damaged their political status or caused them emotional harm. Plaintiffs who had held public office either before or during the time the alleged libel occurred reported that the alleged libel damaged their political status.

However, it is not necessarily the case that plaintiffs who said they suffered financial harm because of the alleged libel were interested in recovering monetary damages from the media. To further gauge the extent of the harm caused by the alleged libel and what it would have taken to rectify the situation, we asked the plaintiffs what could the media have done immediately after the alleged libel appeared that would have satisfied them (Table 3–5). Over 70 percent of the plaintiffs said that they would have been satisfied with a retraction or correction. Another 2 percent of the plaintiffs would have been satisfied with an apology. Less than 4 percent of the plaintiffs said that they would have been satisfied only if the media paid them money damages. These plaintiffs tended to be white-collar employees or professionals who had not reported that the alleged libel caused them financial harm. Only one plaintiff who reported that he suffered financial harm because of the alleged libel said he would have been satisfied only if the media paid money damages. Over 95 percent of the plaintiffs who said the alleged libel caused them financial harm or caused

TABLE 3–5   What Media Could Have Done to Satisfy Plaintiffs

	Number	Percentage
Apologize	3	1.9%
Retract or correct	110	71.0%
Pay money	6	3.9%
Nothing	31	20.0%
Other	5	3.2%

them both emotional and financial harm said that they would have been satisfied with a retraction, correction, or apology. At least shortly after the alleged libel appeared, plaintiffs were more interested in obtaining a retraction, correction, or apology from the media than they were in obtaining money. These findings are supported by an examination of plaintiffs' actions following the publication or broadcast of the alleged libel.

What Plaintiffs Do About the Libel

The plaintiffs interviewed were asked a series of questions about their actions immediately following the publication or broadcast of the alleged libel. After the alleged libelous story appeared in the media, about half of the plaintiffs we interviewed contacted the media, and about half of the plaintiffs contacted an attorney.[10] But regardless of whom was contacted first—the media or an attorney—about 90 percent of the plaintiffs, on their own, through their attorney, or together with their attorney, contacted the media in an attempt to settle the dispute prior to filing their libel suit.[11]

Of those who could recall, nearly three-quarters of the plaintiffs said the media were contacted within two days after publication or broadcast of the alleged libel.[12] About 15 percent of the plaintiffs said the reporter who was responsible for the allegedly libelous story was the person contacted.[13] But most plaintiffs said that someone in a supervisory or management position was contacted. About 46 percent of the contacts were with an editor or news director, 31.3 percent were with the publisher or station manager, and 8.4 percent were with more than one person at the media.

A quarter of the plaintiffs said that the media were contacted in person, another 45.9 percent said the contact was made by telephone, and 3.5 percent said the media were contacted by telephone and letter.[14] About a quarter of the plaintiffs said the media were contacted by letter, usually from a plaintiff's attorney.

Over 78 percent of the plaintiffs who said the media were contacted before the libel suit was filed said that the media were asked to run a retraction, correction, or apology (Table 3–6). Six percent of the plaintiffs said the media were asked to discuss the story with them. Three percent of the plaintiffs said the media were asked to provide space or air time for them to respond to the alleged libel. Only one plaintiff said the medium was asked to pay money damages.

Even those plaintiffs who said they were financially harmed by the alleged libel were more interested in obtaining a retraction, correction, or apology than they were in obtaining money damages. None of the plain-

TABLE 3-6   What Media Were Asked To Do

	Number	Percentage
Retract, correct or apologize publicly	100	78.1%
Apologize in person to the plaintiff	2	1.6%
Pay money damages	1	0.8%
Provide space or air time to plaintiff	4	3.1%
Stop further publication	6	4.7%
Discuss story with plaintiff	7	5.5%
Other	8	6.3%

tiffs who reported that the alleged libel caused them financial harm said the media were asked to pay money damages. And none of the plaintiffs who reported that the alleged libel caused them emotional and financial harm said the media were asked to pay money damages. Nearly 90 percent of the plaintiffs who said that they suffered some financial harm because of the alleged libel said that the media were asked to run a retraction, correction, or apology.

The media refused the plaintiffs' request in 64.8 percent of the cases, and repeated the alleged libel in another 11 percent.[15] However, nearly 24 percent of the plaintiffs did receive a positive response from the media. Twenty-one percent of the plaintiffs were successful in obtaining a retraction, correction, or apology. And 2.5 percent of the plaintiffs did obtain an agreement from the media not to repeat the alleged libel. The reasons plaintiffs sued despite obtaining a correction, retraction, or apology are discussed in Chapters 4 and 5. In a number of instances, the retraction, correction, or apology did little more than repeat the alleged libel.

Plaintiffs were asked an open-ended question about how they felt about the media's response to their request. Nearly all of the plaintiffs who responded to the question said that they were angered or dissatisfied by the media's response.[16] Nearly 57 percent expressed their feelings in terms of anger, and 36 percent said they were dissatisfied. Only 4 percent said that they were satisfied with the way the media responded.

The vehemence with which the plaintiffs responded to the question about their feelings about the media's response is noteworthy. In answering the question, plaintiffs regularly used terms such as "extremely angered," "incensed," "seething," and "very mad." Many of the plaintiffs told the interviewers that it was more than their request being turned down that angered them, it was the way they were treated by the media that contributed to their anger.

Conclusion

As would be expected, most libel suits involve the mass media, usually newspapers. The alleged libel almost always appears in a news story, and the focus of the alleged libel usually deals with a plaintiff's public or political activities or with his business or professional activities.

When asked what upset them most about the alleged libel, most plaintiffs claimed that the alleged libel was false. Plaintiffs reported that the alleged libel caused them emotional harm, damaged their business or personal reputation, or damaged their political status. The type of harm caused by the alleged libel is related to the content of the alleged libel. Public plaintiffs reported that the alleged libel damaged their political status or caused emotional harm. Private plaintiffs said that the alleged libel caused them financial harm or emotional harm.

Nearly all plaintiffs said they would have been satisfied with a retraction, correction, or apology from the media. Even plaintiffs who reported the alleged libel caused them financial harm said they would have been satisfied with a retraction, correction, or apology. Most libel plaintiffs, on their own, through their attorney or with their attorney, contacted the media before filing suit. The media were asked to run a retraction, correction, or apology. Less than 1 percent of the plaintiffs said that the media were asked to pay money damages, and none of the plaintiffs who reported that the alleged libel caused them financial harm said the media were asked to pay money.

As can be expected, most of the plaintiffs' requests are turned down by the media. However, the strong feelings exhibited by plaintiffs about their dealings with the media are especially noteworthy. Over and over again, plaintiffs told the interviewers how angry they were at the media's treatment of them. The strong feelings of plaintiffs towards the media go well beyond simply having their requests turned down. This raises questions about the way the media treat complainants.

Some important implications of the findings presented in this chapter appear to be:

1. Careful attention must be paid to all stories, since many libel suits are the result of seemingly minor stories, often written and edited rapidly, that appear on inside pages of a newspaper.

2. Since most plaintiffs express their concern about the alleged libel in terms of its falsity, news organizations must both stress the importance of

accuracy and establish procedures to deal with complaints about inaccuracy.

3. The role money plays in plaintiffs' decision to sue for libel is complex. However, it does not appear to be the case that most libel plaintiffs see their suit principally as an opportunity to profit at the expense of the media. Even those plaintiffs who reported that the alleged libel caused them financial harm said they were more interested in obtaining a retraction, correction, or apology from the media than they were in obtaining money.

4. Most plaintiffs contact the media about the alleged libel prior to filing suit. Nearly all of them seek a retraction, correction, or apology. From the plaintiffs' perspective, the media all too often seem to aggravate the problem by their reaction. Prompt action by the media to correct errors and considerate treatment of complainants should avert some libel suits.

4

THE MEDIA'S ROLE IN THE LIBEL DISPUTE

A LIBEL SUIT commonly is perceived as something that happens in stages—stage 1, publication; stage 2, a visit to a lawyer; stage 3, filing a lawsuit. Instead of three steps, we found many times a four-step process: publication, *contact with the media*, then a visit to the lawyer, then to court. The significance of the contact with the media is hard to overstate—and this contact occurs in a significant number of cases. It means the press has an opportunity to resolve the dispute before a lawyer enters the picture and before the complainant may even have given serious thought to litigation. A golden opportunity, it might be called.

So what happens? Typically, the subjects are agitated by the news coverage concerning them. When they go to the publication to complain, they are at least hurt and upset. After contact with the media, they are angry, and many are determined to sue. For many of the plaintiffs, the visit to the lawyer is not to decide *whether* to sue, but to engage the lawyer to sue.

The decision to contact the media before contacting a lawyer thus becomes transformed from a golden opportunity for the press to a golden opportunity for the lawyer—especially if he is hired on an hourly-fee basis. Instead of the contact with the media diverting these complainants from court, the contact propels them to court. Overwhelmingly, the plaintiffs told us that their post-publication experiences with the press influenced them to bring suit.

Some people could not be satisfied short of the press bowing and scraping and giving them everything they want—money, an apology, retraction, correction, or whatever—regardless of the merits of the request. Such plaintiffs are a minority of those who sue, however. For the rest, it is more than just failing to get what they were after immediately following publication that seems to be involved. In a significant proportion of the cases, the *way* people were treated when they contacted the media seems to account for, or to be a factor in, their anger and the decision to sue.

What is there about the way the press deals with complainants that antagonizes them? The key part played by the complainant-media contact in the decision to bring suit led us to examine how the press deals with libel-type complaints.[1]

First, we found organizations largely geared to producing the next day's paper instead of coping with the fallout from the previous day's publication. Fielding a complaint represents interference with the organization's prime mission. Few papers systematize the handling of complaints the way they systematize newspaper production. Often, the way complaints are handled does not conform to the way editors think it is done. Absent in most cases are clearly articulated policies and procedures for dealing with complaints, and very little about this is in writing. One consequence is that complaints are haphazardly handled by newsroom personnel who usually have not been instructed on how to deal with them unless the complainant is a lawyer or legal action is threatened; a second consequence is that editors do not even know the volume and character of complaints.

James Gannon, editor, *Des Moines Register*:

> The complaint can come to so many different people at so many different levels at a newspaper. We have a lot of cases where individual reporters get called by somebody complaining. Some of [those complaints] might end up in a libel situation. And I sometimes worry that there are some of those that I don't even know about. It's hard to say how many complaints there really are. . . .
>
> Somebody calls and gets bounced from one person to another—you know, four or five different people in the newsroom—and finally ends up with someone who's on deadline and irritated and saying, "Well, that's just the way we do it, buddy! That's our policy" and, you know, bang, or something like that. And I've had these horror stories told to me—people who have gone through this, and they feel they just don't get a hearing, a real hearing, and they don't get a courteous response. . . . We're not very well organized to do it. The people on the desk will tell you, "Well, yeah, we're trying to put out the paper and these crank calls are coming in and sometimes, you know, you just have to brush them off."

James Squires, editor, *Chicago Tribune*:

My experience has been that what happens [at other papers] is that a reader calls up and . . . first of all they might get the reporter—most reporters are awful about this, they just do not want to admit that they made a mistake. Then the call will go to the city desk, and they don't get a city editor or the managing editor, you get some assistant or some clerk who's busy and on a deadline and in a bad mood anyway, and the reader gets jacked around by this desk person, a nameless desk person that you can never identify for the rest of your life, trying to find out who told that woman to go to hell.

Arnold Garson, managing editor, *Des Moines Register*:

[The system fails because] this is still a newspaper and all those people are trying to do other things while they're trying to handle that complaint, and they've had no special training in terms of doing that sort of thing, although the business does rely on dealing with the public. . . . And it fails because people don't take the time that they ought to take.

A 1984 survey of some 550 newspapers by the Credibility Committee of the Associated Press Managing Editors Association generated responses from 267 papers. Two-thirds of the respondents said they had no written policy on how to handle telephoned complaints and questions.[2] The Libel Research Project had similar responses when it questioned editors at 61 of the newspapers that were defendants in libel suits filed by the plaintiffs who had been interviewed earlier by the project. Only seven of these publications had provided written guidelines to reporters or editors on how to deal with complaints.

Asked by the Project how many complaints had been received about alleged factual errors that had damaged the complainants' business, political, or personal reputation, only two papers could cite complete records. Typical responses were: "no way of knowing," "picked out of thin air," "no record, many just come through the woodwork," "not the foggiest notion," "a wild guess," "impossible to say." A number of the papers did indicate, however, that many such complaints were legitimate.

The disorganized way newspapers cope with complaints is reflected in responses to a question about who at the papers initially receive complaints. More than 90 percent of the editors questioned said that calls come in all over the paper. "God only knows who gets how many," an editor commented. "Unfortunately, people who call are switched all over creation." Only one of the editors reported that the switchboard had been instructed to keep complaints from reporters by referring them to the city desk; only two others said efforts were made to channel complaints away from the person who wrote the story.

The absence of written policies was attributed by about a fourth of the editors interviewed to concern about discovery in libel litigation ("Anything in writing can come back to haunt you") and by others to oversight and belief that too many directives can make the institution "muscle-bound through paper."

Widespread use of electronic technology in newsrooms is likely to further discourage permanent written policies. The electronic systems often permit messages to be sent and displayed on video display terminals. The messaging systems do not automatically leave a permanent record and are not foolproof.

James Gannon, editor, *Des Moines Register*:

> I issued a written policy a week ago on that new writing machine we have over there, but it's not on a piece of paper anywhere—it's an electronic message, so I might be able to search my files and find nothing and yet we've had policy directives.

Interviewing at the *Des Moines Register* was conducted soon after the *Register*'s managing editor electronically messaged the staff to notify him about calls threatening legal action or about calls from lawyers. When reporters were asked during our interviews whether they had been told about procedures for dealing with libel-action threats, several said they could recall no instructions. Those who did see the electronic message about libel threats recalled it differently.

Electronic systems usually can produce paper copies of messages. Staff members who make hard copies and file them would defeat the purpose of electronic messaging if the purpose is to avoid a paper trail.

The lack of written policies produced a consistent result: widespread discrepancies existed between the way editors believe their papers function and the perceptions of other editors, reporters, and desk people.

Robert Pearman, managing editor of the *Omaha World Herald*, said, "All the reporters, all the desk people are told that [if] any mistake [surfaces], I'm to be told immediately. Anyone on the city desk knows it's our policy and they have transmitted it to reporters." The *World Herald*'s reporters are supervised closely by the city desk. Pearman said it had been clearly communicated to the staff that, if someone calls a reporter to complain, the reporter's obligation is to go immediately to the desk.

Interviews with seven reporters and city desk people chosen at random in the *World Herald* newsroom found none who could recall being told how to deal with complaints unless the complaint came from a lawyer. To their knowledge, no other policies, guidelines, or procedures concerning complaints had been communicated to them.

Larry King, *World Herald* metro editor, said that while he expects reporters to inform the city desk about complaints, they had not been told to do so explicitly.

G. Woodson Howe, executive editor, said no instruction had been given to staff unless the call came from a lawyer, in which case there were "explicit instructions" to listen politely and to notify him. "I sort of wish we did [have instructions]," said Howe. "We should follow the same procedure. If I were a reporter and smelled the possibility that the caller would turn it over to a lawyer, I'd cut it off right there." Howe thought it was unclear what actually was happening in his newsroom.

Predictably, in the absence of rules, reporters followed different practices. John Whitesides, a reporter who had been with the *World Herald* for 3½ years, said that he personally would tell the desk about complaints, but he could see how other reporters would not because there were no rules and reporters "definitely" did not have to pass complaints to the desk. Reporter Jerry Mahoney, at the paper 4½ years, said he would inform the desk if a lawyer calls, but he would do so otherwise only if he considers the complaint legitimate or if the caller threatens legal action or demands another story.

Howe, the executive editor, described a blue form on which the recipient of a complaint is supposed to record the time, date, identity of caller and nature of comments. Howe said that the form was not used a great deal and probably would not be used in cases of libel threats because of the time it takes.

Pearman, the managing editor, said he believes the staff conscientiously fills out the complaint form and does so in the case of libel-type complaints. Evan Roth, a reporter on the *World Herald* for a year, said he had never seen the form.

The *Quad City Times* of Davenport, Iowa, like most papers, has no written policy for dealing with complaints. Editor Forrest Kilmer described a procedure that he said had been communicated orally to the staff in periodic meetings. Reporters, said Kilmer, are told not to engage in dialogue with complainants but are advised to say they will notify editors and are told to inform supervisors of the complaint.

Gary Sawyer, Quad City reporter and fill-in city editor, said, "There isn't anything that governs [the way complaints are handled]. We don't have a policy or procedure. It probably hasn't been done because no one's thought about it."

Sawyer improvised his own procedure, which he said consists of determining the nature of the complaint by going through the story with the caller word by word. He wants to know whether the alleged error is factual or one of interpretation and tries not to get into an argument. If he thinks the complainant is reading too much into the story, he may say that. Otherwise, he says, "Let me check. I'll get back to you."

"As a reporter," said Sawyer, "I know my first reaction is, 'They're wrong.' So you try to bring in someone not involved in the story." When he calls back, he tells the caller what he and the editor decided.

"I have my doubts most reporters here do this," said Sawyer. "They seem to turn it into an antagonistic situation long before they have to. I hear about it from reporters. We get together at lunch or at the city editor's desk and they tell me about it. They seem to, without having checked it, decided this fellow is way off base. I don't think they've told him this, but they get the message across." Would they then take the complaint to the desk? "They might or might not. Some complaints stop at the reporter who hopes that if he ignores it the person doesn't go above his head."

Reporters and desk people at the *Quad City Times* said they used "instinct" and their own judgment to cope with complaints because there never had been formal instruction. Many said they would talk extensively with complainants to work out the difficulty. Linda Watson, day city editor, said sitting on complaints "probably could happen, probably does happen," although she thinks reporters understand that they shouldn't— but not because they were told clearly not to.

Newspaper personnel were on different wavelengths not only about how a paper deals with complaints but about how effectively it does so. The editor and managing editor of the *Des Moines Register* both said they were dissatisfied with the way the *Register* responds to complaints, but the metro editor, Charles Capaldo, expressed satisfaction. "It's a good way to handle it. The desk and the staff realize," he added, "that complaints have to be addressed; that you can't just tell somebody, 'Go —— off.' Not anymore."

The pattern of editors at the same paper disagreeing about their procedures, or of editors describing practices and policies that did not conform to the perceptions of reporters and desk people, was encountered repeatedly. It was encountered even at publications that could be expected to be the most systematic in dealing with complaints because they had created the position of ombudsman, or reader representative, to respond to complaints.

Joel Kramer, editor of the *Minneapolis Star & Tribune*, said reporters are supposed to send complaint calls to the paper's reader representative, Louis Gelfand. Kramer conceded that he does not know what actually happens when calls go to a reporter.

Gelfand said that having him notified of all complaints never had been discussed. Although he keeps a log of complaints, he has no way of knowing how many calls to reporters or editors do not get referred to him. Other editors said reporters understand that they should report complaints either to editors or to the city desk.

Tim McGuire, managing editor, said that the initial screening of phone calls results in routing complaints to the reader representative rather than to reporters. The company's phone supervisor agreed that callers with complaints are directed to Gelfand. Of the two copy aides who handle the newsroom phone, however, one said he refers all complaint calls to the reader representative while the other said he forwards some to reporters and others to Gelfand.

Interviews with reporters revealed an undercurrent of dissatisfaction with the reader representative. Reporter Mike Kazuba said that virtually all reporters think having a reader representative is a good idea, but virtually all dislike how it's been executed. He cited lack of evenhandedness and "sacred cows" among the staff as reasons for unhappiness.

Reporter Kate Parry said that she wants to get the reader representative involved in complaints as quickly as possible because she, as a reporter, has a vested interest in the stories that produce complaints. She said reporters "brace" when the reader representative enters the picture instead of thinking, "Oh, good, he'll help me." She suspects that the practices of reporters are "all over the place," with reporters who believe that they had bad experiences with the reader representative being reluctant to steer complainants to him.

Reporter Paul McEnroe said no one told him what to do with complaints, so he devised his own system by using "common sense." While "lots of reporters" dislike the reader representative, McEnroe said, he likes him because he absorbs "lots of crap." After usually trying to go over the complaint with the caller, McEnroe said, he will shift the call to the reader representative.

He added that he hears many reporters tell complaining callers to "talk to my editor." He also has heard callers told, "——you. You're full of——." For reporter Kazuba, who likewise said he had not been told what to do, the *Minneapolis Star & Tribune* was the fourth newspaper he had worked on. At none of them, he said, was he advised how to conduct phone conversations.

Gelfand writes a weekly column in addition to handling complaints. The column discusses the performance of the paper's personnel and criticizes individuals by name. Gelfand agrees that by naming names his column discourages reporters from referring complaints to him. "I do feel it has a negative effect," said Gelfand. "It doesn't help."

Donald (Casey) Jones is assistant to the editor and ombudsman for the *Kansas City Star and Times.* According to Jones, complaint calls should go to him immediately. Reporters, said Jones, are told not to engage in conversation and are instructed to say, "We have one person [Jones] who handles complaints. Let me get you over to him."

The 25-page "guide to policies and procedures of the *Kansas City Star* newsroom" does not mention the ombudsman. "If you find you've made an error in the story," the policy guide states, "notify the desk. Write a correction, make two extra printouts. Write a memo explaining how the error happened." An error follow-up form, however, lists the ombudsman among the seven persons who get copies. [3]

David Zeeck, managing editor of the *Star,* said no instructions had been given to reporters about talking to complainants. Reporters, he said, have considerable latitude. They are supposed to tell immediate supervisors about complaints, Zeeck explained, and Casey Jones would be notified if it is determined that there is a problem.

Rick Serrano, assistant city editor, said that he expects a reporter to notify him about a complaint. Most of the complaints are resolved at this level after he or the reporter checks into them. If the complainant is not satisfied, Serrano tells him to call the ombudsman. Unless the complainant contacted him, the ombudsman would not know about the complaint if Serrano decides that no correction is warranted. Serrano said that he knows to handle it this way because that is the way the city editor does it.

Reporters at the *Star and Times* said that they deal with callers about the substance of their complaints. They expressed a preference for notifying editors, rather than the ombudsman, about complaining calls.

Reporter Bruce Bigelow said he would find out what's bugging the caller and explain his position. He said he would be reluctant to get the ombudsman involved in a controversy. Bigelow described this as a fairly widespread feeling by reporters.

Reporter Molly Rowley said that it's not supposed to be done, but reporters feel that if they can resolve the issue themselves, they do it to avoid "Caseygrams"—the in-house memos or notes Casey Jones writes criticizing reporters and editors, sometimes by name, for errors of commission and omission. Jones believes that, as a disinterested third party looking into complaints, the ombudsman "always should be in an adversarial position with editors and reporters."

Managing Editor Zeeck is supportive of the ombudsman, but he said the ombudsman creates morale problems—sometimes big ones—because "many reporters see his notes as unduly harsh; that they as a staff are being whipped; that this is a punitive lesson." Mike McGraw, special features editor, said that while there is a general understanding that complaints should be routed through the ombudsman, the system is loose since different people do different things, with the result that "I can see our system here resulting in people getting pissed off" by their encounter with the paper. McGraw believes this would be less likely if all complaints went through the ombudsman, but there is "such a resistance" to taking complaints to him. McGraw cited the incident he overheard of an editor telling a reporter, in an implied threat, "Do you want to handle this now or do you want it to go to Casey?"

Of the roughly 30 ombudsmen at work at U.S. newspapers, almost all write columns of media criticism or in-house memos in response to reader complaints. The reactions to the criticism in the columns or memos at the Minneapolis and Kansas City papers suggest that Norman Isaacs, who appointed the first newspaper ombudsman in this country—at the *Louisville Courier-Journal* in 1967—probably is right when he says, "You can have a media critic and an ombudsman, but you can't have both in the same person."[4]

Isaacs' point is underscored by a 1984 study by a senior journalism student at the University of Iowa, Terry Francisco, who found what appears to be a correlation: Ombudsmen who name names of staff members in critical columns or in-house memos by and large get almost all of their complaints directly from complainants while only a small percentage are referred by reporters. As one ombudsman stated, "If I were a reporter, I wouldn't go looking for trouble, either." Francisco found that the ombudsmen who do not criticize staff members by name seem to get higher percentages of complaints referred by reporters.

According to Francisco's study, only two papers with ombudsmen have written policies on how reporters should deal with a complaint involving a question of fairness. Most of the papers do not have policies—written or unwritten—requiring reporters to relay complaints to ombudsmen. One of the ombudsmen commented to Francisco, "How reporters deal with complaints is their own business. My guess is that reporters would try to ignore some complaints." And reporters at some papers with ombudsmen, Terry Francisco found, are encouraged to resolve complaints themselves.[5]

Papers that employ ombudsmen have demonstrated an understanding of the need for a disinterested third party to investigate complaints and to deal with unhappy readers. But a high degree of disorganization exists, it is clear, even at these publications.

A second factor influencing the way the press responds to complaints is its conditioning to resist pressure—economic pressures, political pressures, pressures to keep things out of the paper, and pressures to put things into it. A siege mentality develops in which demands for retraction or other vindication can be regarded as forms of pressure, signals to circle the wagons.

Arnold Garson, managing editor, *Des Moines Register*:

Editors and reporters are pretty hardened people. They have to build up a way to deal with people every day who want something from them. They have to say no every day—to the lady who calls who wants her daughter's graduation announcement in the newspaper, the guy who sends in the picture of his daughter who's a finalist in the Crawford County mid-teen beauty contest. All those people want something from us everyday and we build up a kind of hardened way of saying no to people, and it occurs to me that it's possible that that same attitude, that same mindset that we can build up in being tough and doing our job carries over to a place where it shouldn't—dealing with people after the fact, in connection with news stories in which they've been harmed or wronged . . . a place where we ought to have a good deal more compassion and understanding and take a good deal more time in hearing people out. You say no to somebody and snap your fingers like that and you throw the news release away, or maybe you get in an argument and slam down the telephone because they call at such a pace out here. You shouldn't treat the complainer the same way in an after-the-fact situation.

The inclination to resist pressure is reinforced when a lawyer enters the picture. Scott Whiteside, general counsel, *Kansas City Star and Times*:

The problem with dealing with plaintiffs once attorneys are involved is that there's tremendous pressure exerted on the paper all the time—financial pressure, political pressure to tone down its news stories, not to do certain stories. It's a constant fight against all those pressures that are brought to bear. And so the editors just in their day-to-day business have to have this kind of defensive attitude in some respects. They've got to resist all this pressure and their reflex is to resist. . . . And when that special pressure of legal threat is brought to bear the reflex action is to resist all that much more. That's the posture that they're always in and it takes a lot of confidence to overcome that reflex and to really allow yourself to hear that person who has a complaint and to admit that you're wrong and to run that correction, so you're fighting that kind of built-in attitude that is required by the job in some ways.

The newspaper's lawyer may encounter the same resistance, especially after a story has appeared. Scott Whiteside:

Good, strong, aggressive editors are sensitive to begin with about any lawyer watering down a story or trying to be less aggressive than they think they ought to be. And they say, either implicitly or explicitly to their lawyer, "We're independent and you're not going to tell us how to do a story." But they're more likely to take that kind of a pre-publication recommendation from a lawyer than after publication because the response to pressure is much stronger after publication, the editor's reflex is much stronger, and he really is going to resist the pressure from his own lawyer, if he perceives it as pressure, as much as to pressure from the complaining party. He doesn't like to hear his lawyer come in and say that he ought to bend to pressure.

From the editor's perspective, it may be the company's lawyer who is seen as overly resistant to pressure. James Squires, editor, *Chicago Tribune*:

> One of the things that I do and that I am willing to do and that I'd advocate unequivocally is that newspapers ought to admit when they're wrong. I admit when we're wrong, and if a lawyer doesn't like that, I'm sorry. My hardest time is when the complaint comes from the lawyer. Now when the complaint comes from a lawyer I have to punt it over to another lawyer and I can't do anything about it, so somebody who's got some trouble with the *Tribune* is in a lot better shape coming to complain to me than they are sending a lawyer in here with it, because I can correct, admit my mistake and fix it, and the damn lawyer never will.

Squires' practice of deferring to his lawyer when a complainant's lawyer enters the picture is widespread. If there is any consistency in the generally haphazard way newspapers react to complaints, it is in the extent to which legal pressure in the form of a lawyer's presence causes the staff—from reporter to editor—to bow out and for the company's lawyer to bow in.[6] The same is true, to a lesser extent, when the complainant acting on his own contacts the press and threatens suit.

Half of the interviewed plaintiffs contacted a lawyer rather than the press following publication and left it to the lawyer to initiate contacts with the media. The consequence of the usual press reaction to lawyers is that the complainant may never have the opportunity for what one press lawyer calls "the cathartic bitching session"—the face-to-face meeting with newspaper personnel at which the complainant gets the grievance off his chest and where he may hear a mollifying explanation.

The complainant who does not send a lawyer but whose complaint is laced with threats to sue may be angered by what seems to be unconcern and unresponsiveness but what is actually a defensive legal strategy. A vicious circle may follow in which the press lawyer's advice to be guarded and noncommittal for self-protection heightens the complainant's dissatisfaction and determination to sue.

The resistance-to-pressure syndrome, so evident in the face of perceived legal coercion, is equally or more acute when public officials complain. As a group, these libel plaintiffs are most apt to contact the media before contacting a lawyer.

Donald Jones, assistant to the editor and ombudsman, *Kansas City Star and Times*:

> The prejudice I find in the news business in the kinds of complaints [made by public officials] is just incredible. Someone calls in and says, "I'm a representative

from this and I want to complain about a story." The general reaction, at least in my experience, is "that's self-serving." He's a politician or he's an elected official. He has no justification to complain.

A third factor shaping press reaction to complaints is the defensiveness to criticism that is part of the human condition. Newspeople are no more immune to it than anyone else, and they may be more prone to it because of the public character of their work and the importance attached by journalists and news organizations to a reputation for accuracy.

The degree of defensiveness is suggested by how slow the press has been to adopt the simple practice of placing corrections in a fixed location. Not until 1967 did the *Louisville Courier-Journal and Times* become the first newspapers in the United States to institutionalize corrections by establishing a standing corrections box and by announcing a corrections policy. In a memo to his staff, Norman Isaacs, then executive editor at Louisville, complained about the "paranoid . . . infernally defensive" attitude about correcting errors.[7]

Dan Foley, managing editor, *Quad City Times*:

> Newspapers are reluctant to acknowledge complaints. We're defensive about it. Nobody likes to be criticized. I see it here. I see it everywhere. There's anger that somebody would question us. My immediate reaction is to be defensive about it. Something I have to be careful of when I'm talking to people is that I hear them out, that I try to explain to people what the reason is for what we're doing. I find that very difficult. It's one of my own quirks, something I have to work on, not to respond in a defensive way.

The same editor said that he could not think of anything his paper had done to prevent defensiveness by reporters.

James Squires, editor of the *Chicago Tribune*, told the 1983 annual meeting of the American Society of Newspaper Editors:

> We correct . . . errors. But we have a terrible problem saying we are sorry or explaining our actions. One of the reasons is in Chicago, if you admit something, the opposition will take out an ad and put it on the Kennedy Expressway, pointing it out. We have done that in the past to the *Sun-Times* and they have done it to us. So, in Chicago if you made an error you correct it without admitting that you made it, and without being the least bit sorry for it. That's a terrible policy. That is the greatest threat to our credibility; it is a great danger to our public image.[8]

G. Woodson Howe, executive editor, *Omaha World Herald*:

> A lot of us, including some of us here, are a little defensive about our mistakes, a little too prone to circle the wagons and deny that anybody should feel hurt or that there could be anything wrong about the way we handled the story. It's human nature that reporters, having written the story, have a pride of authorship.

It's probably a little too difficult to persuade them that they were factually wrong or wrong in tone. It's probably not quite so hard to talk their bosses into that idea but even the bosses probably are going to side with the reporter maybe a little bit more than they should. I don't think it's very different here, but it's probably true of the press in general.

I'm not satisfied that we give the aggrieved party full psychic satisfaction in every case. . . . I think they have access, they get an audience. I'm satisfied from that standpoint. I just think that the reception probably is too defensive. We're too unwilling to admit that it might have been a mistake in judgment . . . an account that could have been improved.

Contributing to the problem is the dynamics of the newsroom, where reporters like to feel they have the support of their bosses and where a retraction often is viewed as repudiation.

James Gannon, editor, *Des Moines Register:*

I think it's an important factor in shaping a generally defensive attitude on the part of newspaper people. You know, the natural thing to do is, you want to stand behind your people. They're working hard for you and they're generally doing a good job. You ask an awful lot of them, and you know 99 percent of the time they're right or you like to think they are, and then there's that 1 percent of the time when something is wrong and you hate to have that bring damage to the standing of the person in the newsroom or an editor or the paper. So that's a factor, I think, there in the background and it's true, you have to live with them every day, and you don't have to live with the complainant. And so it's something you wrestle with a lot, and it's a constant battle to put that element kind of on the side and say, you know my job is not to please the staff or to be popular with the staff but to do the right thing—serve the public well, whatever.

James Squires, editor, *Chicago Tribune:*

Junior editors and the reporters just react terribly to a retraction.

On February 9, 1985, *Editor & Publisher* Magazine reported the reaction of reporters at the *Mount Vernon* [N.Y.] *Daily Argus* when the paper's executive editor apologized for coverage of a local campaign meeting. "I have concluded," the editor wrote in the paper, "that we erred in the overall impression we gave of the meeting. We were wrong and we apologize for the error." Three of the paper's four full-time reporters responded in a letter to him: "As journalists, we were under the impression that at a professional newsgathering operation, editors back their reporters when criticism is raised about an accurate story. It now appears that those who scream loudly enough not only will get attention, but a public apology. . . . We feel threatened, knowing that if we do our jobs and are to write a controversial story, we will not receive support from our editors, when crude pressure is applied by critics."[9]

G. Woodson Howe, executive editor, *Omaha World Herald*, who agrees that having to live with the staff "comes into play" in the decision whether to retract, cites "another important reason" for being reluctant to publish retractions and corrections:

> It hurts your credibility. I don't like to see a paper running a whole lot of corrections that aren't called for because every correction does hurt your credibility some. Before I authorize a correction, I want to be persuaded that it really is justified.

Howe's view may not be the prevailing one. Newspapers, says *Los Angeles Times* media critic David Shaw, "have gradually been realizing in recent years . . . that newspaper credibility is more likely to be enhanced than undermined by admissions of error."[10] The same view is reflected in one of the items distilled from the advice of 50 media lawyers for the Associated Press Managing Editors Association: "A correction may give the paper, as a whole, greater credibility in the community—the people realize you are not afraid to admit you are wrong. In some states it will limit the potential damage recovery by the plaintiff."[11]

Most papers publish corrections and many of them set aside a fixed space for the purpose. However, the 1984 Associated Press Managing Editors Association credibility study found that 85 percent of the papers responding to its survey publish fewer than seven corrections a week—less than one a day. "If this were a true measure," commented the editor who reported on the study, Paul Neely of the *Chattanooga Times*, "it would constitute a record of accuracy in American newspapers of which all editors could be proud. It undoubtedly is far from the truth."

"And the real record," he added, "may be worse than what those figures imply." Neely noted that there were 267 responses to the survey of some 550 papers. "On the average," he said, "they probably come from papers that are diligent about accessibility to readers. Newspapers that print corrections only under duress and only on major, legally-troubling matters, may have simply tossed out the survey form."[12]

Published corrections almost invariably deal with factual errors. The complainant who objects to a story's imbalance or negative implications may get less satisfaction. Former *Wall Street Journal* editor Vermont Royster has pointed out that, while newspapers are now willing to "confess they misstated the date of the public school board meeting," most are reluctant to admit to publishing stories that are "basically wrong or misleading or unfair."[13]

Publications use letters to the editor, in addition to corrections in the news columns, to rectify errors. Editors may or may not acknowledge, in an editor's note appended to the letter, that the inaccuracy alleged in the letter was, in fact, an error. [14] *The New York Times* is among the publications that do not customarily acknowledge errors when they are cited in letters published on the editorial page. Omission of an acknowledgment can leave the complainant dissatisfied and leave readers to wonder whether the decision to publish the letter is itself an acknowledgment of error or is simply an effort to provide space for the "other side" to respond.

Editors faced with a complaint sometimes will invite the complainant to express it in a letter to the editor. This may satisfy some complainants, but a published letter, with nothing more, properly can be regarded as a self-serving statement. Significantly, the interviews with libel plaintiffs established that invariably they wanted more than an opportunity to respond; they wanted the publication to *admit* error through correction, retraction, or apology.

The words "retract" or "apologize," when demanded by a complainant, can set off alarm bells. James Squires, editor, *Chicago Tribune:*

> I am as reluctant as the next editor to retract. I'll only retract when I have made an obvious error of fact and that has been stuffed right down my throat. And when we do that we are very sorry and we apologize profusely. A lot of complaints that could end up in libel courts revolve around a person's interpretation of something that was in the newspaper, and they feel aggrieved by the way it was worded or about an imbalance of it or something. We don't have a great reluctance here to clarify something that we said, add another fact to it to put it in a different perspective, to use different words to regret misunderstandings; I mean, it's a lot easier for me to regret a misunderstanding than it is to retract a statement and apologize. . . .

The 1985 draft of a proposed guide for members of the California Newspaper Publishers Association illustrates the dirty-word character of "retraction." Wrote the organization's legal counsel, Joseph T. Francke:

> The healthiest approach with which to begin a corrections policy is to rid your vocabulary of the word "retraction" and ignore it when you see it in a letter demanding a correction. "Retraction" to a journalist has the ring of recantation—of the pressures imposed on Joan of Arc and Galileo. While a "retraction," like a recantation, suggests the coerced denial or abandonment of one's principled beliefs, "correction" does not. The operative word in California's statute on the subject is "correction." Purging your usage of the more emotional term is the first step to a sane policy. [15]

Time Magazine's style for many years made it impossible for the publication to employ the word "apologize." *Time*'s editor, Henry Grunwald, testifying during General Ariel Sharon's libel suit against *Time,* explained:

> The use of the word regret is almost a habit at times. We have used that word traditionally and for many, many years, and really mostly for the sake of

consistency we continue to use that word rather than another word, but there is in our mind no special significance in our using regret rather than apology.[16]

Time nevertheless began to "apologize" for errors, in addition to regretting them, after the Sharon trial.[17]

Of the 267 papers responding to the 1984 Associated Press Managing Editors Association survey, more than 60 percent reported that they do not say they are sorry about an error or do so only when there is a legal reason for it.[18]

Tom Patterson, executive director of the Minnesota News Council, an organization established to receive, investigate and make findings on complaints about press coverage, commented in 1984:

> While I find it a little difficult to understand why so many complainants want to hear an "apology," I find it equally difficult to understand why many editors find it so impossible to say, "I'm sorry that happened." Or even, "I'm sorry you feel that way about it. Our policy is this and our procedures are so. . . ." You can all be sure that when we take complaints against your papers at the News Council, we don't tell any of the complainants to drop dead, or that their complaint is the most ridiculous thing we've ever heard, both statements which complainants have alleged were made to them by editors. We try to show respect for the complainant and for the hurt. . . .[19]

The complainant who asks for a "retraction" may not be thinking in legal terms, but the word has legal implications in the ear of an editor, especially in the many states that have retraction statutes. The statutes usually limit money damages if the media comply with a request to retract. To a news organization, a retraction request sounds like the opening gun of a lawsuit and often triggers the usual defensive response to the threat of litigation—that is, being guarded and unresponsive to the complainant and calling in the lawyers.

In Florida, a retraction request must spell out certain details. Some editors in Florida have become reluctant to discuss retraction requests with complainants for fear of inadvertently perfecting the requests by curing defects through the information they elicit. A statute intended to prevent or to mitigate libel suits, therefore, conceivably can invite suits by making it harder to satisfy complainants through face-to-face discussion.

Editors also may adopt a defensive posture at the word "retraction" because they are mindful that retraction requests have been used to intimidate the press. The Synanon organization in 1978 launched a "retraction project" in which 960 letters citing California's retraction statute were sent to California news organizations demanding corrections or retractions for stories about Synanon. The letters signaled to the press a legal threat without the expense for Synanon of filing lawsuits. The National News

Council, responding to a complaint from United Press International about the "retraction project," concluded:

> It is clear that Synanon is using a law presumably passed to protect publishers and broadcasters . . . as a weapon for coercing the press into silence about Synanon and its affairs. It is also clear that, as a result of the legal harassment, many editors and news directors, especially those associated with small news organizations or limited resources, are refraining from publishing or broadcasting news they deem legitimate affecting Synanon.[20]

Defensiveness is most likely to be a problem when the person who wrote the story or had responsibility for it deals directly with an agitated or abusive complainant. Yet it is commonplace for reporters to be allowed to field complaints about their work.

Although reporters usually are expected to notify the desk of complaints about their stories, "passing on" does not necessarily assure that a disinterested party will hear the complaint. The desk people who learn of a complaint or who deal with it may have been deeply involved themselves in the story and made the decision to retain or delete the portion that led to the complaint.

Joseph Thornton, assistant general counsel, *Des Moines Register*:

> Some readers will call the 800 number. They will not have noticed that there was a byline on the story and they will talk to the first person on the city desk, sometimes that's a dayside editor who hasn't even read the paper or that particular story, or sometimes it's the editor who worked on the story and immediately gets defensive about the pride of authorship and the quality of work. So I'm afraid that there are times that the first opportunity to be accommodating is lost because there's an immediate argument about the accuracy or the tone or the thrust of the story, and positions are taken and lines are drawn. I have had that happen when I called the city desk to inquire about stories and have run into defensiveness. . . .

James Squires, editor, *Chicago Tribune*:

> It's been my experience that when reporters and junior editors do make a mistake, and then are reluctant to acknowledge that and reluctant to apologize, and never let that complaint get high enough into the organization to get the proper response and attention to it, what results is a lawsuit that ultimately brings about a damage claim against the newspaper. . . . I do not make the people who made the error write a retraction and deal with the response. That's where I got into trouble years ago. I learned that they cannot bring themselves far enough along to admit the error with enough flourish to appease the aggrieved party. And by this time they're usually mad, everybody's mad. . . . You can educate [reporters] till hell freezes over and when one makes a mistake in print, there's an incredible tendency, I find, to run away from it and to hide it and to blame it on someone else, and that they can't deal with that. . . . I am comfortable once we identify the call as a

complaint because once we do that, then I feel sure it's going to get to some editor who is not just going to brush it off and throw it away. It's the lost call, the call that just goes to the reporter and never makes it anywhere else—or the call that gets shunted around to four or five phones that never answer—that is where you get into trouble. . . . If I can get that call to the top 20 editors at the *Chicago Tribune* I'm going to significantly reduce my chances of getting sued for libel. . . . Every time I got in trouble it was because some guy was trying to cover his ass and wouldn't deal with the problem.

Donald Jones, assistant to editor and ombudsman, *Kansas City Star and Times*:

By and large, I find that papers are very defensive, very thin skinned. Reporters and editors—and I'm talking about papers of all kinds—are not sensitive to readers. They immediately think that the complainant is a nut or a kook. . . .

Charles Capaldo, metro editor, *Des Moines Register*:

Sometimes newspapers go out the window with the attitude, the haughty know-it-all attitude, that we're right and if you don't like it, sue. That's ridiculous.

Barbara Mack, general counsel, *Des Moines Register*:

Gee, wouldn't it be nice if journalists would be responsible for dealing with people who call in and want to scream and yell and bitch and piss and moan about their story. But the bottom line is that with a newsroom that has 130 or 150 people you are not going to have 150 people who are capable of holding their temper. You deal with large egos, you deal with prima donnas. There are people in that newsroom I would be comfortable knowing that they would get a call challenging them about a story they had written, and I would know that individual would say, 'Tell me everything you want, then let me go away, and then let me respond to you later in the day.' I would trust them to do that. And then there are people in the newsroom I know would be [incapable] of following that kind of protocol.

Michael Guidicessi, assistant general counsel, *Des Moines Register*:

What worries me is all the emotions, the passions, the professional egos that the reporter might have—that the subject who is unhappy and wants to work at it might say, "Let's get this fixed," and the reporter's ego gets in the way and it becomes an emotional issue. They say, "I don't write fiction. I write fact. Once I write it and put it in the paper I'm right." I don't think we're willing to admit very often that we made an error. . . . When a newspaper writes, "This is a correction and we regret the error," that's a lie. We really don't regret the error. We regret that somebody pointed it out to us.

Few editors follow the *Chicago Tribune*'s practice of isolating reporters from corrections. The Iowa Libel Research Project's survey of media defendants found only five papers that do not involve the reporter who did the story in writing the correction. The reporter who writes a story that produces complaints usually rechecks the story.

The expectation that reporters will "pass on" complaints customarily is based on a supposition by editors that reporters understand that they should do so. Fewer than a third of the surveyed media defendants reported having a procedure requiring the desk or an editor to be notified by reporters about complaints. At some papers, editors count on learning about a complaint from the complainant who is expected to take the initiative to go "higher up" if dissatisfied. Well over half of the surveyed media defendants said it was possible for a reporter to deal with a libel-type complaint without an editor finding out about it. Five of these media defendants said they were sued after reporters had hidden the complaints.

Tim McGuire, managing editor, *Minneapolis Star & Tribune*:

> Reporters are as interested in job security as anyone else. They don't want to
> get chewed out. So it's not going to be [their] first tendency to tell the world.

Defensiveness may be found even in cases where the press agrees that a correction or retraction is warranted. Twenty-nine of the 164 libel plaintiffs interviewed sued despite being given some type of redress in the form of retraction, correction, personal apology, or agreement not to repeat the story. The plaintiffs who received a retraction or correction said they were dissatisfied because it was too late or not prominent enough; it made a new error or repeated an earlier mistake; or it was described as the complainant's view instead of being an admission of error. A review of a sampling of cases involving retractions and corrections suggests that these complaints had merit in at least one fourth of the cases, and perhaps in half.[21]

The newspeople we interviewed were not surprised that the complainants were turned off by their contacts with the press. Many were as critical of the press on this score as were the plaintiffs. Relatively few of the editors in the media-defendant survey said they were fully satisfied by the way their staffs handle complaints. Discourtesy was the problem cited most often by editors.

James Squires, editor, *Chicago Tribune*:

> The people who sue us either are jerks looking for a deep pocket and never
> getting anywhere, so they're not that big of a problem—they're a nuisance—or
> people who are forced to sue us because we ignore them and kick them and refuse
> to deal with them.

Tim McGuire, managing editor, *Minneapolis Star & Tribune*:

> Newspeople have the wonderful tendency to be the most arrogant devils in the
> whole world. When they get into a confrontation, they show that arrogance.

Jack Davis, city editor, *Chicago Tribune:* "The rudeness in this business is legendary."

Donald Jones, assistant to editor and ombudsman, *Kansas City Star and Times:*

> You get a quart of sour milk at your local grocery store, put it in a paper bag and you take it back to the check-out counter and say the milk is sour and the guy will say to you either, "Get a new quart" or "Here's your money back." The equivalent of taking a quart of sour milk back to a newspaper is you're lucky if they don't pour it on your head. . . .
>
> Kids come in here and they think this is the way you're supposed to be in the news business, you're supposed to be rude. And if editors aren't smart enough to stop that as soon as it starts—no wonder people don't like us. . . . You hear things like, somebody puts his hand over the phone and yells, "Who the hell gave me this nut? I didn't work last night." The "nut" on the phone hears it.

Arnold Garson, managing editor, *Des Moines Register:*

> I don't know exactly what the hell to do, but I do know that I'm bothered by the fact that we occasionally end up being ruder or [more] discourteous to people than we really ought to be in dealing with them on the telephone.

Joel Kramer, editor, *Minneapolis Star & Tribune:*

> An awful lot of papers are not doing that [being nice to people] very well. . . . From the amount of energy I've seen at papers devoted to the complaint process, it's not viewed as a top priority. A lot of editors don't take the time to do it. . . . There's a lot of arrogance. [But] it's breaking down. The value system is changing. It's no longer considered bad form [among journalists] to care about what the ordinary reader thinks.

And as Kurt M. Luedtke, former executive editor of the *Detroit Free Press,* told the American Newspaper Publishers Association in 1982:

> [R]eporters really don't know how inaccurate they are simply because they assume, as I must say I would, that a story is correct until someone complains. Left out of that equation are all those who don't want to make waves, or who are afraid of offending you, or who don't know how, or who cool down and don't bother, or who are brushed off by whoever answers the phone. Call your city desk some time and see if you like the feeling. [22]

When the Libel Research Project asked plaintiffs what upset them about the article or broadcast that led them to complain to the media, and subsequently to take legal action, they responded overwhelmingly that it was its falsity. Newspeople agree just as overwhelmingly that inaccuracy is a major press problem.

Attend a meeting of editors and chances are you will hear complaints, accompanied by nods of approval from colleagues who had similar experiences, about how the editors were misquoted in their own papers. Studies of press credibility by journalism groups invariably conclude that inaccuracy and unfairness are major parts of the credibility problem.

David Lawrence Jr., then executive editor of the *Detroit Free Press*, wrote in 1984:

> After being interviewed many times in the past decade as a newspaper editor, "damage control" is the way I approach the media. I try to talk slowly enough, and "quotably" enough to get my point across and the facts right. . . . I try to minimize the damage from reporters who have preconceived notions about the "truth". . . . Sometimes I know I'd be better off being less accessible to people I know have made up their minds about the story, but that hardly seems right for someone in the business of asking questions and seeking access. What a shame I feel this way.[23]

Roger Tatarian, former editor of United Press International, wrote in 1982 of how he spoke years ago at a journalism meeting only to be "jolted the next day to find myself generously misquoted in a newspaper of considerable stature. . . . I had spoken from a written text; I knew exactly what I had said, and I knew exactly what had come before and after the key quote. And now I saw how it had come out and [I] could have cried. I began to wonder how often this sort of thing happened, and in talking with editors and publishers . . . over the years, I got an uncomfortable answer: Almost all of them testified, off the record, that they too had been left shaken at one time or another at how their remarks had come out in print."[24]

Phil J. Record, of the *Fort Worth Star-Telegram*, was president of the Society of Professional Journalists, Sigma Delta Chi, in 1984. He traveled extensively during his term and was interviewed frequently. Record commented, "It is an uncomfortable experience for a journalist to be the interviewee instead of the interviewer. . . . My discomfort has turned to genuine concern after having found myself to be the victim of some sloppy, lousy reporting."[25]

Journalism educator and former *New York Times* correspondent Elie Abel complained in a 1984 speech, "As one who lectures from time to time across the land, I have long since learned that words and ideas are frequently misreported by reporters who turn a tin ear to the cadences of American speech or who can't be bothered to check verifiable facts."[26]

"Almost always," observed *Los Angeles Times* media critic David Shaw in 1984, "as we have heard time and time again, anyone who reads a story about something he or she has some personal knowledge of finds a mistake."[27]

Richard Capen, publisher of the *Miami Herald,* told the American Society of Newspaper Editors in 1984, "We put up with far too many errors that shouldn't be in the newspaper in the first place." Capen reported how, in reader "feedback" sessions, readers complain about "errors; stupid errors; embarrassing errors; misleading or incomplete quotes."[28]

Frank Mankiewicz, former journalist and president of National Public Radio, predicted in 1983:

> Sooner or later everybody will know the dirty little secret of American
> journalism, that the reports are wrong. Because sooner or later everybody will have
> been involved in something that has been reported. Whenever you see a news
> story you were part of, it is always wrong. It may be a rather unimportant error,
> but it also can be an important one.[29]

Eugene Patterson, president of the *St. Petersburg* (Fla.) *Times,* admitted in 1984, "There is no question that there's a hell of a lot of carelessness in all of the news media."[30]

One of Patterson's staffers, Rob Hooker, deputy metropolitan editor/projects, commented in a 1984 interview, "You wouldn't believe how many times I hear people in this newsroom who are quoted in a story published elsewhere or figure in it say, 'That's not accurate' or 'That's not quite right.' It's sobering."[31]

Gregory Favre, who was managing editor of the *Chicago Sun-Times* when it changed ownership, had the same experience. Wrote Favre in 1984:

> There have been about a dozen different published versions of several stories
> which happened during that stormy period [at the *Sun-Times*]. . . . Granted every
> story had some things right, at least one had almost everything correct, but not a
> single one had everything right. Help![32]

David Weir, executive director of the Center for Investigative Reporting in San Francisco, said in 1984, "I have had a lot of articles written about me or [about] things I have done, and well over half were just laced with inaccuracies."[33]

Efforts to quantify the frequency of error seem generally to support Weir's experience. In a credibility study commissioned by the American Society of Newspaper Editors in 1984, a cross-section of adults was asked whether the newspaper they read ever had coverage of events they had personal knowledge of. Seventy-three percent responded yes. Of these, about 4 in 10 gave the press generally low marks for both the accuracy and fairness of the coverage they knew about.[34] A *Newsweek* Magazine survey in 1984 found that 37 percent of persons who had been covered by the press felt that the stories contained inaccuracies.[35] "Numerous researchers," reported a 1980 study for the American Newspaper Publishers Association, "have confirmed that about half of all straight news stories contain some type of error."[36]

Lack of confidence in newspaper accuracy is reflected at the *Kansas City Star and Times* in the advice the paper gives to reporters about how to verify facts in news stories. "Use [newspaper] clips as a last resort," says the *Star's* guide to policies and procedures. "If there is an error in the clips, you will perpetuate it."[37] The 1984 Associated Press Managing Editors Association study of corrections found that more than a third of newspapers do not file corrections in their libraries, a fourth do not automatically file the correction with the original story, more than 40 percent do not clip the correction to the original story, and only 10 percent file letters to the editor with the stories the letters are correcting.[38]

Given the accuracy shortcomings that newspeople themselves experience and acknowledge, you would expect them to have placed greater emphasis on assuring that complaints about accuracy are handled properly. After all, when the object of a news story arrives at a newspaper's doorstep with a complaint that the paper got something wrong, he or she is voicing a complaint newspeople know to be too often true. Joel Kramer of the *Minneapolis Star & Tribune* probably is right that journalists no longer consider it bad form to care about what the ordinary reader thinks, but the caring too frequently does not translate into procedures to deal effectively with complaints.

We undertook the interviews with plaintiffs and with newspaper personnel expecting the respective findings to be in conflict. Instead, we found substantial agreement. More often than not, the observations by editors tracked or reinforced the experiences and comments by plaintiffs.

Plaintiffs expressed dissatisfaction with their post-publication contacts with the press. Their experiences with the press, they said, influenced them to bring suit. Yes, said the editors, the press generally is inept in responding to complaints. Nor were the editors surprised that the complainant's contact with the press contributed to the decision to sue. The rudeness, arrogance and defensiveness plaintiffs said they encountered were acknowledged by editors to be common newsroom problems. The criticisms by editors of their own publication's shortcomings, and of those of the press as a whole, were as sharp at times as the criticisms by plaintiffs.

Greater sensitivity and more effective procedures to deal with complaints will avail the press little in terms of preventing libel suits if money is the overriding objective of prospective libel plaintiffs. According to the plaintiffs, however, setting the record straight is the prime objective when they contact the press initially; money figures somewhat more as an objective in their responses when suits are filed, but correcting the record predominates even then.

Editors more often than plaintiffs are inclined to attribute a money motive, but even on this issue editors and plaintiffs tend toward general agreement on the importance to plaintiffs of some form of vindication. We asked them for their reaction to our finding that a large proportion of plaintiffs said that they were predominantly motivated by a desire to have the record set straight, rather than to obtain money.

David Zeeck, managing editor, *Kansas City Star*:

> That's very true. That's certainly been our experience.

James Gannon, editor, *Des Moines Register*:

> I believe in most cases that probably is true, that some sense of justice or setting the record straight probably is more important [than money]. Maybe it's a sense of, you know, punishing a newspaper in the sense of proving that the paper was wrong and they were right, more than the dollars involved.

James Squires, editor, *Chicago Tribune*:

> I am not surprised at that. I mean, that has been my experience.

G. Woodson Howe, executive editor, *Omaha World Herald*:

> I would have to agree with it. It sounds consistent with the experience I've had over many years. . . . There's a lot of plaintiffs' lawyers out there. With them, looking at the one-third sharing of any damage awards, I think their motivation is money. But as for the average guy, I think he just wants to look better in the eyes of his neighbors and his family.

Forrest Kilmer, editor, *Quad City Times*:

> The two suits that were filed against us were for money. Small amounts, but they were people in a poor financial situation and they were after money. Some of the people who have threatened to sue us . . . they want their names cleared and I don't think money was an important angle at all. I don't think that money entered into it.

The Libel Research Project was initiated to determine the feasibility of developing non-litigation methods to deal with libel complaints. The findings lead to the conclusion that an alternative to litigation already exists—in the nation's newsrooms. More editors need to recognize that how they deal with complaints has an important bearing on whether they ultimately are sued for libel. The same attention now given to pre-publication safeguards to prevent libel should be extended to post-publication practices.

James Squires, editor, *Chicago Tribune*:

> I have over the years become a firm believer that even a serious post-publication complaint could best be handled by the newspaper, through its policy,

before it gets to the lawyers and the libel people. I think, in other words, that the best defense against libel in newspapers is the newspaper's response after it's done something wrong.

Our findings argue strongly for editors to:

1. Impress on employees the great power the press has to hurt people. Editors should insist that courtesy in dealing with complaints have high newsroom priority. Instruction in human relations should be part of a journalist's in-house training.

2. Center the responsibility for dealing with complaints in a person with good human-relations skills who is not responsible for news coverage. Editors must be informed and consulted and make final decisions, but, except on smaller papers, they cannot adequately bird-dog complaints. Nor do the qualities that make for good editors necessarily equip them to deal sensitively with people.

3. Develop policies and procedures for addressing complaints, put them in writing, and emphasize their importance.

4. Make sitting on other than a frivolous complaint a firing offense.

Some litigious persons never will be deterred from suing. And, for some persons, the act of suing serves a purpose in itself. But the press ought at least to avoid having complainants who contact newspaper offices leave more aggravated than when they arrived. Simply put, the press must pay the same attention to the post-publication consequences of its stories as it does to getting those stories into the hands of readers.

5

THE DECISION TO SUE

IN THE PRECEDING CHAPTERS we have explored the demographics of libel disputes—who sues, who is sued, for what types of publication, and in light of what types of perceived harm. We have also discussed the steps taken by libel plaintiffs at and after the point of publication, and the nature and consequences of the plaintiffs' interaction with the media.

Beginning with this chapter and continuing through Chapter 7, we will turn our attention to the libel dispute once it has ripened into an irreconcilable conflict. In doing so, we will be interested not only in what various libel plaintiffs do, but in why. We will first explore why plaintiffs sue, how they appear to reach that decision, and what roles the attorneys and media play in the decision to sue. We will then, in Chapter 6, undertake a detailed examination and analysis of the process through which libel claims are litigated and resolved, both by judicial decision and settlement. Our focus will relate not only to constructing a clear picture of how litigation operates as a means of resolving libel disputes, but also to what the litigation process itself tells us about the motivations and objectives of the various parties involved in the dispute. In Chapter 7 we will continue our exploration of why libel plaintiffs sue and what they seek to achieve from litigation. In this connection, we will analyze the suitability of litigation as a means of resolving various types of libel claims, the effectiveness with which litigation achieves the parties' objectives, and the potential for use of non-litigation processes for resolution of libel disputes.

We will begin this extended inquiry with the lawyer, who serves as the entry into the formal legal process. With the lawyer's involvement, the libel dispute will be transformed from a grievance that the parties cannot—

54

or will not—resolve, to a formal claim structured under the rules of the legal system. Our inquiry will disclose that the lawyer's role and influence is remarkably slight; that the plaintiffs—particularly the public plaintiffs—are calling the shots; that the media's arrogance or indifference shapes the plaintiff's decision to sue; and that the plaintiffs sue to deter publication and achieve vindication, with the very act of suit representing the best, and often only, means of response and denial.

THE ROLE PLAYED BY COUNSEL PRIOR TO LITIGATION

Lawyers play an active and central role in any litigation process, and libel disputes against the media are no exception. In the libel setting, however, the timing of the lawyers' involvement and their influence in shaping decisions seem to depart in certain significant ways from patterns to which we are accustomed. The role played by lawyers, and the reasons for any departure in the pattern of lawyers' involvement in other settings, will be discussed in the following sections.

The Initial Lawyer Contact

With the exception of seven plaintiffs who represented themselves in the initial stages of the dispute, all of the plaintiffs in the cases studied sought legal advice prior to initiating litigation. The timing of the contact was bunched at two points, as the following table indicates. Of the plaintiffs who talked to a lawyer immediately following publication—and roughly half of them did—73 percent did so before contacting the media. Of the plaintiffs (36 percent) who talked to a lawyer 7 or more days after

TABLE 5–1   Time of Lawyer Contact

Time	Number	Percent
Before Publication	7	4.9%
Immediately After Publication	69	48.3%
2–7 Days After Publication	16	11.2%
7–30 Days After Publication	31	21.7%
More than 30 days after Publication	20	14.0%

publication, 72 percent had contacted the media prior to seeking advice from a lawyer.

The timing of the lawyer contact bears an independent statistical relationship to a number of other responses that will be discussed more fully later. For present purposes it is noteworthy that more public office holders than other plaintiffs contacted the media before seeing a lawyer, and had decided to sue before seeing a lawyer. Therefore it is not surprising that the group waiting 7 days or more after publication to see a lawyer includes a disproportionate number of plaintiffs who were candidates for political office and public office holders, or persons who were allegedly libeled in connection with public activities. Because they held public office or had very high visibility in the community, these plaintiffs had probably dealt with the press frequently, and would logically be expected to contact the press prior to seeing a lawyer.

The plaintiffs were asked why they contacted the lawyer. The results of this question were coded in terms of their open-ended responses. A surprisingly large number of plaintiffs reported that they went to the lawyer to sue, suggesting that they had decided upon their course of action before consulting with an attorney about their claim. The plaintiffs were also asked in a separate question whether they had decided to sue before going to a lawyer. The responses to this question confirmed that the degree of prejudgment about suit was high. Of the 143 responding plaintiffs, 57 percent (81) indicated that they had decided to sue before seeing a lawyer; 43 percent (62) decided to do so only after consulting the lawyer. The correspondence of responses to these two questions was high, indicating that many plaintiffs decided to sue before seeing a lawyer, but nevertheless sought legal advice on the issue, and responded to the first question accordingly.

The plaintiffs who went to a lawyer having already decided to sue share a number of characteristics. First, they tend to have contacted the media before contacting the lawyer, as discussed above. Second, they tend to have been allegedly libeled in relation to public or political activities.[1]

TABLE 5–2   Reason Plaintiffs Contacted
A Lawyer

Reason Given	Number	Percent
For General Advice	66	45.5%
For Retraction	8	5.5%
To Sue	50	34.5%
Other	21	14.5%

Third, they consist disproportionately of public officials and persons with very high visibility in their communities, who are suing more often to restore their reputation than for money.

Who were the lawyers selected by the plaintiffs? In general, the lawyers were a diverse group with varied experience and varied relationships with the plaintiffs. As background to the analyses that will follow concerning the lawyers' role prior to litigation, their advice, and their influence on the decision to sue, information will be presented on the lawyers' experience with libel litigation and the manner in which they were selected.

To obtain information on the lawyers' prior experience with libel litigation, interviews were conducted with 40 lawyers who represented libel plaintiffs in the survey population.[2] The lawyers' reported prior libel litigation experience is outlined in Table 5–3. The information obtained on the experience of the plaintiffs' lawyers in media libel cases must be viewed with caution, as the population may not be representative. The information, however, permits a few general conclusions. One might have expected that the exceedingly low rate of plaintiff success in litigation would connote a very high rate of inexperience on the part of the plaintiffs' lawyers. The data belie this conclusion, as the rate at which lawyers recommend suit[3] is substantially higher than the percentage of lawyers who report no prior libel litigation experience. One might also have expected to find a certain number of lawyers who "specialized" in libel litigation, but might not have expected to find that as many as 14 percent of the lawyers were very experienced (four or more prior cases), while only three can reasonably be described as "specialists" (10 or more libel cases).

TABLE 5–3   Number of Libel Cases
Previously Litigated by Plaintiffs'
Attorneys

Number of Prior Libel Cases	Lawyers Responding #	%
None	20	50%
One to Three	10	25%
Four to Nine	3	7%
Ten or More	3	7%
Other*	4	10%

*Responses coded "other" represent substantial litigation experience in other fields, including related fields such as privacy actions, allied communicative torts, and the like, constituting the equivalent of a high level of skill and experience.

In view of the information provided by the lawyers, what can be said about their experience? First, it appears that over half had no previous experience with libel litigation. Given the very low incidence of libel suits, this is not surprising. Many of these lawyers may have had experience in complex litigation, however, and such litigation is nearly as specialized and relevant a skill for purposes of a libel suit as is prior libel litigation. Nevertheless, the level of attorney experience seems lower than that reported for general civil litigation, where 78 percent of lawyers describe themselves as "expert" or "somewhat expert."[4] As discussed later, it does appear that the lawyers with no prior libel litigation experience consist disproportionately of lawyers in general practice who represented the private plaintiffs and who worked on an hourly fee basis.[5]

The second and perhaps more noteworthy observation is that 40 percent of the plaintiffs' lawyers had prior libel litigation experience, and an additional 10 percent had related litigation experience. Moreover, about 14 percent had substantial prior libel litigation experience. In light of this, it is difficult to explain the low incidence of plaintiff success in court, the optimistic predictions of success, and the high incidence of contingency arrangements (all discussed in detail in the following pages) exclusively in terms of lawyer inexperience. Inexperience may, indeed, be a substantial contributing factor but, as will be explored in depth, the "how and why" of libel plaintiffs' decisions to sue are infinitely more complex.

Table 5-4 provides information on the way plaintiffs selected their lawyers. As Table 5-4 indicates, plaintiffs seeking a lawyer most frequently went to the lawyer who represented them in other capacities, either personal or business. Few lawyers were selected on the basis of their trial experience or reputation, or their experience as a libel lawyer. Nearly a fifth of the lawyers were selected by referral from other lawyers, however, and it is likely that many of these lawyers were more experienced in

TABLE 5-4   How Plaintiff Lawyers Were Selected

Response	Number	Percent
Self-Represented	7	4.9%
Lawyer Contacted Plaintiff	6	4.2%
Friend and/or Personal or Business Lawyer	84	58.3%
Reputation as Trial Lawyer	8	5.6%
Reputation as Libel Lawyer	14	9.7%
Referral from Lawyer	25	17.4%

TABLE 5–5   Plaintiff Persistence with Original Attorney

Did Plaintiff Change Lawyers, and Why?	Number	Percent
No Change from Original Lawyer	113	74.8%
Changed Because Dissatisfied with Original Lawyer	9	6.0%
Changed Because More Expertness Needed*	14	9.3%
Changed, No Reason Specified	15	9.9%

*The extent to which the third category—changed because more expertness needed—includes lawyer referral rather than client-originated change is unclear from the data.

litigation than the lawyers selected because of friendship or representation in other capacities.

Plaintiffs also were asked whether more than one attorney was engaged during the course of the litigation. Of 107 responding plaintiffs, 82, or 76 percent, indicated that only one lawyer was engaged; and 25, or 24 percent, indicated that a change in lawyers took place. The reasons for the changes are contained in Table 5–5. Two interesting points emerge from Table 5–5. The first is what appears to be a relatively high percentage of plaintiff lawyer changes following the initial engagement of counsel. Attorneys were changed in 25 percent of the cases, a significantly higher percentage of cases than would ordinarily be expected in civil litigation. The changes, moreover, are exclusive of initial referral of a client by the lawyer first contacted (but not engaged) because that lawyer's area of practice did not include libel litigation. Seventeen percent of the cases involved referrals initiated by the lawyer initially consulted, as is reflected in Table 5–4.

The second point raised by Table 5–5 concerns the reasons for change of lawyers. In 9.3 percent of the cases a change in counsel was made because greater expertness in the litigation and libel areas was needed. It is not known from the responses whether all or most such changes were initiated by the lawyers themselves rather than by the clients; but ordinary experience would suggest that at least some changes were lawyer-initiated.[6] In at least 6 percent of all cases the change in lawyer appears to have been initiated by the client, or plaintiff, due to client dissatisfaction. The coded responses, interpreted in light of interview notes, however, suggest that the level of client-initiated change is higher than 6 percent, and may be as high as 15 percent. In addition to the 9 cases (6 percent) involving plaintiff dissatisfaction, no reason was given in 15 cases (10 percent). A majority of these cases, as well as some of the 14 cases in which a change in lawyers occurred because of needed expertness, involved client-initiated lawyer changes.[7] Interview notes do not, however, permit general conclusions to be drawn about the times at which the changes occurred, nor the specific case-related reasons.

The incidence of lawyer change tended to be distributed among all types of lawyers initially selected by the plaintiffs, although the frequency of change was marginally higher for the family lawyer and referral groups than for the established trial and libel lawyer groups. As might be expected, there was a statistically significant difference in the incidence of lawyer change and the type of fee arrangement, with client-initiated change occurring more frequently when the lawyer was engaged on an hourly fee basis. Plaintiffs paying hourly fees are likely to feel a greater stake in the quality and productivity of the lawyers' efforts.

While a 25 percent rate of lawyer change following initial engagement, 6–15 percent of it client-initiated, is high, libel litigation presents certain unique characteristics that might account for the high change rate. First, libel suits are uniquely personal and emotionally charged forms of legal action. Plaintiffs are likely to have strong and relatively unyielding convictions, and be more than normally upset by legal advice that qualifies their right to correct the perceived injustice in any way. A second possible reason for a relatively high rate of lawyer change is the complexity and length of libel litigation. Libel law has become a highly developed, highly sophisticated, area of law, and the litigation of a libel claim with its attendant discovery processes, motions, and constitutional privileges is as complex as almost any other form of personal injury claim. The complexity quite likely accounts for the significant amount of lawyer-initiated change in counsel. The extended nature of the litigation process probably accounts for a good deal of plaintiff dissatisfaction with the lawyers.[8]

Finally, as mentioned above, some lawyer changes relate to the ordinary fee arrangements, discussed in detail below. Seventy-three percent of the lawyers were engaged on a contingency basis—normally a contingency fee coupled with out-of-pocket costs.[9] Client-initiated lawyer change tended to occur with hourly lawyers. In contrast, contingency-lawyer changes were explained by the need for more expertise, or were unexplained. In light of the extended nature of the litigation (the average case lasted about four years) and its complexity, it is likely that some lawyer changes represented voluntary withdrawal by the lawyer.

Whatever the specific reason or set of reasons for the high rate of lawyer change following initial engagement, the phenomenon is not entirely unexpected given the unique characteristics of libel litigation. The high rate of change seems to be related to the nature of the libel action itself. No statistically significant differences in frequency or pattern of lawyer replacement occur depending on the category of plaintiff or the nature of the specific claim made. With the exception noted above, a similar pattern was followed by all groups of plaintiffs, and in all types of libel claims.

The Attorneys' Advice and Counsel

The advice of the attorney took many forms in the cases surveyed. In the following pages the nature of the attorneys' involvement will be surveyed, including the subjects discussed by the counsel with plaintiffs, counsels' involvement in media contacts before suit was brought, counsels' advice concerning suit, and the fee arrangements. Later in this chapter we will analyze the influence of the lawyers' advice on the plaintiffs' decision to sue.

Subjects Discussed by Attorney and Client

Each plaintiff was asked whether the attorney provided information and advice on a series of topics. The responses will be discussed in the following pages, but a note of caution is needed at the outset. In most instances a significant period of time had elapsed between the publication of the alleged libel and our contact with the plaintiffs. The responses, therefore, should be viewed and interpreted with caution, and with the presumption that the discussion of topics is likely to be underreported by the plaintiffs.

In all instances the plaintiffs' attorney discussed the facts of the case and the action for libel with the plaintiffs. Discussion often went beyond libel law and the filing of a lawsuit stemming from the alleged libel, however. Information was not obtained from plaintiffs concerning subjects discussed on a more particularized level, such as the legal theory of the suit, constitutional privileges, and the like.

In most instances, the likely length of the controversy was discussed, and an estimated time period for suit was projected by the attorney. Table 5–6 sets forth the plaintiff responses on this subject. Only about half of the plaintiffs specifically recalled a time frame projected by the attorney prior to litigation. Of those who did recall, the average time projected for the suit was between two and five years (3.9 year mean). This is fairly consistent with the actual results, which yielded an average length of controversy of about four years. [10]

Most of the plaintiffs were apprised by their attorneys of the likely publicity about the plaintiff that would result from bringing a libel action, and the potential for repetition of the libel. Of the 117 plaintiffs who could specifically recall, 84, or 72 percent, reported that the likelihood of pub-

TABLE 5–6   Estimated Length of
Controversy, as Discussed By Plaintiff
and Attorney Prior to Litigation

Estimated Time Before Completion*	Number	Percent
Less than 1 year	6	7.6%
1–2 years	21	26.6%
2–5 years	36	45.6%
More than 5 years	16	20.3%

*36 plaintiffs responded "other" (no codable length of time),
22 were "uncertain"; and 27 refused to answer for a variety of
reasons.

licity was discussed by their attorney. Of the 113 plaintiffs who specifically responded when asked whether the risk of repetition of the libel was discussed, 80, or 70 percent, responded affirmatively.

Alternatives to litigation were mentioned by the attorneys in only 39 percent of the cases, according to the plaintiff responses. Sixty-six plaintiffs, representing 61 percent of the 109 responding plaintiffs, indicated that alternatives to litigation were not discussed by the lawyer with the client in advance of litigation. Of the 43 instances in which plaintiffs reported discussing alternatives, most involved discussion of possible settlement. Nineteen percent of all responding plaintiffs reported that the attorney questioned whether the suit was necessary.

When the discussion of alternatives to litigation and possible settlement or dropping of the claim is compared with the plaintiffs' job at the time of the libel, an apparent pattern emerges. The following tables illustrate the apparent differences between elected officials and professionals, on the one hand, and business proprietors, white collar employees, and public employees, on the other.

Table 5–7 indicates the frequency with which litigation alternatives were discussed with different plaintiff groups.

Table 5–8 indicates the frequency with which the plaintiffs' lawyers discussed settlement or considered litigation unnecessary, broken down by plaintiff job groups.

Both tables indicate a different pattern of consultation between lawyer and client for elected officials and professionals, on the one hand, and other plaintiffs, on the other. Table 5–7 indicates that alternatives to litigation are discussed with elected officials and professionals in 31 and 34 percent of the cases, respectively, while the range for other plaintiffs is 51 to 75 percent. Elected officials and professionals—a category containing a

TABLE 5–7   Did Lawyer Discuss
Alternatives to Litigation?

Plaintiff Category		Yes	No
Elected Official	#	8	18
percentage within category		30.8%	69.2%
White Collar	#	9	3
percentage within category		75.0%	25.0%
Public Employee	#	19	18
percentage within category		51.4%	48.6%
Business Proprietor	#	13	9
percentage within category		59.1%	40.9%
Professional	#	11	21
percentage within category		34.4%	65.6%
p < .04			

fair proportion of persons who are highly visible within the community—
are most likely to have contacted the media before contacting a lawyer,
and to have decided to sue prior to consultation with counsel. In view of
this, it is understandable that the issue of alternatives to litigation is less
likely to arise with these plaintiffs, for they went to the lawyer having
decided to sue, and they felt that there *were no* alternatives to litigation.

Table 5–8 evidences a similar differential pattern between elected officials and professionals, on the one hand, and all other plaintiffs on the
other, but reveals additional insight into the plaintiff motivations and the
lawyer's role in advance of litigation. As noted earlier, the attorneys did
question whether a lawsuit was necessary in roughly 33 percent of the

TABLE 5–8   Selected Alternatives Discussed

Plaintiff Category		Settlement	Lawsuit Unnecessary
Elected Official	#	5	7
category	%	41.7%	58.3%
White Collar	#	5	2
category	%	71.4%	28.6%
Public Employee	#	11	4
category	%	73.3%	26.7%
Business Proprietor	#	4	0
category	%	100.0%	0.0%
Professional	#	6	7
category	%	46.2%	53.8%
p. < .15			

cases. Table 5–8 indicates that 70 percent of those cases involved elected officials or professionals, and that for them the inappropriateness of a lawsuit was mentioned more frequently as contrasted with settlement than for any other group of plaintiffs.

The frequency with which the need for a lawsuit was questioned with elected officials and professionals does not appear to have any relationship to the likelihood of winning, as judged by the actual results reached in litigation. No statistically significant difference in the incidence of victory in litigation occurs with either plaintiff group, although, as would be expected, media win most often when public officials and candidates for office are the plaintiffs.[11] Of course, roughly 89 percent of the plaintiff survey cases finally resolved by adjudication were won by the media (excluding settlements). Notwithstanding this, the higher incidence of suggestions that the suit was unnecessary is likely to have been influenced by the higher standards of privilege and the more complex and prolonged litigation faced by "public" plaintiffs, who are heavily represented in the elected official and professional categories.[12] The persistence of public plaintiffs in the face of frequent recommendations against suit may also confirm the suggestion made earlier, that the "public" plaintiffs have determined at the time counsel is contacted that no effective alternative to litigation (other than not suing) exists.

Each plaintiff was asked whether settlement was discussed, and 77 of the 122 responses (63 percent) indicated that the subject of settlement was raised. The following table provides information on the settlement issue. In cases where settlement was discussed, 30 percent of the attorneys felt that there was a good chance for settlement; 46 percent felt that little or no chance for settlement existed. Generally speaking, the attorneys were pessimistic about the hope for settlement. Information we have obtained on the incidence of settlement tends to confirm their judgment.[13]

The plaintiff responses to questions concerning the subjects discussed with them by their attorney, and the nature of the discussion, suggest that plaintiffs were generally, although not always, apprised of the risks and

TABLE 5–9   Chance of Settlement

Subject Discussed/Prediction	Number	Percent
Discussed/chances good	23	18.9%
Discussed/chances slight	17	13.9%
Discussed/no chance	18	14.8%
Discussed/no prediction	19	15.6%
Not Discussed	45	36.9%

emotional costs of bringing a libel suit, the alternatives that might be available (including no suit), chances for settlement, and the length of the process once litigation is brought. The extent to which the plaintiffs' decision was to sue even in the face of these considerations serves as confirmation of the strength of the plaintiffs' feelings about obtaining recourse for a perceived wrong, and the lengths to which they would go in an attempt to achieve vindication.

Attorney Involvement in Media Contact

Perhaps the first contribution of the plaintiffs' lawyer to resolution of the dispute was contacting the media. Although the media were contacted by the plaintiff, the plaintiff's lawyer, or both in 90 percent of the cases, lawyers were involved in the media contact in only 53 percent of those cases, either alone, with, or in addition to plaintiff contact. The frequency of pre-suit lawyer contact with the media seems surprisingly low, especially in light of the fact that all of the plaintiffs surveyed brought suit. While one would expect, given other plaintiff responses, that a majority of the plaintiffs would be personally involved in the media contact, and a large number of the plaintiffs would contact the media before contacting an attorney, one would also expect that the plaintiff's media contact would be followed by attorney contact prior to filing suit in virtually all cases. The facts reported, however, are inconsistent with the latter expectation. Forty-nine percent of the responding plaintiffs reported that they contacted the media first, before contacting a lawyer. When asked who contacted the media, Table 5–10 indicates that 35 percent of the plaintiffs relied entirely on the lawyer to negotiate with the media. Thirty-seven percent of the plaintiffs, however, appear to have made the exclusive pre-suit contact with the media, almost always prior to contacting the lawyer, and to have approached the lawyer so set on a course of action that the lawyer considered it unnecessary to contact the media on the plaintiffs' behalf before filing suit. An additional 10 percent of the responding plaintiffs brought suit

TABLE 5–10   Media Contact Prior to Suit

Person Contacting Media	Number	Percent
Plaintiff only	53	37.1%
Plaintiff Lawyer only	50	35.0%
Plaintiff and Lawyer	26	18.2%
Neither	14	9.8%

without any prior contact with the media. Instead, the course of action set upon in such cases was a lawsuit. The apparent absence of lawyer contact with the opposing party (through counsel) prior to filing suit diverges sharply from the common practice in civil litigation.[14] As might be expected, a disproportionate percentage of such plaintiffs were public plaintiffs and plaintiffs who had previously filed a lawsuit.

The conclusion that public plaintiffs and those who had previously sued were more actively involved in the media contact—often to the exclusion of the lawyer—is confirmed by an analysis of these plaintiff groups and the media contact. We will turn first to an analysis of the media contact and the plaintiffs' prior litigation experience, focusing on the degree of lawyer involvement with the media. The total level of lawyer involvement in the media contact is similar with plaintiffs who had sued before, and those who had not, although the rate is marginally lower for those with no prior litigation (58 percent) than for those with it (61 percent). The rate at which plaintiffs alone contacted the media is also similar between the two categories. The frequency with which plaintiffs rely exclusively on their lawyers to contact the media is divergent, however, with only 28 percent of those who had sued previously relying only on their lawyer, and 43 percent of those who had never brought a lawsuit relying exclusively on their lawyer to deal with the press. Furthermore, the proportion of cases involving both plaintiff and lawyer contacting the media is much greater (33 percent) among those who had sued previously than among those who had not (15 percent), a result dictated by the higher incidence with which plaintiffs with prior litigation experience personally contacted the media before consulting a lawyer. The different patterns are even greater when comparison is made with those plaintiffs who had previously sued for libel or privacy. These experienced libel and privacy plaintiffs usually contact the media themselves exclusive of their lawyer, and decide to sue before seeing their lawyer.

TABLE 5–11   Media Contact and Prior Litigation Experience

Plaintiff Sue Previously		*Who Contacted Media*		
		Plaintiff	*Lawyer*	*Both*
Yes	#	17	12	14
	row %	39.5%	27.9%	32.6%
No	#	33	34	12
	row %	41.8%	43.0%	15.2%
		p. $<$ .06		

TABLE 5–12   Media Contact and Plaintiff Visibility

	Who Contacted Media		
Level of Visibility	*Plaintiff*	*Lawyer*	*Both*
Very High	21 (45.7%)	15 (32.6%)	10 (21.7%)
Above Average	16 (40.0%)	22 (55.0%)	2 (5.0%)
Average	5 (38.5%)	3 (23.1%)	5 (38.5%)
Below Average	2 (28.6%)	4 (57.1%)	1 (14.3%)
Very Low	1 (14.3%)	2 (28.6%)	4 (57.1%)
	p. < .02		

A similar pattern of response on who contacted the media occurs with "public" plaintiffs (elected officials and those with very high community visibility) in contrast to all other, largely private, plaintiffs. Elected officials and candidates for office rely exclusively on a lawyer for media contact in roughly 36 percent of the cases, while other plaintiffs do so in about 43 percent of the cases. Interestingly, the extent of exclusive plaintiff contact is more clearly distinct when the most public plaintiffs are compared with other, largely private, plaintiffs. Lawyers are involved in media contact in only 41 percent of the elected official and candidate cases, while lawyer involvement rises to 64.4 percent in other cases (white collar employees, 84 percent; business proprietors, 70 percent; public employees, 61 percent; and professionals, 55 percent).

A comparison was also made between the plaintiffs' visibility in the community and the type of media contact. Community visibility is a reflection of both the plaintiffs' public status and the breadth of public attention given the plaintiff as a general matter. The more visible the plaintiff is in the community, the higher the incidence of exclusive plaintiff contact before suit.

Finally, a comparison was made between who contacted the media first and who contacted the media. Not surprisingly, 91 percent of the 59 plaintiffs who contacted a lawyer first either had their lawyer contact the media (78 percent) or contacted the media with their lawyer (14 percent). Most of the instances of media contact by the plaintiff, therefore, occurred before a lawyer was engaged. About 50 percent of the plaintiffs contacted the media first, 70 percent of whom relied exclusively on that contact. In only 30 percent of the cases was the lawyer involved in the contact.

It appears from these comparisons that the more experienced plaintiffs and the public plaintiffs—those who have sued before or who are of very high visibility and therefore are familiar with the media—come to the lawyer with a firm and calculated conviction that litigation is their appropriate recourse. As a consequence, the lawyers are much less involved in communication with the media, or with negotiation of a possible settlement, and, as discussed later in this chapter, are much less influential in the plaintiff's decision to sue. Sixty-five percent of the plaintiffs who decided to sue before going to a lawyer considered the lawyer's advice on the decision to sue to be of little or no importance. In contrast, 67 percent of those who decided to sue after seeing a lawyer viewed the lawyer's advice on the issue to be very important. The lawyers' involvement in the process leading to suit, including media contact, as well as the lawyers' contribution to the decision to sue, is greater with the more private plaintiffs, for whom experience cannot *appear* to substitute for professional advice. [15]

The reduced level of lawyer involvement in media contact when public plaintiffs are involved is both logical and, quite likely, strategically sensible. When a public plaintiff who has contacted the media thereafter engages counsel, it is unlikely that any further negotiations with the media will be fruitful. The public plaintiff, as a general rule, will have a greater chance of success in such negotiations because of past and continuing relationships with the media. The plaintiff's failure, therefore, may often suggest that fruitful negotiations can take place only in a different environment and with different people.

The filing of a lawsuit may alter the environment, for after suit is filed the plaintiff's lawyer is likely to be communicating with media counsel in the context of a specific dispute, the media counsel rather than the editor or reporter is likely to play a central role, and a libel insurance company generally will be notified. Judging by settlement information obtained from a media insurer, negotiation by lawyers with lawyers after suit is filed is not only more likely to be constructive, but is more likely to permit a money settlement. [16] No plaintiff reported a money offer or settlement as a result of media contact, whether the contact involved the plaintiff, the plaintiff's lawyer, or both. While few plaintiffs reported asking for money—at least at the time of initial media contact—many media defendants follow a stated policy of no money settlement. The reported settlement figures, discussed in Chapter 6, appear to be inconsistent with an absolute "no settlement" policy, but they tend to confirm that the timing of settlement occurs after the filing of suit, and often during later stages of the litigation. [17] Few, if any, cases involve settlement prior to the filing of suit. A lawyer—especially one on contingent fee—is very unlikely to negotiate in such a pre-suit atmosphere, especially if the filing of suit can result in a material change in the attitude toward negotiation.

In summary, the lawyers' role in media contact and negotiation follows different patterns for public and private plaintiffs. For private plaintiffs (usually employed in business), the lawyer tends to be more actively involved in the media contact, representing the plaintiffs alone or in the plaintiffs' company. The more public plaintiffs (those with the highest community visibility) present a different situation, for in most instances they will have contacted the media prior to contacting a lawyer. Further lawyer involvement with the media—whether with reporter, editor, or publisher—is much less frequent than with other plaintiffs. Instead, formal legal proceedings tend to be initiated prior to any further negotiation by counsel. It is likely, as discussed later, that negotiation would serve little purpose for public plaintiffs, for whom the very act of suing is of significant value.

Fees and Costs of Litigation

Fee arrangements, of course, were discussed in every case involving engaged counsel. Various financial arrangements appear to have been employed, although they all revolve around one of two fee approaches: hourly and contingency. The variations involve the extent to which the plaintiff would bear costs of litigation other than professional fees.

When asked what fee arrangements were made with their lawyer, 126 plaintiffs responded specifically. Eighteen plaintiffs, or 14 percent of those responding, reported an hourly fee arrangement; 92, or 73 percent, reported a contingency fee arrangement; and 16 plaintiffs, representing 13 percent of those responding, reported "other" arrangements. Based upon interview notes, the group reporting "other" arrangements consists largely of plaintiffs paying a retainer or low base fee plus partial contingency, or plaintiffs whose fee arrangements (usually involving a contingency element), were borne by another party. Including these responses with the contingency group, it appears that up to 108 plaintiffs, or 86 percent, engaged counsel on some form of contingency fee basis. This proportion of contingency arrangements is similar to—although marginally higher than—the 71 percent contingency figure reported for plaintiffs in general civil litigation, and is also most probably similar to contingency fee percentages for other forms of personal injury suits. [18]

TABLE 5–13   Fee Arrangements

Type of Arrangement	Number	Percent
Hourly	18	14.3%
Contingency	92	73.0%
Other (largely combination)	16	12.7%

The heavy preponderance of contingency arrangements is borne out by the reported fees actually paid upon completion of litigation. Of the responding plaintiffs, 47 percent (45) reported paying no fees. Eight percent (8) of the plaintiffs reported fees below $1,000; some of these responses appear to include contingency fee cases dropped prior to litigation in which a minimum fee was assessed, and may also include misunderstandings by responding plaintiffs about the fee or cost basis for the charge. The incidence of no fees or fees below $1,000 in the libel plaintiff population—55.8 percent[19]—is higher than the 46 percent reported for all civil litigation.[20] The difference is explained by the higher rate of plaintiff success (about 90 percent) in general civil litigation as opposed to libel (about 10 percent), and the correspondingly higher incidence of actual fees below $1,000.[21]

Total costs of litigation to plaintiffs were also reported. Seventy-seven percent of the plaintiffs responded; most of the remaining cases were unresolved at the time of the survey. Taking into account the pending cases in which costs were not reportable, the contingency cases in which plaintiffs won in court or by settlement, and the presence of some cases of low hourly fee and contingency arrangements, it appears that at least 16 percent of the plaintiffs' lawyers were engaged on a pure contingency basis (i.e., all fees and costs contingent upon success). This, in turn, would mean that at least 20 of the 108 contingency cases, or 18.5 percent, represented pure contingency arrangements. (The percentage is on the low side because pending cases are not included in the 20 "no cost" cases, but all contingency cases are included in the 108 cases.) In the remaining 81.5 percent of the contingency cases, representing a minimum of 54 percent of the plaintiffs, plaintiffs bore some or all of the costs of representation.

Finally, the plaintiffs were asked whether the costs of litigation corresponded with their expectations. Ten percent of the plaintiffs stated that costs were lower than expected. Fifty-three percent of the plaintiffs indicated that costs were about what they expected. Costs were higher than

TABLE 5–14   Cost of Litigation to Plaintiffs

Reported Cost	Number	Percent
Nothing	20	15.7%
$1,000 or less	18	14.2%
$1,001–5,000	44	34.6%
$5,001–20,000	30	23.6%
Over $20,000	15	11.8%

TABLE 5–15   Fee Arrangements and Lawyer Selection

How Lawyer Was Selected		Hourly	Contingency
Friend, family or business lawyer	#	15	45
	row %	25.0%	75.0%
Trial Reputation, Libel Reputation, Referral	#	3	37
	row %	7.5%	92.5%
	p. $< .05$		

expected for 37 percent of those responding. Actual costs do not seem to have been out of line with plaintiff expectations.

Examining the composition of the plaintiff groups in light of fee arrangements discloses interesting information about the libel plaintiffs. The first comparison is between hourly or contingency fee arrangements and the manner in which plaintiffs selected counsel. The plaintiffs who engaged counsel on an hourly fee basis tended to have sought legal counsel from a friend or from a lawyer representing them on personal or business matters at the time. The other categories of lawyers on an hourly basis tended to be the more experienced lawyers—especially those engaged by referral from another lawyer, presumably because of expertness or ability to handle the case. As the table illustrates, however, most lawyers were engaged on a contingency basis.

The second comparison is between fee arrangement and the "public" status of the plaintiff. A clear relationship exists between "public" plaintiffs and contingency fee arrangements although the relationship is a complex one. Libels concerning business, professional, and private subjects are litigated on an hourly basis 28 percent of the time (12 of 43 cases), while those relating to public or political subjects are litigated on an hourly basis only 9 percent of the time (6 of 66 cases).[22] Plaintiffs legally classified as public figures engaged lawyers on a contingency basis more often than private plaintiffs, and the same held for public officials and candidates in contrast to business proprietors. In the latter two comparisons, however, the "other" and partial contingency groupings, as well as the professional category, make the comparisons statistically insignificant. The comparisons are useful nevertheless, in our judgment, because of their consistency with other comparisons, including actual fees paid.

Plaintiffs who held public office at the time of the libel paid lawyers' fees in less than 19 percent of the reported cases, while those who did not hold public office paid fees nearly 60 percent of the time. Similarly, elected officials or candidates paid fees only 28 percent of the time; public employees did so 44 percent of the time; but business proprietors, professionals, and white-collar plaintiffs paid fees in 67 percent of the cases.

One might intuitively expect the public plaintiffs to retain attorneys on an hourly fee basis more often than the private plaintiffs because of the diminished likelihood of success in litigation for public plaintiffs. One might also expect private plaintiffs to have contingency arrangements more often because of the higher likelihood of winning, and the higher incidence of representation by lawyers with whom they have existing relationships and who therefore might have a greater financial incentive to absorb the risk of loss. Exactly the opposite appears to be the case, however. The precise reasons for the difference are obscure, but may be related to the nonfinancial rewards from representing public officials, including publicity, and to the greater degree of openness and forthrightness that a lawyer with a preexisting relationship can have with his or her client. For such attorneys, more cautious advice may better serve the lawyers' interest in a continuing relationship with the client after the libel case is over. Coincidentally, caution also seems better to serve the client's interests.

The Attorneys' Predictions of Success and Advice Concerning Litigation

The most important aspect of the attorneys' representation of plaintiffs prior to suit involves the advice given about whether to file suit. Plaintiffs were asked about their lawyers' judgments of the likelihood of success in litigation, the lawyers' recommendations concerning suit, and the importance of the lawyers' advice to the plaintiffs' decision to sue. In this section the first two topics will be discussed in detail, with references to the third. Later in this chapter the influence of the lawyer will be considered fully in connection with the reasons for the plaintiffs' decisions to sue. Seventy-two percent of the responding plaintiffs were advised by their attorney that the prospects of success were 50 percent or greater. In light of the actual results achieved in litigation, where roughly 11 percent of the completed, judicially-resolved cases were won by plaintiffs, and 7 percent of the concluded cases were settled, it appears that the attorneys' predictions were wildly overoptimistic. The low frequency of plaintiff success in the surveyed population, moreover, is consistent with the population of media libel plaintiffs as a whole. In all media libel cases adjudicated between 1974 and 1984, plaintiffs won in only 11 percent of the cases that had been finally adjudicated; public plaintiffs won in 10 percent of the cases only, and private plaintiffs in 14 percent of the cases. Of cases filed with insurance carriers, it appears that roughly 10–15 percent are settled.[23] The extremely low incidence of success is widely known and publicized.

TABLE 5–16 Lawyer Prediction of Success in
Litigation

Prediction of Success[*]	Number	Percent of Specific Responses
Very Good	19	15.6%
Good (over 50%)	57	46.7%
50 percent	12	9.8%
Slight	34	27.9%

[*]Forty-two responses were coded "other," "uncertain," or "not applicable."
Responses coded "other" include predictions in non-probabilistic terms,
such as "likely to achieve settlement."

Equally interesting are the 34 plaintiffs, comprising 28 percent of those specifically responding, who sued in the face of their lawyers' predictions that the prospect of success was slight. With this group of plaintiffs it clearly seems that more is at work than the odds of winning when the plaintiffs make decisions concerning suit. To better understand the dynamics of such decisions, the composition of the plaintiff population must be explored.

Certain general characteristics of the plaintiff population should be mentioned first by way of background before exploring particular plaintiff groupings in connection with the predicted likelihood of successful suit. Roughly 50 percent of the plaintiffs contacted the media first before contacting a lawyer. Fifty-seven percent reported that they had decided to sue prior to contacting a lawyer. Seventy-eight percent of the plaintiffs said they sued for reasons unrelated to money damages—to restore their reputation, to deter further republication of the offending statement, or to punish the media.[24] Finally, 57 percent of the plaintiffs were angered as a result of the media contact prior to suit, 93 percent expressed either anger or dissatisfaction with the media response, and 88 percent of the plaintiffs said the media response was a factor in their decision to sue. From these data, which will be analyzed in greater depth below, it appears that the motivations of plaintiffs were significantly more complex than the objective of achieving a judgment in litigation, or money damages awarded by a jury.

Indeed, with a significant proportion of the plaintiff population, money damages seem to have been secondary. Comparing the lawyers' predictions of success with the probable outcome of litigation, therefore, and assessing the plaintiffs' decision to sue even when advised that victory is improbable, may represent an inapt mode of analysis because the lawyers predicting a better-than-even chance of success may have been reflecting in part the *plaintiffs'* objectives rather than measuring their prediction by the yardstick of ultimate judicial resolution. Commencing a libel suit—even if ultimately lost in court—may deter republication effectively, and it is even more likely to publicize the plaintiffs' claim of falsehood and be perceived by plaintiffs as a means of legitimizing that claim through resort to the judicial process. For plaintiffs interested in part in punishing the press, the commencement of a suit, itself, may serve to exact partial retribution. These objectives may in some cases be consistent with the lawyer's interest in representing a visible client or case, even when the prospect of a fee is limited. In any event, the lawyers' predictions, viewed in light of the plaintiffs' *actual objectives*, well may have been quite accurate, although unintended. This is confirmed by the high degree of plaintiff satisfaction with the litigation, even among those plaintiffs who lost, and the overwhelming number of plaintiffs who, if faced with a similar situation, say that they would sue again.[25]

Information about the specific composition of the plaintiff population in terms of the lawyers' prediction of success is exceedingly limited. The attorneys representing private plaintiffs tended to be somewhat more conservative in their advice concerning suit than those representing public plaintiffs. This is interesting, as private plaintiffs have succeeded more often than those in the public group.

The concomitant fact that public plaintiffs—especially elected officials and candidates for office—were represented on contingency and were told by their lawyers that the chances of success were good, may be mildly corroborative of the hypothesis that for this group, who reported suing largely for reputational reasons, the act of suing was itself a vindication of reputation, and therefore the likelihood of success in those terms was high. The lawyer's high prediction of success in cases involving public plaintiffs may further be explained by the visibility of the suit for the lawyer, the appeal of the client's situation, the lack of alternatives for clients who believe that they are compelled to respond in some way, and the likelihood that, having taken the case on contingency, the lawyer may be expected to recommend a course of action implicit in the agreed upon fee arrangement and most likely to yield visibility and revenues.

The lawyers' specific recommendations (as distinguished from predictions of success) were also reported by the plaintiffs. One hundred twenty-six plaintiffs specifically responded, and their responses are given in Table 5–17. As the table indicates, and as would be expected given the survey population, most of the plaintiff lawyers recommended suit.

Because of the dominance of the recommendation that suit be brought, only limited statistical inferences can be drawn from this variable. A few

TABLE 5–17   Course of Action Recommended by
Plaintiff Attorney

Recommendation	Number	Percent
Bring Suit	98	77.8%
Negotiate Prior to Suit	16	12.7%
Do Not Sue	4	3.2%
No Recommendation—Plaintiff's Decision	8	6.3%

comparisons are suggestive, however. When the lawyer recommendation is compared with the fee arrangement, it appears that lawyers on contingency tended to recommend suit more frequently than those on an hourly basis. While the heavy incidence of recommendations to sue makes the differences in the table appear marginal, a notable difference exists between the 50 percent of hourly lawyers who do not recommend suit, and the 22 percent of contingency lawyers who do not recommend suit. One would expect lawyers on contingency to recommend suit, since a lawyer's decision to represent a client on a contingency fee basis would presumably be based on a determination concerning the strength of the case, made in advance of accepting it.

One might, however, have expected a higher rate of advice to negotiate, given the low success rate for the public plaintiffs, most of whom had contingency arrangements. Indeed, the high rate with which contingency lawyers recommended suit, viewed in light of the low rate of success, suggests that the contingency lawyers, in particular, exercised poor judgment or else based their decisions on other factors. This is all the more ironic because, when alternatives to litigation were discussed by the attorneys, the lack of need to sue was mentioned most frequently (in 7 of the 11

TABLE 5–18   Fee Arrangement and Lawyer Recommendation

Recommendation		Hourly	Contingency
Bring Suit	#	8	59
	column %	50.0%	78.7%
Negotiate	#	5	9
	column %	31.3%	12.0%
Do Not Sue	#	1	2
	column %	6.3%	2.7%
No Recommendation	#	2	5
	column %	12.5%	6.7%
	p. < .13		

cases) with the elected official group, who were disproportionately represented on contingency and over 70 percent of whom (10 of 14) paid no fees.

In light of the lawyer recommendations and advice, the plaintiffs were asked how important their lawyers' advice was to their decision to sue. This question is analyzed in detail in a later section of this chapter, but the general responses can be briefly noted here as well, for the question bears on the meaning and importance of the lawyers' recommendations. Of the 141 responses, 40 percent indicated that the lawyer's advice was very important, 18 percent said it was of some importance, 43 percent considered it to be of little or no importance. Nearly half of the lawyers appear to have had little impact on the plaintiff's decision to sue, and 60 percent were less than "very important." The relative unimportance of the attorneys' advice to plaintiffs is consistent with the very high degree of prejudgment about suit that plaintiffs report, as well as the substantial degree to which the plaintiffs are relatively sophisticated in their dealings with the media, and have contacted the media prior to suit. The private plaintiffs—particularly those who sue for money because they have experienced economic loss—comprise the largest proportion of plaintiffs for whom the lawyers' advice is significant. In view of this, it is not surprising that the attorneys' advice about the probable results of the formal legal process is viewed as unimportant, if not irrelevant, by a large segment of plaintiffs for whom vindication of reputation and punishment rather than recovery of economic loss are the most pressing concerns.[26]

A partial explanation for the lawyers' optimistic predictions of success is quite likely related to the reasons for their advice being unimportant. One can read the data as suggesting that the lawyers' financial interests are governing their prediction of success, for without a client no fee can be earned. The difficulty with this hypothesis is that it is not in a lawyer's financial interest to litigate a case on contingency if no significant prospect of success exists, for the lawyer is taking most of the financial risk. If financial interest is at work, one would expect that the hourly fee lawyers would most often express optimism and recommend suit, for their fee recovery is not contingent on success. Exactly the opposite appears to be the case, however, suggesting that elements other than the prospect of fees are governing the attorneys' advice. To the extent that the attorneys are reflecting in their optimistic predictions of success more than self-interest in a fee, their more optimistic outlook may relate to the clients' perceived compulsion to take some form of action and the likely success of litigation in achieving the plaintiffs' *real* objectives rather than those set by the formal legal system. In turn, it may be that for many lawyers the financial motive may lie with the representation of the *client*—often a well-known figure in the community—rather than in the prospect of a fee in that case.

Conclusion

The involvement of lawyers and their role prior to litigation discloses much about the dynamics of the process leading to suit. A few general observations of overriding significance can be summarized by way of conclusion, and as a prelude to the succeeding discussion of the reasons plaintiffs sue. The conclusions, it should be noted, apply only to plaintiffs who sue and who press their suit in litigation. We will discuss certain aspects of claims that are concluded at earlier stages in the next chapter, but the conclusions discussed here do not apply to that larger universe.

1. A conclusion about the experience of the plaintiffs' lawyers cannot be captured in a single generalization. Half of the surveyed lawyers had not previously litigated a libel case, and it might be assumed from this that their advice may be less well informed—especially on matters relating to likely success in litigation—than their more experienced colleagues. It is possible, however, that many of these lawyers without libel experience had prior litigation experience in other contexts that would substitute, at least in part, for direct experience with libel cases. On the other hand, half of the lawyers had prior libel litigation experience, and a quarter of the lawyers had quite substantial experience. Given the low incidence of libel litigation (roughly 2 reported cases per state per year, on average), the level of lawyer experience seems remarkably high.

2. A large group of plaintiffs come to a lawyer after contacting the media and already having decided to sue, a conclusion that applies to all plaintiffs, but most particularly to the more public plaintiffs.

3. For the public plaintiffs, the earlier decision to sue is strongly held and is often based upon prior media contact. In most such instances, the lawyers' influence is slight, the advice given is considered unimportant to the decision to sue, and the lawyers' function is largely restricted to the preparation and filing of suit.

4. Private plaintiffs, particularly those who sue to obtain money damages, are more open to the lawyers' advice, consider it more influential, and rely heavily on the lawyer to handle any contact with the media in advance of suit. They also sue more reluctantly, although they tend to have more strongly held emotional feelings than the more calculating public plaintiffs.

5. In general, the attorneys appear to provide adequate and useful information to the plaintiffs about the risks of suit, the costs involved, and the like. Few plaintiffs, however, are discouraged by this information, least of all public plaintiffs.

6. Most lawyers are engaged on a contingency arrangement, although this is less frequent with private plaintiffs and plaintiffs represented by their

personal or business lawyers, or by more experienced counsel. It also appears that the plaintiffs who value the lawyer's advice most highly pay for it on an hourly basis.

7. The plaintiffs' lawyers overwhelmingly recommend suit. When no suit is recommended, the client is likely to be a public official or to have sued previously. The likelihood of success for these plaintiffs is probably the lowest of any plaintiff group.

8. The plaintiffs' lawyers are highly optimistic in their predictions of success. They seem to be most pessimistic—or realistic—when the plaintiffs' measure of success corresponds with that of the legal system: winning a verdict and damages. For plaintiffs whose reasons for suit are related to vindication of reputation, deterring republication, and punishing the media, lawyers' predictions are most optimistic. Ironically, while the likelihood of success is most slim for these plaintiffs when measured against the legal system's standard, it is greatest when measured against the *apparent* objectives of these plaintiffs. In large measure, these plaintiffs appear to obtain vindication of reputation through the very act of filing suit, which they perceive as a public legitimization of their claim of falsehood. They exact deterrence and punishment, as well, by the act of suing itself. Understood in this context, the lawyers' optimistic advice is likely to have been accurate when measured by plaintiffs' standard of success.

9. Finally, just as the libel suit may in many ways be unique in civil litigation,[27] the lawyers' role may be unique. As a group, libel clients have strong emotional feelings, a clear view of the course to be taken, and objectives unrelated, in part, to the compensatory assumptions underlying the libel tort. Following their engagement by the client, lawyers are changed with great frequency, often involuntarily. It well may be that to a much greater extent than normal, lawyers are unimportant instruments of their clients' presuppositions—actors on a stage where the client is the playwright, producer, director, and choreographer. The lawyer merely follows the script.

THE DECISION: FORCES AT WORK

In the earlier chapters discussion has centered on the actions and attitudes of libel plaintiffs and media defendants at the time of publication and thereafter in advance of litigation. The stages of publication, plaintiff response, media response, and attorney contact are all preludes to the initiation of a lawsuit. In all of the cases studied suit was filed. The surveyed plaintiffs were asked a series of questions about why they thought it

TABLE 5–19   Why Plaintiff Sued

Reason	Frequency	Percent
Restore Reputation	48	30.0%
Stop Further Publication (Deter)	30	18.7%
Win Money Damages	35	21.9%
Punishment & Vengeance	47	29.4%

important to file suit, what they sought to accomplish by a lawsuit, what factors contributed to their decision to sue, and the eagerness or reluctance with which they brought suit. The responses will be analyzed in light of materials discussed in earlier chapters on the harm plaintiffs perceived they suffered as a result of the publication, the impact of media contact on the decision to sue, the role of lawyers, and the stated objectives of the plaintiffs.

What Plaintiffs Sought to Accomplish

Each of the plaintiffs was asked why suit was brought against the publisher of the alleged libel. The responses are set out in Table 5–19. In general, the responses are consistent with the pattern, noted earlier, that a relatively small proportion of the plaintiffs expresses an interest in money. While the proportion of plaintiffs giving money damages as a reason for suit—22 percent—is significantly higher than the roughly 4 percent who stated shortly after publication that money would be necessary to satisfy them, and the 1 percent who demanded payment when they contacted the media (Tables 3–5 and 3–6), it still embraces fewer than one quarter of the

TABLE 5–20   Reasons for Suit and Focus of the Alleged Libel

	Focus of the Alleged Libel			
Reason for Suit	Personal or Private	Business or Professional	Public or Political	Criminal
	col.% (#)	col.% (#)	col.% (#)	col.% (#)
Restore Reputation	20.0% (3)	12.8% (6)	39.4% (28)	44.0% (11)
Deter Further Publication	20.0% (3)	8.5% (4)	26.8% (19)	12.0% (3)
Punish	40.0% (6)	42.5% (20)	22.5% (16)	16.0% (4)
Money	20.0% (3)	36.2% (17)	11.3% (8)	28.0% (7)

p. < .001

plaintiffs who sued. Over three-quarters of the plaintiffs, therefore, claimed non-monetary reasons or motivations as predominant in the decision to sue.

Analysis of the plaintiffs who claimed money as the reason for suit reveals interesting patterns. The clearest pattern occurs when the reasons for suit are compared with the type of activities to which the libel related. Libel suits involving statements about plaintiffs' business and professional activities tended to be brought for money damages or to punish the media. This would be expected, as such plaintiffs are most likely to experience financial harm from the statement and, as discussed later, most frequently express frustration at the media and therefore sue for punishment. The pattern followed by plaintiffs allegedly libeled in connection with private or personal activities is also consistent with the character of harm they are likely to perceive: recovering money damage is not a major reason for suit, but punishment is, for these plaintiffs are likely to have highly emotional reactions to the published statement.

Perhaps most notable is the marked contrast between the plaintiffs allegedly libeled on private subjects and those allegedly libeled in connection with public (civic, etc.) and political activities. Plaintiffs suing on the basis of statements about their public and political activities do so for reputation-related reasons more than two-thirds of the time, and sue to obtain money damages in only 11 percent of the cases.

The pattern of money and, to a somewhat lesser degree, punishment representing the predominant motives for suit in the context of private activities, and reputation being the chief motive when public or political activities are involved, exists generally throughout the other plaintiff groups that fall along "public" and "private" lines. Plaintiffs involved in political activities tend to sue to obtain money less frequently than those involved in civic or other community activities, or those not actively involved in the community. While not statistically significant, the job and legal status of plaintiffs exhibit the same pattern, with public officials and candidates, and plaintiffs legally classified as "public officials" or "public figures," suing to obtain money damages less frequently than other groups, and giving reputation-related reasons for suit most often. As discussed in Chapter 2, the various ways in which we have classified plaintiffs—job, legal classification, subject of the offending statement, and visibility—are all somewhat different ways of exploring the basic libel law distinction between public and private plaintiffs, and testing the extent to which various formulations of this distinction may reflect or explain different behavior and attitudes of plaintiffs. While the pattern of the more public plaintiffs suing for reputation-related reasons exists throughout these groupings, it exists most clearly with the public or private activity to which the allegedly libelous statement pertained. In some ways this distinction appears to be the purest approximation of the theory underlying the constitutional privileges, which were designed to afford greatest protection to discussion of public subjects. [28]

Two general conclusions emerge from an analysis of the reasons plaintiffs sue. The first is that plaintiff motivations are predominantly reputation-related. The data suggest that when money is given as a reason for suit—as opposed to a request for money damages in the legal action—it tends roughly to be the motivating factor in those circumstances when only money will fully compensate for the harm occasioned by a libel. In general, such cases involve plaintiffs who are allegedly libeled in connection with non-public business and professional activities. The lower frequency with which plaintiffs demand money compensation in the days immediately following publication can be explained by the fact that immediate correction can often avoid financial harm, but with the passage of a relatively short period of time between publication and the time the decision to sue is made, any actual economic harm experienced can no longer be remedied by correction alone. Moreover, by the time the lawsuit is filed, the private plaintiffs, who bear litigation costs more frequently than public plaintiffs, will have incurred costs relating to prosecution of the claim.

The second conclusion is that the plaintiffs' reasons for suit bear an ironic relationship to the premises underlying the constitutional privileges. Based on their stated motivation in bringing a libel suit, it appears that the plaintiffs who reported that they sued for reasons unrelated to money damages consist largely of persons holding public office or having high community visibility and influence, who are allegedly libeled in connection with their public activities. This group closely parallels the category of "public figure" plaintiffs who, because of the First Amendment, must establish a higher threshold of fault in order to recover in a defamation action. [29] The constitutional requirement that fault be shown by these plaintiffs is largely based on the need to safeguard against the inhibiting effects of large damage awards on the press. [30] In view of this, there is great irony in the finding that these plaintiffs, in particular, reported that they sue for reasons largely unrelated to money damage. To the extent that such plaintiffs are assumed by the courts to have greater access to the media to defend themselves, and therefore need less protection from the legal system, [31] the fact that most public figure plaintiffs that we studied resort to the courts to defend their reputation suggests that the self-help assumption may be unsound.

A final observation on the reasons plaintiffs gave for suit pertains to the shift in attitude that has occurred between the time of publication and the time of suit. Combining the plaintiffs who sued to restore reputation with those who sought to deter further publication results in 49 percent of the plaintiffs suing for direct reputation-related reasons, with the balance suing for money or vengeance/punishment (both of which may involve a reputational interest, as well). This stands in marked contrast to the plaintiffs' statements of what remedy was needed and sought following publication and at the point of media contact. Immediately following publication, 65 percent of the plaintiffs indicated that their most important concern was the article's falsity. When the publisher was contacted, over 78 percent of the responding plaintiffs sought retraction, correction, or apology from the media. By the time litigation was commenced, 29 percent of the plaintiffs report that vengeance or punishment were their reasons for suing. While the questions the plaintiffs were asked at each stage were framed differently, the shift in responses, combined with direct responses from plaintiffs about the post-publication media contact, suggest a marked change in attitude and motivation. The predominant factor at work with the plaintiffs who ultimately sued for vengeance and punishment and (to a lesser but still material respect) with the plaintiffs who sued for money, appears to be the contact with the media. The impact of the media contact and the related information on the eagerness with which plaintiffs sued, the timing of the decision to sue, and the role of lawyers in that decision, will be considered in the following sections.

The Media's Impact on the Decision to Sue

The striking conclusion that emerges from an analysis of the decision to sue is that the most pervasive influence is the plaintiff's reaction to the post-publication media contact. In Chapter 4 and earlier in this chapter the contacts between plaintiffs and media were described and analyzed in detail. A few general observations about that material bear repeating in connection with the impact of the plaintiff-media interaction on the decision to sue.

The plaintiffs reported that the media were contacted by the plaintiff or the plaintiff's lawyer following publication and prior to commencing a lawsuit in about 90 percent of the cases. Of these plaintiffs, 41 percent contacted the media independently and 20 percent did so with counsel. The other 39 percent contacted the media through counsel alone. In all instances the plaintiffs asked something of the media. Except for one plaintiff, all responding plaintiffs said that they requested correction, retraction, apology, space or time to reply, a halt to further republication of the story, a personal apology, or some other, non-financial remedy. Plaintiffs reported that the media retracted, corrected, or apologized in 21 percent of the cases, agreed not to repeat the allegedly libelous statement in 2 percent of the cases, refused to take any action in 63 percent of the cases, and repeated the story without correction or significant change in slightly over 11 percent of the cases.

Fifty-seven percent of the responding plaintiffs reported that they were angered by the media's response, 37 percent were dissatisfied, 2 percent were ambivalent, and only 4 percent were satisfied (but sued anyway). It is hardly surprising, therefore, that 88 percent of the plaintiffs who contacted the media with a specific request that the media take action to remedy the situation stated that the media response (or non-response) was a factor in their decision to sue.

The strength of the plaintiff reaction to media contact as a factor leading to suit is confirmed by the striking fact that all but one of the plaintiffs who reported anger at the media response said that it was a factor in the decision to sue. Table 5–21 demonstrates the relationship among these variables. Because we do not know the percentage of plaintiffs who did not sue but who reacted strongly to the media contact, our conclusions must be restricted to plaintiffs who actually sued. Table 5–21 reveals a number of things about the media response as an element in these plaintiffs' decisions to sue. First, the table highlights the large proportion of angry plaintiffs, and the very small number of plaintiffs who reported satisfaction with the media's response to their contact. Second, while the number of satisfied plaintiffs is small, the table indicates a clear relationship between the degree of dissatisfaction and the importance of the plaintiff's reaction to the decision to sue.

It should be recalled that public plaintiffs (elected officials, candidates for office, and public employees) are marginally more likely to contact the media themselves, often before seeing a lawyer. Public plaintiffs generally spoke with someone other than the reporter and contacted their lawyer only after having decided to sue. Finally, plaintiffs allegedly libeled in

TABLE 5–21   Was the Media's Response a Factor in the Decision to Sue?

Plaintiff Reaction to Media Response	Yes		No	
	#	%	#	%
Angered	69	98.6%	1	1.4%
Dissatisfied	39	86.7%	6	13.3%
Satisfied	2	40.0%	3	60.0%
Ambivalent	1	50.0%	1	50.0%

$p. < .001$

connection with public activities and whose harm related to their public reputation considered the media response a marginally greater element in the decision to sue than did plaintiffs whose harm was emotional or related to business or professional reputation. Therefore, while the media response was a factor in the decision to sue for virtually all types of plaintiffs, it seems to have been a marginally greater factor for the more public plaintiffs.

In contrast, anger stemming from pre-suit media contact was marginally more pronounced with private plaintiffs than with the public ones. Public official and public figure plaintiffs were marginally less angered by the media response than other plaintiffs who themselves contacted the media, perhaps because the former contacted someone other than the reporter, or simply because of their greater familiarity with the media. The plaintiffs who reported that they were both angered and frustrated and who approached the decision to sue most emotionally appear to consist disproportionately of private individuals or public plaintiffs holding no public office or position, who contacted the reporter rather than someone more likely to provide a positive response to the complaint, and who reported being treated arrogantly.

The hypothesis that the more private plaintiffs tended to feel anger more frequently than public plaintiffs and that their anger had an impact on their decision to sue is borne out by an analysis of the transformation of motivations between the time of publication and the time of suit. This is done by tracing the shifts in the reasons given for suit by plaintiffs allegedly libeled in connection with public activities as compared to private activities between publication of the alleged libel and the decision to sue, isolating only those plaintiffs originally wanting retraction or correction. While all of the plaintiffs listed in Table 5–22 originally expressed retraction or correction as the desired remedy for the alleged libel, and could be expected to sue in order to restore reputation if all circumstances remained constant, their motives shifted in material ways between publication and the start of litigation. The first shift is the movement toward money damages. As discussed in a previous section, money damages are less likely to be viewed as necessary if an error can be corrected promptly. As time passes, however, money damages to compensate for the actual economic consequences of a libel may be necessary. Thus, by the time of suit 23 percent of the plaintiffs reported money as the primary motivation for suing, with the highest incidence of the shift toward money understandably occurring among the plaintiff groups allegedly libeled in connection with private activities.

The more pronounced and interesting shift in motivation occurs with the elements of restoration of reputation and punishment. Nearly three-

TABLE 5–22   Shift in Plaintiff Motive at Time of Suit

Category of Plaintiff Originally Wanting Retraction or Correction Focus of Libel	Reason for Suit		
	Restore Reputation & Deter	Money Damages	Punish
Personal & Private	4 (40.0%)	2 (20.0%)	4 (40.0%)
Business or Professional Activities	5 (16.7%)	11 (36.7%)	14 (46.7%)
Public or Political Activities	35 (71.4%)	7 (14.3%)	7 (14.3%)
Criminal Activities	12 (63.2%)	5 (26.3%)	2 (10.0%)
	56 (51.9%)	25 (23.1%)	27 (25.0%)
	p. < .001		

quarters of the plaintiffs allegedly libeled in connection with their public or political activities gave restoration of reputation (including deterrence of republication) as the reason for suit. This is consistent with the earlier conclusion that these plaintiffs tend to experience less financial harm from the libel and more harm to their influence or their authority in the community. The media response is an important factor in their decision to sue, although perhaps not as emotional a one as with private plaintiffs. Rather, having failed to obtain correction from the media, suing is seen as a logical and necessary step. Restoration of reputation is therefore their chief motive for suing. Only 14 percent of these more public plaintiffs sue in order to punish the media, a significantly lower percentage than the 40 and 47 percent for plaintiffs allegedly libeled concerning their private and business affairs, respectively. In contrast with the public group, only 23 percent, on average, of the private plaintiff groups sue to restore reputation, and 45 percent bring suit to punish the media. Punishment is the single largest reason given for suit by the private plaintiff groups.

These data are consistent with the hypothesis that it is the private individuals who experience the greatest frustration in contacts with the press, whether because of inexperience, contact with the wrong person, or simply ill-mannered responses by the media to persons with whom they have no ongoing relationship. More important, the data suggest that it is the private plaintiff group that is most angered by the media contact and most influenced *by that anger* to sue in order to punish the media.

Finally, a comparison can be made between the actual media response to the plaintiff's contact, whether directly or through counsel, and the

TABLE 5–23   Reported Influence of Media Response on the Plaintiffs'
Decision to Sue

| | Was Response a Factor? | | | |
| | Yes | | No | |
Response by Media	#	%	#	%
Retracted, Corrected, Apologized	20	80%	5	20%
Refused to Make Positive Response	74	95%	4	5%
Repeated Story Uncorrected	14	100%	0	0%
Did Not Repeat Story	1	50%	1	50%
	p. < .02			

extent to which the response was a factor in the decision to sue. This
information is provided in Table 5–23.

As indicated in Table 5–23, all of the plaintiffs who had the allegedly
libelous statement repeated after the media contact considered the media
response to be a factor in the decision to sue. From the plaintiff's perspective, repetition of the libel represents a rubbing of salt in the wound.
Ninety-five percent of the plaintiffs who were refused any positive response by the media considered the media's inaction to be a factor in the
decision to sue. Finally, 80 percent of plaintiffs who received a retraction,
correction, or apology said the media's response was a factor in their
decision to sue. In general, these data are consistent with the hypothesis
that the more negative the response, the greater the likelihood that the
media contact and response will contribute to the decision to sue.

Two further aspects of this issue should be mentioned, however. First,
the fact that the media response was so overwhelmingly a factor in the
plaintiffs' decision to sue, and that even where the response was positive 80
percent of the plaintiffs considered the media contact and response to have
contributed to the decision to sue, suggest strongly that something more
than the substantive response by the media is at work. While we do not
know how many potential plaintiffs received a positive response and decided not to sue, and therefore we cannot measure with certainty the contribution to plaintiff attitudes of the substantive response as distinguished
from the interpersonal dynamics, there is ample evidence to suggest that it
is the latter—the way in which the plaintiff was treated rather than the
substantive response to the plaintiff's request—that played a major role in
the decision to sue. The fact that 27 of the 164 plaintiffs surveyed reported
a positive response, and 21 of them still considered the media response to

their contact to be a factor in the decision to sue, is evidence that the nature of the interaction is most important, for both the proportion and total number of positive responses is significant in relation to the universe of responding plaintiffs. Moreover, in a high proportion of the interviews the plaintiffs noted when responding to questions concerning media contact that the media were "arrogant," "indifferent" to their situation, "aloof," and "insensitive." As discussed earlier, the newspapers that were surveyed confirmed the press' shortcomings in the area of response to complaints.

It must be recognized, as well, that all of the plaintiffs who were surveyed actually sued notwithstanding the media response, and the majority of them said that they were affected principally by the publication's falsity, and wanted correction rather than money from the media. The group of plaintiffs receiving a retraction, correction, or apology and who nevertheless sued presumably represent a subset of a larger universe of potential plaintiffs some of whom decided not to sue in light of a media response that was reasonably related to their perceived harm at the time they contacted the media. One might expect, therefore, that plaintiffs in this universe who *actually sued* would have particularly strong feelings about the media, and that the contact with the media, even though evoking a positive response, would be a major motivating factor. This would be especially likely if most of the "positive" responses were actually imperfect ones, or mere gestures, which only compounded the injury or insulted the plaintiffs. This, indeed, appears to be so, from an analysis of the cases and from plaintiff comments, and suggests that often the inadequate retraction, correction, or apology did not really constitute a positive response. [32] This is also supported by the data which show that 42 percent of the plaintiffs receiving retraction, correction, or apology sued to punish the media—a higher proportion than any other grouping.

The plaintiffs who received a retraction and *did not* consider the media response a factor in the decision to sue, in contrast, may be reflecting an attitude that the act of suing represents a means of legitimating their claim to falsity which is more effective than the apology or retraction actually received. A significant proportion of the retraction cases we studied are consistent with this hypothesis (8 of 22). This would be consistent with the more general conclusion, discussed later, that the prime motivating force behind a large proportion of libel suits is self-help through use of the legal system to legitimate the plaintiff's claim of falsehood. This hypothesis is suggested by the fact that only 14 percent of the plaintiffs who received a positive response gave money as the reason for suit, while 27 percent of those receiving a negative response did so.

The calculus contributing to plaintiffs' decisions to sue media for libel is complex. An array of specific objectives plays a substantial part in the plaintiff's decision, including vindication of claimed falsity through a formal legal action, obtaining compensation in the form of money damages, deterring further republication, and vengeance or punishment of the media. The most pervasive influence, however, seems to have been the plaintiffs' reaction to the media contact and response. This factor was cited by plaintiffs as influencing the decision to sue in over 80 percent of the cases, and in over 90 percent of the instances in which plaintiff contact was made with the media prior to suit.

The Eagerness With Which Plaintiffs Sued

The eagerness with which plaintiffs sued provides additional information about the motivations underlying the libel suit, the objectives with which plaintiffs commence litigation, and the forces that contribute to that choice, including lawyers. Table 5–24 outlines the basic responses from the plaintiffs when they were asked about the willingness with which they brought suit. As Table 5–24 indicates, more than two-thirds of the plaintiffs sued eagerly or willingly.

The plaintiffs' stated reasons for suing bear a relationship to the eagerness with which they sued. These responses are cross-tabulated in Table 5–25. Plaintiffs who sue to restore reputation indicate that they do so most reluctantly. These plaintiffs tend to be public officials or figures allegedly libeled in connection with their public or political activities; they tend to have been less angered by the media contact; and many of them are likely to have continuing relationships with the media being sued.[33] For them the act of suing often appears to be a means of legitimating their claim of falsehood, and a lawsuit is likely to have been the last resort for that purpose.

The plaintiffs who sue most eagerly are those who seek to punish the media and to secure money damages, reasons likely to be grounded in feelings of ill will toward the media. These plaintiffs—particularly those suing to punish—are the ones most angered by the contact with the media, and whose anger appears to have most influenced the decision to sue.[34]

TABLE 5–24   Plaintiff Willingness to Sue

Plaintiff Response	#	%
Sued Eagerly	54	34%
Sued Willingly	55	35%
Sued Reluctantly	48	31%

TABLE 5–25   Plaintiff Reason for Suit Compared to Willingness to Sue

Reason for Suit		Willingness to Sue		
		Eager	Willing	Reluctant
Restore Reputation	#	10	13	22
	row %	22%	29%	49%
Stop Republication (Deter)	#	9	9	11
	row %	31%	31%	38%
Money Damages	#	14	17	4
	row %	40%	49%	11%
Punish	#	20	16	9
	row %	44%	36%	20%
		p. $<$ .01		

   The third group of plaintiffs, those (primarily private individuals) who said they are suing to obtain money damages, virtually all sued either eagerly or willingly, in contrast to the other groups of plaintiffs. Only 11 percent sued reluctantly, in contrast to 20 percent, 38 percent, and 49 percent of the plaintiffs suing to punish, deter further publication, and restore reputation, respectively. In view of the fact that no plaintiff surveyed received money in response to the media contact—only rarely was it requested—the greater willingness to sue among this group is understandable. Their greater willingness to sue also tends to support the judgment that most plaintiffs who gave money damages as a reason for suit were in fact responding to actual perceptions of economic harm.
   A comparison of plaintiffs' willingness to sue with the subject matter of the story provides further information about the plaintiff motivations, and

TABLE 5–26   Plaintiff Willingness to Sue Compared With Subject Matter of the Story

Subject Matter		Willingness to Sue		
		Eager	Willing	Reluctant
Personal/private	#	7	3	4
	row %	50%	21%	29%
Business/prof.	#	21	13	14
	row %	44%	27%	29%
Public/political	#	21	24	24
	row %	30%	35%	35%
Criminal	#	5	14	5
	row %	21%	58%	21%
		p. $<$ .12		

tends to corroborate the conclusion suggested above that private plaintiffs tend, in general, to sue more eagerly than public plaintiffs. Based upon the comparison of willingness to sue and subject matter of the story, it appears that the plaintiffs who sue most eagerly are those allegedly libeled in connection with personal or private and business or professional matters. As noted, they are also those who are most angered by the media response, and those who tend to sue for money damages. In contrast, plaintiffs libeled concerning public or political matters sue less eagerly, are marginally less angered by the media response, and tend not to sue for money damage. The criminal cases appear to follow a pattern unique to that situation.

Influence of the Attorney on the Decision to Sue

The nature of the attorney's involvement, advice given, and influence on the plaintiffs' decisions have been discussed previously.[35] As noted there, and as presented in the following table, a large proportion of plaintiffs indicated that the lawyers' advice was of little or no importance to the decision to sue.

The number of plaintiffs reporting that the lawyer's advice was of little or no importance to their decision to sue appears larger than would ordinarily be expected. The high proportion of plaintiffs so responding can be accounted for in part by a combination of factors. As mentioned earlier, the lawyers' discussions with the plaintiffs seem to have been thorough, for the most part, and the plaintiffs sued notwithstanding this. Particularly in view of the lawyers' frequent discussion of the risks of libel litigation (these would include repetition of the libel in news accounts of the suit, the toll in time and emotion devoted to the suit, and the expense) it is not surprising that many plaintiffs considered their decision to have been largely uninfluenced by the lawyer.[36] The frequent disjunction between the lawyers' advice and the commencement of suit by all plaintiffs surveyed makes likely a lower than normal degree of influence on the part of the lawyer.

TABLE 5–27 Attorney Role in Decision to Sue

Response*	Number	Percent
Very Important	56	40%
Some Importance	25	18%
Little/No Importance	60	42%

*Plaintiffs who proceeded pro se are not included. The remaining responses were not codable.

TABLE 5–28   Subject of Libel and Reason for Seeing Lawyer

| Subject of Libel | | *Why Lawyer Was Contacted* | | |
		Advice	*Retraction*	*To Sue*
Personal/Private	#	8	1	3
	%	67%	8%	25%
Business/Prof	#	28	3	10
	%	68%	7%	24%
Public/Political	#	21	2	28
	%	41%	4%	55%
Criminal	#	8	2	8
	%	44%	11%	44%

$p. < .09$

To explore further the role of counsel in the decision to sue, plaintiffs were asked whether they decided to sue before or after seeing a lawyer. Not surprisingly in light of the 60 percent who indicated that the lawyer was of modest or little importance to their decision to sue, 57 percent of the responding plaintiffs stated that they decided to sue before seeing a lawyer; another 43 percent decided to sue after the consultation. Of those who decided to sue before seeing a lawyer, 65 percent felt the lawyers' advice was unimportant to the decision to sue, and this group comprises 52 of the 60 plaintiffs (87 percent) who considered the lawyer unimportant to the decision to sue.

The plaintiffs who decided to sue even before seeing a lawyer, and who comprise almost 90 percent of those who considered their lawyers' advice unimportant in the decision to sue, fall into two often overlapping groups. Of the first group (plaintiffs who had filed one or more suits prior to the libel action in question), 57 percent considered the lawyers' advice unimportant, compared to 34 percent of plaintiffs who had not previously brought suit. Conversely, 45 percent of the plaintiffs who had not sued previously considered the lawyers' advice very important, compared to 25 percent for those who had sued previously.[37]

The second group who considered the lawyers' advice unimportant to the decision to sue consists of the public plaintiffs—a term used here to embrace those who were libeled in connection with public and political activities, who were elected officials, and who had very high levels of visibility in the community. As Table 5–28 indicates, most plaintiffs libeled in connection with political or public activities see a lawyer "to sue," having decided in advance on that course of action with much greater frequency than other, more "private," plaintiffs.[38] The same pattern holds true with elected officials and persons with very high visibility in the community. Elected officials and candidates for public office contacted the media before a lawyer 56 percent of the time, compared with roughly 46 percent for other plaintiffs. Moreover, elected officials and candidates contacted the lawyer "to sue" 65 percent of the time, compared with 39 percent with other plaintiffs. [39]

Based upon these data, it appears that the plaintiffs who are least influenced by the attorney in the decision to sue are, as a general rule, the public plaintiffs, some of whom have sued before, although not necessarily for libel. These plaintiffs tend to contact the media before contacting a lawyer, and frequently make contact at the editor or management level rather than with the reporter. They tend to be interested in reputational harm, not money, at the point of suit; as a rule they are less angered by the media response (although almost all plaintiffs are angered, and the difference is therefore one of degree); but the media response (as opposed to their anger, as such) plays a marginally more significant role in their decision to sue.

In contrast, those most influenced by the lawyer's advice are the private plaintiffs, many of whom appear to have needed money to compensate for their harm, fewer of whom have contacted the media before contacting the lawyer, but who are more often angered by the media response and who seem to consider that response more emotionally in their decision to sue. Interestingly, the lawyers appear to recommend litigation more frequently to this group of plaintiffs than to the public plaintiffs, although the difference is slight. Economic loss coupled with feelings of frustration and anger at the response of the media, however, tend to override any notes of caution introduced by the lawyer, leading these plaintiffs also to bear costs of litigation in higher proportion than do the public plaintiffs.

Conclusion: The Calculus of the Decision to Sue

A complex set of factors influence the plaintiffs' decision to commence a libel action. While a few generalized conclusions can be drawn, they must be stated cautiously with an awareness that the cases, if nothing else, are highly diverse, that many of the differences among plaintiffs are marginal in character, that the responses are self-reported (although internally consistent with other responses in the data base), and that the implications apply only to plaintiffs who sue. With these qualifications in mind, a few general observations about the reasons for the decision to sue can be offered.

First, the timing of the decision to sue, as might be expected, is not uniform. A significant proportion of the plaintiffs—perhaps 20 percent—

decide to sue before seeing a lawyer *and* before contacting the media. Roughly half of the responding plaintiffs contacted the media before seeing a lawyer. A high proportion of them (largely the public plaintiffs) had decided to sue prior to consulting an attorney. Perhaps as few as 55 percent of the plaintiffs consult counsel for advice concerning whether to sue. Nearly 60 percent of the plaintiffs report that they had decided to sue before seeing a lawyer, although some of them nevertheless sought advice from the lawyer and considered it important to their decision to sue.

Second, the attorneys' advice was relatively unimportant to the plaintiffs' decision to sue, especially in the case of public plaintiffs. Nearly half of the plaintiffs reported that the attorney was of little or no importance to the decision; only about 30 percent considered the attorney very important to their decision. These responses are consistent with the information concerning the timing of the decision to sue. At first glance this would seem inconsistent with the generally complete information the attorney provided the plaintiffs with respect to the length of time the suit would involve, the cost, and the likelihood of republication with accompanying publicity about the plaintiff. But plaintiffs appear not to have been dissuaded by the information supplied by counsel, and in the end most attorneys indicated that the chance of success was 50 percent or better, the chance of settlement was slim, and contingency arrangements would be available. On balance, therefore, the attorneys' advice seems in large measure to have followed the preferences of the plaintiffs.

Third, the chief reason plaintiffs brought libel suits was to vindicate reputation and punish the media, not to obtain money damages to compensate for economic harm. Only about one-quarter of the plaintiffs reported suing to recover money damages, and, as one would expect, these plaintiffs consist largely of private plaintiffs. In most cases the reason for suit tended to comport roughly with the type of plaintiff. Public officials and other plaintiffs with high visibility in their community tended to sue for reputation-related reasons, seeing the lawsuit as a means of vindicating their claim of falsehood. These plaintiffs also tended to be more single-minded and determined in their decision to sue and considered the lawyers' advice unimportant. On the other hand, private plaintiffs sued more predominantly for money or punishment, apparently out of a greater feeling of frustration at the media and anger at the media response to their appeal; they relied more heavily on the lawyer, however, in deciding whether to sue.

Finally, two overriding elements appear generally applicable across the spectrum of cases and plaintiffs. Virtually all of the plaintiffs were chiefly disturbed about the alleged falsity of the published report, and its consequent impact on their reputation. Their reason for suit might have been expressed in terms of reputation, money, or vengeance at the time they decided to sue, but underlying that decision in virtually every instance was a perception that falsity was at the bottom of their grievance, and their action was directed at correcting that falsity.[40] Moreover, in virtually every case the plaintiffs expressed anger or dissatisfaction at the media contact, with anger representing the predominant feeling. In roughly 90 percent of the cases, the media response was a factor in the plaintiffs' decision to sue. Indeed, in view of the various events that generally occurred between publication and suit, and the changed perceptions of plaintiff objectives during that time, it seems that the media response was the most pervasive factor (other, of course, than the publication itself) contributing to the plaintiffs' decisions and actions. The only marked difference between public and private plaintiffs concerns the incidence of economic harm and the influence of the lawyer, both substantially greater with the private plaintiff group.

In a real sense, what the plaintiffs seem to be saying is that the objectives of restoring reputation and punishing the media were largely served by the very act of commencing the libel suit itself.[41] The media's response played a role in their decision to employ litigation for that purpose, because litigation was the only means by which they could publicly respond to the publication and exact retribution for the manner with which they had been treated by the media. The conclusion is consistent with responses discussed later in Chapter 7, which suggest that winning or losing the lawsuit was not determinative of the plaintiffs' perception that the suit had accomplished their objectives, and that the act of suing, itself, represented a form of public vindication and formal legitimation of the plaintiffs' claims of falsity. The conclusion might also explain in part the limited influence of lawyers on plaintiffs, the plaintiffs' indifference to prospects of publicity, delay, and costs associated with litigation, and the decision of those plaintiffs, largely public officials, to sue in the face of legal advice against suit. In a real sense, the bringing of a lawsuit by many libel plaintiffs has relatively little relationship to the legal rules—it is, instead, a highly personal symbolic act.

6

THE LITIGATION PROCESS

In this chapter the process followed in libel suits will be examined from beginning to end. The central focus will be on the functions performed by the legal system, the effectiveness with which the legal system responds to the libel dispute between the parties, and whether the judicial process as presently constituted is an efficient means of resolving libel disputes. Our conclusions will be unsettling to some. The judicial process is geared toward resolving issues that bear little, if any, relationship to the dispute between the parties. The litigation process is inefficient, costly, and cumbersome, as presently constituted. Most striking, however, is the fact there are no real winners in the system—with the possible exception of media lawyers.

COMPOSITION OF THE PLAINTIFFS' CLAIMS

In previous Chapters discussion has focused on who the plaintiffs and defendants were, how they were harmed, or perceived themselves to be harmed, what steps they took in view of the harm, and how and why they ultimately decided to commence litigation to resolve their dispute with the media. Each of the plaintiffs studied, of course, took some form of legal action resulting in suit or settlement. In this and succeeding sections attention will be focused on their lawsuits; on the types of actions brought by the plaintiffs; and on their success in the legal system.

We will first turn to the types of actions brought by the plaintiffs, focusing on the principal legal theories litigated, the legal status of plaintiffs and defendants, the setting in which the allegedly defamatory publication took place (news, entertainment, etc.), and the strength of the legal claim.[1] Analysis of the litigation process and results will follow in a later section of this Chapter.

Privacy cases have been included in the study, and will be discussed briefly, because like defamation they are a communicative tort[2] often involving the media. Moreover, the pattern of litigation and rates of success can be usefully compared with the defamation cases in order to provide a better understanding of the defamation cases themselves. Finally, certain species of the privacy tort are highly analogous to the libel tort, and therefore need to be analyzed to provide a full understanding of the libel action.

Case Composition by Controlling Legal Theory, 1974–84

The total number of cases surveyed and coded[3] between 1974 and 1984 was 909. These cases represent virtually the entire universe of coded libel and privacy cases with formal and reported judicial action occuring in the eleven-year period from 1974 to 1984, inclusive.

The data collected on the 909 cases are broken down in terms of cause of action and legal theory in Table 6–1. The vast proportion of cases are defamation cases. Seven hundred and twelve of the 909 cases, or 78 percent of the total, are defamation cases, and a portion of the cases coded "other" involve a defamation claim coupled with another claim sounding in privacy or another form of communicative tort. Less than 25 percent of the cases are privacy actions. Eliminating the "other" cases, defamation is the main legal theory in 82 percent of the cases; privacy is the main theory in 18 percent.

The privacy cases consist of four distinct types: false light; public disclosure of private facts; appropriation; and intrusion. The false light actions represent 16 percent of the privacy cases, and 3 percent of all privacy and defamation cases over the 1974–84 period. The false light tort is a relative of both the pure privacy tort, which permits recovery for publication of true, but private and embarrassing, facts, and the defamation tort. Generally speaking, statements that concern private subjects that are offensive to the reasonable person, and which through their presentation place the subject in a false, but not defamatory, light, are actionable in

TABLE 6–1 Composition of Defamation and Privacy Cases, 1974–1984

Case Type	Total Coded Cases	Col. %	Media		Non-Media	
			#	Col. %	#	Col. %
Total Cases Coded Media or Non-media, excluding cases coded both	909	100%	665	100%	244	100%
Defamation	712	78%	536	81%	176	72%
False Light	25	3%	21	3%	4	2%
% private plaintiff	68%					
Public Disclosure	58	6%	37	6%	21	9%
% private plaintiff	81%					
Appropriation	53	6%	38	6%	15	6%
% private plaintiff	68%					
Intrusion	23	3%	9	1%	14	6%
% private plaintiff	74%					
Other	38	4%	24	4%	14	6%
% private plaintiff	78%					

states recognizing the false light tort.[4] Unlike the pure privacy tort, false characterization is an element of the false light tort, and unlike defamation, reputational harm is not required.

As this description of the false light tort may suggest, the false light action is difficult to characterize in relation to defamation and privacy. It is also a troublesome tort, for in many instances it forms the basis for a lawsuit when neither a defamation action nor a privacy claim can be made out because reputation has not been harmed and embarrassing private facts have not been disclosed. In this respect the false light tort may represent the closest formal approximation to a legal action for publication of false facts.

The 25 false light cases during the 1974–84 period represent only the cases in which the false light claim was the main legal theory. False light claims were made in conjunction with other claims in many more cases, although in only 17 additional cases were these claims deemed sufficiently colorable to be tried or addressed in the judicial resolution of the case.

The tort of intrusion was the main legal theory in 23 cases studied, representing 15 percent of the privacy cases, and 3 percent of all privacy and defamation cases. The intrusion tort typically concerns invasion of privacy or private areas by physical means, and the nub of the action is the "trespass" rather than subsequent publication.[5] The tort, therefore, is not, strictly speaking, a communicative one, although many of the cases concern alleged physical intrusion as part of a process leading to eventual publication. In addition to the 23 cases noted above, "colorable" intrusion claims were coupled with other privacy claims in 17 other cases. No intrusion claims deemed "colorable" were coupled with defamation claims in the cases studied.

Seventy percent of the privacy cases consisted of the more purely "private" communicative torts of public disclosure of embarrassing private facts and appropriation of likeness without consent. The public disclosure action exists for unreasonable public disclosure of true but not newsworthy embarrassing private facts about a person.[6] The 58 public disclosure, or "pure" privacy, cases represented 37 percent of all privacy cases, and 6 percent of all defamation and privacy cases between 1974 and 1984. In an additional 29 cases "colorable" public disclosure claims were coupled with other legal theories (largely false light and intrusion).

Appropriation claims represented an almost equally large proportion of the privacy claims, consisting of 53 cases in which appropriation was the main legal theory, or 33 percent of all privacy cases and 6 percent of all privacy and defamation cases. The appropriation action is based upon the publication of true pictures or other representations of a person for the private, and usually commercial, use of the publisher, without consent.[7] The range of circumstances in which the tort has been applied is exceedingly broad, and the technical complexities of the cause of action are significant and varied in jurisdictions recognizing the tort. The distinguishing features of the tort when contrasted with the public disclosure action are that the representations need not be private and embarrassing, and the harm is typically commercial, rather than emotional, in character.[8] In addition to the 53 cases in which appropriation was the main legal theory, 11 other cases involved "colorable" appropriation claims coupled with other claims, largely false light and public disclosure actions.

The composition of defendants in the general population of all defamation and privacy claims yields largely expected patterns. Of the 909 total cases, 665 (73 percent) involved media defendants.[9] The media defendant composition of the privacy and the "other" (largely privacy) cases is significantly different than for the defamation group. One hundred and five privacy cases, representing 66 percent of coded privacy cases, involved media defendants. For the "other" cases, which consist almost exclusively of cases with two principal legal theories sounding in privacy, 24 cases representing 63 percent of cases coded "other" involved media defendants.

While privacy claims might be expected to involve a higher proportion of non-media cases because of the private or personal character of the information involved in most such actions, wide disparities exist within the different groups of "privacy" actions. In general, these disparities are explainable in terms of the nature of the published material at issue in the cases, and the distinct interests represented by each form of privacy tort. False light cases, which are closely related to defamation claims and often involve publication of material in a fictionalized form for general or popular consumption, [10] involved media defendants 84 percent of the time, by far the largest percentage of any group of cases. Appropriation claims, which often involve the commercial and therefore general dissemination of material, were brought against media defendants in 72 percent of the cases. In contrast, public disclosure and intrusion cases involved proportionally fewer claims against media. [11]

Composition of Defamation Cases, 1974–84

Defamation cases represented over 78 percent of the cases studied in the 1974–84 period, and information was collected on each case regarding the status of the plaintiffs, the defendants, the publishing setting in which the alleged libel occurred (news, entertainment, literature, and non-media), the principal legal issue upon which the case turned, and a subjective but nevertheless consistent and systematic judgment concerning the legal strength of the claim. In the following pages the composition of the media and non-media defamation cases will be analyzed in terms of each criterion.

The general data for all coded defamation cases with a reported judicial decision between 1974 and 1984 are contained in Table 6–2.

Plaintiff Status

Each of the defamation cases surveyed was coded for the plaintiff's legal status, a criterion that is central to the system of constitutional privileges applied in public defamation cases. For purposes of constitutional privilege, plaintiffs are categorized by courts into two general categories: public plaintiffs and private plaintiffs. [12] Each of these categories, in turn, can be subdivided. The public plaintiffs consist of public officials, public figures, and public figure corporations (or entities). Private plaintiffs consist of private individuals and private corporations (or entities). The status of the plaintiffs triggers varying levels of constitutional privilege—extra proof requirements that limit the likelihood of plaintiffs winning and therefore protect the interest in free expression of the publisher/defendant. Generally speaking, the more "public" the plaintiff (and presumably the statements made about the plaintiff), the higher the privilege and the greater the protection for the published statements that are being challenged. [13]

Public officials are those plaintiffs who hold public office, whose public responsibilities are related to the alleged libel, and who therefore are in

TABLE 6–2   Composition of Media and Non-Media Defamation Cases, 1974–1984

Case Type	Total Coded Cases	Col. %	Media #	Media Col. %	Non-Media #	Non-Media Col. %
Defamation Cases Only						
Plaintiff Status	663	100%	497	100%	166	100%
Public Figure	199	30%	161	32%	38	23%
Public Official	146	22%	119	24%	27	16%
Public Corp.	30	5%	23	5%	7	4%
Total Public	375	57%	303	61%	72	43%
Private Individual	249	38%	164	33%	85	51%
Private Corp.	39	6%	30	6%	9	5%
Total Private	288	43%	194	39%	94	57%
Setting of the Libel						
Total Coded Cases	691	100%	530	100%	161	100%
News	488	71%	451	85%	37	23%
Entertainment	33	5%	31	6%	2	1%
Literature	41	6%	39	7%	2	1%
Other–non-media	129	19%	9	2%	120	75%
Main Legal Issue Adjudicated						
Total Coded Cases	549	100%	423	100%	126	100%
Plaintiff Legal Status	225	41%	188	44%	37	29%
Privilege Application	235	43%	180	43%	55	44%
Strict Liability	2	0%	—	0%	2	2%
Truth or Falsity	87	16%	55	13%	32	25%
Strength of Claim						
Total Coded Cases	694	100%	519	100%	175	100%
Petty	563	81%	422	81%	141	81%
Non-petty	131	19%	97	19%	34	19%

a position to influence the resolution of issues of public importance or interest related to the alleged libel.[14] Public figures are persons who, by virtue of widespread fame or notoriety or through their voluntary efforts, attempt to influence the resolution of public issues related to the subject of the alleged libel.[15] Public figure corporations (or entities) are those non-individual plaintiffs who satisfy the same criteria applicable to public figures.[16] In order to succeed in a defamation action, public officials or public figures must prove actual malice by clear and convincing evidence.[17] Actual knowledge of falsity or reckless disregard of serious doubts concerning truth at the time of publication, rather than negligence or gross negligence, must be established to prove actual malice.[18]

Private plaintiffs, both individual and corporate, consist of all plaintiffs not qualifying as public officials or public figures, either because they hold no office or have no general notoriety, or because the allegedly defamatory statement bears no relationship to their public office or position of public influence. Private plaintiffs must establish negligence to succeed against a media defendant in a defamation action.[19] In actions against non-media defendants, or concerning material published for a special private purpose to a highly restricted audience, the constitutional rules seem to permit strict liability—recovery upon a showing of defamation and harm, in the absence of truth as a defense—although a significant number of states require a showing of negligence in these cases as well.[20] We will refer to these two situations as actions against media and non-media defendants respectively.

In addition, the Supreme Court has recently held that plaintiffs bringing libel claims against media defendants involving publications that do not involve highly limited and restricted circulation must bear the burden of proving the actual falsity of the challenged statement.[21] This burden alters the common law rule that truth was a defense, and requires that an additional element beyond subjective falsity be proved to succeed. Most libel plaintiffs, in other words, will have to prove that the statement was false (actual falsity), and also that the publisher doubted its truth and acted negligently or recklessly, in light of those doubts *at the time of publication* (subjective falsity). The way in which actual falsity must be proved was left uncertain in the Court's decision.

When either the negligence or malice level of privilege applies to a case, the plaintiff who fails to prove either malice or negligence cannot succeed, even though an otherwise valid claim of unjustified reputational disparagement and injury exists. During the period from 1974 through 1984, 57 percent of the defamation cases involved public plaintiffs, who would have to satisfy the highest level of constitutional proof to suceed in the lawsuit. Thirty percent were classified as public figures—individuals whose position or conduct was influential with respect to the controversy surrounding the alleged libel. An additional 5 percent of the public plaintiffs were classified as public figure entities, largely corporate. A third subcategory of public plaintiffs consists of public officials. They comprised 22 percent of the total plaintiff population.

Since the Supreme Court's 1974 decision in *Gertz v. Welch,*[22] the significance of the distinction between public officials and public figures has been eroded. After *Gertz* the public figure classification in media libel cases has legally subsumed the public official group with the public figure criterion generally applied to all public plaintiffs. The *Gertz* criteria focus on the nature of the individual's influence on public debate surrounding the subject of the libel, rather than on the office held by the individual.[23] The distinction between public officials and public figures continues to be relevant after *Gertz*, however, in the limited context of non-media cases.[24]

Notwithstanding its limited relevance after *Gertz*, many courts continue to apply the public official standard in media defamation cases. The incidence with which this takes place, moreover, suggests that this is more than an ad hoc or episodic practice. In media cases, 39 percent of the public plaintiffs are so categorized under the public official criterion. When the incidence of public official plaintiffs in media cases (where the category is subsumed in the public figure test) is compared with the incidence in non-media cases (where the distinction is legally relevant), the proportion of public official plaintiffs is virtually identical, with 39 percent for media cases and 38 percent for non-media cases. The proportion of public official cases does not seem to have changed dramatically over the 11-year period of the study, although one would expect to see a change over time in the media defendant cases in light of the *Gertz* decision. The data therefore suggest that notwithstanding the Supreme Court's reformulation of public defamation privileges in *Gertz*, the public official plaintiff category is still being applied in media defamation cases.

The public libel plaintiff group can also be divided into claims brought by individuals and those brought by corporations or other entities. Of the total public plaintiff case population, 92 percent of the cases were brought by individuals, and 8 percent by corporations or other organizations. This pattern was roughly consistent in both the media libel cases, in which 92 percent of the cases were brought by individuals, and the non-media cases, in which 90 percent of the cases were brought by individuals. The incidence of claims by individual plaintiffs in public libel cases (cases brought by public plaintiffs) was marginally higher than in private cases, where 87 percent of all claims were brought by individuals, and 85 percent of media cases involved individual plaintiffs. Most striking, however, is the difference between libel claims and civil litigation in general, where the incidence of individual claims is about 50 percent.[25]

The interest protected by libel law accounts for the high incidence of individual claims in libel cases. The primary interest secured by the defamation tort is that of reputation, and this interest has been historically associated with the *individual's* interest in reputation. While the law of libel does not foreclose protection of an organization's or group's interest in reputation, the cultural heritage of the tort, as well as its classic application, has focused on protection of the reputation of persons.[26] The reputational interests of corporations, commercial enterprises, and other collective entities has found protection in other torts more directly shaped around the specific settings in which such reputational concerns arise, *e.g.*, trademark, common law copyright, unfair competition, appropriation, and trade libel or product disparagement.[27] While data were not collected on these tort actions as part of this study, it is likely that a significant number of defamation-like claims for non-individual reputational harm are brought under these different causes of action.[28]

In addition to the composition of defamation cases by public or private plaintiffs and by individual or corporate plaintiffs, data were collected on the incidence of media and non-media defendants within these groups. Of the 377 coded public plaintiff defamation cases, 80 percent (303) involved media defendants. The incidence of media defendants within each of the public plaintiff subcategories was generally consistent, with media defendant cases comprising 81 percent of the public figure cases, 82 percent of the public official cases, and 77 percent of the corporate public figure cases. In contrast, media defendant cases comprised only 67 percent of the private plaintiff defamation cases, and a distinct difference exists in the composition of media defendant cases between individual and corporate claims. Sixty-six percent of the private cases brought by individuals involved media defendants, while 77 percent of the private cases involving corporate plaintiffs involved media defendants. The higher incidence of media defendants in corporate plaintiff cases suggests that corporate plaintiffs are more likely to be classified as private rather than public plaintiffs for privilege purposes. The lower incidence of media defendants in claims brought by individuals in private rather than public cases is consistent with the private/public distinction itself, as one would intuitively expect claims based on private matters not the subject of public controversy to occur more frequently in a setting of limited or special purpose publication.[29]

In conclusion, the composition of defamation cases in terms of public or private claims is consistent with other studies that have reported on defamation litigation. The pattern of media and non-media defendants within the public and private groups is also consistent with results one might expect given the assumptions underlying applicable legal doctrine. When this pattern is broken down in terms of individual as opposed to corporate plaintiffs, however the patterns diverge. In material respects it appears that the coporate plaintiff cases are unique, and many of the unique patterns that emerge from those cases may be explained, at least in part, by the conclusion that the public/private plaintiff distinction is being blurred in corporate cases, or the same criteria are not being applied by courts for corporate, as opposed to individual, plaintiff claims.

Setting of the Libel

The population of libel cases from 1974 through 1984 was categorized in terms of the "setting of the libel." This level of categorization was general in character, relating not to the specific type of news or other media involved, or to the medium in which it existed (newspapers, broadcast, etc.), but rather to the general character of the statement judged in its setting. The categories used for this approach were news,[30] entertainment,[31] literature,[32] and all others, consisting largely of non-media publications.[33] More detailed information pertaining to the setting of the claims was assembled for the 164 cases selected for the plaintiff survey. Extended analysis of this data is contained in Appendix A, and it will be repeated here only to the extent that it provides useful explanatory information concerning the general survey results.

Of the 691 coded defamation cases, 81 percent (562) involved publications in the news, entertainment, or literature settings. The vast bulk of these cases, moreover, arose in the context of news. News cases comprised 87 percent of the news-entertainment-literature group, and 71 percent of all cases. Entertainment cases, all but two of which were coded "media," represented 5 percent of total defamation cases, and cases involving literature represented 6 percent of the total population of defamation cases.

When cases involving media defendants are considered separately, the prominence of libel actions based on statements made in the news setting is even more dramatic. Eighty-five percent of media cases involve news, 7 percent involve literature, and 6 percent involve entertainment. While the proportion of cases arising from the entertainment setting may seem surprisingly small, it is understandable in view of the preponderantly fictional character of entertainment, and the greater factual authoritativeness associated with news and literature.

Further information about the media cases—which consist almost exclusively of cases arising in the news, entertainment, and literature settings—is provided through the plaintiff survey. Seventy percent of the 164 plaintiff survey cases involved newspapers, 11 percent involved periodicals, and 18 percent involved radio or television broadcasters.

Main Legal Issue Adjudicated

The common law tort of libel was premised on the relatively straightforward notion that persons whose reputation in the community has been injured by a disparaging statement made about them could seek redress for the loss of reputation.[34] The libel action, accordingly, focused on whether a statement had been made and communicated to others (publication), whether the statement was libelous (disparagement), and whether the reputation of the subject of the statement had been harmed as a consequence (reputational harm). If these elements could be shown, and if neither justification nor truth could be shown by the person making the statement, the person harmed could recover for libel (or slander, in the case of the spoken word).[35]

Since the United States Supreme Court decision in *New York Times v. Sullivan*[36] in 1964, however, libel cases are no longer as straightforward in theory, and they are immensely more complex in practice. As a result of the *Sullivan* decision and many that followed, an additional layer of complexity in the form of constitutional privileges has been superimposed on the libel, or defamation, tort. The privileges, which have two dimensions relevant for present purposes, are as a practical matter adjudicated in most cases, and usually *prior to addressing the common law issues of publication, disparagement, and reputational harm.*[37]

The first question to be addressed is the level of constitutional privilege applicable to the case, judged by the legal status of the plaintiff and whether the defendant's identity is media or non-media.[38] If the plaintiff is a public figure, public official, or public figure entity, the privilege of actual malice applies to the case.[39] If the plaintiff is a private plaintiff, whether individual or corporate, but the defendant is classified as media, the privilege of negligence applies to the case.[40] If the plaintiff is private and the defendant non-media, state law governs the case, and may permit recovery based on the common law rule of strict liability (no fault need be proved) or on negligence.[41]

The second constitutional privilege question is the application of the level of privilege to the facts of the case. If the constitutional privilege is actual malice, for example, the plaintiff must show, in addition to the common law elements of publication, disparagement, and reputational harm, that at the time of publication the publisher believed that the challenged statement was false, or actually entertained serious doubts about its truth and acted recklessly in publishing in the face of those doubts.[42] If the privilege is negligence, the plaintiff must show that at the time of publication the publisher acted negligently in proceeding to publish in light of what was or reasonably should have been known concerning the reliability of the material.[43]

Neither of these privilege issues relate squarely to the issue of the actual falsity of the published statement or to the harm occasioned by it. Because they are generally raised in pretrial motions and, if the subject of trial, are addressed with and usually prior to a decision on the common law elements, the privilege issues are preliminary elements that the plaintiff must prove before getting to the falsity and reputational questions. They are not designed to make adjudication of the libel action more reliable, but instead are instruments designed by the Supreme Court to safeguard the First Amendment interest in freedom of speech by guaranteeing a robust and open marketplace for public expression. Libelous speech, according to the Court, can be "punished" constitutionally through a common law libel action, but the First Amendment requires that some libelous speech—that which is non-negligent or non-malicious—be privileged in order not to deter non-libelous expression by the prospect of liability.[44]

The extent to which the constitutional privileges play a role in libel actions, and the nature of that role, has not been assessed previously. In light of the fact that privilege issues, especially if unsurmounted by the plaintiff, have the effect of extinguishing an otherwise valid common law tort action, and may resolve the controversy without the issues of falsity, disparagement, and harm being addressed, it is most pertinent that we should assess the pervasiveness of the privilege issues and the extent to which they are dispositive in litigation. To obtain some measurement of this issue, the defamation cases were coded in terms of the main legal issue adjudicated. The categories established were truth or falsity, and strict liability—both of which would roughly represent adjudication of issues beyond constitutional privilege (falsity, disparagement, and reputational harm)—and the plaintiff's legal status and application of constitutional privilege (either negligence or actual malice).[45]

For defamation cases between 1974 and 1984, constitutional privilege represented the *main* legal issue adjudicated in 84 percent of the cases. Forty-one percent of the cases principally involved (and usually turned on) a determination of plaintiff status for constitutional privilege purposes, and 43 percent principally involved application of the privilege to the facts of the case following a plaintiff status determination. An additional 16 percent of the cases focused primarily on truth or falsity, and an appreciable proportion of such cases involved antecedent constitutional privilege determinations. If one assumes that the privilege issue was dispositive in a significant proportion of the cases in which it was the main legal issue adjudicated, as the data on case results discussed later tend to bear out,[46] the pervasive presence of constitutional privilege issues, as well as their determinativeness in litigation, seems apparent.[47]

When the cases are separated into two groups, one involving media defendants and the other non-media defendants, the role of constitutional privileges is even more apparent. Understandably, in non-media cases constitutional privileges are less frequently the main issue adjudicated. Up to 27 percent of such cases do not involve such issues, as the bulk of non-media cases brought by private plaintiffs are governed by state law rather than constitutional privilege.

Virtually all media cases, by definition, involve constitutional privilege issues,[48] and here 87 percent of the cases focus mainly on constitutional privilege issues. The remaining 13 percent of the cases address truth or falsity as the primary focus, with the constitutional privilege issues having been successfully surmounted by the plaintiff in most such cases. Inasmuch as roughly 20 percent of the seriously litigated media libel cases reach trial[49]—where truth or falsity (rather than what was known about truth at the time of publication) is likely to become highly relevant—it is a fair inference that most of the 87 percent of media cases involving privilege issues are disposed of on those issues, with an evidentiary trial on defamation counts never taking place.[50] It is probable, therefore, that nearly 87 percent of media libel cases chiefly focus on the constitutional privilege issues and are in fact disposed of on those issues without trial and prior to any adjudicative determination of falsity and reputational harm.

While many of the cases resolved on privilege grounds may involve claims of falsity that are or would be unchallenged, or allegations of reputational harm that would be acknowledged, disposition of the cases on privilege grounds forecloses any test of falsity and, more important, forecloses its materiality and thus precludes examination of the essentially circumstantial issue of the presence and consequence of reputational harm in the minds of the readers or listeners. It is also clear, as discussed later, that many such claims involve highly disputable claims of falsity and tenuous grounds for reputational harm.[51] Exploration of these basic common law issues is practically foreclosed in litigation until privilege issues are resolved, and most media libel cases never get past the privilege stage. The pervasive role of constitutional privileges seems beyond dispute.

Strength of the Claim

An effort was made in the coding of the defamation cases to include a measure of the factual strength of the claim asserted. It was anticipated when this measure was defined that absolute conclusions could not be drawn from analysis of this factor. Nevertheless, it was deemed useful to define a set of criteria that, while subjective, could be applied with reasonable consistency, and that attempted to reflect a judgment about the libel claim in terms not reflected in the actual case results.

For coding purposes, therefore, all claims were classified as "petty" and "non-petty." This determination was based on two factors: the apparent strength of the plaintiff's claim of reputational disparagement based on the known facts of the case; and the materiality of the alleged harm to plaintiffs in reputational and/or financial terms. These judgments were to be made independently of applicable legal doctrine or questions of privilege. In short, the equitable, rather than legal, strength of the claim in light of the ascertainable facts was being measured.[52]

The reason for the coding on this criterion was twofold. First, the common law and, to a much greater extent, the constitutional law rules that are applicable to libel claims are highly technical, and in major respects these technical rules determine the outcome of cases but have no bearing on the strength of the *defamation* claim itself.[53] A rough measure of the divergence of legal rules from the factual strength of a plaintiff's claim of defamation at common law can therefore be derived from the coding. Second, review of a large body of decided cases left the clear impression that many libel claims were "petty" or "frivolous" on the facts.

An example might be *Lawlor v. The Gallagher President's Report*,[54] which involved the discharge of a Gulf & Western vice president for employee relations. In a company newsletter it was stated that Lawlor had been discharged because he and some subordinates had started their own executive recruiting firm without authorization, that this constituted a conflict of interest, and that Lawlor's firm had "extracted fees for the placement of executives" with G&W. Lawlor's libel claim was successful in the district court because his firm had not received fees for placements with G&W. Lawlor had been discharged, however, for setting up the firm without authorization (indeed, in the face of instructions not to do so), and because of the conflict of interest present in his ownership of the recruiting firm (which used the resumes of unsuccessful applicants to G&W without G&W consent, and from which Lawlor obtained financial advantage) and his capacity as vice president for employee relations with G&W.

As a technical matter—and only as a technical matter—Lawlor might make out a claim that the challenged fact was false, and that it should have been known to be false when published. Negligence could therefore be established, but the finding of liability in Lawlor's libel action seems justifiable only if one disregards the substantive interests reflected in libel law itself. It is highly doubtful, in other words, that the increment of harm to Lawlor's employability flowing from the falsity of the statement that his firm received fees from G&W was significant; at the very least, the presence and materiality of harm is an issue of considerable moment in the case. G&W did not recommend Lawlor for employment elsewhere—a fact which resulted in his loss of jobs independent of the publication at issue in the case. Prospective employers would likely be mainly influenced by the facts that Lawlor was fired, that the reason was the unauthorized creation of a personal executive placement firm in violation of instructions and company policy, and the conflict of interest G&W saw in that situation.

The *Lawlor* case is illustrative of many cases that appeared, after extensive review of judicial decisions, to involve claims that are "petty" when judged by the facts of the case and the materiality and nature of the alleged harm to reputation. In coding the cases, therefore, systematic and relatively consistent judgments were made in each instance concerning the factual strength of the claim of falsity and disparagement, and the materiality of claimed harm when judged in the circumstances. The criteria could then be employed to ascertain generally the relationship between judicial result and the factual strength of the defamation claim, and the types of cases in which stronger or weaker claims are made.

Analysis of the cases in terms of strength of the claim yields some interesting observations. For the universe of coded defamation cases from 1974 through 1984, 81 percent were deemed petty (weak factual claims), and 19 percent were coded non-petty (strong factual basis for claim). The relative composition of strong and weak claims is identical for media and non-media cases. The factual strength of a claim therefore seems largely a function of the *plaintiffs'* decision to sue, and is not more or less inherent in the mode or medium of publication. Moreover, the plaintiff's decision to sue in light of the strength of the claim does not seem to be affected by the defendant's media or non-media status.

While litigation results will be discussed in detail in the following section of this chapter, brief discussion of the subject in terms of the strength of claim criterion is appropriate at this point. The "pettiness" coding tends to follow rather closely patterns of ultimate success in the judicial system, and the patterns are similar whether the cases involve media defendants or non-media defendants. Of total defamation cases finally resolved, only 6 percent of those coded "petty" were won by the plaintiffs. For media cases alone, 95 percent of the "petty" group were won by the media defendants. In marked contrast, 48 percent of defamation cases coded "non-petty" were won by plaintiffs; and 45 percent of "non-petty" cases involving media defendants were won by the plaintiffs. [55] Recognizing that the coding of "pettiness" represents a subjective judgment, and that the analysis must take that into account, it appears that the incidence of "error" (cases in which liability is imposed on petty claims) is only 6 percent for the population of petty claims, and 5 percent for the case population as a whole. This group would consist of the type of claims illustrated by the *Lawlor* case, where the factual basis of material reputational disparagement or identifiable harm is very weak, but the technical legal rules of privilege may permit, ironically, success in litigation.

On the other hand, the incidence of error in the form of failure to obtain relief for a factually strong claim of libel is very high. For the group of non-petty claims, the incidence of such error is 52 percent, and this group represents about 10 percent of the total defamation cases. These cases consist of claims that are factually forceful in light of the common law interest in redressing reputationally disparaging statements that produce material unjustified harm. In view of the fact, discussed earlier, that the plaintiffs' failure to succeed in such cases is largely a product of the constitutional privileges of malice or negligence, the cost of denying recovery in order to avoid inhibiting other protected expression under the First Amendment is borne by perhaps as many as one of every two libel plaintiffs whose otherwise strong factual claims for relief are foreclosed.

It bears repeating that the conclusion about the cost to valid claims of constitutional privileges is derived from data that, while consistently generated, fall far short of any exacting standard of absolute accuracy. The constitutional privileges clearly exact a cost in terms of foreclosed valid defamation claims, and the analysis of the strength of claims criterion bears this out. That such a cost would be exacted was clearly and explicitly understood by the Supreme Court when the privileges were first crafted, and while the cost could not be quantified, the Court balanced it expressly against the benefit of less inhibited public discussion. The strength of claim analysis described above does not purport in any scientifically reliable way to quantify that cost precisely, but it nevertheless suggests the conclusion that factually strong defamation claims are foreclosed by privilege rules in material numbers.

At the risk of overextrapolation from the data, a final point should be made about the "strength of claim" analysis. If one assumes that an adjudicative process directed specifically at truth or falsity and reputational harm would yield a more direct relationship between litigation results and the strength of the underlying claim, that the petty cases won by plaintiffs would therefore have been lost, and the non-petty cases lost on privilege grounds would have been won instead, the total number and proportion of plaintiff wins would not have changed significantly. Plaintiffs actually won 6 percent of the petty cases, for a total of 28 cases. Plaintiffs lost 52 percent of the non-petty cases, for a total of 39 cases.[56] From a total of 693 cases, the incidence of plaintiff wins if falsity and material reputational harm were determinative would increase by only 11 cases, or less than 2 percent.

A further analysis of the strength of claim data can be made in terms of the plaintiffs' legal status, as summarized in Table 6–3. The comparison of strength of claim with plaintiff legal status yields a clear and consistent difference between public and private defamation actions. While 84 percent of claims brought by public plaintiffs were "petty," and this proportion is essentially constant for all public plaintiff subcategories, fewer claims (76 percent) brought by private plaintiffs were "petty." The higher incidence of "petty" claims brought by public plaintiffs suggests either that in coding the cases a different standard of factual strength was being employed for public cases, or that some degree of systematic difference in plaintiff motivation occurs between public and private plaintiffs. While the coding was conducted in a way designed to avoid the public character of the claim from being taken into account, the inherent subjectivity of the coding makes certainty on this point impossible.

TABLE 6–3   Strength of Claim and Plaintiff Status
Defamation Cases (Media and Non-Media), 1974–84[57]

Plaintiff Status	Petty		Non-Petty	
	#	%	#	%
Public Figure	160	84%	31	16%
Public Official	122	83%	25	17%
Public Entity	27	90%	3	10%
Total Public	309	84%	59	16%
Private Individual	191	77%	58	23%
Private Entity	27	69%	12	31%
Total Private	218	76%	70	24%

Based upon the earlier analysis of the reasons plaintiffs sue, the role of counsel, and the demographic composition of the plaintiff population, however, there is substantial reason to conclude that at least part of the reason more "petty" claims are brought by public plaintiffs concerns the plaintiffs' approach to the decision to litigate. Public plaintiffs tend to rely less heavily on lawyers; they tend to contact the media themselves, respond less emotionally to the contact, but make the decision to sue early and in advance of seeing an attorney. Public plaintiffs also appear to sue more often for nonfinancial reasons, and the objectives they set for suit tend more heavily to relate to vindication of reputation and correction of falsity, as such. Their suits, in short, may tend more often to relate to public or political ends rather than to wholly personal or financial harm.[58] While these differences, discussed at length in Chapter 5, are marginal, the difference in the incidence of petty claims is also marginal. To the extent that these features of the public plaintiffs' decisions to sue may be manifested by more marginal degrees of falsity in the challenged publication, or more marginal degrees of consequent disparagement and harm to the plaintiff, they would tend to be reflected in strength of claim criterion applied in the analysis of the cases.

RESULTS ACHIEVED IN LITIGATION

The widely known truth that the odds of winning a defamation suit are poor, at best, did not discourage libel plaintiffs in the cases studied. No doubt many reasons account for the persistence of libel plaintiffs, but two seem paramount. First, the concept of what constitutes victory in libel litigation is determined by a more complex equation than the general statement that nearly 90 percent of the plaintiffs lose. The second reason for plaintiff persistence is that the incidence of victory is much higher than the simple won/loss statistics suggest. Nearly 90 percent of the plaintiffs may lose in court, but a significantly larger proportion win, even though the judicial standard for victory would suggest otherwise, because they believe they have substantially vindicated their reputation by the very act of bringing suit. [59] In the following pages the results achieved by plaintiffs in litigation will be assessed from both of these perspectives.

The Incidence of Success in Court

Information pertaining to the incidence of plaintiff success in litigation was assembled from two primary sources: analysis of virtually all libel and privacy cases between 1974 and 1984, and information provided by the 164 plaintiffs surveyed. As mentioned previously, the privacy cases are included and discussed briefly for comparative purposes.

Defamation and Privacy Cases, 1974–84

Before proceeding to a specific discussion of rates of success in specific types of circumstances, data assembled from the analysis of all cases from 1974 to 1984 will be briefly analyzed. The data are presented for all defamation and privacy cases in Table 6–4.

The rate of plaintiff judicial success was 14 percent for all finally concluded defamation and privacy cases involving media and non-media defendants between 1974 and 1984. When this general universe of cases is broken down by plaintiff legal status and media or non-media defendants, both of which are key elements triggering constitutional privilege, patterns emerge that tend to confirm the expected operation of the privilege rules. Cases involving public plaintiffs, which are governed by the rigorous actual malice privilege or its equivalent in the privacy setting, have a 12 percent success rate, which is somewhat although not significantly lower than the 14 percent rate for the population as a whole. Cases brought by private plaintiffs, which are governed by a lower standard of privilege, if any at all, have a success rate of 17 percent.

These data follow a consistent pattern when the public and private plaintiff groups are broken down into subcategories, with the notable exception of the public figure corporation or entity. The success rates for individual (as opposed to corporate) public figure and public official plaintiffs are essentially the same at 13 and 12 percent respectively, which tends

TABLE 6–4   Defamation and Privacy Cases, 1974–84 Litigation Results

Case Type	Total Cases		Resolved Cases Only				Pending Cases[60]	
			Pro Pl.		Pro Def.			
	#	% col.	#	% row	#	% row	#	% total
Plaintiff Status								
Total Coded Cases	860	100%	91	14%	547	86%	222	26%
Public Figure	236	27%	23	13%	159	87%	54	23%
Public Official	158	18%	14	12%	102	88%	42	27%
Public Corp.	33	4%	1	5%	21	95%	11	33%
Total Public	427	50%	38	12%	282	88%	107	25%
Private Individual	388	45%	47	16%	240	84%	101	26%
Private Corp.	45	5%	6	19%	25	81%	14	31%
Total Private	433	50%	53	17%	265	83%	115	27%
Defendant Status								
Media Defendant	668	72%	58	12%	426	88%	184	28%
Non-media Defendant	243	28%	35	18%	155	82%	53	22%

to confirm the fact that most such cases after *Gertz v. Welch* are legally synonymous. Public figure corporations, however, succeed in only 5 percent of the cases. While the relatively small number of such cases may partially account for the disparity in success rate, the lower rate for public corporate plaintiffs also tends to support the conclusion suggested earlier that privilege standards are apparently being applied differently to corporate plaintiffs than they are to individuals. In light of the earlier discussion, the different treatment seems to occur in the public/private classification of corporate plaintiffs. The fact that the corporate plaintiff success rate in private cases is only marginally higher than the individual rate makes any clear conclusion difficult, however, as one would expect the rate of success for private corporate plaintiffs to be correspondingly higher than private individual claims if categorization were the only factor influencing the different rates in the public case setting.

Analysis of the proportion of cases pending at the time of the study (1984) yields interesting but limited observations. First, of the various private and public plaintiff categories, the highest rate of pending cases— cases not *finally* resolved by unappealed judicial decision or settlement[61]— occurs in the corporate setting, with 33 percent of the public figure corporate cases pending, and 31 percent of the private corporate cases pending.

The higher rate of unresolved corporate cases may be an indication of the difficulty courts are experiencing in applying the plaintiff categories and privilege rules in the corporate or entity setting.[62] The second observation is that the general rate of pending cases is essentially the same for public and private plaintiffs as a whole, but when the cases are divided between media and non-media defendants, a difference in the rate of pending cases emerges. Twenty-eight percent of media defendant cases were pending at the time of the study, while only 22 percent of non-media cases were pending. Given the large number of cases in each population, and the consistent application of the pending criterion, the difference in rate of pending cases is significant.

The explanation for the difference seems to lie in the applicability of constitutional privilege, with cases involving privilege issues taking longer to resolve than those not involving privilege.[63] Defendant status is a better surrogate for the application of privilege than is plaintiff status, and therefore the difference in pending rate emerges in that comparison.[64] The influence of privilege rules is further borne out by an analysis of the pending rate for media defamation cases and non-media defamation cases. All media defamation cases involve constitutional privilege issues, and 29 percent of these cases were pending. Non-media defamation cases, on the other hand, often involve no constitutional privilege issue, and only 6 percent of these cases were pending.[65] Privilege rules account for a substantial proportion of the appellate court involvement in libel cases—much of which occurs before trial.[66] It is not surprising, therefore, to see the stark difference in the rate of pending cases when cases involving privilege issues are compared with cases to which privileges are inapplicable.

A final observation concerning success rates pertains to defendant status. While the relevance of the defendants' media status to the constitutional privilege is ambiguous at best, under the formal legal rules, the status of the defendant as "media" or "non-media" seems to play a role in the application of constitutional privileges. This is borne out in practice by the lower plaintiff success rate in cases brought against media defendants. Plaintiffs succeeded in 12 percent of the defamation and privacy actions brought against media defendants, and in 18 percent of such actions brought against non-media defendants. While the Supreme Court has only recently addressed whether the application of constitutional privileges in private non-media cases is explicitly contingent on the media status of the defendant,[67] it appears from the data that such a distinction is in fact influencing the approach of courts in the adjudication of cases. This is dramatically confirmed in the defamation setting discussed below, where the success rate for private plaintiffs was 23 percent in non-media cases, and 14 percent in media cases.

Privacy and Related Cases, 1974–84

Selected information was collected on privacy cases involving a published judicial order during the 1974–84 period. Privacy cases include the torts of public disclosure of private facts, false light, intrusion, and appropriation.[68] Information pertaining to litigation results for these cases is set out in Table 6–5.

It is apparent from Table 6–5 that the incidence of plaintiff success in privacy cases is higher than that for defamation claims. Plaintiffs succeed in 18 percent of the privacy cases, while the success rate is only 14 percent for the combined population of defamation and privacy actions, and 13 percent for defamation cases.[70] Similarly, 17 percent of the privacy claims against media defendants were successful, compared with success rates of 12 percent for all defamation and privacy cases, and 11 percent for media defamation cases. The success rate for non-media privacy claims (20 percent) was also higher than for all non-media claims (18 percent) and non-media defamation claims (18 percent).

The higher plaintiff success rate in privacy cases is somewhat surprising, for the constitutional restrictions on recovery in many forms of privacy action are significant, if not nearly insurmountable. This is especially so in the public disclosure and false light settings. Because the public disclosure tort permits recovery for the publication of private, yet true, facts, the circumstances under which liability can be imposed on truthful publication are highly restricted in view of the First Amendment speech and press guarantees.[71] While the false light action avoids this difficulty through the requisite element of fictionalization, the false light tort does not require a showing of reputational harm,[72] and therefore has weaker roots in interests traditionally reflected in the communicative tort area. In light of these considerations, one would expect the incidence of plaintiff success to be

TABLE 6–5   Privacy and Related Cases, 1974–84 Litigation Results

| | Total Cases | | Resolved Cases Only | | | | Pending Cases[69] | |
| | | | Pro Pl. | | Pro Def. | | | |
Case Type	#	% col.	#	% row	#	% row	#	% total
Non-Defamation Cases								
Total Coded Cases	196	100%	27	18%	124	82%	45	23%
Media Defendant	129	66%	17	17%	83	83%	29	23%
Non-media Defendant	67	34%	10	20%	41	80%	16	24%

TABLE 6–6   Plaintiff Success by Main Legal Theory

| | Plaintiff Success Rate, Final Cases | | |
Main Legal Theory	All Cases	Non-Media	Media
Defamation	12.6%	17.5%	10.8%
False Light Privacy*	16.7%	50.0%**	11.5%
Public Disclosure Privacy*	6.6%	12.0%	2.8%
Appropriation	33.3%	33.3%	33.3%
Intrusion	22.2%	10.0%	37.5%

*Includes false light or public disclosure claims coupled with other privacy claims, but representing the chief theory of recovery.
**The total number of cases is four, and therefore the rate is not a reliable indicator of success rate.

lower in privacy cases than in defamation cases, for the public disclosure and false light cases represent a large portion of privacy claims.

Table 6–6 provides a breakdown of success rates by type of privacy claim.

Analysis of the data in terms of the specific type of privacy claim reveals the reasons for the difference in success rates between privacy and defamation claims. The plaintiff success rate for public disclosure privacy actions is quite low (6.6 percent), and is even lower for media cases (2.8 percent). Interestingly, the success rate for false light claims is high (roughly 17 percent), but virtually all of the successful cases involve non-media defendants, where the success rate is 50 percent compared to 12 percent for media cases (the number of non-media false light cases is very small). The largest contributing influence to the high rate of plaintiff success in privacy cases, however, is the high success rate for the two remaining forms of privacy actions. Plaintiffs succeed in 22 percent of the intrusion cases, and in 33 percent of the appropriation cases. In each case, moreover, the success rate against media defendants is strikingly high. While these cases comprise less than half of the privacy claims, the higher rate of success in the appropriation and intrusion areas increases the overall privacy success rate significantly.

A final observation on the privacy cases should be made concerning the relationship between plaintiff success rate and defendant status. Plaintiffs won 17 percent of the privacy cases brought against media defendants, and 20 percent of the privacy cases brought against non-media defendants. While the higher rate of plaintiff success against non-media defendants is expected and is consistent with the pattern for all types of cases surveyed, it is notable that the disparity in success rate between media and non-media cases is comparatively small. In absolute terms, the spread in success rates for media and non-media cases is only 3 percent, and in comparative terms the media success rate is 85 percent of the non-media success rate. In contrast, the defamation case success rate for media claims is 10 percent, and for non-media claims it is 15 percent. The absolute spread in rates is 5 percent, and the media success rate is 66 percent of the non-media rate, compared to 85 percent for privacy cases.[73]

Given the large number of cases surveyed, the difference in plaintiff success rate in privacy cases is significant, and requires explanation. The answer seems to lie in the greater legal significance of the plaintiff status issue in defamation cases as compared to privacy cases. For defamation and privacy cases combined, public plaintiffs succeed in 12 percent of the cases, while private plaintiffs succeed in 19 percent of the cases. For defamation cases, however, the differential increases, with 10 percent of the public plaintiffs succeeding and 18 percent of the private plaintiffs succeeding. When only non-media defamation cases are considered, moreover, it appears that 11 percent of the public plaintiffs succeed, while 23 percent of the private plaintiffs win.

These differential success rates suggest that defamation cases, as a group, exhibit great sensitivity to the plaintiff's status in light of the related constitutional privileges. This is particularly evident in the non-media setting, where the clear disparity in success rate in light of plaintiff status most closely reflects the presence (with public plaintiffs) or frequent absence (with private plaintiffs) of constitutional privilege. In contrast, the generally high success rate in privacy cases is not as significantly influenced by the media or non-media character of the defendant, or by the public or private status of the plaintiff.

While it is difficult to generalize about public and private plaintiff success rates in privacy cases, the rate of success across all privacy claims is the opposite of that seen in the defamation setting. Public plaintiffs are more successful, as a group, than private plaintiffs in privacy cases. Table 6–7 provides a detailed breakdown.

Public plaintiffs succeed in 26 percent of the privacy cases, while private plaintiffs succeed in only 16 percent. This disparity reverses the pattern found in the non-media defamation setting and in the defamation setting in general. With the exception of the false light tort, moreover, the pattern of higher success by public plaintiffs is consistent across the various privacy actions. It appears, therefore, that the plaintiff and defendant status considerations that are critical in the defamation setting play a significantly reduced role in the privacy context, and this is especially true with the intrusion and appropriation torts. The explanation appears to be that constitutional considerations apply uniformly to all privacy cases regardless of plaintiff status, and that plaintiff status, which is not an explicit element in the constitutional privileges applicable to privacy claims (except false

TABLE 6–7 Success Rate by Plaintiff Status, Privacy Cases, 1974–84

Type of Claim	Plaintiff Wins	Total Resolved Cases	Plaintiff Success Rate
I. All Privacy Cases			
Public Plaintiffs	9	35	26%
Private Plaintiffs	18	115	16%
II. Types of Privacy Cases			
False Light			
Public Plaintiffs	0	3	0%
Private Plaintiffs	3	12	25%
Public Disclosure			
Public Plaintiffs	1	10	10%
Private Plaintiffs	1	39	3%
Appropriation			
Public Plaintiffs	5	11	46%
Private Plaintiffs	9	30	30%
Intrusion			
Public Plaintiffs	2	5	40%
Private Plaintiffs	2	13	15%
Other (Combined Privacy Claims)			
Public Plaintiffs	1	6	17%
Private Plaintiffs	3	21	14%

light cases), in fact plays no implicit role in adjudication. Moreover, it appears that constitutional privileges have a relatively smaller impact on the adjudication of privacy claims, perhaps because a privacy invasion may be perceived as inflicting greater harm on those persons whose lives are otherwise public.

Defamation Cases, 1974–84

The main focus of this study concerns defamation actions against media defendants. To obtain comparative information concerning possible differences in litigation results between media and non-media defamation claims, information has been assembled on all coded defamation claims during the 1974–84 period, on non-media claims as a group, and on media claims as a group. In the following two tables, information on litigation results for all defamation claims and for non-media claims have been compiled separately.

TABLE 6–8   Defamation Cases, 1974–84 Litigation Results, Media and Non-media Cases

| | Total Cases | | Resolved Cases Only | | | | Pending Cases[74] | |
| | | | Pro Pl. | | Pro Def. | | | |
Case Type	#	% col.	#	% row	#	% row	#	% total
Defamation Cases								
Plaintiff Status								
Total Coded Cases	661	100%	64	13%	420	87%	177	27%
Public Figure	199	30%	14	9%	142	91%	43	22%
Public Official	146	22%	14	13%	92	87%	40	27%
Public Corp.	30	5%	1	5%	21	95%	8	27%
Total Public	375	57%	29	10%	255	90%	91	24%
Private Individual	247	37%	30	17%	145	83%	72	29%
Private Corp.	39	6%	5	20%	20	80%	14	36%
Total Private	286	43%	35	18%	165	82%	86	30%
Main Legal Issue								
Total Coded Cases	548							
Plaintiff Status	225	41%	9	6%	136	94%	80	36%
Privilege Applic.	234	43%	41	24%	132	76%	61	26%
Strict Liability	4	1%	2	50%	2	50%	0	0%
Truth or Falsity	85	16%	7	9%	73	91%	5	6%
Setting								
Total Coded Cases	687							
News	487	71%	34	10%	315	90%	138	28%
Entertainment	32	5%	3	13%	20	87%	9	28%
Literature	41	6%	2	7%	26	93%	13	32%
Other–non-media	127	19%	22	21%	81	79%	24	19%
Strength of Claim								
Total Coded Cases	693							
Petty	563	81%	28	6%	408	94%	127	23%
Non-Petty	130	19%	36	48%	39	52%	55	42%

Before turning to the media defamation cases, a few general observations can be made about the total population of defamation cases, and the non-media cases in particular For the total population of defamation cases, plaintiffs' rate of success was 13 percent. Public plaintiffs succeeded in 10 percent of the public defamation cases, and private plaintiffs succeeded in 18 percent of the private cases.

TABLE 6–9   Non-media Defamation Cases, 1974–84 Litigation Results

| | Total Cases | | Resolved Cases Only | | | |
| | | | Pro Pl. | | Pro Def. | |
Case Type	#	% col.	#	% row	#	% row
Total Coded Non- Media Cases (Final)	131	100%	24	18%	107	82%
Public Plaintiff	54	41%	6	11%	48	89%
Private Plaintiff	77	59%	18	23%	59	77%

When the non-media defamation cases are isolated, the pattern of plaintiff success rates follows familiar and expected patterns. As a group, plaintiffs in non-media defamation cases are more successful than defamation plaintiffs in general. Eighteen percent of non-media actions are successful compared to 13 percent of all defamation actions. The different success rates for public and private plaintiffs in non-media cases are stark and revealing. Private plaintiffs win nearly one-quarter of the defamation actions brought against non-media defendants, and this is the highest success rate for any plaintiff or defendant grouping of defamation claims. This subcategory of cases includes all of the instances in which constitutional privileges are nonapplicable, and the common law tort prevails.

In contrast, public defamation plaintiffs in non-media cases succeed in 11 percent of the cases. This is roughly the same success rate applicable to public plaintiff defamation claims in general. It is also roughly the same success rate applicable to public plaintiff claims brought against media defendants. The identity of success rates in public cases against media and non-media defendants is significant, for it confirms the consistency with which the constitutional privileges are being applied. In both sets of cases the plaintiffs' public status governs the constitutional privilege rules, and the same actual malice privilege is applicable. One would expect, therefore, to find nearly identical success rates notwithstanding the different defendants involved in each group. Confirmation of this expectation suggests that the constitutional privilege rules are being properly applied, and are yielding intended—or at least consistent—results.

The data also indicate that, with the exception of the subset of public plaintiff cases, the non-media defamation cases have a different success rate as well as a different composition of success than the media defamation cases. The media status of the defamation defendant, in short, influences the outcome of cases independently of other factors. More particularized information concerning the nature of these differences is provided in Table 6–10, pertaining to media defamation cases only.

A total of 494 media defamation cases occurring between 1974 and 1984, inclusive, were coded. The composition of these cases in terms of plaintiff and defendant groupings, legal theory applied, and other factors has been discussed previously. Three hundred and fifty-three of the cases, or 71 percent, had been finally concluded by settlement or formal judicial

TABLE 6–10   Media Defamation Cases, 1974–84 Litigation Results

| | | | Resolved Cases Only | | | | | |
| | Total Cases | | Pro Pl. | | Pro Def. | | Pending Cases[75] | |
Case Type	#	% Col.	#	% row	#	% row	#	% total
Plaintiff Status								
Total Coded Cases	494	100%	40	11%	313	89%	141	29%
Public Figure	160	32%	12	9%	115	91%	33	21%
Public Official	118	24%	10	11%	78	89%	30	25%
Public Corp.	23	5%	1	7%	14	93%	8	35%
Total Public	301	61%	23	10%	207	90%	71	24%
Private Individual	163	33%	13	13%	91	87%	59	36%
Private Corp.	30	6%	4	21%	15	79%	11	37%
Total Private	193	39%	17	14%	106	86%	70	36%
Main Legal Issue								
Total Coded Cases	419	100%						
Plaintiff Status	187	45%	6	5%	115	95%	66	35%
Privilege Applic.	179	43%	30	22%	104	78%	45	25%
Truth or Falsity	53	13%	2	4%	49	96%	2	4%
Setting								
Total Coded Cases*	518	100%						
News	449	87%	31	10%	290	90%	128	29%
Entertainment	30	6%	3	14%	19	86%	8	27%
Literature	39	8%	2	7%	25	93%	12	31%
Strength of Claim								
Total Coded Cases	516	100%						
Non-Petty	97	19%	23	45%	28	55%	46	47%
Petty	419	81%	17	5%	306	95%	96	23%

*An additional nine media cases involved alleged libels falling outside the three coding categories.

decision by 1984, when the survey was completed. Of the cases finally resolved, libel plaintiffs who sued media defendants succeeded in only 11 percent of the cases, a significantly lower rate of success than that applicable to libel actions against non-media defendants (18 percent) and to privacy and related actions against media defendants (17 percent) or non-media defendants (20 percent).[76]

In media libel cases two layers of privilege apply.[77] First, the presence of a media defendant assures in virtually all cases that a minimum privilege of negligence will govern adjudication of the case.[78] In other words, all plaintiffs suing media defendants must at least prove that the allegedly defamatory statement was published negligently in order to recover. Recovery under the common law rule is foreclosed for non-negligent but unjustified publication of defamatory statements injurious to reputation. The second layer of privilege applies in cases brought by public figure or public official plaintiffs. In this group of media libel actions the privilege of actual malice applies, requiring the plaintiff to show that the publication was reckless in light of known falsity or actual and serious doubts concerning falsity at the time of publication.

In view of these two layers of privilege, one would expect to see different incidences of success when the cases are grouped in terms of privilege application, with a lower incidence of success in the public plaintiff actions in view of the higher standard of privilege in those cases. Moreover, because some form of constitutional privilege applies in all cases, one would expect to see a smaller disparity in success rates between these groups than between the public and private non-media cases, where the highest standard of privilege applies for public plaintiffs, and no constitutional privilege applies to many private plaintiff cases. The data are consistent with these expectations. In media defamation cases, public plaintiffs succeed 10 percent of the time, and private plaintiffs, who face a lower privilege requirement, succeed 14 percent of the time. Excluding the corporate plaintiffs which, for reasons discussed previously, exhibit certain unique characteristics in the privilege setting, the pattern remains the same, with the success rate for public plaintiffs at 10 percent, and for private plaintiffs at 13 percent. The disparity in success rate in these two groups (10 percent v. 14 percent), moreover, is much smaller than that between public and private plaintiffs in the non-media setting (11 percent v. 23 percent).[79]

Judged by ultimate success in litigation, therefore, the privilege rules are generating expected and significant results, reducing the success rate almost in half from 23 percent to 14 percent by the requirement of negligence, and by as much as 60 percent from 23 percent to 10 percent by the requirement of actual malice. These differences in success rate are consistent with the suggestion, developed earlier, that the cost of constitutional privileges in terms of extinguishing previously successful libel actions may be as high as 50 percent.[80]

In order to determine whether the rate of plaintiff success in media libel cases has changed over time, the cases were analyzed longitudinally by the date of final judicial resolution. While grouping the cases by this criterion will not necessarily reflect differences that might depend on the date of the libel or the initiation of suit in particular cases, the large number of cases studied will allow a sufficiently systematic review over time to indicate the presence of any general trends.

A discernible pattern of reduced plaintiff success over time appears when the media defamation cases are grouped by year of final disposition. Plaintiff success rates range from a high of 29 percent to a low of 7 percent, but the 29 percent rate exists at the beginning of the period, and sample size and proportion of unresolved cases appear to influence the success rate. Excluding 1975, the rate of success is more consistent, but nevertheless declines over the period covered.

A second pattern is a consistent increase in the proportion of media defendants over time in the defamation setting. In 1975, 68 percent of the defendants were classified as "media." This proportion rises to 94 percent by 1983.[82] Part of this rise can be associated with the bunching of pending, and mostly media, cases prior to 1980, but it does not appear that this phenomenon fully accounts for the fairly consistent rise in media cases. While the bunching of cases in the 1980–82 period may also have had some impact on the decline in plaintiff success, it seems clear that, based

TABLE 6–11   Media Defamation Cases[81]
Plaintiff Success 1975–83 (final cases)

Year*	Plaintiff Wins		Media Wins	
	#	% Final	#	% Final
1975	4	29%	10	71%
1976	4	17%	19	83%
1977	4	15%	22	85%
1978	4	11%	32	89%
1979	2	12%	15	88%
1980	4	8%	47	92%
1981	4	8%	48	92%
1982	5	7%	72	93%
1983	4	9%	40	91%

*The years 1974 and 1984, for which only partial data were collected, have been deleted from the analysis.

on the date of most recent judicial action, plaintiffs have faced increasingly difficult obstacles to success against media defendants in defamation actions.

Concomitant with an increasing proportion of media libel cases is a consistent increase in the total number of defamation and privacy cases between 1975 and 1982.[83] The population of finally-resolved cases rises consistently from 35 to 120 during this period, and this pattern also occurs with total cases, including those still pending. A substantial decrease in the case population occurs in 1983, not only for finally-decided cases, but for all cases, including those still pending.[84] The extreme rate of decrease does not necessarily signal a reduction in libel filings, as the cases included are restricted to those with a judicial opinion or published order, although if the trend persists this conclusion could be drawn with some confidence. Instead, the decrease most likely reflects a decrease in the incidence of judicial activity in libel cases, and particularly a decrease in multiple judicial actions in the cases. From 1975 to 1982 a significant increase in the incidence of pretrial motions on privilege issues, and multiple appeals at the pretrial stage, was widely perceived. The data bear this out, for libel cases involve an uncommonly high commitment of judicial resources. The growth in judicial activity is consistent with this. With the recent reduction of pretrial activity resulting from a number of Supreme Court opinions,[85] cases which had been telescoped into the 1980–82 period (even though begun much earlier) were either concluded at that point or proceeded to trial. Assuming that the incidence of trials has increased, one would expect the level of judicial activity in the form of published opinions or orders to decrease in large part, or to be deferred.

In view of this, it appears that the incidence of libel actions may not have changed as dramatically as the data drawn from published judicial decisions might suggest. Instead, the processing of the cases has changed. The substantial pretrial and appellate involvement until 1979 may have bunched the cases, or telescoped them into the 1980–82 period. While constitutional privilege issues still require substantial pretrial activity, the relaxed standard for overcoming motions for summary judgment or dismissal has likely had the effect of directing more cases with disputed fact issues to trial. As a consequence, the level of judicial activity by opinion or published order seems to have tapered off, but this does not establish that the underlying number of actions commenced has decreased.

The uncertainties about the timing of cases permits only two limited conclusions to be drawn from an analysis of cases over the 1975–83 period. First, the incidence of plaintiff success in all cases appears essentially stable, but plaintiffs have been less successful over time in defamation cases against media defendants. Second, the number of cases grew substantially from 1975 to 1982, and dropped precipitously after 1982, and the proportion of media cases increased over the same period. A large part of this change, however, appears to relate to shifts in the processing of litigation rather than the underlying incidence of libel suits.

In order to obtain a finer breakdown of the factors contributing to plaintiff and defendant success in media libel cases, other criteria were also coded as part of the case survey. For present purposes, the three main factors are (1) the main legal issue adjudicated in the case, (2) the setting of the media defamation—news, entertainment, and literature—and (3) the strength of the claim.

In the constitutional privilege setting, legal analysis follows two steps. First, the legal status of the plaintiff must be ascertained in order to define the level of privilege applicable to the case. Second, the constitutional privilege, once identified, must be applied to the facts of the case. The issues of truth or falsity and defamation are generally determined after the privilege inquiries, and only if the applicable privilege is surmounted by the plaintiff. The distribution of cases in Table 6–10 bears out this sequence. It is noteworthy that 87.5 percent of the cases turn largely on the privilege issues of plaintiff status and privilege application. Only 12.5 percent of the cases are substantially focused on the issues of truth or defamation. [86]

The privilege cases are divided evenly between those primarily involving plaintiff legal status, or level of privilege, and those primarily involving application of the privilege standard to the facts. The incidence of success between these two groups of privilege cases is strikingly different, however. In cases whose principal focus is plaintiff status and level of privilege, only 5 percent of the plaintiffs ultimately succeed. In effect, many of these plaintiffs' cases are contingent on the first privilege question, and an adverse determination on the privilege issue poses a burden of proof obstacle that cannot be overcome, even if the *defamation* claims are factually strong. The plaintiffs who succeed on the level of privilege issue (establishing the lowest possible level of privilege), or whose cases are strong on the privilege issue as well as the common law defamation claim, fall into the second group, where the principal legal question is the application of privilege in light of the facts. Those plaintiffs who have proceeded through the first "filter" of privilege succeed in 22 percent of the cases.

Two observations can be made about the success rates in privilege cases. The first is that the threshold privilege question has a powerful influence on the sorting out of successful and unsuccessful claims. Because the level of privilege question has little, if anything, to do with the defamation claim itself, the influence of the plaintiff legal status criterion is all the more striking, and somewhat troubling. Fully 45 percent of the media libel cases are foreclosed on plaintiff status grounds without the factual strength of the defamation claim or the materiality of the harm to reputation being assessed in a trial.[87] Second, the constitutional privilege issues are having a pervasive influence on the adjudication of media defamation actions. The principal issue in 88 percent of the cases is privilege-related, and more often than not the questions pertinent to constitutional privilege determinations are distinct from those applicable to the underlying defamation claim.[88] For example, in a random sample of 64 public official and public figure cases, the truth or falsity of the challenged statement was addressed in only 24, or 38 percent, of the cases. For those 24 cases, however, the statement was found to be false in 10, or in 42 percent of the .cases. The pervasiveness of privilege issues, even in successful cases, leads one to wonder whether the privileges are now driving the tort.[89]

The media defamation cases were also analyzed in terms of the setting of the alleged libel—whether it occurred in the context of news, entertainment, or literature. The predominance of cases involving news has been noted and discussed previously.[90] For our present purpose, the comparative rate of plaintiff success is of interest. While the rates of success vary marginally in the news (10 percent), entertainment (14 percent), and literature (7 percent) settings, the most notable observation is consistency of success rate among these case groupings. Because of the relatively small number of cases in the entertainment and literature groups, the rate of success for statistical purposes is indistinguishable.

Finally, the media defamation cases were grouped according to the factual strength of the defamation claim, without regard to privilege considerations. The implications of this factor have been discussed at length.[91] For the present it is worth noting that more than half of the factually strong common law defamation claims (material falsity and material harm) were unsuccessful, and in over 90 percent of such cases this was due to privilege considerations. The conclusion previously suggested—that the cost of constitutional privileges is foreclosure of up to 50 percent of the otherwise valid common law claims—is corroborated by the relative rate of success in cases involving privilege (10 percent for actual malice cases, 14 percent for negligence cases)[92] when compared with those not involving privilege (23 percent).[93]

Whether the free speech values achieved by the privileges are worth the cost in foreclosed claims cannot be measured statistically. This question, instead, is one of value and judgment. More precise knowledge of the cost, however, can help to sharpen that judgment and focus the inquiry. Moreover, analysis of the cases provides one further insight pertinent to the ultimate balance struck. It appears that 5 percent of the factually weak media libel claims (non-material falsity *or* non-material harm) were successful despite the privileges—or perhaps, ironically, because of them.[94] When the rate of weak but successful claims is compared for cases governed by the highest privilege of actual malice and cases governed by the lower negligence privilege, no significant difference emerges.[95] This suggests that the risk of permitting recovery in weak cases is not significantly increased with the lower negligence privilege. In terms of this risk, therefore, the actual malice privilege may be unnecessary.

The Course of Litigation

Two sources were employed to obtain data on the incidence of defamation litigation, the incidence of success by plaintiffs and defendants, and the relationship, if any, between success or failure and the parties to the action, the issues adjudicated, and selected factual variables. The first survey, discussed in the preceding pages, consisted of an analysis of defamation and privacy cases with judicial opinion between 1974 and 1984, inclusive. The second involved case-specific information collected from the 164 plaintiffs interviewed.

Incidence of Success: Plaintiff Cases

While the number of cases from which the plaintiff survey information was drawn was significantly smaller than the number for the general case survey discussed above, the results achieved in litigation are generally consistent with those reported for all the media defamation cases. To obtain information on overall plaintiff and defendant success rates, information was obtained from plaintiffs and from published legal records in cases brought by the plaintiffs who were interviewed. Table 6–12 outlines the incidence of success in these 164 cases.

The incidence of success by plaintiffs or defendants is best reflected as a percentage of cases reaching final resolution. Of the 164 total coded

TABLE 6–12   Results Reached in Plaintiff Survey Cases: Media Defamation Cases

	# Cases	% Cases Finally Decided
Total cases surveyed	164	
Cases finally resolved	130	
Cases won by media	108	83%
Cases won by plaintiff by final judgment	13	10%
Cases won by plaintiff by settlement[96]	9	7%
Total won by plaintiff	22	17%

cases, 130 cases had reached a final conclusion at the time of the survey. Eighty-three percent were won by the media defendant, 10 percent by the plaintiff through final judicial order, and 7 percent by the plaintiff through settlement which, in many instances, followed a judicial decision adverse to the media defendant.

While the rate of plaintiff success for finally resolved cases—17 percent—is higher than the 11 percent rate reported for all media defamation cases, two factors explain the disparity. First, different criteria are being reflected in the case result determination. The general case data base reflects only the judicial determinations of success. In contrast, the plaintiff survey data base includes settlements as well. The rate of judicial success by final judgment for the plaintiff survey cases is 10 percent, and the rate of success by settlement is 7 percent. The general data base includes only those settlement cases in which a final published judicial order exists, and such cases would be coded by judicial result as wins or losses, not as settlements. As a result, some of the actual settlement cases are not reflected in the success rate for the general case data, as the final judicial order may have been favorable to the media defendant, but a settlement might nonetheless have been agreed upon in exchange for the plaintiff foregoing any further appeal. The second reason for the success rate difference stems from the inclusion of settlement cases drawn from insurance files in the 164 case data base. Each of these cases involved formal judicial action, but the settlement cases when included in the general group of plaintiff cases may not fully represent the incidence of settlement. Efforts have been made to correct for this, but it is possible that some marginal distortion persists.

Because of the differences in source data, it appears that the 17 percent plaintiff success rate reflected in the plaintiff data, which includes settlement activity that is not reflected in the case data, is closer to reality than the 11 percent rate reported for all cases. Notably, the rate of judicial success is virtually identical with both sets of data. Because the plaintiff data reflect settlements that cannot be determined from judicial reports, and include settlements favorable to plaintiffs following adverse judicial decisions, the actual success rate is likely to be closer to 17 percent than 11 percent. The incidence and timing of settlements beyond deductible reported by a major media insurer, and information about settlements obtained from newspapers,[97] also bear out the conclusion that the true plaintiff success rate is higher than 11 percent.

How Plaintiffs Lost

In view of the low rate of plaintiff success reported in both the plaintiff and general case data bases, information on the stages involved in litigating media defamation claims can provide valuable insight into the critical determinants of success and failure. Such information also provides specific information on the role of constitutional privileges in the adjudication of defamation cases. Four principal sources were used to compile information on the procedural course ordinarily followed in libel litigation: a random sample drawn from libel cases from 1974 through 1984; the cases in our plaintiff survey; information compiled from 941 insured claims filed with a media libel insurer; and a survey of the libel suit experience of 175 newspapers, conducted by the *Iowa Law Review*.

LITIGATION STAGES: LIBEL CASES, 1974–84

A randomly selected group of 188 libel cases from 1974 through 1984 were analyzed in terms of the stages through which litigation passed and the point of final disposition in the 143 resolved cases.[98] The information is compiled in Table 6–13. The information pertaining to the course of litigation and the point of disposition of cases will be discussed thoroughly in the following section in conjunction with similar information pertaining specifically to media libel cases drawn from the plaintiff survey. At this point, a few general observations will suffice.

In light of the high incidence of pretrial judicial activity on the merits, perhaps the most notable statistic is the small number of cases that reaches trial. For surveyed defamation cases from 1974–84, including public and private plaintiffs and media and non-media defendants, 76 percent of the cases were finally and judicially resolved in advance of trial.[99] Virtually all of these cases were resolved on grounds of privilege issues raised in motions for summary judgment or to dismiss. In 62 percent of the cases resolved in advance of trial, appeal was taken from the district court's pretrial ruling, and in 11 percent, more than one appeal was taken. Only 35 cases, or 24 percent of those that were finally resolved, reached trial.

Of the cases that reached trial, plaintiffs won 61 percent. Plaintiffs won 89 percent of the cases tried before a jury, and 45 percent of those tried before a judge. In a remarkable 91 percent of the cases tried, appeal was taken, with the defendant (media) prevailing on appeal in 67 percent of the cases finally resolved. These cases, of course, involved appeals by plaintiffs as well as defendants. For cases in which the plaintiff won at trial, the defendant prevailed on appeal 62 percent of the time. Of the cases appealed following trial, 15 percent involved two levels of appeal.

The other notable observation to be drawn from Table 6–13 is the extremely high incidence of appeal, and the heavy use of appellate judicial resources in libel cases. In 140 of the 188 total cases, or 75 percent, at least one appeal was taken. The total cases included 45 still in litigation (not finally resolved), and it is likely that many of these cases will involve

TABLE 6–13　The Course of Litigation: Libel Cases 1974–84

Point of Final Disposition	Number	% Final Resolution	% Total Cases
Total Cases	188		100%
Total Finally Resolved	143	100%	
For Cases Finally Resolved:			
Point of Disposition			
Pretrial Disposition			
District Court, motion	41	29%	
Pretrial: 1 appeal	55	38%	
2 appeals	11	8%	
3 appeals	1	1%	
Total Pretrial	108	76%	
Total Tried	35	24%	
Posttrial Disposition			
Disposition by Trial	3	2%	
Posttrial: 1 appeal	28	20%	
2 appeals	4	3%	
Total Posttrial	32	22%	
All Cases			
Incidence of Appeals			
Cases with 1 appeal	111		59%
Cases with 2 appeals	27		14%
Cases with 3 appeals	1		1%
Cases with 5 appeals	1		1%
Total Cases with Appeal Taken	140		75%
Total Appeals	173		

appellate review prior to completion. Sixteen percent of the cases involved more than one appeal. For cases finally resolved at the time of the study, 69 percent involved at least one appeal. In both groups, the incidence of pretrial appeal outpaces that of posttrial appeal by a margin of two to one. Because virtually all appeals are based on constitutional privilege issues, it is clear that privileges are dominating the adjudication of the tort.

MEDIA DEFAMATION CASES

Information on the course of litigation with specific reference to libel actions against media defendants was drawn from the plaintiff survey cases included within the 188 cases covered by Table 6–13. The survey drawn from the plaintiff interview cases included information on the stage of litigation at which plaintiffs or defendants prevailed. The number of cases in which plaintiffs prevailed was too small for analysis, but information about media defendant victories has been assembled in Table 6–14, and usefully supplements the information in Table 6–13 by focusing specifically on media libel cases.

The information outlined in Table 6–14 is generally consistent with that provided earlier in Table 6–13, covering all libel cases. The most notable difference is the incidence of trial, which is 25 percent in all libel cases, and 19 percent in media libel cases. Because of the higher incidence of constitutional privilege issues giving rise to pretrial motions in media cases, this difference is expected, and in any event it is not substantial. Other differences, to the extent that they are material to the following discussion, will be noted where appropriate.

The information in Table 6–14 indicates that more than half of the media defendant victories result from summary judgment. Fifty-eight percent of media victories, and 50 percent of the 99 cases finally resolved by judicial order or settlement, are resolved through summary judgment. An additional 23 cases, or 27 percent of media victories, are resolved by other dismissal in advance of trial.

Only 13 cases, representing 15 percent of media victories, were tried prior to final resolution. Adding to this the 6 plaintiff victories by final

TABLE 6–14   How Media Defendants Won Cases with Final Resolution

	Number	Percent
Total Media Victories	86	100%
Summary judgment		
summary judgment—trial level	17	20%
summary judgment—appeal level	33	38%
Other dismissal		
trial level	13	15%
appeal level affirmance	10	12%
Trial judgment for defendant		
jury verdict for defendant	1	1%
judge verdict for defendant	2	2%
Trial judgment for plaintiff		
jury verdict rev'd on appeal	9	11%
judge verdict rev'd on appeal	1	1%

legal action, all of which were tried, it appears that only 19 percent of the finally resolved media defamation cases were adjudicated at trial. Of the 19 cases that were tried before a jury or judge, media defendants won only 3, or 16 percent. Thirteen of the 19 cases were tried before a jury, and in only 1 such case did the media defendant win at the trial level. Media defendants won at the trial court level in only 2 of the 6 cases tried before a judge. Interestingly, the incidence of defendant success at trial for the general population of libel claims was somewhat higher, as noted earlier, but the pattern of success in jury and bench trials was essentially the same. [100]

The picture of media defamation litigation painted in Tables 6–13 and 6–14 yield a number of conclusions. The first pertains to the role played by constitutional privileges. Of the 99 finally resolved media libel cases, 86 were won by the defendant. Seventy-three cases were finally resolved in advance of trial. This represents 74 percent of all final cases, and 85 percent of the cases won by media defendants. Similarly, Table 6–13 indicates that 76 percent of the libel claims were resolved in advance of trial. Roughly 84 percent of all the cases resolved before trial were concluded on constitutional privilege issues, and in advance of any adjudication of the underlying claim of defamation, reputational harm, or truth or falsity. The privilege standards, therefore, are sifting out an extraordinary proportion of cases in advance of any fact adjudication.

Whether the dominance of privilege determinations prior to trial is good or bad, or greater or lesser than might be expected, cannot be determined. To the extent that the privileges were intended as instruments to filter out cases, the data suggest that they are accomplishing this goal, perhaps with a vengeance. To the extent that operation of the privileges was intended to sort out the strong defamation claims from the weak, as well as to reflect constitutional policies, the evidence of their effectiveness is somewhat ambiguous. On the one hand, the number of weak claims that pass through the privilege filter is small. As reported earlier, 94 percent of the cases judged factually weak ultimately fail, and 80 percent of these appear to be filtered out at the privilege stage of litigation. This is confirmed by the high degree of plaintiff success at trial, discussed below. On the other hand, as many as half of the factually strong *defamation* claims are filtered out by privilege requirements (85 percent of post-trial appeals are decided on privilege grounds, and all strong claims that are lost, lose on privilege grounds). It remains to be determined whether this level of foreclosed claims is acceptable or avoidable.

The level of pretrial disposition also raises questions about the level of appellate resources devoted to initial privilege determinations. For libel cases as a group, 62 percent of the cases resolved in advance of trial involve at least one level of appeal. [101] Of the 73 media libel cases involving pretrial disposition, 43 involved at least one level of appeal from the pretrial determination, again in advance of trial. [102] In other words, 60 percent of the pretrial privilege determinations require the commitment of appellate as well as trial court resources. As indicated in Table 6–13, moreover, roughly 17 percent of these cases involve more than one level of appeal at the pretrial stage.

The level of appellate court involvement on pretrial issues in libel cases is extraordinary when judged by experience in any other form of civil litigation. [103] When the incidence of pretrial appeal is combined with the incidence of posttrial appeal reported in Table 6–13, it appears that at least one appeal is taken in 75 percent of all finally resolved libel cases, and it is possible that the incidence of appeal is greater in the media libel case group. Viewed in light of the infrequency of plaintiff success, it seems that the investment of judicial resources in libel cases is vastly disproportionate to the purposes served by the tort of defamation as presently constituted.

The second group of observations pertains to the trial of defamation claims. Thirty-five of the 143 final libel cases, or 24 percent of the claims involving formal judicial action, were tried. [104] Similarly, of the 99 finally resolved media libel cases, 19 were tried—the 13 cases reported in Table 6–14, and six additional cases won by the plaintiff. Only 19 percent of the media defamation cases, therefore, reached trial.

The proportion of cases reaching trial is notable not so much because the figure is high or low, but rather because of what it reflects about the libel litigation process. As a general rule, only about 8 percent of filed civil litigation claims reach trial. [105] The data reported in Tables 6–13 and 6–14 provide no information about claims that are dropped in advance of trial or formal judicial decision. Thus, the 20 percent trial figure for media libel cases cannot be compared with information pertaining to civil litigation in general. The same is true to a lesser extent with settlement information, for the case data reported above would not catch settlements made prior to formal reported judicial action.

Two pieces of information, however, lead us to believe that the incidence of settlement is significantly lower in media libel actions than in civil litigation as a whole. First, information collected from newspaper defendants in the 164 cases indicates clearly that settlement is infrequent, even at early stages of the legal process. Many media defendants follow a policy of not settling. The very low incidence of reported retractions and corrections confirms this. Only 6 percent of the reported media libel cases involved retraction or correction, or an offer to do so. The level of non-financial settlements in the insurance cases also suggests a low incidence of retraction prior to litigation. Second, as reported in greater detail in a later section, information obtained from insurance files indicates a 10 percent incidence of settlement beyond deductible for all covered claims, including settlements prior to and after litigation. This is confirmed as well by a survey of newspapers which were sued for libel, where a settlement rate between 8.7 percent and 12.4 percent was reported.[106] In contrast, for civil litigation in general over two-thirds of filed claims are settled.[107] While the settlement statistics are not exactly comparable, the great disparity in the settlement rate, coupled with the high incidence of pretrial *judicial* resolution, makes the uniqueness of libel cases apparent.

THE DISPUTE PROCESS: A COMPARISON
OF LIBEL AND GENERAL CIVIL CLAIMS

The apparent and significant differences between the incidence of trial, settlement, and appeal between libel cases and civil litigation as a whole are suggestive of profound differences throughout the litigation process from beginning to end. To ascertain the nature and timing of these differences, as well as their apparent causes, information was collected about the stages of the litigation process for both classes of dispute.[108] The comparative picture of litigation in each context is summarized in Figure 1A, below, and the specific process followed by libel disputes is later represented in detail in Figures 1B and 2.

The figures depicting the pattern of general civil litigation as contrasted to libel litigation, from grievance to trial, are based on information drawn from various sources. The statistics related to general civil litigation plaintiffs were drawn from information found in the Wisconsin Study and the Annual Report of the Director of the Administrative Office of the United States Courts (1984). The libel litgation data have been drawn from information provided by a media insurance company and from an analysis of 188 media libel cases included in the study.

The information is presented in the form of pyramid-shaped continuums which trace the behavior of the potential plaintiffs. The base of the pyramids represents the number of grievances that arise. The pyramids then ascend and narrow as they account for the ratio of those individuals who interact with the potential defendants, seek legal counsel, file a claim, and are involved in pre-trial litigation. Ultimately, the pyramids' peaks represent the number of plaintiffs who have pursued a judicial resolution of their grievance to trial and post-trial appeal.

In general civil litigation, the vast majority of individuals who have grievances do not pursue the matter to the point of litigation. In fact, less than half of all potential general civil litigants even confront the potential

Figure 1A. *Comparative Litigation Processes for Libel and General Civil Litigation**

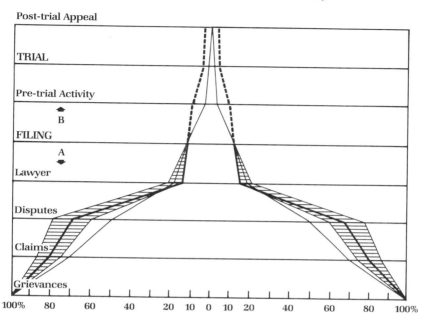

Post-trial Appeal

TRIAL

Pre-trial Activity

B

FILING

A

Lawyer

Disputes

Claims

Grievances

100%   80   60   40   20   10   0   10   20   40   60   80   100%

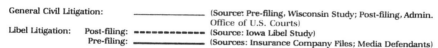

General Civil Litigation:		——————————	(Source: Pre-filing, Wisconsin Study; Post-filing, Admin. Office of U.S. Courts)
Libel Litigation:	Post-filing: ===========	(Source: Iowa Libel Study)
	Pre-filing: ——————————	(Sources: Insurance Company Files; Media Defendants)

*General civil litigation information post-filing pertains to federal court litigation.

defendant with their grievance. And only 10 percent seek a lawyer. Of the group that is advised by counsel, about half file complaints, and less than 8 percent of the filed complaints eventually go to trial.

The pattern generally experienced in civil matters appears to contrast sharply with the trend in libel complaints. Because we could not obtain reliable information on the number of people with grievances (perceptions of wrongful harm), we have generally followed the same pattern for libel plaintiffs prior to the filing of a suit as exists for civil litigants in general. We have, however, modified the pattern slightly in two respects to reflect our intuition based upon the known attitudes of libel plaintiffs and ad hoc information provided by the media defendants whom we interviewed. First, we suspect that a higher proportion of libel complaints come to be filed lawsuits than is true with civil litigation in general (although we do not reflect this on Figure 1A). We base this assumption on the conclusions that libel plaintiffs seem to be quite determined in their course of action before seeing a lawyer, that roughly half of the lawyers are inexperienced, that many of them see representation of the client as an advantage independent of the likelihood of victory, and that settlement activity prior to trial and filing is lower for libel cases than for other types of civil litigation.

The second assumption is that many of the grievances do not reach lawyers, although they involve contact with the media publisher. The defendants we spoke with had no way of tracking the number of complaints about alleged injurious falsity that were received, but they estimate that perhaps as many as 20 or 30 complaints were received for every lawsuit filed. Interestingly, many of the defendants also indicated that a high proportion (25–50%) of such complaints (claims) have validity. We reflect on Figure 1A, therefore, our assumption that a relatively high proportion of grievances (perceived wrongs) result in contact with the media (claims), that a high proportion of such grievances are unresolvable at that level (disputes), but that a relatively lower proportion of such unresolvable grievances result in lawyer contact than is true for civil litigation in general. It bears repeating, however, that these patterns are based on our intuition, not on statistical information.

The central differences between libel disputes and civil litigation, and the differences upon which we have generally comparable data, occur at and after the point of filing suit. For the population of cases involving a reported judicial order, [109] it appears that libel plaintiffs who approach lawyers are highly committed to the litigation of their claims. More than one-third of plaintiffs who sued had decided to do so even before they contacted an attorney. Once the plaintiffs file complaints, there is a 60 percent likelihood that the matters will be judicially resolved either through pre-trial decision on the merits of the claim, or after trial. Incredibly, one-fourth of the complaints go to trial. While plaintiffs win at trial roughly 60 percent of the time, virtually all of these trial judgments are subsequently appealed, and plaintiffs lose 70 percent of the appeals. Plaintiffs ultimately lose nine out of ten cases. In general, libel plaintiffs appear to be remarkably persistent, and pursue their claims to formal judicial resolution (pre-trial judgment or trial) in a remarkably high percentage of cases, and in the face of almost insurmountable odds.

While the information from which the charts were constructed has been drawn from various sources, and often represents extrapolation from incomplete data, the general shape of the pyramids is reflective of the libel and civil litigation processes. In the following sections, the stages of pre-litigation and litigation process will be explored in greater detail, and specific comparisons between libel litigation and general civil litigation will be drawn where comparable data are available.

The Grievance Stage to the Filing Stage. In Figure 1A, the pattern of plaintiff activity is traced from the point a grievance arises until the disposition of the claim. Specifically, portion "A" of Figure 1A represents this activity up to the filing of a complaint. This section reflects our judgments about the different attitudes held by the two types of plaintiffs. The libel plaintiff not only appears to be much more likely to confront the defendant ("dispute" category) but may also, for reasons discussed below, be more likely to eventually institute legal action ("filing" category).

The Wisconsin Study revealed that generally 71.8% of those individuals who have a grievance will make a complaint to the opposing party. Subsequently, a dispute arose from two-thirds of these confrontations. A prominent explanation for why half of the grievances do not become disputes is that an initial reaction of anger often cools and yields to rational thinking. Pursuing a grievance, whether it be through the courts or an alternative route, often requires much time, emotion, and money. Consequently, the individual may make a cost-benefit assessment in his or her own mind and simply walk away from the matter deciding it would not be worth the effort and resources required to continue.

Clearly, the average potential plaintiff in general civil matters is not bound and determined to litigate his or her claim. Rather, individuals are generally very willing to negotiate a settlement prior to filing. In fact, a lawyer may have been sought to perform these negotiations. Settlement discussions, of course, presuppose that there is some merit to the claim. Nonetheless, a good number of these claims may simply be dropped because the right to a cause of action is purely illusory.

The most dramatic shift in the elimination of potential general civil litigants occurs at the point of filing. Only 11.2 percent of the grievances that become disputes end up as filed complaints. This significant disposition of disputes at the pre-filing stage is not unforeseeable. Plaintiffs ordinarily sue to obtain some material compensation for a wrong they feel they have suffered at the hands of the defendant. Litigation is simply a means toward achieving that end. And it is, of course, a very costly one in terms of resources. If litigation can be avoided, so much the better. Furthermore, the filing of a complaint may only serve to alienate the defendant. Putting the opposing party on the defensive may be self-defeating since it is likely to inhibit the progress of settlement negotiations.

It is hard to quantify the pool of individuals with grievances from which libel plaintiffs emerge. Many of those who contact newspaper offices and television stations have grievances which are not actionable. For example, one person may feel that the sequence of action in a cartoon is incoherent. Another may complain about the impropriety of a caption to a picture. Or still another person may not like the anchorwoman's hairstyle. Nonetheless, there are many aggrieved people who call and express their displeasure concerning what they consider an erroneous representation of themselves or some institution they are affiliated with. Many of these complaints are actionable. The great majority can be dealt with and the problem disposed of after the grievance surfaces and a satisfactory response is made. There are, nevertheless, complaints which persist. Either the defendant is unresponsive, which only inflames the problem, or the plaintiff simply cannot be appeased. Consequently, the potential libel plaintiff who seeks out a lawyer often does so for the purpose of filing a suit rather than attaining advice as to the prudence of pursuing litigation.

Considering the objectives of libel plaintiffs, the pattern of activity that we have inferred from grievance to filing is foreseeable. For them, litigation is more than simply a means of obtaining material compensation. For many libel plaintiffs it is an end in itself. By filing a complaint, the plaintiff demonstrates indignation for the attack on his character. The complaint serves as a public denial of the legitimacy of the disputed material. The intangible benefit that the libel plaintiff receives from the filing of the complaint apparently overrides the high probability of failure that would ordinarily deter potential civil plaintiffs.[110]

It should be noted that a libel plaintiff may be motivated by the prospect of a financial windfall. Proof of defamation often requires proving malice on the part of the defendant. If successful, the plaintiff may recover a substantial amount in punitive damages despite the inability to show much in the way of actual injury.

There are, of course, instances of settlement prior to the filing of a libel complaint, although they seem rare—2.5 percent of the insured claims on which we have information. In contrast, 31 percent of insured claims are simply dropped prior to suit, with no evidence of settlement. The pre-filing settlements and dropped claims likely occur for a number of reasons. The plaintiff may have realized the weakness of the libel claim, or it might have been determined that the cost of litigation simply outweighed the possible benefits that could be garnered. It is also probable that satisfactory retractions, corrections, or apologies were made by the media. Whatever the reasons, the apparent rate of pre-trial settlement and dropped claims seems low.

The Filing Stage to Judicial Resolution.   Portion "B" of Figure 1A, also highlighted in Figure 1B, demonstrates the continued tenacity of the libel plaintiff once a complaint has been filed. It should be noted that the libel case data are based largely on suits that involve a published judicial decision, rather than on a universe of all filed suits. Because we know from the

Figure 1B. *Comparison of Libel and General Civil Claims Post-Filing Through Post-Trial Appeal*

Post-trial Appeal

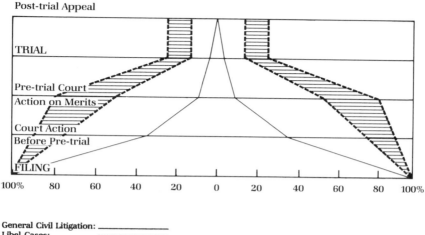

General Civil Litigation: _____
Libel Cases: ▬▬▬▬▬▬▬▬

insurance file data reported in the next section that settlement activity does occur both prior to and after lawsuits are filed, and because there are suits, indeterminate in quantity, that are not published in any of our data sources, we recognize that the limited number analyzed may introduce bias into the analysis. Our conclusions are therefore limited only to suits with reported judicial activity, although we believe it likely that the underlying patterns shown by our limited data are indicative of patterns of litigation common to all filed libel suits that are seriously pursued.[111]

Some sort of pre-trial action directed toward the *merits* of the claim occurs in roughly 80% of the sampled libel cases, with commensurately high incidences of pre-trial appeal, trial, and post-trial appeal. Figure 1B graphically represents the different patterns followed by general (federal) civil litigation and libel cases.

Figure 2 displays in greater detail the various levels of pre-trial motions and appeals in libel cases. Of the complaints involving pre-trial rulings in the district court, pre-trial appeals are taken 52 percent of the time, and 21 percent of these involve a second level of appeal. Twelve percent of all second level appeals are pursued to yet a third level of appeal. After trial, an even more pronounced tendency to appeal is exhibited in libel cases.

The pattern of litigation in libel cases contrasts markedly with the pattern for general civil litigation.[112] Only about 35 percent of filed complaints (lawsuits) involve court action prior to pre-trial (usually discovery-related, not focused on the merits of the claim, and not published), 11 percent involve subsequent action by the court prior to trial, and only 4 to

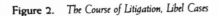

Figure 2.   *The Course of Litigation, Libel Cases*

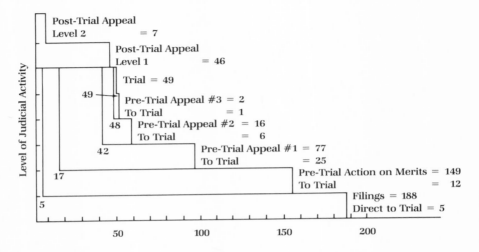

8 percent eventually get to trial. In contrast, for libel cases involving a published or lawyer-reported order, about 25 percent reach trial, and we believe that this rate is indicative of, although higher than, the larger proportion of filed suits that are seriously pursued.[113]

General civil litigation plaintiffs remain very willing to settle their claims out of court even after the complaint has been filed. The Wisconsin Study reported a settlement rate of more than 50 percent for filed complaints, and this group of cases does not include suits that are simply abandoned after filing.[114] This level of settlement activity is consistent with the high number of filings (48 percent) which are terminated without any court action whatsoever, although some of these cases are probably dropped without settlement. While the filing of a complaint will sometimes alienate the defendant and make settlements less attainable, it may at times have the reverse effect. It might be necessary for the plaintiff to file a lawsuit to demonstrate the seriousness of his claim. Often a defendant may know of a number of potential plaintiffs with good claims; to hold the amount paid out to a minimum, the defendant may decide to compensate only those who file a lawsuit. Most important, with the filing of a suit costs begin to mount and more complete information about the complaint is obtained through discovery. These factors often provide a conducive environment in which to negotiate and settle.

In the case of libel plaintiffs, however, no such phenomenon occurs. Once the parties are joined by the filing of a complaint, the previous reluctance to settle at pre-trial seems to intensify. The lines have been drawn and the settlement offers, if any, have been made to the fullest extent. In many instances, the litigation appears to be a struggle for principles: the plaintiff's reputation opposing the defendant's commitment to its practices, its reputation, and its ideology of freedom. Not all cases, however, involve such a noble struggle. There are some plaintiffs who are wholly concerned with the recovery of actual economic damages. There are also plaintiffs for whom the lawsuit is primarily an opportunity for a monetary windfall through punitive damages. Nonetheless, whether the suit is filed on the grounds of principle or in pursuit of financial relief, only one-fifth to one-quarter of these claims are settled or dropped prior to pre-trial activity directed to the merits of the claim.

As reflected in Figure 2, the tenacity of the libel plaintiff continues through the pre-trial stage. Of the complaints that receive an initial pre-trial ruling, half engage in pre-trial appeal. And 21 percent of those appeals go on to a second level of pre-trial appeal. There are even instances of third level appeals at the pre-trial level. This amount of pre-trial activity is astounding considering that three-quarters of the pre-trial decisions favor the defendant. Undaunted, the libel plaintiff battles on. One-quarter of all complaints filed by these individuals ultimately go to trial. And of that group, almost two-thirds involve one or more levels of pre-trial appeal. For the cases that reach trial, an astonishing 90 percent of the trial judgments are appealed.

Once again, the dramatic difference between the libel and general civil litigation plaintiffs is apparent. Over two-thirds of the general civil litigation cases are resolved after filing but before any pre-trial involvement of the court. Another 22 percent are settled during or after the pre-trial stages, but prior to trial. Thus, less than one-tenth of the claims that involve court action go to trial, compared to 20–25 percent of libel cases involving reported judicial action. For civil litigation, tried cases represent between 4 and 8 percent of all complaints that are filed. The trial judgment is appealed in roughly 10 percent of the civil cases, compared to as many as 90 percent of the reported libel cases.

THE LITIGATION PROCESS: CONCLUSIONS

Our inability to obtain reliable data on all filed libel suits leaves large gaps in our knowledge about the libel litigation process. In light of this, our conclusions are limited to what we know about reported libel suits, and to our judgment that patterns exhibited for such cases are not fundamentally at variance with patterns we would expect for seriously pursued suits. In addition, we have discussed our intuition about the larger universe of cases at selected points, explicitly indicating the intuitive basis of such judgments where offered. Our inability to generalize our conclusions to the full universe of filed libel suits, however, should not detract from the observations that can be made.

The principal point to be drawn from the comparative analysis of libel and general civil litigation is the shape of the "pyramid." The incidence of settlement in libel cases appears to be lower than in general civil litigation. The incidence of pre-trial judicial activity on the merits in libel cases is much greater than for general civil litigation. A higher proportion of such libel cases are finally disposed of on the merits at the pre-trial stage. Finally, a much greater incidence of post-trial appeal seems characteristic of libel cases, although on this point we cannot be certain, as we do not know of all the tried cases, and the possibility exists that many defendant wins at trial are not appealed and are therefore not reported. With these qualifications in mind, we can hazard some general conclusions about the libel litigation process in media cases.

The comparison of general civil litigation with libel litigation discloses a litigation process in media libel cases that appears in many ways to be unique. While many libel claims, or complaints, are dropped prior to their ripening into a lawsuit, few of them involve settlement, unlike experience in civil litigation in general. For civil litigation in general, nearly 90 percent of "disputes" (redress for a grievance sought and rebuffed) are settled or dropped prior to filing a lawsuit. [115] For libel disputes, 31 percent of insured claims are settled or dropped prior to filing a lawsuit. [116] The decision to proceed to litigation seems driven more by emotion and lack of alternatives than by a calculated judgment about the strength of the case. Once in litigation, media libel cases are only infrequently settled, at least prior to a decision adverse to the media defendant. Many of the filed cases may languish and ultimately be dropped—often because the filing of a suit, without further action, accomplishes plaintiff objectives—but those that proceed through litigation tend to force a judicial conclusion rather than reach a conclusion through settlement. While one might expect a high incidence of trial as a result, relatively few trials occur. Eighty percent of the cases with a reported judicial order are concluded by judicial action prior to trial, with most such cases involving at least one level of appeal. In light of these circumstances (particularly the fact that, unlike civil litigation in general, formal pre-trial judicial action on the merits occurs in a high proportion of the cases), the incidence of trial seems very low, and can be accounted for only because of the pervasive influence of the constitutional privileges.

For the 20 to 25 percent of reported libel claims that survive privilege analysis and reach trial, the rate of plaintiff success is quite high. For all libel cases, plaintiffs win at trial 61 percent of the time; 89 percent of the jury trials are won by plaintiffs, and 45 percent of the bench trials. Appeals are taken in 91 percent of the tried cases, and the defendant prevails in 67 percent of the appeals after trial.

The media cases follow a similar pattern. Of the media libel cases that were tried, 85 percent resulted in a verdict for the plaintiff. In each of these cases the plaintiffs had to prove not only defamation but also negligence or actual malice. Sixty-three percent of these cases were reversed on appeal, largely on privilege grounds. Most of the cases were tried before juries. Of the three cases tried before a judge, two resulted in verdicts for the media defendant. Because of the small number of bench trials, however, no significance can be attached to the lower rate of plaintiff success in such cases.

The high rate of plaintiff success at trial has been the subject of considerable discussion, with occasional suggestions that heavy use of summary judgment and other pretrial dispositions is needed to avoid the bias juries exhibit toward libel plaintiffs. Analysis of the data, however, belies this conclusion. Constitutional privilege requirements apply to every media libel case, requiring each plaintiff to demonstrate either negligence or actual malice, and to make an adequate showing in advance of trial on these issues to overcome summary judgment or dismissal. Every case that reaches trial, therefore, will have had to overcome the initial obstacles posed by the privileges. Because the privilege standards appear to operate quite effectively in filtering out factually weak claims,[117] the cases that are tried are likely to be the strongest claims. It is not surprising, therefore, that the plaintiff success rate is high at trial. The strength of the plaintiffs' claims, not the vagaries of jury prejudice, seems to account for plaintiff success.

One might, however, interpret the high rate of reversal after trial as some evidence that jury bias rather than the merits of the case account for plaintiff success. An examination of the post-trial reversals, however, reveals that they are almost exclusively based on privilege-related issues such as the applicable level of privilege, jury instructions, and the like, rather than on the factual strength of the defamation claim. This confirms the conclusion suggested previously that the role of privileges in the adjudication of defamation claims is pervasive, and the impact of privileges is not confined to the factually weak cases.

In contrast to general civil litigation, it seems that a higher percentage of libel cases reaches trial, and this difference is likely attributable to a lower overall rate of settlement after suit is filed. On the other hand, in view of the fact that a strikingly high percentage of libel claims are pressed to judicial decision on the merits, it is striking that only 20–25 percent of the cases reach trial, and that plaintiffs enjoy astounding success at trial, whether before a jury or, it appears, a judge. Virtually all of the trial court reversals in favor of media defendants are based on privilege determinations. Roughly 80 percent of the judicially-resolved cases never reach trial, and almost all are concluded on privilege grounds. The overwhelming majority of cases are resolved as a matter of privilege in advance of trial, usually without adjudication of the facts from the perspective of common law doctrine, and those cases that do go to trial and yield a verdict for the plaintiff are often resolved as much on a determination of actual malice or negligence as on a determination of truth or falsity or reputational harm.[118] In up to 45 percent of tried cases, the focus at trial seems to have been on state of mind at the time of publication—actual malice or negligence—rather than on underlying truth or falsity of the published statement. The issue of truth or falsity is the major focus in only 13 percent of the media libel cases; privilege issues predominate the adjudication of 87 percent of the claims. The incidence of success for plaintiffs and the basis of judgments made in the cases, combined with the infrequency of trial, suggest that the tort of defamation in media cases might best be characterized as a tort of abuse of privilege rather than defamation as understood at common law.

The Incidence of Non-suit and Settlement

The plaintiff survey and case survey groups did not provide complete information on the timing and incidence of settlement, nor could we establish the frequency of adjudicated claims in relation to total initial disputes. In order to obtain information on these and related subjects, material was obtained from the coded case files of a major media libel insurance company. The number of case files is large and reflects claims that are nationwide. The material is not necessarily representative of all claims, however, because it involves only one insurance company, and does not include disputes or claims against uninsured publishers. Nevertheless, though the information is not necessarily representative, it is most informative and probative. The information provided in Table 6–15 sheds a great deal of light on the litigation process from its beginning (with the filing of a claim brought to the attention of the insurer) to its end.

First, as would be expected, many libel complaints are formally registered but never result in a filed action or in a negotiated decision not to sue. Of the 941 insured claims, 292, or 31 percent, are simply dropped in advance of litigation.[119]

Second, the actual rate of plaintiff success for media libel cases in which suit is filed is significantly lower than the rate of success for cases in which formal reported judicial action occurs. It appears that up to 649 of

TABLE 6–15   The Course of Media Libel Claims as
Reflected In Insurance Files

Disposition of Claim	Number	Final Insured Percent
Total Claims	1352	
Total Insured Claims	941	100%
Filed Insurance Claims not Prosecuted by Lawsuit (no suit, no settlement)	292	31%
Claims Prosecuted to Judicial Resolution		
Concluded pursuant to terms of judicial resolution		
For defendant	281	30.0%
For plaintiff	8	.8%
Dormant, last action for defendant	90	9.5%
Claims Settled & Voluntarily Withdrawn (includes settlements pre-suit, pre-trial, and post-trial)		
Voluntary non-suit, no $	24	2.5%
Settled within deductible	154	16.4%
Settled beyond deductible	92	9.8%
Indemnified and Disclaimed Claims	411	

the 941 cases involved a filed lawsuit (or would have in the absence of successful settlement), and 379 were prosecuted to judicial conclusion. Plaintiffs prevailed in court (exclusive of settlements following a judgment) in 8 of the 379 cases, or 2.1 percent of the time.

Third, it appears that the level of settlement activity is higher than the plaintiff survey cases suggested. Some form of "settlement" occurred in 270 of the 941 insured cases, or 29 percent of the time. Financial settlement, however, occurred in fewer than 246, or 26 percent, of the insured claims (not all cases settled within deductible appear to have involved money). Settlement beyond the deductible occurred in 92 cases, or 9.8 percent of all insured claims. For the smaller group of up to 649 filed lawsuits, financial settlement occurred in up to 38 percent of the cases, and settlement beyond deductible occurred in up to 14 percent.[120]

Finally, if we consider the settlements beyond deductible and the plaintiffs' judicial wins to represent material plaintiff victories in litigation, the rate of plaintiff success in these cases is 10.6 percent, represented by 8 judicial victories and 92 settlements. Interestingly, this rate of overall success is strikingly close to the rate of success reported for all media libel claims involving reported judicial decision. In other words, the higher incidence of settlement in the larger population of claims does not appear to influence the general rate of plaintiff success, which remains strikingly low. This is also perhaps the best perspective from which to judge the incidence of settlement in media libel claims when compared to civil litigation in general. Judged in this way, the 9.8 percent rate of material settlement is exceedingly low.

These observations are generally confirmed by a survey of the libel litigation experience of 175 newspapers conducted by the *Iowa Law Review*. That survey reveals a reported liability rate of 4.9 percent, and a settlement rate of 8.7 percent for all libel claims brought over the ten-year period from 1975 to 1985.[121] Like the insurance information, the Law Review data include libel claims that are not reflected in the general data base of cases that involve a published judicial order, and therefore provides a broader view of the litigation process. Also like the insurance information, the rate of liability (4.9 percent for all cases; an estimated 6.9 percent for final cases) is lower than for the general data base—as would be expected because of the larger number of claims not involving published judicial order and because some of these settlements will have followed a final judicial decision adverse to the media, which would be coded as a plaintiff win in the general case data base—and the rate of settlement (8.7 percent for all cases; 12.4 percent for final cases) is higher. On an overall basis, however, the 15–20 percent underlying rate of plaintiff success by judicial decision and settlement is consistent with that reported for the subgroup of claims with judicial order as reported in Table 6–12 *supra*.

PERSPECTIVES ON LITIGATION: LAWYERS, FEES, AND COSTS

The composition of defamation and privacy claims, the controlling legal theories, the legal steps through which the lawsuit passes, and the incidence of ultimate success explain a great deal about the defamation action. This information also sheds light on the objectives and motivations of the parties to the action. Beneath the surface of these general statistics, however, lies a great deal of additional information about the dynamics of the litigation process and the actions and objectives of the principal parties to it. In this section, information obtained from plaintiffs and plaintiff lawyers about the experience and involvement of the lawyer in litigation, the fee arrangements, and the costs of litigation to plaintiffs will be discussed. In significant measure, analysis of this information will draw upon material previously discussed concerning the composition of plaintiffs, the basis for the suit, and the role of the lawyer prior to suit.

The Lawyer in Litigation

The composition of the plaintiff lawyers, and their role or influence, have been discussed in Chapter 5, but can usefully be summarized here. Most lawyers were selected by plaintiffs because of prior representation of the plaintiff or personal friendship. Only 15 percent were selected specifically because of their reputation and experience as a trial or libel attorney; 17 percent were engaged following referral by another attorney, most likely because of experience in litigation, or because the original attorney deemed the case unacceptable and referred the client to another, probably younger, attorney who would be more likely to accept it.[122] Based on information provided by plaintiffs and the lawyers themselves, it appears that roughly 50 percent of the lawyers were not experienced in litigation or libel law, and many of these lawyers may have been relatively young and generally inexperienced.[123] It is not surprising, therefore, that the initial attorney was changed prior to the conclusion of litigation in roughly 25 percent of the cases,[124] with plaintiff dissatisfaction or the need for greater experience causing that change in up to 15 percent of all cases.

It would be unfair to assume that any substantial causal link occurs between the lack of plaintiff success in libel cases and the inexperience of the lawyers who represent those plaintiffs. Our data (which is limited on this point) disclose no relationship between ultimate success and lawyer experience in libel litigation. Inexperience probably does, however, play a part in the libel litigation process at the initial screening stage. Many of the actions commenced stand little chance of success, and this fact is bound to be obvious at the time of filing. Such actions are nevertheless brought, and this can be explained in part by the lawyers' lack of familiarity with the complexities of libel law and the burden of libel litigation.

To be sure, the plaintiffs' adamance, as earlier suggested, seems to play a major role in the decision to sue despite the odds against victory, and this is attributable to the plaintiffs' feeling of helplessness and sense that suing will, itself, vindicate reputation. But this explanation cannot fully account for the phenomenon, as the lawyers in many "legally" hopeless cases are engaged on contingency arrangements. With the prospect of remuneration dependent on judicial rather than moral victory, one would expect such lawyers to hesitate to sue notwithstanding the clients' wishes unless, as seems probable, many of the lawyers are not aware of the difficulties of the litigation process, or the value of the case lies in its visibility and the potential to represent the client again. The best explanation, therefore, seems to lie in a combination of lawyer inexperience, the interesting character of libel law, and the possible business value in representing a visible libel plaintiff. These factors, combined with the strong-willed determination of the client, may often cause a breakdown in the initial litigation screening process which is so heavily dependent on an attorney's sound legal judgment and advice.

Fees, Costs, and the Incentive to Litigate

In Chapter 5 we analyzed in detail information concerning the level and incidence of lawyers' fees, and the cost of litigation to libel plaintiffs; we will now explore more fully the implications of this information for the litigation process. There is reason to believe that lawyer fees and litigation costs significantly influence both the incidence of litigation and its course.

By far the most common fee arrangement was the contingency fee. Over 80 percent of the libel plaintiffs engaged their lawyers on this basis, and this held true, generally, whether or not the plaintiff selected the lawyer based on trial or libel reputation.[125] Contingency fee arrangements were more common with public plaintiffs than private plaintiffs.[126] The disparity is greater with actual fee costs to plaintiffs. Seventy-two percent of public office holders paid no fee. Only 33 percent of the private plaintiffs, however, paid no fee, and 56 percent of the non-office holding public plaintiffs paid no fee.

Many of the contingency fee arrangements required the plaintiffs to share or absorb costs of litigation. Only 16 percent of the plaintiffs bore no costs whatsoever, and 75 percent of these plaintiffs were public office holders. There were no business proprietors and only one professional among the group with no costs. In general, however, the litigation costs borne by plaintiffs were quite low, with 30 percent of the plaintiffs experiencing no costs or costs (including fees) under $1,000, 35 percent with costs between $1,000 and $5,000, 24 percent bearing costs between $5,000 and $20,000, and 12 percent with costs in excess of $20,000. As would be expected in view of the high proportion of contingency arrangements, 54 percent of the plaintiffs experiencing the highest costs succeeded in litigation, either through settlement or final judgment. Based on plaintiff responses, we estimate the average cost of litigation for all plaintiffs to be $7,015.00.[127] Again, public plaintiffs tend to experience the lowest litigation costs. Average costs ranged from lows of $4,400 and $5,400 for public employees and elected officials, to $8,600 and $9,200 for professionals and business proprietors, respectively.

The incidence and level of fees and costs for plaintiffs suggest a number of conclusions about the litigation process. The first observation flows from the generally low level of cost to plaintiffs. A decision to sue involves a calculus of risk involving more than the legal judgment concerning likely success. Financial risk, emotional commitment, and cost are common and economically useful elements that tend, in a generally systematic way, to play a screening function in the litigation setting. When the out-of-pocket costs to plaintiffs are very low even in the event of loss, an element of the risk calculus is reduced or eliminated. Put differently, it appears that for many libel plaintiffs the decision to sue is essentially cost free, and therefore risk free in financial terms. When this fact is combined with the low risk of a judicial determination that the allegedly libelous statement is true,[128] the predictable delay in litigation, and the plaintiffs' strong convictions that the act of suit is itself a form of reputational vindication, it is not surprising that the plaintiffs' decision to sue is relatively easy and risk-free. Small wonder, in short, that these plaintiffs sued, even with weak claims; small wonder too that most plaintiffs report that they would sue again if given the chance.[129] In substantial respects, there often exist strong incentives to sue for libel, and very few disincentives.

The relatively cost-free environment in which plaintiffs sue also appears to contribute to the plaintiffs' persistence once suit is brought. The many levels of appeal through which most plaintiffs progress pose little risk of clear loss for the plaintiff, as the conclusion that the defendant wins because of privilege can be as face-saving for the plaintiff as it is satisfying for the defendant. Inasmuch as the lawyers are typically engaged on a contingency basis, their incentive to persist in litigation—to a point, at least—is perfectly consistent with the plaintiffs' indifference from a risk of loss or cost standpoint. It is not surprising, therefore, that libel actions often are pressed to judicial resolution, and that these cases persist for an average length of about four years, and involve on average more than one level of judicial decision.

Finally, the absence of disincentives to bringing suit is most pronounced with public plaintiffs, where "pure" contingency arrangements predominate, leaving the plaintiff virtually cost-free in financial terms. In these cases, interestingly enough, the public plaintiffs appear to sue for reasons substantially unrelated to economic harm. Instead, these plaintiffs, who feel most strongly about the need to sue, say they do so for reputational reasons. They are least likely to win substantial money damages if successful, but they bear essentially no costs. It is ironic that the suits least likely to succeed, and therefore most susceptible to financial disincentives to litigation, are those in which virtually no disincentives exist. The public plaintiff who is able to hire a lawyer on contingency fee frequently has no reason not to sue.

CONCLUSIONS

From the information we have analyzed on the litigation process, so rich with implications, a few overriding conclusions emerge, and provide significant insight into the nature of public defamation litigation.

1. Remarkably few libel plaintiffs win in litigation, and even fewer win in suits brought against media defendants. The reason for this is twofold: first, many factually weak claims are brought without any realistic prospect of success; second, the impact of constitutional privileges has been profound, for the privileges are determinative in roughly 80 percent of the cases, and foreclose as many as 50 percent of the factually strong defamation claims. There is little escape from the conclusion that the constitutional privileges have come to dominate, if not supplant, the common law tort of defamation.

2. Most libel plaintiffs define the central issue in terms of the truth or falsity of that which was published. Because of the overwhelming use of pre-trial proceedings, and the dominant emphasis on issues of constitutional privilege, the question of *actual* truth or falsity is only infrequently addressed in the adjudication of the cases. The actual adjudication of the claim, therefore, has very little relationship to the plaintiffs' chief stated concern. Yet the commitment of judicial resources to libel suits is, by almost any standard, vast.

3. Many factually-weak defamation claims are brought despite little prospect of success. This is largely attributable to the lack of disincentives to suit, and the irrelevance of existing disincentives to the plaintiffs' objectives. Because most lawyers who sue[130] are engaged on a contingency basis, and many absorb not only fee losses but litigation costs as well, the average cost of litigation to the plaintiff is very small. For two-thirds of the plaintiffs, total costs were less than $5,000; for nearly one-third, costs were less than $1,000. For the plaintiffs with the greatest *legal* obstacles to recovery, the costs were the lowest. For many plaintiffs, a lawsuit is therefore an inexpensive way to challenge credibility and impose substantial costs on the media.[131] Moreover, the disincentives of emotional stress and likely failure to recover damages seem to have little deterrent effect on most libel plaintiffs. They sue because they have nowhere else to turn, and suing is therefore a means of emotional release, not stress. More significantly, success in court is not the sole measure by which they judge success, for it is the symbolic act of bringing suit itself that plaintiffs view as producing significant vindication of their claim of falsity.[132] There is little risk that a plaintiff's effort to legitimize the claim of falsehood through formal legal action will be impugned, for the formal legal process rarely reaches a conclusion in less than four years, and the conclusion it reaches at that point rarely concerns truth or falsity. The plaintiff can be confident that the claim of falsity will rarely be formally rejected.

4. If, as we believe, many libel plaintiffs—particularly the public plaintiffs—view the act of suing as an effective form of response and redress, a central premise upon which the constitutional privileges are based is cast in doubt. In the *Gertz* case the Supreme Court explained the higher privilege accorded statements about public plaintiffs in terms of their voluntary assumption of the risk of libel and their greater access to the media for response and denial. It may be, however, that their greater access is more imagined than real, and that response through the media is viewed as self-serving and therefore less effective than suit. In any event, there is reason to doubt that the disincentive of more onerous privilege rules has a significant relationship to the actions or objectives of many plaintiffs, as *suing*, rather than winning, provides a direct and effective form of self-help.

The impression most clearly conveyed from analysis of the litigation process is that of a formal legal action having little real relation to the objectives and the actions of the initiating party. While the legal system has evolved complex rules for the litigation of claims, and while these rules seem largely to be operating in predictable ways, they have only the most tenuous relationship to the motives and conduct of those persons for whom the cause of action is provided. In other words, the actual results achieved in the formal legal process may be substantially irrelevant to many plaintiffs. In ironic ways, those formal rules facilitate and support the decision of libel plaintiffs to pursue the case, even when the prospect of *judicial* victory is nonexistent.

7

RETROSPECTIVES: THE PURPOSE OF SUIT AND THE FEASIBILITY OF ALTERNATIVES

IRONIES ABOUND IN libel law. Foremost among them are that most libel suits fail, yet suits persist; that constitutional privileges present onerous obstacles to success in public cases, yet public plaintiffs continue to sue; that litigation is often prolonged, emotionally trying, and, in some cases, expensive, yet these costs are willingly borne; that reputation is the legal interest being protected, yet, as Robert Sack notes, "[t]he few plaintiffs who succeed resemble the remnants of an army platoon caught in an enemy crossfire."

In this chapter we will explore the plaintiffs' retrospective views of the litigation experience, and whether the plaintiffs would be generally receptive to non-litigation processes to resolve their libel dispute. Our conclusions are that success in court is not the sole measure by which plaintiffs judge the utility of the lawsuit. While frustrated by the judicial process, many plaintiffs accomplish reputational repair by suing (even though unsuccessfully). The lawsuit is viewed as an effective form of public vindica-

152

tion, and alternatives will not be employed unless they provide a suitable substitute for that primary motivation.

RETROSPECTIVE VIEWS OF LITIGATION: WHAT LITIGATION ACHIEVES

Most plaintiffs lost in court.[1] A small fraction won, but even for these plaintiffs the terms of judicial victory were disappointing. Plaintiffs who won in court obtained an average of $80,000 in damage awards.[2] Excluding two large awards, however, the average award was $20,600, a sizeable portion of which was committed to fees and costs. Plaintiffs who settled their claims obtained an average of $7,000, an amount which must also be reduced for fees and costs.[3] By most standards, plaintiffs' financial victories were of modest proportions.

Why, then, do plaintiffs persist in pursuing libel actions? We have in previous chapters uncovered several reasons, based on an analysis of the plaintiffs' actions prior to bringing suit, their motivation for suing, and other factors. While the information on which we relied, viewed collectively, presents a relatively clear and striking picture of the plaintiffs' motivations and objectives, information directly related to these issues was also obtained from the plaintiffs in a series of questions seeking retrospective views of the litigation process.

In the following pages, we will present and analyze the plaintiffs' responses to a series of questions bearing directly on their motivation.[4] Plaintiffs were first asked whether anything was accomplished by the lawsuit and, if so, what. Plaintiffs' degree of satisfaction with the litigation process was also explored, as were the specific aspects of the plaintiffs' satisfaction and dissatisfaction. Each plaintiff was asked: "Now that the suit is over, if you were faced with a similar situation, what would you do differently, if anything?" Finally, each plaintiff was asked whether alternative forms of non-judicial resolution, if available, would be acceptable or preferable to a lawsuit, and what preconditions would be necessary for each plaintiff to be willing to employ a non-judicial alternative.

A detailed analysis of their responses yields a clear and general conclusion. Judicial success is not the sole measure by which plaintiffs judge the utility of the lawsuit. Many plaintiffs are extremely frustrated by the judicial process, but feel that they accomplished something by suing (even though unsuccessfully), and virtually all of them report that they would sue again if faced with a similar situation. Non-judicial alternatives would be welcomed by most plaintiffs, but only if their interest in reputation and determination of falsity could be vindicated publicly. The lawsuit is viewed as a form of public vindication, and alternatives will not be employed unless they provide a suitable substitute for that primary motivation.

What the Lawsuit Accomplished

In order to ascertain the plaintiffs' attitudes about the lawsuit and the objectives they set for it, plaintiffs' feelings about what the lawsuit accomplished were explored. Of greatest interest, of course, were the perceptions of the plaintiffs who lost the lawsuit and thus failed to obtain a money judgment.

Each losing plaintiff was asked whether anything was accomplished by the lawsuit. Sixty-seven of 106 losing plaintiffs (63 percent) responded affirmatively.[5] These plaintiffs felt that the lawsuit served some positive and constructive purpose *unrelated to its judicial resolution* and independent of their failure to obtain any form of financial reward. If we presume that the breakdown of pending cases will generally mirror those already resolved, and if we add the 22 cases won or settled by plaintiffs, it appears that in roughly two-thirds of the cases the lawsuit achieved objectives set for it by the plaintiffs, even though 83 percent of the plaintiffs lost in court.

The losing plaintiffs who felt the lawsuit accomplished something were then asked what they felt was accomplished. Their responses are presented in Table 7–1.

The most significant aspect of the plaintiffs' response is that it confirms the conclusions drawn earlier about the reasons plaintiffs sue. Forty-one percent of the losing plaintiffs whose suits had accomplished something felt that the lawsuit served to defend their reputation. These plaintiffs, in other words, indicated that the suit itself, independent of its outcome, represented a significant means of legitimizing their claim of falsehood. An additional 40 percent of the plaintiffs expressed their belief that the suit effectively deterred or halted further publication, thus protecting reputational interests, and 9 percent responded that the lawsuit, although unsuc-

TABLE 7–1[6]   What Was Accomplished Despite Loss

Response	Number	Percent
Reputation Defended	24	41%
Support from Family and Friends	5	9%
Further Publicity Stopped	23	40%
Media Punished	6	10%

cessful, achieved support from family and friends—the very groups with whom plaintiffs' reputational interests are often most acute. Combining these three responses, 90 percent of the losing plaintiffs who said that something was accomplished, and 48 percent of all losing plaintiffs, stated that the lawsuit achieved reputation-related objectives.[7] In this connection it is notable that of the plaintiffs who lost but indicated that the suit had achieved something, only 10 percent stated that punishment of the media was the goal accomplished. Punishment and money seem—in retrospect at least—to play a relatively minor role in the interests of this group of plaintiffs.

The role of money and punishment as motivating factors may, however, play a greater role for the 37 percent of losing plaintiffs who felt that nothing was accomplished by the lawsuit—the disappointed losing plaintiffs consisted disproportionately of the plaintiffs with low community visibility whose loss often took more direct economic form and who sued for money. In contrast, the data suggest that the plaintiffs who lost but felt something had been accomplished consisted disproportionately of the highly visible, public plaintiffs who, as indicated earlier, tended not to sue for money, but for reputational reasons. It is ironic that the public plaintiffs, whose suits are intended to be discouraged by the constitutional privileges, are the very plaintiffs expressing the highest degree of satisfaction with litigation, even when their suits are unsuccessful.

Plaintiff Satisfaction With Litigation

Plaintiffs were also asked their feelings about the litigation experience in both general and specific terms. These questions elicited plaintiff attitudes concerning the process and its participants, independent in large part of their own personal objectives in bringing suit. Responses were drawn from all plaintiffs, rather than only from those who lost.

Of 151 codable responses, 52 (or 34.5 percent) expressed satisfaction with their litigation experience. An additional 52 plaintiffs, again 34.5 percent, expressed dissatisfaction, and 47 plaintiffs, or 31 percent, expressed extreme dissatisfaction. Roughly two-thirds of the plaintiffs expressed dissatisfaction, and many of these plaintiffs come from the group (comprising 66 percent of all plaintiffs) who won, settled, or lost but felt the suit accomplished something.

When the precise bases for the plaintiffs' feelings of dissatisfaction are examined, the reason for the apparent disjunction between perceived accomplishments of the suit and feelings of dissatisfaction with litigation emerges. The thrust of the dissatisfaction expressed by the plaintiffs seems

TABLE 7–2   Comments About Litigation Experience

Response	Number	Percent
Valuable Experience, Goals Met	39	25%
Angry & Bitter	13	8%
Critical of Media	6	4%
Critical of Media and Judicial System	34	22%
Critical of Judicial Power	44	28%
Other	20	13%

related to their frustration with the unresponsiveness of the judicial system to their claimed harm. It is quite consistent, given this interpretation, for many plaintiffs to feel that the lawsuit accomplished their objectives—or part of them—yet to express dissatisfaction with the legal system's failure to recognize those objectives and formally respond to them. In essence, plaintiffs who accomplished something by the lawsuit, but who lost and express dissatisfaction at the experience, appear to be reflecting through their responses that the lawsuit serves as a useful instrument for their reputational objectives, but that the formal legal system has frustratingly little bearing on the accomplishment of those objectives.

The clearest indication of this is the overwhelming sense of dissatisfaction and bitterness directed, in retrospect, at the judicial system. At the time of commencing suit, a major motivating factor was the plaintiffs' feelings of anger at the media, often compounded by the perceived arrogance or ineptitude of the media response to their plea. Remarkably, the plaintiffs' sense of anger and frustration seems to have radically shifted by the end of the litigation process from the media to the judicial system. Of the plaintiffs expressing dissatisfaction (excluding those coded other), 80 percent direct it in whole or in part toward the judicial system.[8] This strongly suggests that a disjunction exists between the plaintiffs' objectives—some of which are achieved despite the formal judicial decision—and the rules and results of the judicial process, and that it generates great frustration.

The Rightness of the Action Taken

As a final measure of the plaintiffs' objectives and motivations, the plaintiffs were asked what they would do if faced again with the situation, knowing of their actual experience. The responses are given in Table 7–3. It is clear from the table that the libel plaintiffs are attitudinally wedded—

TABLE 7–3   Plaintiff Action if Faced With Similar
Situation Again

Response	Number	Percent Specific Response
Not Sue	7	5.5%
Pursue Non-litigation Alternative	10	7.9%
Sue Again	87	68.5%
Sue, with better lawyer	16	12.6%
Sue, exert more control	7	5.5%

whether volitionally or not—to litigation as the single most effective means of achieving vindication of their reputation. Even after the experience of litigation, in which most plaintiffs lost and toward which most plaintiffs express dissatisfaction, 86.5 percent of the plaintiffs who specifically responded to the question stated that they would sue again if faced with a similar situation. In the absence of an alternative process, 95 percent of the plaintiffs said they would be likely to sue again, and this proportion holds for those plaintiffs who lost. Indeed, nearly 80 percent of the plaintiffs who lost and said nothing was accomplished by the suit indicated that they would sue again, although 40 percent of them would do so only after engaging a different lawyer or exerting more control.

The proportion of plaintiffs who say that they would sue again is very high for all elements of the plaintiff population, but some marginal differences occur. Ninety percent of the elected officials and candidates for public office state that they would sue again, even though the incidence of judicial success was the lowest with this group, and the existence of economic rather than reputational injury was small. For the other categories, the breakdown is as follows: for public employees, 88 percent; for white collar employees, 78 percent; for business proprietors, 89 percent; and for professionals, 89 percent.

Further analysis of the composition of plaintiffs who state that they would sue again reveals some insights into the litigation process and plaintiff motivation. We first analyzed the plaintiffs who lost in litigation, and the action they would take if faced again with the same situation. Eighty-four percent of these plaintiffs said that they would sue again. Fifty-nine percent stated that they would do so without changing lawyers or playing a more active role in the litigation, 18 percent would get a better lawyer, and 7 percent would exert more control. Sixteen percent would either "not sue" (7 percent) or "pursue non-litigation alternatives" (9 percent).

When these responses are separately analyzed for losing plaintiffs who thought something was accomplished by the suit, and those who thought nothing was accomplished, the level of plaintiff dissatisfaction with counsel becomes apparent. Plaintiffs who thought something was accomplished responded that they would sue again 86 percent of the time. Only 11 percent of these plaintiffs would get a better lawyer or exert more control in a second suit; 75 percent would sue with the same lawyer. Plaintiffs who thought nothing was accomplished also stated that they would sue again— amazingly, 79 percent of the time. Only 39 percent, however, would do so without change of lawyer or greater client control; 29 percent would sue again only after hiring a better lawyer, and 11 percent would exert more control in the suit. While all plaintiffs—even those who lost and who thought nothing was accomplished—responded that they would sue again in the vast majority of cases, most of the plaintiffs who thought nothing was accomplished by their first suit expressed dissatisfaction with their lawyers or with the course of litigation, and would therefore change lawyers or play a more active role in the second action.

Who are the plaintiffs who would change lawyers or exert more control prior to suit, if faced again with the same situation? As might be expected, they appear largely to be the private plaintiffs who suffer the greatest financial harm from the alleged libel and who exhibit the greatest frustration toward the legal process. Eighty-nine percent of the individual plaintiffs classified as public figures or public officials responded that they would sue again; 84 percent of the private individuals said that they would sue again. For public plaintiffs, however, only 12 percent would get another lawyer (8 percent) or exert more control (4 percent); 77 percent would sue again without any change in representation. In contrast, only 56 percent of the private plaintiffs would sue again without change in representation. Instead, 20 percent would change lawyers, and an additional 8 percent would exert more control.

Similarly, 90 percent of the elected officials or candidates for office responded that they would sue again if faced with the same situation, and only 15 percent would do so after replacing counsel or exerting more control over the suit. In stark contrast, while 78 percent of the plaintiffs classified as white collar employees indicated that they would sue again, only 33 percent would do so without some change in representation. Nearly 45 percent of these plaintiffs would either change lawyers (11 percent) or exert more control (33 percent). Finally, 88 percent of the plaintiffs with contingency arrangements said that they would sue again, and 71 percent would do so without change in representation or exertion of greater control over the suit. For plaintiffs with hourly fee arrangements, 80 percent responded that they would sue again, but only 40 percent would do so without change of representation. Instead, 27 percent would change lawyers, and 13 percent would exert more control. Interestingly, only 4 percent of the plaintiffs with contingency arrangements indicated that they would *not* sue again, compared with 13 percent of those with hourly fee arrangements.

The plaintiffs' responses when asked what they would do differently, if anything, were they faced with a similar situation again, should not necessarily be viewed as predictive of their future action or indicative of their resolve to employ suit in response to alleged libels. Their significance, instead, lies in what they suggest about the objectives being achieved by suit. Generally, plaintiffs appear to view litigation as an effective response to alleged libel because bringing suit achieves significant vindication and, perhaps more important, because no other means of obtaining or claiming vindication exists from the plaintiffs' perspective. Public plaintiffs, in particular, seem to view suit as an acceptable form of response, certainly more effective than a public statement denying the alleged libel; and they exhibit a remarkable degree of satisfaction with the way in which the litigation—and their lawyer—achieved legitimation of their claim of falsity. Understandably, it appears that the private plaintiffs exhibit the greatest frustration, both with the effectiveness of litigation in achieving their more frequently financial objectives, and with their lawyers.

Non-litigation Processes and Plaintiff Attitudes

The plaintiffs' responses to a series of questions about alternative non-judicial processes as a substitute for litigation will be analyzed in depth in a subsequent part of this chapter. Certain aspects of the plaintiff responses, however, are directly pertinent to the plaintiffs' objectives for litigation, and should be discussed in general terms at this point.

When asked whether they would consider a non-litigation alternative to resolution of the libel dispute, the vast majority of the plaintiffs responded affirmatively. Seventy percent of the plaintiffs said they would consider such an alternative, and an additional 13 percent indicated that they would do so with certain qualifications. Only 14 percent expressed no interest in alternative processes, and less than 3 percent were uncertain.

The features of the alternative process in which plaintiffs expressed interest reveal the reasons for bringing suit and the prime objectives libel plaintiffs seek to accomplish. The desirable alternative process was described to plaintiffs as having four key elements: (1) promptness; (2) fairness; (3) yielding a finding on the dispute (alleged falsity and harm); and (4) publication of the outcome. The interest in alternative processes expressed by plaintiffs was clearly based on these features. When asked why they would consider such a process, 95 percent of those who would consider alternative processes explained their interest specifically in terms of avoiding suit (28 percent), reducing cost and time (13 percent), achieving a more just outcome (28 percent), and having that outcome made public (26 percent). Only 5 percent expressed a need for money damages. Moreover, of the 13 percent of plaintiffs who qualified their interest in non-litigation alternatives, less than half (42 percent) would require the availability of money damages, and 37 percent conditioned their interest in terms of publication of the outcome. Indeed, *no more than* 20 percent of the plaintiffs stated that the availability of money damages would be a precondition to use of *any* alternative process. Since this group includes individuals, not all of whom would necessarily demand money, it is likely that the true proportion of plaintiffs who would demand money damages is significantly lower.

These and related data will be analyzed in greater detail later in this chapter. Their significance for present purposes, however, lies in what they reveal about the plaintiffs' objectives in litigation. The overwhelming impression drawn from the data is that most plaintiffs are chiefly concerned with the underlying falsity of the challenged statement, and seek a prompt and fair process for publicly setting the record straight. Only 24 percent of the plaintiff responses can be differently interpreted: the 14 percent who expressed no interest in alternatives, and the 10 percent who would precondition their interest in an alternative on the availability of money damages. Moreover, more than half of these plaintiffs won in litigation, settled, or experienced financial harm compensable only through money damages. Elected officials, however, exhibit the greatest disinterest in non-litigation alternatives (33 percent), although two-thirds of this group would consider such alternatives. The willingness of this group to sue again even in the face of an alternative tends to confirm the conclusion that, for public officials in particular, the act of suing achieves public vindication, even though they lose more often than other plaintiffs. Very few plaintiffs seem to have based their disinterest in alternatives on a desire to punish the defendant through litigation.

The overall picture presented by the plaintiffs' responses reflects a set of objectives that are generally frustrated by the litigation process and legal rules. Most plaintiffs appear to be chiefly concerned about falsity, they want to set the record straight, they would welcome a process directed to the heart of the dispute, and they seek prompt and public resolution. The view that libel plaintiffs are persons with no confidence in their claim and who manipulate the legal process for personal ends seems both simplistic and overbroad in light of the cumulative weight of their responses. The fact that the majority of cases were deemed insubstantial when judged by standards of material falsity and reputational harm does not undermine this conclusion, for "insubstantial" *defamation* claims may, and often do, involve statements that are incorrect or incomplete[9] and are legitimately perceived by plaintiffs as causing emotional harm.

Rather than suing for improper or manipulative reasons, most plaintiffs seem to resort to litigation as a means of self-help and legitimation of their claim. The legal process itself encourages such use, through its delays, relative inexpensiveness, and low risk of loss on the merits of the dispute (falsity or truth); and the fact that plaintiffs employ litigation for these very reasons should not lead one to impugn their motives. Nor should the motives of all plaintiffs be suspect because some plaintiffs use the legal system's delay and failure to address falsity to pursue a meritless claim.[10] Rather, these facts only serve to confirm the conclusion that most—but not all—plaintiffs sue for the simple reason that they have no effective alternative for redressing perceived reputational harm. The judicial system, not the plaintiffs, should bear principal responsibility for this situation.

Conclusion

The general conclusion to be drawn from these data seems clear. We have seen that the private plaintiffs are most likely to experience significant economic harm from a libel. Yet, when figures for private and public plaintiffs are compared, a smaller proportion of private plaintiffs state that they will sue again if libeled again. They are also most dissatisfied with their lawyers, most frustrated by the litigation experience, and most likely to pay the bill. Private plaintiffs, in short, are being most directly and effectively discouraged by the rules and results of the legal system.

In contrast, public plaintiffs face the greatest legal obstacles to recovery, yet they seem generally satisfied with their lawyers, significantly less frustrated by the litigation process (even though they win less frequently than the private plaintiffs), and more inclined to say that they would sue again. Their harm is most often reputational rather than economic, and they rarely pay significant lawyer fees. For them, the libel action is an essentially free good, and they are not significantly affected by the rules and results of the legal system, even though those rules are very much designed to discourage them from suing.[11]

It is not low fees alone, however, that lead the vast majority of the public plaintiffs—as well as a somewhat lower percentage of private plaintiffs—to say they would sue again. It is, instead, a perception that despite all its frustrations litigation is an effective—indeed, the only effective—means of achieving self-help in relation to their reputational, as distinguished from economic, harm. The act of suing, itself, represents a public and official form of response and denial, legitimating the plaintiff's claim of falsity more effectively than any other form of self-serving response, reply, or denial. The delay in judicial decision, coupled with resolution on grounds of privilege rather than truth or falsity, assures plaintiffs a face-saving explanation for the almost inevitable media victory. The risk that the truth of the challenged statement will be confirmed in litigation is slight.

For most libel plaintiffs, the act of suing achieves reputational objectives. Its effectiveness is confirmed by the fact that roughly 84 percent of the *losing* plaintiffs responded that they would sue again if faced with the same situation. There can be little doubt that, in actual practice, the libel action is serving very different purposes than those set for it by the legal system, and apparently serving them well. Strangely enough, the villain in the act—if there be one—may be the very constitutional privileges designed to discourage suit and protect the press.

ALTERNATIVE NON-JUDICIAL PROCESSES: PLAINTIFF ATTITUDES AND OBJECTIVES

The overwhelming majority of libel plaintiffs expressed interest in non-litigation alternatives for resolution of their libel suits. Seventy percent of the plaintiffs responded that they would consider such an alternative, and an additional 13 percent indicated that they would do so with certain qualifications. Only 14 percent expressed no interest in alternative processes, and 3 percent were uncertain. The significance of these responses must be analyzed in light of the plaintiffs' equally overwhelming response that they would sue again if faced with the same situation. This analysis tends to confirm the view that most plaintiffs' concern is focused on falsity, and that their chief interest is setting the record straight—purposes now at least partly achieved through the act of suit itself.

Under What Circumstances Would the Plaintiffs Avoid Litigation?

Most of the plaintiffs, who ultimately wound up dissatisfied with their litigation experience, simply had not considered alternative non-judicial processes in advance of suing. In part this is because 60 percent of the responding plaintiffs' lawyers did not discuss alternatives to litigation. In larger part this was because few such alternatives exist, and even fewer would serve satisfactorily to achieve the plaintiffs' goals. We know, for example, that of those plaintiffs' lawyers who did discuss non-litigation alternatives, half discussed settlement, and one-third told their clients that suit was unnecessary. Further, rather than present non-litigation as a viable alternative, 72 percent of the lawyers indicated that the chance of success in the lawsuit was 50 percent or better, and the chance of settlement was slim. Because so many of the plaintiffs if again faced with the same situation responded that they would sue, the likely conclusion is that those plaintiffs whose lawyers did suggest alternative non-judicial processes saw the alternatives as an unsatisfactory means to restore their reputations.

This conclusion is confirmed by the plaintiffs' responses when asked why they would consider a non-litigation alternative that would involve a prompt, fair, and public determination of the conflict. Although the plaintiffs may not have had a clear picture of the alternative non-judicial processes available to them, the plaintiffs through their open-ended responses did express an interest in non-litigation alternatives containing certain elements. Thirty-two plaintiffs (24 percent) would employ a non-litigation alternative in order to avoid suit. This response at first may seem difficult to reconcile with the overwhelming number of plaintiffs who responded that they would sue again if faced with a similar situation, even though that response is more a reflection of attitude than a prediction of future behavior. Perhaps it can be explained by the fact that their interest in suing again reflects the plaintiffs' beliefs that there are few viable alternatives to suit. When asked if they would be interested in a *viable* alternative, even those who would sue again in the same situation responded that they would consider a non-litigation alternative if it meant the possibility of avoiding suit. For these plaintiffs, the lawsuit itself seems to have served little purpose.

Closely allied with the interest in avoiding suit, another 15 plaintiffs (11 percent) stated that reducing cost and time was a precondition to a

TABLE 7–4   Reason Why Plaintiff Would
Elect an Alternative to Litigation

Conditions	Percent	#
Avoid Suit	24%	32
Reduce Cost & Time	11%	15
More Just Outcome	24%	32
Outcome Publicized	27%	36
Damages Available	10%	14
Other	4%	5

non-litigation alternative, and 32 (24 percent) would have considered a non-litigation alternative if it would produce a more just outcome. These two responses reflect significant interests in making the non-litigation alternatives more prompt and fair, qualities that were obviously seen to be missing from their litigation experiences. It seems clear that a large residue of dissatisfaction specifically directed at the litigation process remains for most plaintiffs (79 or 57 percent in these three groups), and that they would prefer in most cases to choose a meaningful alternative to litigation as a process for resolution of their dispute.

Thirty-six plaintiffs, comprising 27 percent of those responding, would have considered alternative non-judicial processes if the outcome were publicized. It is highly likely that this is an appreciably larger group of plaintiffs than the 36 who specifically mentioned publicity as a condition, for the question asked plaintiffs described the process as involving a "public" determination. Because so many of these plaintiffs eventually lost their lawsuits, the "outcome publicized" precondition reflects the plaintiffs' interest in restoring their reputations by some public proclamation—something they felt that the act of suing for libel had not accomplished to their satisfaction. Once again, the data suggest that there remains a significant group of plaintiffs who, if given the opportunity for a meaningful publication of the outcome, would not have chosen litigation.

Finally, 14 plaintiffs, comprising 10 percent of those responding, would consider alternative non-judicial processes if they provided for damages. These plaintiffs consist disproportionately of private individuals who appear to have suffered actual money damages to their businesses or in their professions. Although the legal system provides access for these plaintiffs to bring their libel claims, they found that their libel suits did not satisfy their economic harm. Coupled with the fact that these plaintiffs are in most cases paying their lawyers' fees, it should not be surprising that money damages appear as a significant precondition to the non-litigation alternative for them.

While for 83 percent of the plaintiffs non-litigation could be a viable alternative, a small group of 23 comprising 14 percent of all plaintiffs would choose litigation rather than a non-litigation alternative, even if conditioned on the availability of money damages. It seems, therefore, that there remains an entrenched minority of libel plaintiffs who would choose litigation over the non-litigation alternative, although a small proportion of this group consists of plaintiffs who won or settled, and therefore might be expected to prefer the judicial process.

The pattern that emerges from the plaintiff responses is that plaintiffs overwhelmingly express interest in an alternative to litigation. The essential characteristics of the alternative are promptness, fairness, resolution of the underlying dispute concerning falsity, and publication of the result. Notably, money seems to play a distinctly secondary role in the plaintiffs' judgment about alternatives.

Which Plaintiffs Would Consider Non-Litigation Alternatives?

When the plaintiffs' legal classification is compared with the circumstances in which plaintiffs would consider alternative nonjudicial processes, no significant patterns emerge, other than those previously mentioned. However, when the media response to the plaintiffs' initial contact is compared with the circumstances in which plaintiffs would consider non-litigation alternatives, a trend emerges. For example, in those cases in which the media refused the plaintiffs' demands or repeated the story uncorrected, 47 percent of the plaintiffs placed specific conditions on their interest in non-litigation alternatives.[12] In contrast, when the media retracted, corrected or apologized, or did not repeat the story, only 30 percent expressly conditioned their interest.[13]

While the size of the groups involved may make these responses inconclusive, the direction of the data suggests that the more negative the media response to the plaintiffs' contact, the more likely the plaintiffs are to demand an affirmative act—such as publicizing the outcome or giving the plaintiffs money damages—as a prerequisite to a non-litigation alternative. This hypothesis suggests a complex dynamic between the libel plaintiffs and the media defendants. At the very least it suggests that the more responsive the press was to a plaintiff's contacts—even though, in many cases, the response was viewed as inadequate—the more receptive the plaintiff might be to alternative non-judicial processes. This hypothesis is consistent with our earlier conclusion that media response was the most pervasive factor contributing to the plaintiffs' decision to sue and other actions. It follows that the plaintiffs' perception of the media response would color their own attitude toward non-litigation alternatives.

The data also suggest that whether or not the plaintiffs had seen a lawyer before deciding to litigate would have an important impact on their receptivity to non-litigation alternatives. Most of the 60 plaintiffs who said that they decided to sue after seeing a lawyer expressed an interest in a fairer, more just, and less time-consuming alternative to litigation. Fifty-three (88.3 percent) would be interested in a non-litigation alternative. Only 10 of these (19 percent) would have conditioned their interest on publication of the outcome, while only 1 plaintiff (2 percent) would have asked for money damages as a prerequisite. On the other hand, those plaintiffs who said that they had decided to sue before seeing their lawyers were primarily interested in non-litigation alternatives with a specific affirmative act as a precondition. Sixty-five of these 79 plaintiffs, or 82 percent, would consider non-litigation alternatives, but 21 of the 65 (32 percent) would consider non-litigation only if the outcome were publicized, and 11 (17 percent) would do so only if money damages were available.

We know that most of the plaintiffs who decided to sue before seeing their lawyers were public plaintiffs for whom the influence of the lawyer on the decision to sue was slight. It is not surprising, in light of this, that the largest group of plaintiffs who decided to sue before seeing their lawyers, and who would have also considered non-litigation as an alternative, are public plaintiffs who want the outcome publicized. Private plaintiffs, however, also sought conditions in non-litigation alternatives, though largely in terms of availability of damages. [14] Plaintiff status, therefore, may not fully explain the different receptivity to non-litigation alternatives depending on the timing of the decision to sue. An additional explanation may be that the involvement of lawyers before the plaintiffs decided to sue had a leavening influence on the plaintiffs' objectives in litigation, and helped make them more receptive to non-litigation alternatives. [15]

Plaintiffs' Objectives and the Non-Litigation Alternative

The most important means of understanding the plaintiffs' willingness to accept non-litigation alternatives is by comparison with the reasons plaintiffs sued. This comparison is provided in Table 7–5. Of the 39 plaintiffs who said they sued to restore their reputations, 11 plaintiffs (28 percent) would have accepted non-judicial alternatives to avoid the lawsuits; 3 plaintiffs (7 percent) would have required that cost and time be reduced; 8 plaintiffs (21 percent) would have wanted more just outcomes, while 16 plaintiffs (41 percent) would make publication of the outcome a prerequisite to accepting a non-judicial process. For these plaintiffs, there was no need that money damages be a precondition. Rather, their reputations could have been restored by non-litigation alternatives which avoided suit and published the outcome.

Of the 23 plaintiffs who reported that they sued to obtain money damages, 9 (or 39 percent) would condition use of a non-judicial alternative on the availability of money damages. This result is expected, and is notable only because it is low. The other 14 plaintiffs would, at least in retrospect, have different objectives in the non-litigation situation from those they had in their lawsuits. Of equal interest is the fact that the largest

TABLE 7–5   Why Plaintiffs Who Sued for Particular Reasons Would Choose a Non-Judicial Alternative

	Why Plaintiff Sued			
	Restore Reputation	Win Money Damages	Punish & Vengeance	Deter and Stop Publicity
Avoid Suit	11	4	8	8
	28%	17%	20%	33%
Reduce Cost & Time	3	0	5	7
	7%	0%	12%	29%
More Just Outcome	8	6	11	7
	21%	26%	27%	29%
Outcome Publicized	16	4	14	1
	41%	17%	34%	4%
Money Damages Available	1	9	3	1
	3%	39%	7%	4%
		$p. < .001$		

group of the 41 plaintiffs who sued to punish the media would require that the outcome be publicized (14 or 34 percent). Only 3 of these plaintiffs (7 percent) would have required that money damages be available, which tends to confirm the view that "punishment" as a reason for suit is heavily influenced by the media interaction with the plaintiff, but is unrelated to the presence of financial harm to the plaintiff. Indeed, the vast majority of plaintiffs who sued to punish the media appear, in view of their interest in non-litigation alternatives, to have surprisingly benign objectives. From all this it appears that even those plaintiffs who initially sued with perhaps the most vindictive of motives are essentially receptive to non-litigation alternatives. Furthermore, it may point out a fundamental problem with current libel litigation: By forcing the parties to define the dispute as a conflict between press irresponsibility and free expression, the judicial process may create more controversy than it resolves.

Conclusion

The plaintiffs' responses to alternative ways of resolving their dispute show that the complex calculus of the plaintiffs' motives and actions permeates not only all facets of their lawsuits, but also reaches into their receptivity to non-judicial alternatives. At the surface of this complexity is the plaintiffs' likely uncertainty about the specific features of a non-litigation alternative. We cannot be certain whether they conceived of a mediated non-judicial result or some nirvana where all the objectives they set for their libel suits were fulfilled. Obviously, what constitutes a meaningful alternative would have to be as individual as the lawsuits themselves. Notwithstanding this ambiguity, several observations can be cautiously advanced.

1. The plaintiffs' responses that they would sue again if faced with the same situation do not overshadow their interest in alternative non-judicial processes. The fact that they sued and say they would do so again may reflect little more than the fact that non-litigation alternatives are essentially nonexistent today.

2. The initial contacts with the media influenced the kind of preconditions that the plaintiffs would place on non-litigation processes. The more negative the media response to the plaintiff, the more harsh the alternative demanded.

3. The plaintiffs' objectives changed dramatically from the time their suits were initiated to the point at which we inquired about alternatives to litigation. Particularly important is the fact that a number of those plaintiffs who in their lawsuits had set out to obtain money or to punish the media would, in a non-judicial setting, choose less antagonistic objectives. Because these milder objectives—while real—are expressed retrospectively, we cannot conclude that plaintiffs who have not experienced a libel suit would be equally receptive, at least in the absence of a less negative experience with the media. Information on this issue will be gathered in the next phase of the Iowa Libel Project, when specific non-litigation processes will be tested.

Retrospectives on Litigation: Implications

The plaintiffs' responses on their retrospective attitudes toward litigation largely confirm inferences drawn earlier from our dicussion of the conduct of plaintiffs and defendants before and during litigation. The main implications of the data seem clear:

The core of the libel dispute is falsity. In defining the dispute in terms of fault rather than falsity, the legal system engenders great frustration and contributes to the cost and complexity of litigation.

Plaintiffs use the lawsuit as a means of response, and to legitimate their claim of falsity. They seem to view the act of suing as an effective means of vindication, notwithstanding the fact that they lose—ultimately—in court.

Plaintiffs express a clear interest in a process that is directed straightforwardly to the truth issue, and that is directed toward correction rather than money.

In view of this, and in view of the expensiveness, cumbersomeness, and indirection of the current legal process, fundamental reshaping of the libel system and the constitutional privileges should be considered, and alternative non-judicial processes should be seriously explored.

8

MEDIA DEFAMATION RECONSIDERED: THE NEED FOR CHANGE

IN THIS CHAPTER the possibilities for reform of the libel tort will be explored. Beginning with an overview of the current libel litigation process, we will analyze the common law and constitutional elements of libel law in light of the empirical information collected in the study. Our conclusions are sure to be met with resistance. The actual adjudications in libel cases do not reflect any systematic, rational protection of reputation. Nor do they reflect any systematic effort to ascertain the truth or falsity of materially damaging statements. Finally, they do not consistently safeguard the First Amendment values of open discussion and editorial freedom. Instead, the essence of today's libel law is directed, not at truth, nor to protection of reputation, but instead toward enforcement of press responsibility. In terms of legal doctrine and judicial decision making, the libel suit is perhaps best described as a tort for abuse of constitutional privilege, not libel or reputational repair.

The blame for this state of affairs—if blame be appropriate—rests with the legal system, with the constitutional privileges as well as the common law, and not with the plaintiffs or the media defendants. The cure rests also with the legal system. In broad outlines, we suggest that the focus of libel suits be falsity, not fault, and that the objective should be correcting falsity with truth, not money. We suggest that the many proposals which attempt to direct libel litigation toward the truth issue should be seriously considered. We also outline, for illustrative purposes, a new tort that could replace the present libel action, focusing efficiently and directly on the truth issue, without significant constitutional privileges, and with the objective of setting the record straight rather than awarding money damages. Along with other reform proposals, such a new tort, the broad outlines of which we describe, should be seriously explored, as we believe it reflects not only sound constitutional theory, but sound public policy as well.

PLAINTIFF EXPECTATIONS AND REALITY

The common law of defamation is grounded on the premise that factual statements about an individual (or group) can be harmful to the individual's reputation, can cause consequential economic and emotional harm, and in such instances should be legally compensable in the absence of justification for publication.[1] Implicit in this straightforward statement of the law of defamation are three central assumptions:

1. that reputation adequately describes the nature of the plaintiff's interest;

2. that plaintiffs want compensation and can be adequately compensated for harm to their interest by money damages; and

3. that "justification" is necessary as a rule limiting liability and money damages when the challenged statement is warranted by public policies that override reputational harm.

The latter proposition carries two connotations: First, that money damages when applied will deter unacceptable or unjustified conduct in the future; and second, that financial penalties, whether compensatory or punitive, should therefore be applied only when publication results from conduct by defendants that is unacceptable or unattended by independent policy justification.[2]

The constitutional law of defamation builds on these assumptions, adding another of its own. Constitutional principles have been held to require that when otherwise actionable defamatory statements concern a public person, the press' liability should exist only upon a showing of fault—in the case of public figures, actual malice; for private persons, negligence.[3] The assumptions underlying the fault privileges are that defamation actions by public persons will only succeed when the publisher was knowingly reckless or negligent, that public plaintiffs will be deterred from commencing libel actions, and that expression will be more open and robust when it is freed of the inhibitions of potential liability.[4]

While centuries of experience with the legal concept of defamation, and two decades' experience with the constitutional privileges, might suggest at least that these assumptions comport with reality, it is remarkable how little is actually known about the extent to which they reflect actual experience. It is even more remarkable how little else we know about the actions and motivations of parties to a defamation action, and the process that is followed before and during litigation. Our study of libel cases between 1974 and 1984 leads us to conclude that many of the assumptions underlying current libel law are open to serious question, and others may simply be wrong. The greatest disjunctions between the law's assumptions and our measure of practical reality occur in the contexts of why plaintiffs sue, and what they achieve in litigation: what plaintiffs want, and what plaintiffs get.

What Plaintiffs Want

While defamation law assumes that plaintiffs sue to remedy reputational injury, and employ litigation as a means of obtaining compensation for the economic and emotional harm that flows from reputational injury, the plaintiffs indicate that neither the harm actually perceived nor the motivations actually at work are quite so simple. The information obtained from plaintiffs and their lawyers in defamation cases involving the media is most revealing.

Each of the 164 plaintiffs surveyed was asked what the media could have done to satisfy him or her during the period immediately following the publication or broadcast. Nineteen percent (31) of the plaintiffs indicated that nothing could have satisfied them; 4 percent (7) were uncertain; 73 percent (119) of the plaintiffs indicated that the media could have done something to satisfy them following publication; only 4 percent (6) mentioned money. In one formulation or another, 95 percent (113) of the specific responses, and 69 percent of all plaintiffs surveyed, sought correction of alleged falsity rather than money damages during the period immediately following publication.[5]

Contacts with the publisher prior to suit were reported in 129 of the 164 cases surveyed.[6] Plaintiffs contacted the media directly and in advance of contacting an attorney in 52 percent of the cases. The remaining 48 percent contacted an attorney before contacting the media, thereafter contacting the publisher personally or through their attorney.[7] Most media contacts by the plaintiffs were made in person or by telephone, and in virtually every case the plaintiff was able to contact the person with whom he or she wanted to speak.[8] One hundred and twenty-eight plaintiffs who contacted the publisher directly, with counsel, or through counsel were able to recall what was requested of the publisher. Only one of the 128 plaintiffs requested money; the remaining 127 plaintiffs all sought correction or an apology, although this was expressed in various terms because no prompting was used by the interviewers. One hundred plaintiffs reported asking for a retraction or public apology, 2 sought a personal apology, 4 sought time or space for comment on the story or broadcast, 6 requested that publication be stopped, and 7 sought discussion or explanation of the story.[9]

In describing the media's response to the action requested by the plaintiffs, 122 plaintiffs provided specific information. Twenty-six said that the publisher fully or partially retracted or corrected the story or apologized for it. Three defendants agreed not to repeat the story or fact. No publisher acceded to a request for space or time to respond. The remaining 93 plaintiffs, or 76 percent, indicated that the media declined the plaintiffs' request, and in 14 of these cases the objectionable story was subsequently republished.[10]

Each of the plaintiffs was asked how he or she felt about the media's response. Of 125 plaintiffs who responded, 57 percent stated that they were angered by the publisher's response or lack of response, 37 percent indicated dissatisfaction, using such terms as "unfair," "irresponsible," and "inadequate," and 6 percent reported "ambivalence" or satisfaction, but sued nevertheless.[11]

While one would expect that a group of plaintiffs who actually instituted litigation would generally express dissatisfaction with the media's response to their contact, one is struck by the very large proportion of plaintiffs who expressed *anger* as distinguished from just strong feelings of dissatisfaction. Two other responses also reveal the apparent motivating forces at work before litigation is begun. When asked whether the publishers' response to the plaintiffs' contact was a factor in their decision to sue, 127 plaintiffs responded, and 115 of them, or 91 percent, indicated that it was a factor.[12] Moreover, 81 of the 143 plaintiffs responded affirmatively when asked specifically whether they decided to sue before contacting an attorney.[13]

Each plaintiff was asked to specify the reasons for initiating a defamation action. The reasons given, and their disjunction with the plaintiff's expressed interest in correction immediately following publication, further suggest the change in plaintiff motivation between publication and suit. Of the 160 plaintiffs who provided specific reasons, without prompting, for bringing suit, 30 percent (48) stated that suit was brought principally to correct error or clear their reputation, and 19 percent (30) stated that they sued to deter further publication. Thus only 49 percent of the responding plaintiffs expressed their primary reason for bringing suit in reputation-related terms.

Just over 50 percent of the plaintiffs, therefore, stated that they sued primarily for reasons other than, or in addition to, reputation. Twenty-nine percent (47) of the plaintiffs described their objectives in terms of punishment. An additional 22 percent (35) said they sued to obtain money damages.[14] While immediately following publication 95 percent of the responding plaintiffs indicated that correction of falsity was their objective,[15] only 49 percent explained the subsequent decision to bring suit strictly in terms of correction of falsity; over half the plaintiffs brought suit for other or additional reasons, including punishing the media or obtaining money damages.[16]

Plaintiffs were asked two questions about their reaction to the offending article. They were first asked what upset them about the article.[17] Of the 157 specific responses given, 68 percent (106) stated that they were upset by the article's falsity; 28 percent (44) were upset by the publication's impact on their reputation; and 4 percent (7) were upset because the article invaded their privacy or dealt with private matters. Plaintiffs were also asked to explain the damage or harm caused to them by the publication.[18] Of 155 plaintiffs specifically responding, 14 percent (22) said they were harmed financially; 22 percent (34) stated that they were harmed emotionally and financially; 27 percent (42) indicated that the harm was emotional; and 37 percent (57) expressed the damage in terms of their standing in the community, over one-third of them implying they lost political status. A majority of the plaintiffs therefore expressed harm in non-financial terms.

These and other data have been analyzed in great depth in earlier chapters. We recount it here in simplified form for a more limited purpose. The body of information obtained from the plaintiffs in defamation cases brought against the media raises difficult questions about the assumptions defamation law makes regarding the conduct of plaintiffs and their motivating purposes, at least in the context of actions against the media. Defamation law is premised on the plaintiff's interest in reputation, a concept that is distinct from falsity, embracing instead only certain *legally* protected interests, in one's good name in the community. Relatively few plaintiffs, however, express their own interests in precisely such terms. Rather, plaintiffs' immediate reactions and stated interests are couched in terms of falsity, a term which certainly expresses reputational concerns, but reflects a more complex mixture of objectives. When asked to break down their interests following publication, the plaintiffs seemed to relate "falsity" as often to emotional distress or financial loss as to reputation in the community. Moreover, 23 of the 57 plaintiffs who did relate their feelings of harm to reputation did so in terms of damaged political status, an interest all but foreclosed from recognition in current defamation law. When the question of plaintiff interest at the time of commencing litigation is considered, reputational interests as such account for less than one-half of the suits brought, according to the plaintiffs themselves. A sizeable proportion of the suits (19 percent), according to the plaintiffs, are chiefly brought to deter further publication—a reputation-related purpose, but not one that is necessarily consistent with compensatory assumptions of the libel tort. [19] The remaining actions are brought to obtain monetary damages or to punish the publisher, with punishment (29 percent of the cases) being a more important expressed reason for bringing suit than money (22 percent of the cases).

This suggests two conclusions of significance. First, "reputation" does not adequately reflect the complex mix of plaintiff interests at the time of publication. Their chief concern is with falsity, and their chief interest is in setting the record straight. Second, between publication and the initiation of suit a series of events and interactions occurs which substantially transforms the plaintiffs' perceptions and motivations, fundamentally changing the nature of the suit and perhaps the role served, albeit unwittingly, by the law of defamation. Plaintiffs do not necessarily employ litigation because the *legal* process will correct error or clear their reputation; they do so to stop further publication, to obtain money or achieve vindication of their claim of falsity, and to "get even." Reputation, in short, is an apt, but oversimplified, reflection of actual plaintiff interests.

The second assumption of defamation law is that plaintiffs want compensation and that they can be satisfactorily compensated through money damages for the harm caused by publication. Information obtained from plaintiffs, however, puts a very different cast on this proposition, at best. It seems clear from plaintiff responses that the primary and almost exclusive interest of plaintiffs following publication is correction of perceived falsity, not damages or any other form of compensation. This is borne out by the plaintiffs' recollection of their objectives immediately following publication, as well as by their description of what they or their attorney asked the publisher to do when contacted in advance of litigation. Many plaintiffs expressed feelings of satisfaction or accomplishment with litigation, even though they lost, and most said that, knowing what had happened, they would sue again if faced with a similar situation. It is noteworthy, as well, that when asked whether, in light of the litigation experience, the plaintiffs would be willing to consider a non-litigation alternative involving a prompt public finding on the question of falsity without going to court, at least 82 percent of the plaintiffs stated that they would consider such an alternative. Less than 15 percent of the plaintiffs stated that they would not consider such an alternative.[20]

These responses by plaintiffs indicate that compensation and money damages do not reflect their actual desires following publication, nor do the plaintiffs seem, viewing the events in retrospect, to consider damages necessary to an acceptable or even preferable resolution of the dispute. Indeed, in light of the expressed interests of the plaintiffs, "compensation" seems to ill-fit their interests. Money and damages do, however, enter into their motivation more distinctly after pre-litigation contact has been made with the publisher, and after counsel has been engaged. At this point, however, fewer than one-quarter of the plaintiffs give money as the reason for suit, and in some of these cases money only serves as a surrogate for motives distinct from obtaining compensation, such as deterrence and punishment of the publisher. The responses suggest that, in roughly three-quarters of the cases, non-compensatory motives play a predominant role at the point of bringing suit. To the extent that this reflects defamation plaintiffs generally, it leads to the conclusion that the compensatory assumptions or objectives of defamation law may be largely unimportant to the vast majority of plaintiffs.

Money damages do, of course, play a role in the motivation of certain libel plaintiffs, and these are largely the private plaintiffs who have experienced economic harm from the publication being challenged. Curiously, it is these plaintiffs who seem to be most uncertain about whether to sue, who tend to pay the highest lawyer fees, and who, in retrospect, are least inclined to sue again if faced with the same situation.[21] In contrast, the public plaintiffs do *not* tend to want money but sue eagerly, rarely pay lawyers' fees, win less often, but would sue again if faced with the same situation. In short, it seems that the assumptions and operation of the legal process *least* fit the motivations of the minority of plaintiffs who experience legally compensable harm.

The law's conceptions of what plaintiffs want seems far removed from the actions of plaintiffs in media defamation cases today. To the extent that the law's assumptions and the plaintiffs' expectations correspond, moreover, the underlying motivations of plaintiffs seem substantially distinct from those more benignly presumed in the common law of defamation. The actual perceptions, interests, and conduct of persons libeled in the press seem infinitely more complex than the straightforward approach of the law, and the true goals being accomplished in the litigation appear strikingly different from those reflected in the public policies supporting the common law doctrines.

The picture painted by actual experience suggests two generalizations:

1. Most plaintiffs do not seek compensation for reputational harm; instead, they seek public vindication of the truth.

2. Most plaintiffs do not sue to obtain compensation for the harm experienced; they sue to achieve vindication, to deter future publication, and to get even.

What Plaintiffs Get

Data obtained from the libel plaintiffs depicts an apparent and stark contrast between the plaintiffs' motives (what plaintiffs want) and the formal results achieved—what plaintiffs get. But it also discloses the ironic fact that most plaintiffs, even though frustrated and unhappy about the experience, express a willingness to sue again, thereby reflecting a conviction that litigation accomplished important objectives. To understand this irony we must look to the objectives that govern the plaintiffs' actions from the beginning of litigation to its conclusion.

The decision to bring suit is perhaps the most critical step taken by plaintiffs, for having commenced a defamation action, forces unrelated to the merits of the action may make it difficult for plaintiffs to withdraw. Fifty-seven percent of the responding plaintiffs who were represented by counsel indicated that they had decided to bring suit before contacting an attorney.[22] All of these plaintiffs, of course, contacted an attorney prior to the actual filing of an action, and appear from the responses to have been apprised of the risks attendant to litigation, including further publication and disclosure about the plaintiff, the costs of litigation, and the extended character of the litigation process in media defamation cases. Notwithstanding this, 43 percent of the plaintiffs indicated that the attorney's advice had little or no bearing on the decision to sue, and 18 percent stated that the advice was only of "some" relevance. Only 40 percent of the plaintiffs—largely the private plaintiffs—indicated that the attorney's counsel played a significant role in the decision to bring suit.[23]

The plaintiffs' expressed sense in retrospect that litigation accomplished important objectives must also be interpreted in light of the formal legal results they had experienced. The incidence of success by the plaintiffs was discouragingly, but predictably, low. In 130 of the 164 plaintiff cases surveyed, final judgment or settlement had been reached. Of the 130 plaintiffs whose cases had been completed, 83 percent (108) lost. Only 3 of these plaintiffs dropped their claim; the remaining 105 lost only after proceeding to trial court judgment and, in most cases, appeal. Thirteen of the 130 plaintiffs won their suits, and 9 plaintiffs settled. Whether through judgment or settlement, only 17 percent of the plaintiffs prevailed.[24]

The plaintiffs who prevailed in litigation obtained an average of $80,000 damages, although this average was greatly distorted by two large awards.[25] If these two awards are disregarded, the remaining plaintiffs received an average award of $20,600. The plaintiffs who settled received an average of $7,000. Adding together the total amount of successful judgments and settlements and applying them to all completed libel actions covered by the survey, the average amount obtained by plaintiffs was $7,869; excluding the two large awards, the average dropped to $2,392.

Plaintiffs also provided information on the total cost of litigation.[26] In 16 percent of the cases the plaintiffs bore no cost at all, as the cases were taken on a pure contingency basis. In an additional 57 percent of the cases the plaintiffs paid only certain costs, with the attorney acting on a contingency basis with respect to fee.[27] For all plaintiffs, including those on full or partial contingency arrangement, the estimated average cost was $7,015. The average attorney fee for all plaintiffs, including those with contingency arrangements, was $3,468.

While average recovery and average costs for all plaintiffs whose cases were finally resolved are not, in themselves, meaningful statistics, their comparison sheds some light on the economics of media defamation litigation. For the total group of surveyed plaintiffs with claims that had been finally resolved, the average recovery was $7,869, while the average cost was $7,015. The cost figures represent only the out-of-pocket cost to the plaintiffs, not the true cost of litigation (much of which was borne by attorneys engaged on a contingency basis) nor the non-party costs associated with use of judicial and other resources. The limited incidence of success in the adjudicated cases and the low level of apparent recovery in the roughly 15 percent of cases that are settled suggest that, from a strictly financial point of view, media defamation cases cost plaintiffs roughly as much on average as they achieve in damage award or settlement. On the other hand, the average cost is not high in light of the plaintiffs' intense interests, and a large proportion of plaintiffs bear costs under $1,000.00.[28]

While, as a group, the plaintiffs stated that they were aware from the outset that the litigation process could be prolonged, they were nevertheless frustrated by the extent of time consumed, and the number of levels of judicial action. On average, it took roughly 4 years from the date of publication to achieve final resolution of the lawsuit.[29] Four percent of the cases took 8 years or more, 25 percent took between 5 and 8 years, 29 percent took between 3 and 5 years, 34 percent took between 1 and 3 years, and 7 percent were resolved within 1 year from publication. In 30 percent of media libel cases the action was resolved after the first level of judicial proceeding. Seventy percent of the cases judicially resolved employed two or more levels of judicial action (trial court and at least one appeal), with at least 13 percent involving two or more appeals.[30]

In view of the results achieved in the legal system, perhaps the most interesting responses obtained from the plaintiffs involved their feelings of satisfaction with the litigation process when viewed in retrospect. Of the 151 plaintiffs who responded specifically, 6 percent (9) expressed extreme satisfaction, 28 percent (43) expressed satisfaction, 34 percent (52) expressed dissatisfaction, and 31 percent (47) expressed extreme dissatisfaction.[31] About 34 percent of the plaintiffs viewed the process in retrospect with satisfaction, either because they won the suit or obtained favorable settlement, or because notwithstanding ultimate loss the plaintiffs felt that at least some of their objectives had been met. Of the plaintiffs who lost, a remarkable 67 percent thought that the suit accomplished something.[32] Thirty percent of the 108 losing plaintiffs felt that their reputation had been defended notwithstanding the ultimate judgment, 5 percent received support from friends and associates, 10 percent felt the media had been punished, and 26 percent felt that the suit had deterred further publication.[33]

Roughly 66 percent of the plaintiffs expressed dissatisfaction with the litigation in retrospect, for reasons ranging from cost, time, emotional trauma, and unfairness. But when the plaintiffs were asked whether, in light of their experience, they would bring suit again if the same thing happened, 87 percent of the plaintiffs said that they would sue again.[34]

It is difficult to account for the continued persistence of media defamation actions in light of the extremely small likelihood of success, and even more difficult to explain the large degree of expressed willingness on the part of unsuccessful defamation plaintiffs to resort to litigation again even though most such plaintiffs expressed dissatisfaction with the process. The responses obtained from the plaintiffs do not fully resolve this issue, but certain limited inferences are suggested by the data.

First, most plaintiffs say that they want to correct the falsity and clear their reputation immediately after the publication. Bringing suit may, itself, accomplish this objective from the plaintiff's perspective, and part of the reason for this may, ironically, be the very delay associated with final resolution. A more immediate prospect of failure might better discourage some plaintiffs, for friends and associates might draw stronger inferences from a prompt resolution on the question of truth or falsity. The failure of the judicial process to rest judgments on truth or falsity, as opposed to privilege issues, coupled with the lack of prompt adjudication, minimize the risk of loss to the plaintiff's reputational interests. This may serve to eliminate from the plaintiff's consideration a relevant and important element in the decision to sue.

Second, at the point of commencing litigation, reaction to the media in the form of desire for punishment and vengeance plays a significant role for many plaintiffs, and the act of bringing suit, coupled with the cost of the suit to the media, may itself provide satisfaction in spite of the result. The desire to exact retribution and vengeance no doubt plays a part in many litigation settings, but media defamation plaintiffs seem to have a particularly acute desire to penalize. Public defamation litigation provides a predictably effective means of imposing costs on the media, both financial and reputational, and the effectiveness with which such a goal can be achieved is substantially unrelated to success or failure on the merits. The heavy incidence of contingency arrangements suggests that the plaintiffs' attorneys serve as gatekeepers, eliminating wholly frivolous actions seeking only punishment. On the basis of our limited data this appears to be the case, but there remain a large number of facially colorable claims where the prediction of success requires, at a minimum, a subtlety of understanding beyond the ken of most lawyers—and the preponderance of lawyers in media defamation actions appear not to have been involved in defamation litigation before. The combination of non-predictiveness and plaintiff objectives that are not entirely dependent on success in court may account in part for the persistence of plaintiffs in bringing actions, and also for their apparent willingness to sue again.

Finally, in a real sense plaintiffs have no other place to turn than to a defamation action, and given the strength of their emotional feelings most plaintiffs would prefer any process—even one they acknowledge as painful and probably unproductive in a legal sense—to doing nothing and by inaction confirming the published facts. It is revealing in this regard that 82 percent of the plaintiffs indicated that they would seriously consider a nonjudicial process leading to a prompt and fair public finding of the facts were such a process available.[35]

When one asks what plaintiffs get in media defamation litigation, therefore, one must be prepared for answers on two levels. In terms of the law's assumptions and the prospect of successfully establishing liability as the law dictates it, plaintiffs get precious little. Very few succeed, and in most cases the out-of-pocket costs to the plaintiff exceed the award. Because liability rests largely on adjudication of privilege rather than falsity, more than half of the plaintiffs view the judicial process as producing unfair and inadequate results. On a different level—unrelated to the specific resolution of the case, or to the need for compensation in money terms—the plaintiffs get what they seek in a remarkable percentage of the cases, and would sue again knowing that the result would be the same. The act of suing, by itself, represents a real form of personal vindication, serves to legitimate the claim of falsity, exacts a penalty on the media for conduct perceived to be unfair to the plaintiff, and provides an outlet—the only outlet—for the plaintiff's frustrations. The irony is that the plaintiff's objectives persist and are accomplished regardless of, or in spite of, the law and its assumptions.

Conclusion

When judged in terms of what libel plaintiffs want and what libel plaintiffs get, there appear to be marked disjunctions between the assumptions of the legal system and actual experience in litigation. The law assumes that people sue to obtain protection for their reputation through a formal judicial decision. They do. But their specific objectives are to correct falsity, complete the record, and get even; vindication through formal judicial decision, while desired, is not necessary to substantial accomplishment of these objectives. The law assumes that people sue to be made whole through damages; instead they do so to legitimate their claim and to get even. The law assumes that constitutional privileges deter suit and protect uninhibited expression; instead, the privileges may encourage suit and protect the plaintiff by fostering delay and ignoring the question of falsity. The law assumes that bringing suit is expensive for the plaintiff and is done only after careful consideration; instead, bringing suit is relatively inexpensive, and plaintiffs often have little choice but to bear the cost in the absence of any alternative. Finally, the results achieved in litigation suggest that most plaintiffs lose; instead, most plaintiffs succeed, although not on the law's terms, and most report that they would sue again if faced with the same situation.

Ironically, the media defendants contribute to the differences between the law's assumptions and the realities of libel litigation. The media defendants express an institutional interest in truth. On an everyday level, however, they often tend to deal with libel complaints in a way that forecloses private solution and encourages suit. For the media, little by way of adverse results in litigation is lost by this strategy; the constitutional privileges provide substantial shelter from liability, and permit the troubling issue of truth or falsity to be avoided. Much is lost by the media, however, in the form of litigation costs, attorney fees, and insurance premiums. Much may also be lost in terms of credibility. From the media defendant's point of view, the winners are not the media, not the insurance companies, and surely not the First Amendment, if truth be its guide; the main winners are the media lawyers.[36]

The differences between the rules of the legal system and the actual conduct of plaintiffs who invoke them are substantial and profound. The differences go to the very heart of the libel tort. In many respects, the differences have been fostered by the very system of constitutional privileges that was intended to harmonize the common law defamation action with current notions of free expression. As such, the focus of reform should be directed not toward further modification of privilege rules, but rather toward a fundamental re-examination of the libel system itself, so that it may better reflect the legitimate concerns of those harmed by false fact, while at the same time protecting the interests of the publisher as well as the public in free and open expression, including the correction of falsity.

THE NEED FOR REFORM IN THE LAW OF LIBEL

Four principal conclusions emerge from an analysis of libel litigation and the actions and motivations of the parties to it. It is around these conclusions that changes in our present methods of resolving libel actions must be shaped:

1. The dominant interest expressed by libel plaintiffs is correction of falsity, or setting the record straight. Plaintiffs' interest in the libel process, therefore, is focused on the question of truth or falsity.

2. The interaction between media and plaintiffs, following publication, often fosters rather than discourages litigation. This may be the most important single factor explaining the large number of "petty" claims that ripen into lawsuits.

3. The issue of truth or falsity of the challenged statement is rarely adjudicated in the lawsuit. Instead, privilege issues dominate adjudication of virtually all claims, including many of those that are successful.

4. Most plaintiffs win by suing; they do not sue only to win in court. Plaintiffs sue to correct falsity, to deter republication, and to get even. The act of suit, itself, represents the only available form of self-help through which plaintiffs' claims of falsity can be legitimized and vindicated through the invocation of formalized judicial scrutiny. Because the legal process rarely addresses falsity, and even less frequently responds promptly, the suit serves to legitimize plaintiff claims irrespective of their actual merit, with little risk that the truth of a statement will be confirmed.

Whether viewed singly or as a whole, these conclusions demand a fundamental and searching re-examination of the law of libel. They suggest that the libel process is largely unresponsive to the very dispute being adjudicated, and that a substantial part of that unresponsiveness is of the law's own making.

In the following sections the rules and procedures applied in libel actions will be analyzed in light of the major conclusions reached in this study. The primary focus will be on the issue of falsity as an element of the cause of action; the impact of privilege rules on the adjudication of libel; the significance and meaning of reputation as an element of the libel tort today; and the influence of procedural requirements on the libel suit. On the basis of this analysis, we will discuss the need for reform of the libel action, and the features such reform should contain. Finally, the constitutionality of the needed reform will be analyzed in light of the guarantees of freedom of speech and of the press.

Falsity and the Transformation of the Common Law

New York Times v. Sullivan[37] first brought the First Amendment to bear on the common law tort of defamation, imposing a set of constitutional privileges on the common law doctrine; and it did so in the interest of fostering a robust discussion of matters of public moment relating to self-government and to the exigencies of life in an organized and free society. *Gertz v. Welch*[38] substantially modified and recast the *Sullivan* privileges, increasing their complexity and changing their theoretical complexion in fundamental ways.

In many respects, the constitutional privileges have themselves transformed the common law of libel. The most far-reaching and pervasive consequence of this transformation has been the introduction of new forms of "falsity" in the adjudication of the tort. First, through the fault-based privileges, *subjective falsity*—what the publisher thought about truth or falsity *at the time of publication*—has been made an element of the libel action in virtually every case.[39] This element relates, however, to whether the challenged communication is privileged, *not* to whether it is defamatory. Second, the concept of *actual falsity*—the underlying truth or falsity of the published statement—has been infused into the tort. At common law, actual falsity, if relevant at all, was presumed from a well-pleaded defamation complaint.[40] The burden of proof by evidence was on the defendant, who could raise and prove the defense (or justification) of truth. Over the past 10 years this rule has been modified or supplanted by two new rules that were increasingly applied in a number of jurisdictions. The first of these is that the plaintiff must plead and prove the challenged publication's falsity, by some evidence, as an element of the common law tort.[41] The second variant imposed in an increasing number of cases is that proof of falsity by the plaintiff is constitutionally required, for liability cannot rest on truth. [42] Notwithstanding both the constitutional and logical infirmities of such a constitutional rule, [43] it has met increasing acceptance. Finally, in the 1986 decision in *Philadelphia Newspapers Inc. v. Hepps*, the Supreme Court held that plaintiffs in most media defamation cases must bear the burden of proof of falsity. [44]

For purposes of this discussion, the nuances of these variants on falsity are less important than the complexities that they have introduced in the adjudication of libel claims. These complexities, and their apparent consequences in libel cases, will be explored in the sections that follow. Attention will first be given to the data collected on the incidence of adjudication of subjective falsity and actual falsity; on the effect these determinations are having on the course of the libel suit's litigation; and on the results reached in libel cases. The theoretical as well as practical implications of the "falsity issue" will next be explored in some depth. Thereafter three issues closely interrelated with the falsity question will be discussed, to better assess the legal theory governing libel adjudication today, and its shortcomings. These issues, in order, will be the legal importance of reputation; the system of plaintiff- and defendant-based privilege categories; and the concomitant proceduralism of the present public defamation tort. Finally, we will outline a reformulation of the common law tort itself, and its practical and constitutional implications will be briefly explored.

The Role of Falsity in Libel Litigation

It has been noted several times already that the question of *actual* falsity—as opposed to a publisher's belief concerning truth at the time of publication, based upon information then available—is only infrequently addressed in the litigation of libel claims. It has further been suggested that *actual* falsity represents the gravamen of the plaintiff's claim. Before discussing the reasons in legal doctrine for the failure of courts to adjudicate truth or falsity, and the implications this state of affairs holds for the current status of the defamation tort, we will summarize the basis for our underlying conclusion that truth or falsity is rarely addressed.

It should be noted that the cases studied preceded the *Hepps* decesion, [45] which placed the burden of proving falsity on most plaintiffs in media libel cases. While it is hoped that *Hepps* will result in greater emphasis on actual truth or falsity in libel cases, the failure to address truth or falsity in litigation seems largely to be a function of the fault privileges, not the burden of proof on the truth question. It should also be noted that many of the cases studied were adjudicated under the *Hepps* rule, which had been adopted in various forms in many jurisdictions prior to the Supreme Court's recent decision.

The incidence with which the issue of actual truth or falsity is addressed in litigation can first be explored in terms of the role of constitutional privileges. On this point, the statistical evidence drawn from the plaintiff survey and the survey of libel cases, though largely indirect, is compelling. In libel cases generally, roughly 75 percent of the seriously litigated claims are resolved in advance of trial. [46] A review of the cases and the principal legal ground for decision discloses that the decisive issue in virtually all such cases is privilege-related. Specifically, these cases are resolved on motions to dismiss or for summary judgment, the claim being that a constitutional privilege applies and requires that the plaintiff demonstrate a factual basis for the publisher's negligence, or actual malice. [47] These issues involve the publisher's state of mind on the issue of truth or falsity *at the time of publication*, not the underlying truth or falsity of the challenged publication. To overcome the privilege, the plaintiff must plead sufficient evidence on the privilege, or "fault," issue—which does not concern *actual* falsity—in advance of any adjudication of falsity as an element of the basic defamation action.

Even after trial of the defamation action, where the issue of truth or falsity is often addressed, over half of the plaintiff verdicts are reversed on appeal. [48] Here again, the predominant ground for reversal is constitutional privilege—the absence of negligence or actual malice. [49] Combining the decisions reached on privilege grounds in advance of trial with those reached on appeal following trial, 87 percent of all media libel cases are resolved on privilege grounds. [50] Because adjudication of privileges is legally distinct from the issue of actual truth or falsity, and because as a practical matter the privilege decision imposes a burden that most plaintiffs cannot overcome, falsity seems rarely to be addressed in the litigation process, and even more rarely to be material to the resolution of the claim.

This conclusion is corroborated by the responses of plaintiffs to the broad series of questions discussed in earlier chapters. Without reviewing those responses in detail here, it is plain that a large proportion of the plaintiffs are chiefly interested in the falsity of that which was published, not in the fault of the publisher. It is also clear that most plaintiffs are frustrated at the failure of the litigation process to address the falsity issue forthrightly, and that plaintiffs overwhelmingly express a keen interest in a process which would afford the opportunity for a prompt, fair, and public test of truth.

To obtain a more direct measure of the frequency with which the questions of truth and falsity are addressed, even obliquely, and the effect on the litigation when the issue is broached, 188 randomly selected defamation cases decided between 1974 and 1984 were analyzed and coded.[51] The results are reported in some detail below. In general, it appears that the issue of truth or falsity is explicitly broached in nearly half of the cases, but it is adjudicated in an evidentiary setting in only 16 percent of the cases. Where the question is "fully" adjudicated, plaintiffs are remarkably successful, both in advance of trial and in trial. On post-trial appeal, however, plaintiff success was demonstrably reduced, as privilege considerations regularly overrode verdicts for the plaintiff on the underlying defamation claims. Perhaps most interesting—and comforting—is the fact that the defendant publishers won every case in which truth or falsity was fully adjudicated and the challenged statement was found to be true. Equally comforting is the fact that where doubt existed on the truth issue, publishers prevailed so long as the issue of truth or falsity was directly addressed. Where truth or falsity was not adjudicated, however, yet doubt on the question seemed probable from the pleadings and facts, publishers did not necessarily prevail. The issue of *actual* truth, it seems, was more a friend than a foe of the defendant.

The Incidence of Adjudication of Falsity

Of the 188 cases surveyed, 155 could be coded in terms of the presence of an adjudication of falsity (the remainder consisted predominantly of actions based on statements of opinion rather than fact, and a few that were in the early stages of litigation and therefore it could not be determined whether falsity would be adjudicated). Each case was also analyzed to determine, in light of the factual materials available, whether the publication was likely true or false.

Of the 155 coded cases, truth or falsity was specifically addressed in 70 cases, comprising 37 percent of all claims and 45 percent of the cases in which the opinion privilege was not involved. In 43 percent of these 70 cases, the challenged statement was deemed false; in a majority of the cases (57 percent) it was found to be true, or materially so. In contrast, the truth or falsity of the challenged statement was not addressed in 63 percent (118) of the cases. Excluding the opinion cases, truth or falsity appeared to have been unexplored in 85 cases, representing 55 percent of all coded non-opinion cases. When these 85 cases were assessed in terms of probable truth or falsity in light of known facts, 24 cases (28 percent) were deemed probably true, 7 (8 percent) were probably false, and in 54 cases (64 percent) probable truth or falsity could not be judged. It appears that cases involving falsity are more likely to have that issue addressed directly (largely because, as discussed below, these cases tend to go to trial), while cases in which the challenged statement is likely true are less likely to address the question. To an uncertain extent, this may be a product of the requirement, existing in only some jurisdictions prior to 1986, that falsity must be pleaded and proved as an element of the tort.

When the nature of the adjudication of falsity is explored, a number of patterns emerge. The first concerns the point at which falsity is adjudicated. Twenty-six of the cases in which truth or falsity was adjudicated went to trial. This represents 53 percent of the cases tried, and is surprising only in that 47 percent of the cases tried appear not to have involved an adjudication of the underlying truth or falsity of the challenged statement; instead, the focus was the reasonableness of the decision to publish in light of what was known at the time of publication. The remaining 44 cases in which truth or falsity was addressed represent 31 percent of the cases not tried, and 41 percent of the non-opinion cases that were not tried. In these 44 cases the determination of truth or falsity was made without an evidentiary trial; the challenged statement was determined to be false in 13 cases, true in 30 cases, and uncertain in one case. The falsity or truth determination in these cases was based upon the pleadings or required preliminary showings, and ultimate resolution of the cases was almost always based on privilege grounds rather than on the challenged statement's underlying truth or falsity.

The issue of truth or falsity tended most frequently to be addressed in cases involving private plaintiffs and media defendants. Truth or falsity was addressed in 49 percent of the media cases, in contrast to 33 percent of cases brought against non-media publishers. Because a slightly higher proportion of non-media cases went to trial (29 percent v. 25 percent), a higher percentage of the media determinations of truth or falsity would have been nonevidentiary in character, and accompanied by a disposition on privilege grounds. For private plaintiffs, truth was addressed as an issue in 55 percent of the cases, in contrast to 35 percent of the public figure cases. Breaking these elements down further, it appears that the public or private character of the plaintiff has more to do with the adjudication of falsity than the media status of the defendant. Truth is addressed in a majority of the media cases involving private plaintiffs, and in a distinct minority of media cases involving public plaintiffs. This difference cannot be explained by a higher rate of trial in private plaintiff cases, as more cases are tried involving public plaintiffs (30 percent) than involving private plaintiffs (25 percent).

THE CONSEQUENCES OF ADJUDICATING TRUTH OR FALSITY

More significant than the incidence and completeness of the adjudication of the truth or falsity of the challenged statement are the consequences that flow from that adjudication. An assessment of the consequences must differentiate between a determination of truth or falsity in advance of trial—where an evidentiary determination will generally not have been made in an adversary proceeding—and such a determination at and after trial. Following a preliminary discussion of case results, therefore, we will analyze the specific consequences of adjudicating truth or falsity prior to and following trial.

The adjudication of underlying truth or falsity appears to have a relationship to the result reached in the case, although the relationship is complex and the number of cases from which one can draw conclusions is small. For cases with final judicial resolution in which truth was addressed, plaintiffs won 17 percent of the time (10 of 60 cases)—a higher rate of success than for final cases as a whole. Where the challenged statement was judicially determined to be false, plaintiffs won in 43 percent of the cases (10 of 23 cases). Where the statement was found to be true, no plaintiffs won. For the total number of plaintiff wins (12 cases), 83 percent (10) involved an adjudication of falsity. In contrast, only 35 percent (36) of the defendant wins involved an adjudication of truth. In a remarkable 96.4 percent (53) of the cases *not* involving a determination of truth or falsity, the defendants ultimately won.

A few conclusions based on these data can be ventured. First, it appears that having underlying truth or falsity addressed is highly important to libel plaintiffs, and particularly to those plaintiffs who are classified as private and therefore must overcome only a negligence rather than actual malice privilege. Second, where truth or falsity was adjudicated and the publication was determined to be true, defendants always prevailed. Defendants also prevailed in a majority of the cases (57 percent) in which the publication was deemed false. This suggests that the risks attendant upon the adjudication of truth for the media defendant are not great, assuming that the adjudication of truth or falsity is reliable, and that the consequences of inability to ascertain truth are acceptable. As to the former point, a review of the cases in which full adjudication of truth was undertaken suggest a high degree of reliability, but the ultimate test would involve those cases in which the evidence is close, and those cases tend not to have been adjudicated. As to the consequences of an inability to ascertain truth, the 96 percent defendant success rate suggests that the law would be sensitive to the defendants' interests in the context of uncertainty.

The third and final conclusion suggested by the data is that the constitutional privileges play a major role in the adjudication of libel cases, even where truth or falsity is placed in issue. Defendants won in the face of a determination of falsity of the challenged publication 57 percent of the time, and the vast majority of such cases involved constitutional privilege determinations—i.e., that while false, the statement was not published with negligent or reckless indifference to doubts actually entertained by the publisher.[52] In nearly 60 percent of the finally resolved cases no consideration was given to truth or falsity, and in roughly 70 percent of the cases in which the issue was broached it was not thoroughly adjudicated, as 85 percent of these cases were decided on privilege grounds. For both groups of cases, the defendants succeeded over 95 percent of the time, virtually always because of privilege issues which preempted or subordinated the question of underlying truth or falsity of the published statement.

Determination at the Pre– and Post–Trial Stages

The effect of a determination of truth or falsity at the pre-trial stage suggests that such a determination may function more effectively as a filter for factually strong claims than do the privileges. Of the 96 cases involving motions for summary judgment, 39 addressed truth or falsity. Plaintiffs prevailed in 9 of the 39 cases, or 25 percent of the time. In contrast, plaintiffs prevailed (overcame motion for summary judgment) in 15 of the 56 cases in which truth was not addressed, or roughly 27 percent of the time. The same pattern of greater plaintiff success when truth or falsity is *not* addressed occurs with appeals from pre-trial rulings. When truth or falsity was determined, plaintiffs prevailed in 23 percent of the pre-trial appeals. In the absence of any focus on truth or falsity, plaintiffs prevailed in 38 percent of the pre-trial appeals. These data suggest that pre-trial motions on privilege grounds (which almost all such cases involve) may not be as protective of the media defendant as some have thought, at least as compared to a process going directly to falsity rather than fault. It suggests also that a determination of truth or falsity may serve the defendants' interests as well as the plaintiffs' expressed desires.

An analysis of the cases that were tried indicates that the issue of truth or falsity is addressed less frequently than would be expected, and that the reliability of the trial judgment may be impaired by the absence of a determination on the question of truth or falsity. Of the 48 cases that were tried, 26 (or 54 percent) appeared to involve an adjudication of truth or falsity. When that issue was addressed, plaintiffs won 22 percent (2 of 9) of the cases in which the publication was found to be true, and plaintiffs won 14 of the 17 cases (82 percent) in which it was determined to be false. In sum, plaintiffs prevailed in 16 of the 24 cases involving adjudication of truth or falsity. For cases in which the underlying truth of the publication appeared not to have been determined (the trial turning, instead, on fact issues related to privilege and state of mind at the time of publication only), plaintiffs prevailed in 13 of the 22 cases. This was a similar rate of plaintiff success (59 percent) to that for cases in which truth or falsity was adjudicated (66 percent). Of course, many of these cases may have involved an actual or *de facto* admission of falsity; others seem to have involved the defendant's decision not to attempt the dangerous defense of truth.

Post-trial appeals tended to function largely as a means of correcting trial judgments in those cases that did not involve an adjudication of truth or falsity. No plaintiffs prevailed on appeal in the face of a determination of the truthfulness of that which was published. Sixty percent of the plaintiffs who won in trial on the basis of proof of falsity of the publication succeeded in post-trial appeals. In contrast, for cases not involving the adjudication of truth or falsity (13, or 59 percent, of which had been won by plaintiffs at the trial level), only 2, or 9 percent, of the plaintiffs ultimately prevailed. In 10 of the 12 initially successful plaintiff cases, or 83 percent, trial verdicts for the plaintiffs were reversed on appeal.

A few observations from this pattern of plaintiff and defendant success can be noted. The first observation is that the adjudication of truth or falsity appears to have little effect on plaintiff success at trial, but it does assure that no publisher is held liable when the underlying statement is true. The second observation is that for those cases in which the statement is judged false, the plaintiff success rate is surprisingly low. While 82 percent of such cases were won by plaintiffs at trial, 40 percent of these victories were reversed on appeal because of privilege—because, in short, the publisher made a material error, but did not do so knowingly.[53] In short, defendants won in the face of a finding of falsity in 47 percent of the tried cases. The third and final observation is that the constitutional privileges play a pervasive role even in the adjudication of cases that go to trial. Where actual truth is not specifically addressed, plaintiffs were successful at trial, but the defendants ultimately won 91 percent of the cases, usually on appeal and virtually always on grounds of privilege. In 50 percent of the tried cases the issues turn on questions of privilege *to the apparent exclusion of any determination of truth or falsity*. Nearly half of the cases in which the publication is deemed false are decided for the defendant because of privilege.

Viewing these data as a whole, it is far from clear that focusing on the underlying truth or falsity of the challenged statement does disservice to the publishers' interests. While no true statements were made the subject of liability, 2 statements whose truth or falsity went untested did result in liability. It seems clear, however, that the plaintiffs' expressed frustration with the failure of the litigation process to get to the heart of their concern is well grounded in fact. Questions of privilege—state of mind and fault—rather than questions of truth or falsity and reputational harm, dominate the adjudication process, and do so to the complete exclusion of truth or falsity in the clear majority of the cases.

The Focus on Subjective Falsity

The concept of falsity was introduced into the defamation tort's operation through the constitutional privilege rules. The introduction of falsity in its varied forms has been perhaps the most complicating change effected by the Supreme Court, and it has had the most widespread and fundamental consequences. Many of those consequences have been unanticipated and carry implications that only now are becoming clear. In this section the origins of falsity in the public defamation tort will be outlined against the common law background; the reasons for the introduction of falsity will be surveyed; the highly complex form in which falsity now plays a role will be outlined; and the consequences will be identified and assessed.

The Conflict Between Actual Falsity and Subjective Falsehood

Perhaps the greatest point of confusion in the decided cases surrounds the precise meaning of falsity as part of the public defamation tort, and its logical relationship with the defamation action. The common law of defamation did not include falsity as an element of the tort; truth was an affirmative defense. [54] The best explanation for this is that the tort was one for disparagement of reputation, not for falsity, nor for disparagement through falsity. Reputations are not necessarily *true*, but they are nonetheless entitled to legal protection against disparagement in the absence of a showing, through truth, that the reputation was undeserved. Thus, under this view, falsity was not relevant to the cause of action itself. A different view would treat falsity as a *sub silentio* element of the tort, but one which is presumed by a well-pleaded complaint establishing reputation, establishing publication, and finally establishing that disparagement of reputation occurred through the publication. [55] In logical terms, this view treats reputation as reflecting truth; this is a questionable premise, but perhaps one that reflects a difference of little practical consequence in the common law.

The changes wrought by the constitutional law altered the common law tort in two material ways. First, for virtually all media libel cases, actual falsity is a constitutionally-required element of the tort, and plaintiffs bear the burden of proof. [56] Second, fault was introduced, by which the conduct of the publisher is to be judged in terms of his or her subjective knowledge of the falsity or truth issue *at the time of publication*. This could be proved either intrinsically or extrinsically. [57]

The introduction of fault and falsity, when coupled with the tort's historic focus on reputation, has created an inevitable and inherent tension within the new public defamation tort. This is because the concepts of reputation, actual falsity (or falsity in fact), and subjective falsity (negligence or malice in light of what was believed about falsity at the time of publication) are in many instances mutually exclusive concepts; to require their confluence to be established as a predicate to liability is either to require the impossible or to transform the tort in preference for one or more of the three to the exclusion of the others.

Reputation is not always based on truth, or the whole truth, and the common law recognized this by focusing on reputation rather than falsity and acknowledging the relevance of truth only as a defense (or justification) *directed to the legitimacy of the disparaged reputation.* Moreover, reputation is predicated on the *audience* interpretation of words that are expressed. The issue of fault, however, is point-in-time based, focusing on judgments in *advance* of publication, and therefore by logical necessity excludes the relevance of audience interpretation, which occurs subsequent to publication. Fault, or negligence and gross negligence, *when directed toward falsity,* therefore requires the sacrifice of audience interpretation and therefore reputation as a governing criterion for liability, leaving negligent falsehood judged at the time of publication, rather than reputational disparagement, as the gravamen of the cause of action.

Falsity in fact—that is, the actual falsity or truth of that which was published—is not a point-in-time determination. If provable, falsity is falsity whether it was known or ought to have been known at the time of publication. Actual falsity, moreover, is contingent on *audience* understanding of the message alleged to be false. Falsity in fact is therefore logically distinct from negligent falsehood, as the latter concept relates only to the facts and circumstances at a given point in time in advance of publication, and therefore antecedent to audience interpretation. Falsity in fact, therefore, is more consistent with the common law interest in reputation, assuming that the falsehood goes to the legitimacy of the reputation as a legal interest—for it matters not for common law purposes that the fact of falsity or truth is discovered after the fact. It is reputation that the common law is protecting, not truth. Fault formulated as negligent falsehood is therefore incompatible with reputation as both a logical and practical matter.

The inconsistency of the three elements of reputation, falsity in fact, and fault often requires, in the adjudication of actual cases, that a court find a way to harmonize them by preferring one or more elements to the others. The Supreme Court has provided clear guidance on this issue, although without knowing the consequences, by its designation of *fault* as a *constitutional* privilege. Therefore, in cases where the factors conflict, reputation and falsity in fact tend, as a matter of constitutional law, to be sacrificed or submerged. Once sacrificed, the essence of the cause of action becomes a tort action for abuse of constitutional privilege—an action for negligent or grossly negligent publication in light of what was known about truth at the time of publication. This action is even less than a far distant cousin of the defamation tort.

This analysis might be less discomforting if the actual incidence of liability were restricted to cases in which all the three elements of reputational disparagement, falsity in fact, and negligent falsehood coalesced. This appears not to be the case, however, as actual falsity is fully adjudicated in only 14 percent of the cases, and liability has been imposed in the absence of a determination of actual falsity,[58] and in the absence of an adequate adjudication of reputational harm pursuant to common law standards.

FALSITY, FAULT, AND REPUTATION: THE UNIMPORTANT
RESIDUUM OF ACTIONABLE LIBEL

By its recent decision in *Philadelphia Newspapers Inc. v. Hepps*,[59] the Supreme Court has held that most plaintiffs in libel cases against media defendants must prove falsity as a precondition to recovery, both in public figure and private individual settings. In most media libel cases, therefore, a confluence of the three elements discussed above—actual falsity, negligence or subjective falsity, and reputational harm—ought to be and generally is required as a precondition to recovery. While the actual scope and meaning of the plaintiff's burden of proof on falsity remains unclear,[60] we must consider whether a tort based on falsity, fault, and reputational harm represents a proper and sensible approach in public defamation cases, yielding not only predictable but acceptable results.

To address this question one must ask what is being achieved by a tort for reputational harm which shows actual falsity as well as negligence or actual malice at the time of publication. Such a tort will allow recovery for reputational harm, but only where the challenged publication is false in fact. To the extent that falsity is applied to screen out cases in which the falsity undercuts reputation, the result is not dissimilar to the common law concepts except that the burden of falsity is shifted to the plaintiff. To the extent that the falsity issue is viewed in isolation, as appears to be the case in many instances,[61] a showing of falsity may permit recovery even where reputation ought not to be recognized, and the absence of falsity as a technical matter may preclude recovery where reputation is materially injured and specific truth or the absence of specific falsity does not adequately respond to the reputational interest.[62]

The requirements of actual falsity and negligence or actual malice will result in cases of falsity and reputational harm going unvindicated because the publisher's conduct was reasonable at the time of publication when judged by a negligence test; or was unreasonable but the publisher was not aware of falsity, or did not act recklessly in light of serious doubts about falsity at the time of publication. Therefore, instances of negligence or recklessness will be excused in light of non-falsity. Likewise, instances of falsity and reputational harm will go uncompensated if negligence or actual malice do not exist.

The tort which remains under this confluence of criteria fails consistently to vindicate legitimate reputational interests and to deter negligent or reckless conduct by publishers. To be sure, liability is only imposed when the publisher acted unreasonably or with subjective awareness of falsity, but it is not imposed in all such cases. If deterrence of unreasonable or reckless conduct of publishers is a major policy served by the public defamation tort, this end is not consistently achieved.

The common law tort, of course, was not designed to deter recklessness of the publisher, but to compensate persons harmed by the publication. A tort requiring the confluence of reputational harm, actual falsity, and negligence or actual malice clearly falls short of this objective, as the constitutional elements of proved falsity and negligence or actual malice will preclude recovery even in the face of legitimate reputational harm as defined at common law. Moreover, the application of the highest constitutional privileges to persons of substantial reputation tends to foreclose liability in those instances of greatest reputational harm, leaving the incidence of liability for cases involving harm of narrower compass. The tort remains active, therefore, only in the least pressing instances of harm.

The constitutional negligence and actual malice privileges have been established for the purpose of fostering expression; what remains of the tort, however, is difficult to justify on this ground. First, the incidence of permitted recovery seems so narrowly confined to relatively inconsequential harm that the preponderant impact of the tort is to shield publishers from liability, a result better achieved through eliminating the tort altogether rather than maintaining a relatively unimportant residuum.

Second, the expression which is typically being protected in the public libel cases is false fact relating to public people or to issues of public importance. Given the apparent predominance of such cases, which is suggested by the fact that over 80 percent of the defamation cases are decided on privilege grounds and 57 percent of the plaintiffs are public officials or public figures,[63] serious questions exist as to whether the legal system's chief focus should be geared to protecting falsity on issues of public importance.

Finally, what remains of the defamation tort, after the falsity and fault requirements have been surmounted, raises important questions about the very ends of expression the tort is designed to achieve and foster. While the tort purports to protect publishers against the chilling impact of liability, the conduct of plaintiffs in bringing defamation actions, and their motives in doing so, suggest that this purpose is not being achieved. More fundamentally, the privileges may have the consequence of deterring correction on the part of publishers, in part for fear of liability, and preventing access by the readers or viewers to the truth in those instances where material falsity exists. The origins and focus of the fault-based privileges have obscured this dimension of public interest in expression, and the actual adjudication of cases has even more effectively diverted attention from this issue.

The issue of actual falsity, even when required to be established by the plaintiff, may disserve the general expressive interests in true statements of fact. In actual application, falsity is a matter which goes to the published statement itself. It is not generally considered in the context of reputation; rather, in light of the negligence and malice privileges, it goes to the statement alleged to be defamatory, judged in isolation. Questions concerning the *materiality* of falsity—whether the falsity is technical only, unimportant in its relation to reputation, or of any *public* significance—and audience interpretation, tend, like reputation, to be lost in the predominant focus on the question of falsity.[64] In its narrow context, the issue of falsity bears little relationship to the statement's material falsity in terms of the public interests of free expression, including the interest in disclosure of falsity or truth when known.

What remains of the common law tort under even the most rigorous set of constitutional criteria, therefore, is a largely empty residuum that fails to accomplish well any of the common law or constitutional interests. The constitutional requirements severely narrow the instances of liability to those in which the common law interests are least pressing. The cases involving most pressing reputational harm and greatest public interest in the subject matter of the action are virtually foreclosed, with the consequence that personal injury is uncompensated and public interest in further discussion on a topic is constitutionally discouraged.

The Receding Emphasis on Reputation

While the heart of the defamation tort at common law was reputation, the recent cases suggest that the interest in reputation has become obscured and is often lost in actual adjudication. In major respects this is due to the constitutional privileges, which have had two consequences. First, the privileges in actual practice have become the first and predominant issue to be adjudicated, shifting the focus to subjective state of mind, plaintiff identity, and the publisher's procedure. None of these issues bears on reputation as such, but they divert attention in the litigation of cases from the reputation question, even when cases proceed to trial. Second, the privileges are based, fundamentally, on falsity, even though it is a limited species of fault-based falsity. This emphasis tends in practice to transform the pure and direct common-law reputation interest into one infected by falsity. In subtle ways reputation has thereby been transformed as an element of the tort, when it is considered at all.

The Conflict Between Fault and Reputation

The receding emphasis on reputation is closely intertwined with the privileges and with falsity. The subtle interrelationship can perhaps best be illustrated through the case of *Lawlor v. The Gallagher President's Report*,[65] discussed earlier. Lawlor, it may be recalled, was the vice-president of employee relations for Gulf & Western Corporation, a large conglomerate. In early 1973 it was discovered that Lawlor and some of his subordinates had set up their own executive recruiting firm outside Gulf & Western, had used resumes and applications submitted to Gulf & Western in the conduct of this business, and had sought to place such applicants with other companies on a commission basis. Lawlor had been instructed not to establish the company, and he violated Gulf & Western's conflict of interest policy in doing so. He was discharged because of the action.

The President of Gulf & Western stated that Lawlor's discharge resulted from the conflict of interest involved in establishing the company; and The Gallagher President's Report further stated, in describing the situation, that Lawlor had "extracted fees for the placement of executives" with the company. Lawlor's defamation suit was based on both statements. In imposing liability of $45,000 on the business news publication, the district court held that Lawlor was not a public figure for purposes of the defamation action; that the president's statements were true and therefore not libelous; and that the statement in the newsletter was defamatory because it incorrectly implied that Lawlor obtained fees for the placement of executives with Gulf & Western, and the reporter negligently failed to corroborate the facts prior to publication.

The *Lawlor* case illustrates the impact of the privileges and the focus on falsity on the interest in reputation. Judging from the extended discussion of the evidence in the district court's opinion, there appears to have been little or no discussion of the impact of the statement published in the newsletter on Lawlor's reputation in the relevant business community. Discussion of the consequences of the publication is reserved exclusively for the court's determination of the amount of damages, and even here the question exists in terms of the financial consequences of Lawlor's difficulty in obtaining another position after having been fired from Gulf & Western.

The focus on privileges through determination of Lawlor's status as a public figure or private person, and thereafter through discussion of falsity and negligence in the newspaper account, dominated the court's attention. In the end, the court's decision seems to have been based on negligent falsehood in virtually complete isolation, a focus so narrowed as virtually to ignore the surrounding circumstances as they bore on the issue of reputation and on the appropriateness of legal redress in such a situation.

In short, the *Lawlor* case, which was subsequently remanded on appeal, [66] represents an abuse of privilege case. There appears to have been little consideration of the incremental contribution of the false statement to the already damaged reputation of Lawlor because of conflict of interest and discharge from Gulf & Western. Nor is there any indication that people were asked to testify about how their view of Lawlor was significantly diminished by virtue of the newsletter statement itself. [67] The court's award of damages was not premised on any substantial evidentiary determination that the newsletter statement was largely, or even materially, responsible for Lawlor's inability to obtain employment; indeed, the evidence suggested that it was Gulf & Western's appropriate refusal to recommend Lawlor in light of the conflict of interest that foreclosed his employability. [68]

Understandably, the court considered with some care the question whether Lawlor was a public figure for purposes of the suit, concluding that he was not. On balance, this conclusion may be the correct one; but the fact that the answer cannot be determined easily is symptomatic of the problem occurring in public libel cases, for the distinction between public and private persons defies all but the most abstract generalizations, and tends because of its ultimate importance in the case to so consume the courts' energies that it diverts attention from the basic common law issues, and the basic common law interests. [69]

In the *Lawlor* case the plaintiff's status, like the issue of falsity, seem largely irrelevant to a proper resolution of the case under common law policies. At best they are small components of the case, not large ones. Because they assumed a large dimension, the result is difficult to comprehend when viewed as a whole in light of the tort interests, and the resolution of the case disserved the law's interest as well as the interest in reputation.

From Private Reputation to Public Duty: Public Defamation and Press Responsibility

The introduction of fault into defamation law by way of constitutional privileges has not only worked substantial practical changes in the character of the common law tort and its adjudication, but it has also spawned a fundamental shift in the cause of action. The logic of fault in public defamation cases demands that the action reflect policies bearing on the press' responsibility, rather than on the individual reputational interest of the plaintiff or on the free-expression goal of the Constitution.

Under the system of constitutional privileges, liability can be imposed on a publisher of defamation only upon showing actual malice or negligence, depending on the identity of the subject of the statement.[70] The chief reason for this heightened standard of recovery is that public plaintiffs are better able to obtain access to the media to defend themselves, and that the inhibitions stemming from potential damage awards require that the honest or inadvertent error should be protected in order to encourage robust expression. The chief effect of the heightened standard for recovery is that liability should be imposed only if the publisher or broadcaster is at fault; and this is but a formulation of the proposition that if the press acts responsibly it cannot be sanctioned under the First Amendment, notwithstanding the truth or falsity of its statements or the harm inflicted on an individual. Therefore the answer to the simple but fundamental question about the public goals of public defamation law privileges is that the tort, as shaped by the privileges, is enforcing responsibility on the press.

Whether a tort action should attempt to accomplish this, and whether as a private cause of action it is an acceptable instrument to this end under the free press guarantee, are questions that have been addressed elsewhere.[71] For present purposes, however, the inquiry is a narrower one, going only to the actual nature of the public defamation action today. The tort as presently shaped and enforced is clearly directed at enforcing press responsibility, and the fact that the privileges only serve to shield the press from liability in the absence of irresponsible conduct does not change this basic fact. The privileges have had the consequence of refocusing the entire cause of action in this direction.

It is important to understand the origins and precise nature of this shift in the emphasis of the defamation tort, and its larger consequences. Prior to the constitutional privileges, the common law defamation tort was predicated on strict liability.[72] While the rule of strict liability was frequently moderated in special settings by common law privileges,[73] the essence of the tort was that liability could rest in the absence of fault. As a consequence, the scope of inquiry at trial was largely focused on what was published, not why it was published or how it was published. Fault, in other words, did not have to be found.[74]

With the introduction of fault as a predicate to liability in the *Sullivan* case and its progeny, it became necessary to determine not only whether reputation was unjustifiably harmed, but also whether the publisher's action in inflicting the harm was *blameworthy*. While the blameworthiness or fault criterion was introduced in a legally specific and narrow setting—knowledge of falsity at the time of publication, and "reasonableness" of the publication in light of that knowledge—the concept of fault directly and inevitably has drawn courts into judgments concerning professional and ethical standards of journalism. With the broadening scope of the privileges and the introduction of negligence in the *Gertz* case, courts have been playing an ever expanding (although unintended) role in setting the standards of professional conduct (while often denying any intention to do so).[75]

At the same time, the journalism community plays, at best, a modest role in articulating meaningful principles of conduct and judgment. Increasingly, in large part out of a fear of liability, news organizations are unwilling to commit policies and procedures to writing as part of an effort to deny courts the raw materials with which to enforce the journalistic community's own standards.[76] Two great ironies have arisen from this state of affairs. First, journalists are leaving courts and juries freer reign in developing their own standards by which conduct is to be judged in litigation. The second irony is that the primary reason that courts are explicitly creating and enforcing professional norms—the motivating force behind the developing shift in enforcement of journalistic standards from the profession to the courts—is the *Sullivan*[77] case, which introduced "fault" in the defamation tort in order to protect the profession's independence in contributing to robust and wide open discussion and debate on matters of public moment.

It is small wonder, then, that the individual reputational interests have tended to become obscured or lost in the actual adjudication of the public defamation cases.[78] As Robert Sack has concluded:

> The few plaintiffs who succeed resemble the remnants of an army platoon caught in an enemy crossfire. Their awards stand witness to their good luck, not to their virtue, their skill or the justice of their cause. It is difficult to perceive the law of defamation, in this light, as a real "system" for protection of reputation at all.[79]

It is likewise not surprising, upon reflection, that a fair assessment of the tort today is that it is one for abuse of privilege, or for enforcement of responsibility, rather than for vindication of narrow and private interests in reputation, or for broader public interests in truth. Responsibility, judged at the time of publication, has nothing to do with truth or falsity itself; it concerns only what was done and known in a snapshot of history. Responsibility likewise has nothing to do with private reputation, at least to the extent that it is judged—as it is too often judged today—strictly in light of the conduct and knowledge of the publisher without reference to any obligation owed to an individual who may be the subject of the press' attention. The result, ironically, is that liability can rest upon a finding of actual malice or negligence, but in the absence of proof of reputational harm,[80] and without proof of falsity.[81]

The Confusing Maze of Categorical Rules

The principles enunciated in the *Sullivan* line of cases and in *Gertz v. Welch* have taken the form of a highly structured system of categorical constitutional privileges. Distinctions must first be adjudicated on the basis of the plaintiff's identity as a public official, public figure, private person, or public or private entity. For those cases involving private plaintiffs, the identity of the defendant as media or non-media must be ascertained, an inquiry which involves not only the breadth and purposes of the statement's distribution, but also an assessment of the public significance of the statement in light of that distribution.[82] These steps determine the level of privilege applicable to the case. Thereafter, the privilege itself must be adjudicated in terms of either actual malice or negligence, with attendant issues relating, for example, to scope of discovery and availability of evidence.[83]

The interstices of these rules have been explored elsewhere in this study, and have been exhaustively discussed in the literature and in innumerable judicial opinions.[84] In the following pages, a more limited inquiry is undertaken. This inquiry addresses the following issues: the extent to which the plaintiff distinctions are being adjudicated consistently and in light of a theoretically justifiable standard; the manner in which courts are approaching the issue of fault under the constitutional privileges; and the impact of the fault-based categorical privileges on the underlying defamation action and the policies served by the public defamation tort.

The central distinction in the system of constitutional privileges is drawn between public plaintiffs on the one hand, and private plaintiffs on the other. With public plaintiffs a higher level of constitutional privilege attaches to the publisher's conduct, and the plaintiff must overcome this higher privilege by demonstrating "actual malice" on the part of the publisher. Actual malice is a subjective standard, requiring either direct or extrinsic proof by the plaintiff that the defendant published the allegedly libelous statement with knowledge of its falsity or in reckless disregard of serious doubts (actually entertained at the time of publication) about the statement's truth.[85]

Private plaintiffs, in contrast, must overcome a privilege of negligence when the allegedly defamatory remark was published by a media defendant,[86] and in many jurisdictions the negligence privilege has been extended to both media and non-media defamation actions in which the plaintiff is not a public official or figure.[87] To succeed in such a case, the plaintiff must establish that the publisher acted unreasonably in light of what was known at the time of publication about truth or falsity, or about the strength of authority for the published statement.[88]

The distinction between public and private plaintiffs is central to the ultimate resolution of most defamation actions, for it dictates the level of privilege borne by the plaintiff on issues supplemental to the elements of the defamation cause of action. Moreover, as a general rule the privilege issue is adjudicated in advance of trial, typically on a motion for summary judgment; and the largest proportion of the appeals in public defamation cases occurs at this stage as well, rather than after trial.[89] Thus, as a practical matter, the plaintiff status and privilege issues resolve most of the cases brought, and do so prior to trial on the defamation action itself.

The pattern of decisions between 1974 and 1984 confirms these conclusions and provides additional insight into the litigation process in defamation actions. Of the defamation cases studied (media and non-media), 549 cases had proceeded far enough to identify the main legal issues adjudicated in the case. Of these cases, 84 percent (460) involved substantial issues relating to the constitutional privileges. In 41 percent (225) of the defamation cases, the definition of the plaintiff's status for purposes of the privileges was an important contested issue as judged by district court or appellate opinions; an additional 43 percent (235) turned on the related issue of application of the privilege in the facts of the case.[90]

The importance of the privilege issue to the defendants is clearly shown in the rates of success by plaintiffs.[91] Of the 661 total defamation cases, 484 had reached final judgment. The overall rate of plaintiff success in finally-resolved cases was 13.2 percent. In cases involving public official or public figure plaintiffs, the rate of success was 10.2 percent. In cases involving private plaintiffs, the corresponding success rate for plaintiffs was 17.5 percent. For public plaintiffs, the media or non-media identity of the defendant had no significant impact on the plaintiff success rate. For private plaintiffs, the rate of success against non-media defendants was 23 percent, and against media defendants 13.8 percent.[92]

As part of the plaintiff survey, information was gathered on the procedural aspects of the litigation in a selected group of 114 media defamation cases during the same period.[93] Eighty-six of the 114 selected cases had been finally resolved in favor of the defendant at the time the procedural information was gathered. Of the 86 cases, 73, or 85 percent, were finally resolved before any trial—either on motion for summary judgment or for dismissal. Forty-three, or 59 percent, of the cases resolved by summary judgment or dismissal involved at least one level of appellate review. Only 13 of the 86 cases won by defendants, or 15 percent, ever got to trial. Virtually all of these cases involved contested issues of privilege.[94]

These statistics drawn from decided cases between 1974 and 1984 confirm much of what has generally been assumed about public defamation litigation after *Sullivan* and *Gertz*. The application of privileges superimposed on the common law tort by the Supreme Court's opinions decisively influences the results of litigation. The privilege questions, beginning with the touchstone issue of plaintiff identity, dominate the attention of courts in defamation cases, and do so to the practical exclusion of the underlying common law in a large majority of cases. For media libel claims that are pursued to the point of at least one level of judicial action on the merits, only 25 percent of the claims reach trial. Actions won by media defendants, representing 89 percent of the cases brought against them, reach trial only 19 percent of the time. The remaining 81 percent are resolved at the trial or appellate court level on pre-trial summary judgment or dismissal, largely on grounds of privilege.[95]

In view of the central role played in public defamation cases by the distinction between public and private plaintiffs, it is disconcerting that this question, perhaps more than any other in the cases, has generated so much confusion and inconsistency in its application by the courts. The issue is one that has drawn courts into the most subtle and minute determinations, and has required judgments at the pre-trial stage concerning particularized and specific questions about the plaintiffs' history, actions, and their relationship to the challenged publication. In broad terms, this has yielded a patchwork of decisions that are wholly case- and fact-specific, and that defy even the best of efforts to draw general patterns or rules in all but the most highly abstract form.[96]

The reason for this state of affairs is perhaps best found in the lack of clear theoretical basis upon which the distinction between public and private plaintiffs rests, and the uneasy relationship that exists between the present approach to the issue and the underlying defamation law policies. The earlier *Sullivan* and *Rosenbloom*[97] approach to the application of constitutional privileges had the virtue of theoretical clarity and consistency, although it raised other concerns and lacked practical manageability.[98] Under those cases, constitutional privileges, applied to publications, related to the public self-governing ends of the First Amendment.

The *Gertz* reformulation of these rules attempted to avoid the open-ended character of the *Rosenbloom* formulation, shifting instead to a focus on the plaintiff rather than on the issue involved in the publication, and resting distinctions among plaintiffs on an ordered set of rules pertaining to the plaintiff's stature in the public eye. The measure of the plaintiff's stature, moreover, was primarily qualitative rather than quantitative. As a secondary element, the media or non-media identity of the defendant was built, at least implicitly, into the privilege system.[99]

The actual adjudication of the *Gertz* rules since 1974 reflects two general problems with the Court's rules. First, the assumption that a rigorous and objective set of plaintiff-identifying rules could be consistently applied in real cases with meaningful results seems to have been wrong. Courts are not applying the rules consistently. Further, it is now clear that beneath the symmetrical and straightforward texture of the *Gertz* rules lies a morass of relevant, highly-particularized, and fact-based distinctions applicable in different measure to each specific case; trial and appellate courts are obliged to assemble this information in making a judgment of constitutional fact and privilege in advance of trial. The clarity that the Court hoped to establish with the *Gertz* case is not developing, and the highly circumstantial nature of the issue makes the prospect of clarity remote.[100]

The second problem created in the *Gertz* rules is the absence of a clear and sensible theoretical relationship between the rules and the constitutional policies being served by the privileges. This problem, of course, has served to compound the difficulties of application of the rules discussed above. The *Gertz* rules were neither derived from nor explained on adequate theoretical grounds. Rather, as a practical matter, they represented an attempt to respond exclusively to the problems that attended the *Rosenbloom* rules. But in their absence of independent theoretical rationale, the new rules lost constitutional force because they represented a departure of substance from the pre-existing rules.

The *Gertz* rules cannot be rationalized in terms of the public self-governing ends of the First Amendment, because they do not draw clear distinctions along that line; yet they purport to represent a practical reformulation of the objectives and rules of *Rosenbloom*. The Court went to great lengths in *Gertz* to state what the rules were designed to avoid, and how they were to apply mechanically, but the only real explanation given for the new regime was practical, not theoretical—those who introduce themselves into public issues are considered to have waived a certain degree of protection, and are assumed by their involvement to have greater access to self-help in counteracting falsity. Neither premise is necessarily true as a matter of logic or fact. More significantly, neither premise seems to reflect the actions or perceived self-interest of the actual plaintiffs. The rules do not sensibly fall along lines governed by a waiver concept, whatever its origin. In any event, plaintiffs most suited to a waiver rule sue because the initiation of suit, itself, vindicates their claim, and represents the most effective, if not the only, form of self-help. In practice, if not in theory, the *Gertz* rules appear to be based on fundamentally flawed assumptions.

Proceduralism and the Reign of Privilege

Hutchinson v. Proxmire: A Case Study

The consequences of present-day rules of privilege on the litigation of defamation claims, and the lack of theoretically clear bases for the constitutional privilege rules, can perhaps be illustrated through a selected case. The case is *Hutchinson v. Proxmire*,[101] decided by the United States Supreme Court in 1979.

Hutchinson was a behavioral science researcher engaged in federally-funded research on stress in animals, using monkeys in his studies. He was the "beneficiary" of Senator Proxmire's Golden Fleece award for wasteful government spending on "worthless" research to determine when monkeys clench their teeth. To quote part of the press release:

> Dr. Hutchinson's studies should make the taxpayers as well as his monkeys grind their teeth. In fact, the good doctor has made a fortune from his monkeys and in the process made a monkey out of the American taxpayer. . . . [in] view of the transparent worthlessness of Hutchinson's study of jaw-grinding and biting by angry or hard-drinking monkeys.

In fact, Hutchinson's research was quite legitimate. It was funded by a number of federal granting agencies, and was of great interest to NASA, among others, in connection with the causes of stress in humans and their reactions to it. Hutchinson sued for defamation, and prevailed. Hutchinson was deemed not to be a public figure, and therefore liability could and did rest upon a finding of negligence on the part of the publisher—in this case Senator Proxmire.

Before turning to the implications of the *Hutchinson* case for defamation law in general, a few observations can be made about the Court's approach to the case. First, the analysis of whether Hutchinson was a public figure seems wholly unenlightening, and largely if not completely irrelevant to the issues in the case. This case amply illustrates the impossibly subtle, if not arbitrary, distinctions courts are drawing between public and private persons under present defamation law. The analysis of this issue takes place in a virtual vacuum, as nowhere is there any discussion of the *reason why* the public figure question is relevant to the interests in the case. Yet the answer to this question, for all practical purposes, determines the outcome of the case.

Second, the question of the type and extent of reputational injury caused by the statement is virtually submerged in the case. By the time of appellate review, that issue remains unaddressed in any careful analytical fashion.

Finally, by virtue of the constitutional privilege standards, the result in the case turns almost entirely on the issue of falsity, and the resolution of the falsity issue turns largely on an assessment of the speaker's conduct and motive based on what was and should have been known at the time of publication rather than the actual truth or falsity of the challenged statements. It seems virtually certain in this case that Hutchinson's primary motivation for suing was to clear his name. In this respect Hutchinson's motivation is similar to that of most of the libel plaintiffs surveyed. Falsity is the chief issue to plaintiffs, not the motive of the speaker or the reasonableness of conduct at the time of publication. The result, interestingly enough, is quite understandable under existing defamation standards, as reputation is in fact hardly considered, the question being largely one of knowledge of falsity at the time of publication; and the conclusion that Hutchinson was not a public figure, while not the product of satisfying analysis, is plausible under existing caselaw.

Whether the *Hutchinson* case was rightly or wrongly decided under the current approach to libel cases, however, is beside the point. Instead, the important point is that the Court's very approach is symptomatic of the larger problems the case illustrates. Had Hutchinson been deemed a public figure, the result would have been against him, yet one must wonder why a difference of such subtle degree should have such a profound impact on the result. In reputational terms, Hutchinson's claim to injury would arguably be stronger if he is deemed a public figure, yet this finding would yield the opposite result.

Clearly the public figure issue is based on a different set of interests, expressed in First Amendment terms, but in a sense one must accept this on faith as the analysis never reaches this issue, and the general theory and principles underlying the public figure privilege have rightly been criticized as unexpressed and indiscriminate. It is appropriate, for example, to conclude that speech on issues of public importance should be encouraged and protected; but is the plaintiff's status as a public figure the proper measure of that rule, and is the subjective intent and motive of the publisher an acceptable way to weed out instances of unprotected speech falling within the principle? If we can no longer explain away the courts' approach to these unanswered questions by reference to the need to protect reputational interests—because such interests are no longer really at work—then the structure of rules and privileges built around reputation should be discarded and the whole issue re-examined.

Without the foundation of reputation, there seems to be no basis for imposing liability on speech merely because it is false. That is, however, precisely what courts seem to be doing today in light of the conclusion that reputation is not being seriously considered in the cases, and in view of the fact that the cases simply cannot be explained in any systematic fashion by reference to the interest in reputation. In the absence of another justification for government intervention in such instances as Hutchinson's, therefore, defamation law should be formally interred, as it actually expired some years ago.

It is possible, however, to view such cases as Hutchinson's as instructive of another, markedly different, and more narrowly tailored approach to instances of falsity published widely. We might view the First Amendment interest, which has stricken defamation, as the much more complex question that it actually is; then the issue in such cases as Hutchinson's could be defined, not exclusively in terms of prohibitions of speech and protection of falsity in public and private discourse, but rather in terms of the underlying purposes of the free speech and press guarantees, and the self-governing hypotheses which underlie them. Couldn't an approach be crafted by which the freedom to speak, even falsely, is fully protected, but the interest in counteracting falsity with true fact can at the same time be assured in limited settings where the falsity, if uncorrected, might seriously distort reputation and disserve the public interest in *full* expression and the process of self-government?

The *Hutchinson* case might best be approached in such terms, the question being whether the statement, as understood in the real communication process, was actually false, and whether its reputational consequences as well as its public relevance is of such moment as to warrant correction. There are many other instances in which the case for correction is much more compelling, such as factual allegations concerning a political candidate or a public official. [102] It is ironic—if not worse—that the constitutional privileges constructed by the Supreme Court foreclose any effective vindication of a public First Amendment interest in the very cases in which that interest is most compelling, yet those privileges permit recovery and the sanctioning of false expression only in the cases where the interest in truth on any but an individual level is most attenuated, and where in any event that interest is hardly acknowledged.

The Public Tort of Abuse of Privilege

The simple formulation of the tort of defamation has been radically transformed by constitutional law, and in ways that were unanticipated and unintended. The common law tort was firmly grounded in reputation;

truth was an affirmative defense, not because falsity was otherwise presumed, but because reputation based on truth, no matter how damaging, ought not to be discouraged as a matter of public policy. Liability was strictly determined rather than based on the publisher's fault. Privileges were narrowly tailored to fit certain substantive policies favoring open expression in particularized settings, not broadly categorical ones.

The constitutionalization of the common law has swept much of this common law aside. Reputation seems largely to be ignored or treated half-heartedly in the public defamation cases. The tort instead seems focused almost exclusively around falsity rather than reputation. Presently, however, the focus is *around* rather than *on* the question of falsity because the constitutional privileges foreclose as a practical matter the forthright consideration of falsity of the published statement itself. *Subjective* or *vicarious* falsity is a better description of the public defamation tort's focus, as the issue of falsity is most often formulated in terms of the subjective knowledge or belief of the publisher, coupled with the publisher's course of action prior to publication. The strict liability character of the underlying tort, as well as most specific privileges, have been submerged by sweeping categorical privileges requiring that fault be determined in virtually every public case.

What emerges from the Supreme Court's decisions and an assessment of the totality of decided cases is a reformulated public defamation tort best described as abuse of privilege through reckless publication of a factual statement about another. In substance, the privileges themselves have become the cause of action. The new tort reflects the ironic conjunction of two central premises of current public defamation law: first, the central focus of the tort is subjective belief about falsity, not actual falsity, or its materiality; and second, the privileges shift emphasis from reputation to the publisher's beliefs about falsity. Liability, therefore, can be and occasionally is predicated on a determination that the publisher *thought or should have thought* that the statement was false, *whether or not it was actually and materially false.*[103]

The actual course of decisions suggests that liability can be imposed on "truth" as long as doubts were entertained about truth at the time of publication and the factual statement was recklessly published. This observation, combined with the lack of consistency reflected in the actual determination of recklessness, raises constitutional concerns of the highest magnitude. While the expressed basis for the constitutional privileges was to protect published *falsity* in the absence of recklessness or negligence, the actual result seems also to protect the publication of *truth only insofar* as the publisher can establish it or the publisher's conduct falls short of recklessness or negligence.[104] This turning of the constitutional tables is exacerbated by the disincentives to the defense of truth, for failure in that defense carries the risk of prejudice; the publisher is often not best situated to provide evidence on truth as such, and the privileges provide incentives to the publisher to direct all efforts toward seeking their shelter.

Finally, notwithstanding this substantial transformation of the defamation tort, there is no evidence to suggest that the new formulation of the tort comports more fully with plaintiff interests, more effectively selects out those cases in which liability *should* be imposed by its own criteria, or avoids the often byzantine and impenetrable quality of the common law privileges. Moreover, there is reason to believe that the reformulated tort disserves the publisher's interests by fostering intrusion into the newsroom, and countenances the imposition of liability in instances flatly inconsistent with the constitutional principles around which the new tort has been shaped.

The focus on issues of publisher conduct and state of mind to the exclusion of the substantive elements of reputation, harm, and actual falsity and truth represent a proceduralization of the common law tort. Issues of constitutional privilege do not bear upon the strength of the underlying cause of action. To the extent that such issues bear an uncertain relationship to constitutional principle and theory, they represent little more than a network of procedural impediments to be overcome in litigation. In any event, they appear in practice to divert attention from the common law interests, even in successful cases; to take on a substantive force of their own; and to dominate the litigation.

The privileges, however, have done more. They have generated an additional type of proceduralization that has added great complexity and expense to public defamation litigation. The privileges have made editorial material relevant to the cause of action;[105] they have spawned litigation on discovery, disclosure, and jurisdictional issues; and they have caused an enormous commitment of pre-trial and appellate resources to the adjudication of public defamation claims.[106] It now commonly if not almost inevitably happens that prolonged discovery will precede trial of the action, that issues of access to editorial material will be pressed in court, and that claims of privilege and protection from disclosure will consume a large proportion of the time of lawyers, trial judges, and appellate tribunals—all in advance of any consideration of the merits of the defamation claim.

In assessing the consequences of the procedural elements of the defamation action, as well as the clear problems associated with disgorgement of the journalistic and editorial processes of the publishers, it is critical that the source of these problems be understood. While it would be wrong to conclude that these problems were never experienced at common law, it would be equally wrong to assign the responsibility for the present state of affairs to the common law. The responsibility, ironically enough, lies with the constitutional—not the common—law. The single most sweeping change introduced by the constitutionalization of media defamation law was the introduction of *fault* as a necessary, and primary, element in every case. Finding fault requires assigning blame, and that judgment must and does rest on a conclusion drawn about the subjective awareness of the writer and editor, and the process involved in the gathering, assimilating, and interpreting of information, and the writing or producing and editing of the published statement. It is, therefore, because of the need to find fault that the editorial process must be disgorged, that the steps leading to publication must be explored, and that the actual frame of mind of the principal parties to the publication must be ascertained. It should be noted that this is not happening because plaintiffs are principally concerned about fault; they are not. It is the defendants whose interests the privileges are designed to serve. But the very privileges designed to safeguard editorial freedom, ironically, have required the searching judicial examination of the editorial process.

In respect both to the application of privilege rules and the extended pre-trial process, the need to assign fault as a constitutionally required precondition to recovery for defamation has shifted the focus of the tort and led to increasing emphasis on procedure rather than substance in its litigation. Ironically, the proceduralization of defamation has shifted costs to the defendants, not to the plaintiffs, and the procedural obstacles have deterred publishers more than plaintiffs. For plaintiffs, suing is cheap. Most plaintiffs win by suing, they do not necessarily sue to win. The obstacles to ultimate recovery are frustrating and bothersome to plaintiffs, but they are not in the end an effective deterrent. The most effective deterrent to the frivolous or ill-motivated claim—an efficient, fair, *and prompt*, determination of the truth or falsity of that which was published—is effectively foreclosed by the privileges and procedures themselves.

Setting the Record Straight: A Direction for Reform

While the source of many of the concerns expressed here about the present status of defamation law is the imposition of constitutional privileges on the common law doctrines, the solution to the resulting problems does not lie in reformulation of the constitutional privileges. The basic system of constitutional privileges reflects in generally appropriate ways the specific First Amendment interests implicated by the common law formulations of the tort and the damage remedies they permit. It cannot be denied that, as presently formulated, the tort of defamation demands privileges that are chiefly designed to safeguard against the censorship and unwarranted punishment of expression which, while false, reflects processes of publication that should be respected.

That this system of privileges has had the additional consequences of skewing the practical application of the common law tort, and of shifting judicial focus from reputation toward privilege issues, is as much the result of the common law's intractability as it is of a misconceived view of constitutional privileges. A greater degree of reformulating and readjusting of the constitutional privileges has taken place than most would care to admit, and in the end this effort has achieved little in the way of more satisfactory results. This is because the problem lies not primarily with the privileges, but with the underlying law of defamation. It is, therefore, to the defamation tort, itself, and the adjudication process it demands, that we must look for reform, not to the constitutional standards.

A wide variety of reforms—many of very recent vintage—have been proposed for the litigation of defamation suits. The various proposals, and their authors, will not be cataloged here. It is sufficient for present purposes to state that the reforms include proposed mini-trials on the question of falsity; bifurcated verdicts on the elements of defamation, falsity, and privilege; declaratory judgment suits on the question of falsity alone; and modification of the underlying common law tort. These and other proposals share an important common ingredient: they each attempt to focus all or part of the litigation on falsity, unencumbered by fault.

It is not our intention to survey or analyze the many proposals that have been made. Each raises difficult issues, including the practicability of adjudicating truth in certain contexts, the possibility that more, rather than fewer, disputes will be encouraged, and the likelihood of their modification once placed in the political arena. These and other questions should be the focus of further research; we will touch upon them only briefly, if at all, in the pages that follow.

Notwithstanding the many questions that remain to be addressed, we believe that the various proposals warrant serious consideration. They represent alternative means of accomplishing the important objective of focusing straightforwardly on whether the offending publication is true or false, thereby directing attention toward the central question for the parties to the suit as well as for the public, whose interest lies in accurate as well as open expression.

In the following pages we outline and analyze the general elements of a reformulated defamation action. In doing so, we make no claim of originality. Nor do we suggest that the action we describe would be superior to other reforms that have been or will be proposed. Instead, we outline a new tort action simply as a convenient means of focusing on the two elements that we consider central to future reform: emphasizing the issue of truth or falsity; and eliminating money damages in favor of a remedy that goes directly to curing reputational harm.

The Action to Set the Record Straight

The libel plaintiff's chief interest is achieving a public determination of the falsity of the reputationally harmful challenged statement. The defendant's chief interest is freedom from costs and liability, freedom from intrusion into the editorial process, and freedom to publish that which reason suggests should be published. Neither of these interests is being well served in theory or practice today. For these reasons, we will outline a reformulation of the defamation tort free of present constitutional privileges. We have given the tort a new name—setting the record straight—so as to avoid needless confusion with existing rules. It would remain, however, a personal cause of action arising from publication harmful to reputation, the purpose of the action being to set the record straight. The basic outlines of the tort will be set out below, and more thorough discussion of selected issues will be addressed in subsequent sections.

The essence of the tort would be an action brought to remedy individual reputational harm by setting the record straight. The tort would apply to all libel actions, whether previously denominated "public" or "private." The plaintiff would be required to plead and prove the following elements of the cause of action: the material falsity of a specific, defined, factual statement that concerned the plaintiff, that was published, and that caused reputational harm to the plaintiff in the view of other persons who heard or read it. The only significant departure in this formulation from the common law of libel is the requirement of proof of falsity, which satisfies certain constitutional concerns and which avoids most of the problems associated with the present constitutional privilege for opinion. [107]

The remedy available in the action would be limited to publication of the results of the fact finding process, and this remedy would be available to the plaintiff and the defendant alike. Money damages would not be permitted; the fees and costs of litigation would be borne, respectively, by each of the parties. The constitutional privileges now applied in defamation cases would not apply to the action to set the record straight. This is because, as discussed more fully in a later section, there would be no need for the privileges. Because the issues in the case would focus exclusively on the *actual* truth or falsity, with the burden placed firmly on the plaintiff, there would be no need to explore or render any form of judgment on the process leading to publication. The judgment reached would explicitly disavow any implication of fault or impropriety on the part of the publisher. Nor would the judgment prevent further publication on the very factual issue adjudicated. The finding of the court or tribunal would be published. If the defendant were unwilling to publish the finding of the court, the defendant would have to bear the cost of having it published elsewhere.

The approach reflected in the reformulated tort is structured to achieve the overriding goal of responsiveness to the legitimate and *real* objectives of the principal parties to the libel action: the plaintiff, the defendant, and the public's interest in the free exchange of ideas. While the setting the record straight tort, as well as the other proposed reforms which share common elements, appear straightforward and simple, there are many implications which must be explored further. The major implications will be discussed in the following sections.

Plaintiff Interests and Defamation Law

The legal transformation of defamation law by the constitutional privileges stands in stark contrast to the private purposes being served through public defamation law today. The legal theories and rules appear only to have the most tenuous relationship to the actions of plaintiffs. Thus the problems associated with defamation law today are not simply the legal peculiarities of a transformed tort for abuse of privilege, and the lack of systematic enforcement of legal rules that are fully consistent with freedom of expression; they also involve the apparent irrelevance of the legal rules to the objectives being accomplished by plaintiffs in litigation.

The chief interest of plaintiffs lies in vindicating reputation through proof of falsity; it does not lie in obtaining damages for loss suffered, nor in playing a part in modifying the general functions or processes of the press. The publisher's conduct, in the view of plaintiffs, is wrong principally because what was published was false; fault and responsibility are not at issue, but correction is. The remedy sought is likewise simple, ranging from personal apology, to correction of error, to acknowledgement of mistake.

As a rule, those plaintiffs who sue do so because direct and simple relief for error is not forthcoming. In some cases that may be because there was no error, but in other cases ultimately resulting in suit the reason may simply be that the publisher will not suitably apologize or correct the error, if it is material. A clear pattern emerges from the plaintiffs who sue the press for defamation: when they contact the news organization immediately after publication, they often meet an arrogant or inept response.

In large measure plaintiffs ultimately sue because they have no other alternative. The lawsuit is a means of striking back for a perceived error— whether understandable or not—which is not acknowledged. The lawsuit also is a means, and the only means, of vindication by self-help, and many plaintiffs see legal action as the only way to dispel that which has been published. The legal system serves this objective well in its indecision. Rarely is the simple question of publisher error ever resolved, and rarely is any resolution promptly reached. Fault, privileges, and subjective state of mind have forestalled adjudication of the merits of the dispute.

In the end, it is ironic that the legal system has gone to great lengths to protect expression and adjudicate close questions of privilege, and yet these lengths have little real bearing on the litigation process. While, thanks largely to lawyers operating on contingent fees, the legal rules do discourage many cases that will clearly fail the hurdles of legal doctrine, plaintiffs whose cases pass this screening test seem largely indifferent to the legal rules, for those rules have little to do with their motives in bringing suit. Plaintiffs sue because they feel that they must do *something*, because they have no other alternative available to them, because suing is perceived as a form of self-help in counteracting the defamation, and because they are outraged at the indifference to their feelings expressed in the response of the publisher to their contact.

While the realities of the litigation process may be no different with defamation than other forms of action, it is striking that a fundamental difference exists as to the relief sought by the plaintiffs. Most plaintiffs are not motivated strictly by money. More important, most do not care about using litigation to assess legal fault. They want the record set straight. The legal system translates this motive into financial terms, and the publishers force the plaintiffs to the legal system. Most plaintiffs in civil litigation may be ignorant of and indifferent to legal niceties. In defamation cases, however, the plaintiffs are not necessarily ignorant of the legal rules; they are often indifferent to them because winning or losing the suit is not the chief motivating factor.[108] The act of suing, itself, represents vindication and retribution. This is not only supported by what plaintiffs say; it may be the only possible explanation for a continuing phenomenon of litigation in the face of overwhelming odds.

In the public defamation setting today, therefore, we see a theory of liability that has experienced fundamental transformation by virtue of constitutional privileges. At the same time we see a pattern of plaintiff behavior suggesting that the law is simply an instrument for objectives largely divorced from the doctrine or policies. This dichotomy exists in most, though not in all, cases. It counsels either frustration and indifference in response, or an effort to reform the libel system so that it better reflects the real interests and actual conduct of plaintiffs as well as the legitimate concerns for freedom of expression shared by defendants and the general public alike.

The Disservice of Rules of Privilege

Among the principal ends of the First Amendment are truth and the availability of information and opinion which will contribute to political freedom and democratic self-governance.[109] Falsity is of value only as an instrument to the ascertainment of truth and exchange of views through open expression in the marketplace of ideas. As the Supreme Court has often stated, there is no First Amendment value, as such, in false fact.[110]

Defamation poses special problems in light of these principles. The fact is that in most cases an allegedly defamatory statement's most pressing claim to constitutional protection under the First Amendment—that it concerns an issue of public importance or relates to an influential person—is dependent on its truth. Yet in cases involving the most pressing claim to protection, truth or falsity need not be examined, and generally are not. The privileges are typically adjudicated in advance of the determination of truth or falsity, rendering truth or falsity practically irrelevant. Even with the recent requirement that plaintiffs bear the burden of proving falsity, a review of the actual decisions suggests that the actual malice and negligence issues will practically dominate the decision on falsity.[111]

If, therefore, the constitutional and public significance of the allegedly defamatory statement is contingent in many cases on truth or substantial truth[112] (or at least on the absence of *material* falsity), or (when truth is unascertainable or effective means of correction are operative) on its contribution to discussion leading to truth, the effect of the constitutional fault privileges is to foreclose straightforward consideration of a central question from the perspective of constitutional principle and policy. Such an approach significantly undermines the purposes of both constitutional and common law policies, and it makes intellectually indefensible the claim that existing constitutional rules are necessary in order to protect public interests in expression and self-government.

To illustrate the problems just outlined, we draw on *Rebozo v. Washington Post*.[113] Former President Nixon's friend claimed that an account of his selling, on behalf of the re-election campaign, securities which were known by him to be stolen, was false. The public importance of this factual allegation, even when viewed through the surrogate question of Rebozo's status as a public figure or public official, cannot be determined in the abstract; nor, as present approaches imply, can it be determined by indulging the assumption that it is true. If it is simply false that the securities were stolen and that Rebozo believed them to be stolen, the published statement is clearly not of public importance, whether "importance" be predicated on considerations of public policy or on constitutional interests in free expression. Its only value would lie in its effective correction. Furthermore,

Rebozo's "status" for constitutional purposes has nothing to do with the question of the importance of the false factual statement, unless we are to take the position that even the most loosely conceived drivel on the subject of a person in the media spotlight is to be valued; the Supreme Court has stopped far short of such a proposition.

It is instructive to outline the actual adjudication of the *Rebozo* case in light of the constitutional significance of the statement's falsity. As the circuit court properly analyzed the *Rebozo* case under existing law, the factual statement having been published and an allegation of libel having been made, the initial question to be addressed was the status of the plaintiff. This decision had to be made in advance of and irrespective of any determination of falsity. The court properly concluded under existing law that Rebozo was a public figure at the time of publication and that the actual malice standard applied. Accordingly, truth or falsity was again made legally irrelevant, the sole issue being whether the fact was published recklessly—with subjective knowledge of falsity in terms only of what was known at the time of publication; or by a process under which the publisher harbored serious concerns about falsity and published nevertheless, or was so grossly lax in fact-finding that such a subjective state of mind could be attributed to the publisher.

The immense difficulties associated with proving the malice issues have been dealt with elsewhere. For the present moment we must assume such findings are capable of being adjudicated,[114] and concern ourselves with the consequences of the methodology employed in the *Rebozo* case and the many others it represents.[115] The first consequence is that with the application of the constitutional privilege, the issue of truth or falsity will never be determined in the case, for it has been made practically, if not legally, irrelevant. The nature of the cause of action has become one for abuse of privilege.

Assuming that the statement is actually false, publication will have been protected and recovery denied; and this despite the fact that, were falsity to have been shown, the conclusion should have been that a false fact is not so protected by the First Amendment as to foreclose its correction. This is an important point to repeat, for the effect of a successful claim of privilege in such a case is to foreclose not only liability, but a determination of falsehood which can then be, and may be required to be, published. The privileges, then, may legitimate falsehood and thereby foreclose expression, without the cost of such foreclosure having been weighed in the balance.

If, on the other hand, the statement is true, and if Rebozo were required to bear the burden of disproof on that issue, and were required to do so directly without the complication of proof of fault (publisher *belief* about falsity), he might not have brought the action, for it would then perhaps prove too much. In the absence of that risk, recovery could be had by Rebozo even if he knew the statement to be true, because there is a basis upon which he can establish reckless disregard for the truth by the reporter and editor even though the statement is true; also, at the time of the case, the burden of showing truth rested with the defendant publisher, and proving truth is most often difficult, if not impossible. Even under current law, which would require that Rebozo prove falsity, the actual malice issue may permit him to succeed; proving that the publisher doubted truth and published recklessly—while not the same as proof of falsity—will as a practical matter represent a convincing case for the jury on the falsity question. In such a case the law requires, as a direct consequence of constitutional privileges, that falsehood be vindicated through imposition of liability on truth.

The second consequence of the fault issue foreclosing inquiry into the statement's truth or falsity, or effectively substituting for such a showing, is that the public interest in expression and information in the marketplace is strangely ignored. If the facts of the Rebozo story are false and, as is likely, the privileges foreclose liability, the interest in truth is surely compromised, for the legal effect of foreclosed liability is to legitimize and protect the published falsity. While this does not preclude publication of truth— whether by Rebozo or others—in the future, and while publication of the truth is not *legally* deterred, it is deterred as a practical matter by removing any incentive to its publication and by providing a legal basis upon which truth's integrity can be challenged. This is a consequence which the law ought not to ignore, even though it may not intend. Legitimation of falsehood by a judgment for a defendant on grounds of privilege is a direct and practical, although unintended, consequence of our present approach to libel cases.

One might seek comfort from this conclusion in view of the limited nature of the legal system's determination, coupled with an understanding that the legal decision means no more than that the editorial procedures, while sloppy, cannot be judged legally reckless; one might also hope that broad discussion of such editorial processes would temper the asserted practical consequences of the decision. But even if effective public understanding at this level could be achieved, the system of privileges dashes this hope as well, for constitutional privileges also operate to disable Rebozo as well as the trier of fact from obtaining very much information about the editorial and reportorial processes. [116]

Comfort might also be sought in the argument that Rebozo is always free to introduce evidence of falsity, even though he may not be required to do so. Unfortunately, however, this would often not be possible, as the privilege issue is almost always considered in advance of trial on the merits, and its determination will often foreclose even the opportunity to present evidence on any point other than state of mind. If the plaintiff fails on the privilege issue, the case is ended. If the plaintiff succeeds in proving abuse of privilege, there may be little incentive to introduce additional evidence on the issue of actual truth or falsity, for as a practical matter the actual malice finding will satisfy the plaintiff's burden on the falsity issue.

The public's interest in having falsehood counteracted may therefore be effectively foreclosed under the current state of defamation law. While this may be an occasion for sympathy for Rebozo under the hypothetical facts given, it is an occasion for even greater sympathy for First Amendment interests which the constitutionalized law of libel seems to have forgotten through its system of privileges and its focus on the parties to the controversy, to the exclusion of larger concerns.

It would be simpler and more consistent with First Amendment concerns to adjudicate falsity *in the first instance*, unencumbered by the question of fault. If the statement is found to be false, the statement itself does not deserve or need First Amendment protection in and of itself, but its correction is a matter of constitutional moment. Such a case should be ended at this point, as the public interest has been served, and served well. If, however, we persist in insisting on money damages, privileges could be brought into play in the interest of imposing liability only on conduct that meets some standard of unreasonableness. Whatever the result at this stage, the First Amendment interest and public interest in free expression will have been vindicated, and the point of public interest will have been properly fixed on the correction of falsehood rather than on the falsehood itself, which is behind us in any event, as it has already found its way into the marketplace.

If, on the other hand, the statement is found to be true, even if only by virtue of the absence of convincing proof to the contrary by the plaintiff, adjudication of this question *at the beginning* of the case would avoid the risk that truth will be undermined by imposition of liability on the publisher for abuse of privilege. Moreover, First Amendment concerns would then be directed at the important point of protecting published truth or legitimate uncertainty from liability or correction, and away from issues of privilege which serve as less than perfect measures by which to adjudicate First Amendment principles. Truth would be forthrightly vindicated in such a case—surely a more pleasant prospect than the current state of affairs—but its vindication would not foreclose further publication to the contrary, or even subsequent revelation on that score, a possibility in any case in which the legal system withholds its heavy hand only in the absence of sufficient proof to warrant its use.

Defamation and the Whole Truth

One troubling aspect of the current libel doctrines is their tendency in the adjudication of a case to preclude determination of the whole truth, when full disclosure would not only shed light on the legal dispute but would also serve better the constitutional interests in expression around which the various privileges have been shaped. This result occurs because the present cause of action limits narrowly the relevant questions in the case to the injury caused by a publication and the circumstances surrounding the publication. In cases most likely to involve general public interests in the whole truth, adjudication of truth is virtually foreclosed, the focus being shifted entirely to the process of publication rather than its substance. Examining the question of truth or falsity directly and at the outset, unencumbered by privileges based on fault, would allow a determination of the direction in which constitutional interests in expression should fall, and would also reveal the extent to which the truthfulness or falsity is conditional or incomplete. This, in turn, would allow one to consider whether revealing the condition or completing the truth ought to be part of the judicial resolution in the interests of First Amendment values.

The points just made can be briefly and well illustrated by the case of *Reilly v. Gillen*.[117] In that case Reilly was a candidate running for re-election to the city council, and Gillen was his opponent. Several days before the election Gillen mailed an undertermined number of letters containing a copy of a 23-year-old newspaper article reporting that Reilly had been charged with conspiracy. Not mentioned in the letter was the fact that the charge had later been dismissed and Reilly had been exonerated. Reilly lost the election, sued for libel, and recovered damages against only one of the defendant republishers.

What is instructive about the *Reilly* case is the effect of defamation rules and constitutional privileges on exactly what was adjudicated in the case. The main focus of the case was the proper application of privileges: whether a qualified privilege applied by virtue of republication; whether Reilly was a public figure capable of succeeding only upon a showing of actual malice; whether the defendant knew of or harbored serious reservations about the statement's falsity at the time of publication. In the end, liability was predicated on the reckless manner in which Gillen published the statement, having had reason to know of its falsity or seriously to doubt its truth in light of subsequent events.

The imposition of liability on the basis of these legal considerations achieved only partial satisfaction for Reilly, as one of the defendants was freed from liability because actual malice could not be established. Equally as significant, however, the court's action—shaped by the issues addressed in the case—yielded virtually no satisfaction to other and equally pressing public interests in information and expression: the interest in truth, and in disclosure of the surrounding circumstances of dismissal and exoneration which may have made literal truth misleading, and left the real truth disguised in the absence of information never published. In short, what is missing in the court's perfectly legal approach to the cause is the whole truth.

The imposition of liability will not assure a remedy to the constitutional parties in interest—the public who would care to read the whole truth. Yet we cannot escape the force of their interest by calling the case a purely private cause of action. It is a cause of action publicly endorsed and created; it is based on the public consequences of expression in terms of the perceptions and attitudes of the readers; and it is interlaced with privileges and doctrines whose express source and purpose is the protection of free expression. The phrase "private cause of action" is descriptive only of what is, not what ought to be.

Safeguarding Freedom of Speech and Freedom of the Press

Multi-dimensional issues surround the constitutional validity of reforms directed toward the falsity issue, including the tort of setting the record straight, as they all focus on the adjudication of truth or falsity and eliminate or suspend the privileges based on fault. The question of constitutionality must first respond to the view that the privileges spawned by the *Sullivan* case and its progeny are necessary to protect free expression and a free press notwithstanding the absence of First Amendment value in false fact itself. Imposition of liability on falsehood would discourage robustness of expression which is instrumental to First Amendment theory, implicit in the historical origins of the guarantee, and inextricably linked to our experience over the past two centuries.[118] Second, a constitutional analysis must account for the proposition that with respect to the press in particular, the adjudication of truth or falsity with a view to its confirmation or correction may directly conflict with the central principle of editorial freedom.[119] Finally, it must be determined whether the adjudication of falsity, no matter how structured and no matter how accepted it seems to be in current defamation law, can be squared with the guarantees of free speech and press when the instrument of adjudication is government.

These are serious problems of fundamental proportion which must be fully addressed and resolved in advance of any reform directed toward the issue of falsity rather than fault. They must, moreover, be resolved in their full dimension, rather than solely through a process of reasoning by analogy from decided cases or from doctrine. To this end, a number of specific arguments in support of a reformulated tort focusing on falsity should be noted, but not considered determinative of the broader constitutional concerns to which we shall thereafter turn. These arguments address the question whether the imposition of liability in the form of correction of material deemed false would be foreclosed under existing constitutional doctrine. First, the adjudication of truth or falsity is in fact now countenanced in defamation cases, although for reasons discussed above the question is directly adjudicated only infrequently. [120] While a determination of falsity is not a constitutional precondition to liability in all libel actions today, courts are increasingly mandating it, and the Supreme Court has required it in most media cases. [121] Second, the workings of defamation law strongly suggest that the imposition of fault and liability in the form of actual and punitive damages (as also the lesser remedy of correction) on false and reckless expression is constitutionally permissible even under the most robust view of the First Amendment. [122] To be sure, the requirement in most cases that recklessness be shown is viewed as a limiting rule, but it seems equally clear that liability can be imposed on truth if recklessly published. [123] Finally, the facts that liability can be imposed on an exercise of editorial judgment by the press; that induced correction has not been declared unconstitutional; and that correction of previously published facts confirms rather than restrains editorial judgments—together preclude the argument that a reformulated tort for setting the record straight is clearly foreclosed by presently decided cases. [124]

The larger question, however, is whether constitutional concerns *ought* to be viewed as preclusive notwithstanding existing doctrine. This requires us to look more expansively to the purposes of the First Amendment guarantees of speech and press. Each can be taken in order, starting with the speech guarantee.

The purpose of the speech guarantee is to assure freedom of expression and thought, and this is done, as the Supreme Court reminds us, through a "profound national commitment to the principle that debate on public issues should be uninhibited, robust, and wide-open." [125] The debate must permit "vehement, caustic, and sometimes unpleasantly sharp attacks on government and public officials," and must be permitted to extend to all "issues about which information is needed or appropriate to enable the members of society to cope with the exigencies of their period." [126]

It is this conception of the speech guarantee that accounts for the resolution of the seditious libel controversy, [127] that compels special rules all but foreclosing government restraint of speech in advance of its publication, [128] and that informs the privileges of actual malice and negligence in the public defamation cases. As to the latter observation, rules governing allegedly defamatory expression must, at least, leave room for uninhibited, robust, and wide-open statements, even statements of a factual character only, lest failure to *know* truth—often a metaphysical matter—will discourage taking desired risks in its assertion. The principle that safeguards these concerns is editorial judgment: if the decision to publish is a product of reasoned choice and selection of material and format, it is protected under the First Amendment as an exercise of editorial judgment. Actual malice and negligence, which are concerned with the process of subjective judgment, define the line between editorial judgment and calculated indifference to the interest in reasoned discussion.[129] Only unforgivable publication having no respect whatsoever for truth can be penalized.

Can a tort predicated on the interest in setting the record straight on factually erroneous statements that harm an individual's reputation be squared with these principles and admonitions? There is good reason to believe that it can be, assuming that the burden of disproof lies squarely with the plaintiff, that fault plays no part in the cause of action, and that relief is limited to the vindication of truth in respect to factual statements alone. At base, the reason for this conclusion is the *compatibility* of the tort (or the allied reforms) with the ends of the speech guarantee itself.

One must start with the fundamental proposition that with respect to public matters debate must be uninhibited and robust. Present defamation law both inhibits debate and discourages its robustness through the prospect of extended and costly litigation, the possibility of substantial damage awards, and the potential disgorging of editorial processes and judgments in the course of litigation. How often these consequences occur, whether the perception of their likelihood comports with reality, and whether they are justified are matters relating as much to perception as to fact.[130] Based at least on perception there seems little room for arguing that these factors play no significant and inhibiting role. A tort of setting the record straight would substantially avoid these problems, as the more straightforward cause of action could greatly simplify the trial process, and might encourage other and less formal processes to be employed. It may also facilitate a far greater incidence of private resolution by the parties, as the impediments of advice of counsel would be removed.

The setting the record straight concept, whether in the form of a new tort or as a modification of existing law, would avoid the inhibitions flowing from substantial damage awards and the need by the publisher to defend against a finding of *fault*. No damages would be permitted, and fault would be irrelevant, the sole objective being to permit the subject of the article to have the record set straight. This would likewise clarify the judgments to be made and the forces to be considered in advance of publication. Reasonable care as dictated by standards of the journalistic profession itself, for example, would presumably be applied to publication decisions, not because the law requires or incorporates such standards, but rather because the profession itself embraces them. The job of articulating standards of reporting would be the province of the profession, where it belongs, no matter how imperfectly that responsibility has been exercised in the past. [131]

Finally, the absence of damages and the concomitant elimination of fault sweeps away the need for present constitutional privileges, especially those whose other edge penetrates the substantive editorial processes of the newsroom. [132] It is well to remember that the problems attendant to broad discovery relating to the reporters' and editors' state of mind, the material included and excluded, sources of information, and the bases for editorial judgment, are not the consequence of the common law, but rather result largely from the constitutional law and its requirement of recklessness or negligence as a precondition to liability. In this respect the *Sullivan* case is something of a hollow victory for free expression, for in limiting liability it withdrew confidentiality for the editorial process. By eliminating fault as an element, reforms directed toward the truth issue, including the tort of setting the record straight, would simplify the adjudication process and, equally as important, remove the present apprehensions which may have had an inhibiting and moderating influence on expression.

Freedom of expression finds its fullest and most pressing command in the injunction against prior restraints—prohibitions of speech in advance of its publication. [133] This principle, of course, is a corollary of the command that speech be uninhibited and robust; the prospect of injunction will deter expression more directly than the prospect of subsequent punishment. The tort of setting the record straight (and the other reform proposals it represents) is responsive to the command against prior restraint and its corollary command that open expression be encouraged, for it leaves previously-made speech unrestricted and unpunished—an improvement over the present situation. Through its purpose of setting the record straight without determination of fault or liability, the tort's concept encourages wide-open speech, making the rationale of protecting uninhibited expression more forceful by virtue of the possibility of correction. For once the tort would provide a full and complete justification for an absolute prohibition on prior restraint with respect to false factual statements damaging to the reputation of another. And it avoids the real danger under present law that falsity may be unintentionally legitimized and competing speech discouraged or snuffed out.

The most compelling case, however, is not the consistency of the tort with the First Amendment speech guarantee, but its congruence with the guarantee's very purposes. The First Amendment does not guarantee uninhibited and robust expression as an end in itself, but rather as an instrument by which information is available to the members of society about issues bearing on the exigencies of their period, be they political, social, economic, cultural, or personal in character.[134] False fact—particularly that which may be legitimized—has no value *as such* when measured against this ultimate policy, and the Supreme Court's repeated statements to that effect are clearly correct.[135]

This is not to say that the end of the First Amendment is truth. As the late Professor Bickel said, truth is too elusive, too subject to fallibilities, too "relative" to embody with mathematical and moral certainty in the constitution. Rather, the end of the First Amendment is speech.[136] It is equally clear, however, that there exists such a thing as falsity which is capable of proof as to some assertions of fact, notwithstanding its frequent difficulties of proof and its relativity in view of the surrounding circumstances. Falsity need not be provable in all cases for its vindication in some to be worthwhile to an injured party. When it is unprovable, an action should not lie. But where error can be established, false fact on a public matter and relating to an individual should not be legitimized, as it can be under present law. More fundamentally, the disclosure of true facts in the face of published falsity represents speech on an issue and should be as entitled to protection as falsity, if not more so. A tort whose function is to adjudge falsity in the limited confines of factual statements damaging to the reputation of an individual represents nothing more than further speech contributing to the information needed by members of society to enable them to cope with the exigencies of their period. Truth competing with prior factual statements, even if only a species of truth determined through adjudication, contributes to the dissemination of information upon which personal and public decisions are made and actions are taken, and therefore contributes to the First Amendment.

While the reforms that would focus on the issue of falsity, which we have illustrated through a discussion of a tort of setting the record straight, can in our view be harmonized with the speech guarantee, a distinct set of constitutional considerations pertaining to the press must also be taken into account. Here the concerns are additive, but are also distinct from freedom of expression as an individual right, relating instead to the function and effective operation of "institutional public speech"—which we shall call "press"—in a free democratic society. The applicable principles have been variously described, but boil down to three: preserving the press' "checking" function, or its responsibility independently to monitor and report on centers of public and private moment in society; preserving editorial freedom as a necessary incident to its checking role; and preserving the press' separateness from government, but not its independence from law in general, through a principle of neutrality which prohibits singling it out for imposition of a burden or conferral of a benefit.[137] It is the first two principles that are of present concern, as neither defamation law nor a reformulated tort of setting the record straight singles out the press.

An adjudication of falsity without a determination of fault and free of the prospect of damage awards would, if anything, enhance the press' position as an institution whose mission is to serve as an informational check on public and private affairs. The removal of inhibitions in advance of publication, discussed above in connection with speech principles, would effectively free the press in its publication and in its exercise of editorial judgment. Moreover, the checking principle does not connote checking as an end in itself, but rather as an instrument for accomplishing the ultimate goals discussed previously—providing information to members of society to enable them to cope with the exigencies of their period. The flow of more information through adjudication of falsity with respect to reputationally damaging facts that were reported about an individual does not disserve this ultimate goal, as the objective of the guarantees is speech and information.

Yet the press, in the view of many, performs an additional function of monitoring public affairs which is independent of the rights of the readers or viewers under the speech guarantee. This role of the press serving as a center of influence independent of government is protected and assured by the principle of editorial freedom—the freedom to make judgments about when to publish and what to publish free of government influence. It is here that the apparent conflict of constitutional principle with the various reform proposals focusing on falsity is most acute, and it is here that the strongest language of the Supreme Court can be found, starting with the Court's invalidation of the Florida right to reply statute in *Miami Herald Publishing Company v. Tornillo.*[138]

Notwithstanding the absoluteness with which editorial freedom has been protected, the limited adjudication of falsity anticipated by the various proposals presents a different situation than that with which the Court has dealt, and arguably can be reconciled with editorial freedom as well. The *Tornillo* and related cases dealt with opinion, not fact, and with the newspaper's obligation to make its pages available for a point of view different from that arrived at as a matter of editorial judgment. The protection of editorial judgment as a matter of constitutional protection for the press is, at its core, protection for point of view.[139] Freedom of point of view is a central element of the press' role as a distinct center of influence. The remedy of adjudicating falsity without determining fault, and publishing truth or correction, does not involve point of view directly, although it may do so indirectly because a point of view may be contingent on the false fact. To the extent this is so, correction will implicate the publisher's point of view, but only in the publisher's own terms because the reliance on fact to support opinion is a judgment already made, and made freely, by the publisher at the time of original publication.

To be sure, however, the remedy of correction by further publication will, independently of the point of view issue, require publication by the press when it might otherwise choose not to do so. One response to this concern would be to forego required correction by the publisher as an element of remedy. Vindication by the injured plaintiff would still be obtained, but in narrower terms unless the publisher or another publisher chose to write about the factual error. Another response would be to view the limited need to correct factual error as conforming in most instances with editorial judgment previously made. At the time of initial publication the fact at issue was freely deemed worthy of publication by the publisher, and the same can be said of the selection of facts and the relevance of the facts reported to the substance of the article or broadcast. Required correction of factual error by the publisher or in another publication at the publisher's expense, therefore, is consistent with and may complement the previous free editorial judgment about selection and materiality of facts and worthiness as news. If editorial freedom in *substance* means that judgments about worthiness for publication, manner of presentation, and material to be included be free from government influence, the reformulated tort of setting the record straight can be reconciled with the First Amendment, as correction of fact confirms the very judgments already freely made. If, on the other hand, editorial freedom confers an absolute right to control what is printed, where it is printed, and when it is printed free from subsequent review of its falsity and reputational harm, and free of the obligation to correct or pay for the cost of publishing the adjudicated facts elsewhere, the full remedy of correction cannot be constitutionally enforced. The latter view, however, does not find support in the cases that have been decided or in the applicable First Amendment principles; were it to do so, the tort of defamation as we now know it could not exist.

The final constitutional issue related to the proposed tort of setting the record straight is the validity under the First Amendment of adjudication of truth or falsity by government through its judicial arm, even though limited to disproved factual statements injurious to an individual's reputation. The principle concern would parallel the Sedition Act controversy: the prospect that by incorporating truth in law the government can make only certain ideas lawful.[140] A legal determination of "truth" in the course of litigation could carry this spectre with it.

The force of this view is contingent on that which is legally determined, and its force and effect. Without doubt, the imposition of liability for defamation represents an adjudication of fact closely analogous to that which would be required under the reformulated tort, yet such concerns have not arisen. The reason they have not arisen lies in the explicit and limited effect of a judgment, and in the observation that what is adjudicated is most decidedly *not* truth.

Both current defamation law and the tort of setting the record straight represent adjudication of a private dispute, and the remedy is both legally and constitutionally limited to the interests of the private parties to the controversy. The dispute relates to the factual accuracy of a statement of fact, its consequences, and the appropriate remedy to the party injured by the publication. The tort of setting the record straight is in no sense different in these respects from defamation, as the consequence of adjudicating falsity as between the parties is of legal effect only as to them, and the remedy of correction is tailored to the plaintiff's interests as they have been determined to exist in fact. That the remedy also serves broader interests in expression should not be understood to mean that the judgment carries broader legal force and effect, nor that the judgment in any way shuts off further publication on the same subject.

It is also a misapprehension to view the defamation tort, the setting the record straight action, or any of the related reform proposals, as representing an adjudication of "truth." Instead, it represents an adjudication of falsity in fact, and it does that only if the plaintiff can bear a heavy burden of proof on that issue. This is no small distinction in theory or in fact, as the most that is decided is that the stated fact or facts were deemed incorrect through an established and impartial adversarial process. Other views of the facts are not foreclosed; indeed, disagreement with the determination of falsity by the original publisher is neither foreclosed nor subject to any subsequent liability.

If we are to foreclose defamation actions as well as those reforms explored here we must do so notwithstanding the limited nature of the adjudication, notwithstanding the many contexts in which facts are found, albeit imperfectly, and notwithstanding the contribution that such an adjudication, properly understood, can make to the goals of the First Amendment. A decision to foreclose an action to set the record straight would also have to acknowledge that in doing so we would not resolve the problem of truth and falsity in public discourse; we would merely shift it. Absolutely foreclosing the judicial branch from adjudicating falsity, no matter how limited the context, would not have the effect of leaving the question of truth open for continued debate, or at least it would not do so to any greater extent. Instead, it would leave resolution of the question in the hands of the publisher, a result generally to be preferred but certainly not required by the First Amendment in the context of a limited inquiry into the truth or falsity of a factual statement causing serious reputational harm to an individual.

9

THE NEED TO EXPLORE NON-LITIGATION ALTERNATIVES

OUR EXAMINATION of libel suits against the media was undertaken to better understand the dynamics of the libel dispute, and the actions and objectives of the parties to it. We have probed more deeply than those before us, employing a variety of research methodologies and applying social science research techniques to the legal system in relatively unprecedented ways. We have attempted to make our interpretations and conclusions clear, as well as the data on which they are based, so that others can assess our judgments and explore beyond them. While there is much we know about libel disputes and suits, there is much more that we do not know, and we hope that our efforts will help to define the important issues that remain.

Given our objective of thoroughly examining the libel dispute from beginning to end, and given the scope that such an objective dictates, our analysis has covered a broad range of specific but interrelated material, and a seamless web of specific conclusions. Certain general or overriding conclusions can be identified.

228

1. The dominant interest of most libel plaintiffs is correction of falsity, or setting the record straight. If it is to reflect the plaintiffs' interest and their actual conduct, therefore, libel law must focus directly on the question of falsity.

2. The manner in which the press deals with plaintiffs following publication unnecessarily fosters litigation. The press, therefore, has some self-examination to do.

3. The libel tort is now one for enforcement of press responsibility, not for injury to private reputation. This turning of the constitutional privilege tables may encourage litigation. If the libel litigation process were redirected toward falsity and reputational harm, with the plaintiff having a heavy burden of proof, most privilege issues could be greatly simplified or even eliminated, and the risk to plaintiffs that falsity could not be proved would provide a powerful *and needed* disincentive to suit.

4. Most plaintiffs win by suing; they do not necessarily sue to win in court. The very act of suit, itself, represents the only non-self-serving form of response through which plaintiffs' claims of falsity can be legitimized and vindicated through the invocation of formalized judicial scrutiny. Because the legal system only rarely addresses the underlying dispute about falsity, and even more rarely responds promptly, plaintiffs face little, if any, risk that the truth of a statement will be confirmed. The system most disadvantages those whose interest is in truth and most advantages those to whom truth is a threat.

The law of libel seems to have disturbingly little relationship to the real actions and objectives of the parties; what is decided in litigation may be substantially irrelevant to the actual dispute, and the legal rules are encouraging the very conduct that is sought to be discouraged, and discouraging the conduct sought to be encouraged. In seeking solutions, our approach should be shaped by the insights that emerge from the actual process of libel litigation.

Whether viewed singly or as a whole, our conclusions demand a fundamental and searching re-examination of the law of libel. They also demand a clear-minded assessment of the effectiveness with which the constitutional privileges respect legitimate private interests in reputation, serve the ends of freedom of the press, and foster full and robust public discussion concerning issues of public moment.

Our principal conclusions and our suggested responses have been largely directed toward libel law and the process of judicial resolution of libel disputes. Because of tradition, the peculiarly American habit of "going to court," and the equally American faith in law, it is likely that legal reform is the most practical and pressing response to the libel problems being faced today. The ultimate objective of the Iowa Libel Research Project, however, is to assess non-litigation alternatives for libel disputes. This book represents only the culmination of Phase I of the Project.

The information we have gathered is of relevance beyond the confines of judicial disputes. We know more about libel disputes than we know about virtually any other form of civil litigation. We know a great deal about the personal interests, stakes, and actions of the parties between the point of publication and the initiation of suit. We also have suggested that the direction of legal reform should be toward straightforwardness and simplicity. In combination, these considerations suggest that libel disputes may provide a hospitable context for less formal, non-judicial, processes for adjudication, negotiation, or mediation.

A full scale analysis of the adaptability of libel disputes to non-litigation processes is well beyond the scope of this book, and we have yet to develop the information base upon which we can confidently reach conclusions about the features of such processes and their practical feasibility. At the risk of venturing into uncharted terrain, however, it is fitting to explore in general terms the implications for such alternative processes of the information collected here, for the knowledge obtained about libel disputes permits some general observations about the amenability of libel disputes to non-judicial resolution, and the various contexts in which such non-judicial processes might operate. Our comments will be limited to selected observations about the susceptibility of libel disputes to non-judicial processes, and the likely value of employing such processes. The detailed analysis and testing of alternatives will be undertaken in the next phase of the Iowa Libel Research Project.

There is reason to believe that the current attractiveness of alternative, non-judicial dispute processes is based in part on misconceptions of the litigation process, at least in the civil context. The authors of the Wisconsin Civil Litigation Study, the first and most comprehensive study of civil litigation, expressed concern that those encouraging the use of non-litigation processes may see the litigation process as one that only involves formal process and imposed resolution of disputes.[1] Instead, the authors noted that *negotiation*, not formal litigation, dominates the judicial process, and that the utility of non-judicial processes that are structured around negotiation may be limited as an alternative to litigation. Most civil cases involve negotiation, most are settled without imposed judicial resolution, and most of the work of lawyers is devoted to negotiation, not to trial.[2] These facts do not mean that non-litigation processes are unworthy of exploration, but they do suggest that the reasons for employing them, the processes they employ, and the benefits yielded must take these facts into account.

The care with which non-litigation processes should be justified and structured applies in the specific context of libel suits as well as to civil litigation in general. There are, however, some significant apparent differences between libel suits and most other forms of civil litigation that should be noted, and that have particular relevance to the prospects of non-litigation alternatives for the resolution of libel claims. First, our data suggest that the pattern of negotiation and settlement in libel cases departs dramatically from that found in most other forms of civil litigation. While we have no direct and comparable evidence of the time libel lawyers devote to negotiation, we do know, for example, that a high proportion of libel plaintiffs whose cases are ultimately adjudicated decide to sue before seeing a lawyer, that the rate of settlement appears to be substantially lower than that applicable to other forms of civil litigation, and that the vehicle of a lawsuit is an important (although symbolic) ingredient of the plaintiffs' motivation, for such a suit represents a form of legitimizing the plaintiffs' claim *because* it invokes the formal machinery of the judicial system. While some of these features of libel litigation may make more difficult the consent of the parties to a non-litigation process, they suggest, on the other hand, that the yield of a non-litigation alternative in terms of cost and efficiency may be significantly greater than for most other forms of civil litigation, where alternative channels such as negotiation are already actively operating beneath the surface of the formal process.

Second, the libel dispute seems more exclusively to concern a clash of principles than an argument concerning compensation for financial or economic harm. As the plaintiffs tell us, and as common sense suggests, money is neither the ideal remedy nor, for that matter, a necessary one in many—perhaps most—libel disputes. Indeed, the best remedy would not involve money; it would involve prompt correction and apology. While most other forms of civil litigation may involve clashes of principle in varying degrees, they also frequently involve disputed claims over money, and money is often a necessary element of the resolution. The predominance of principle over money may make it more difficult to obtain the parties' consensus on a non-litigation process, but the possibility that money can be eliminated as a necessary ingredient of that process may greatly simplify the dispute with which such a process must deal.

Finally, there are fairly clear incentives built into a non-litigation alternative for virtually all participants in the libel suit. For most plaintiffs, an alternative process getting promptly to the heart of the dispute (falsity) should be attractive, assuming that the result is fairly arrived at and published. This would provide the very relief that the vast majority of plaintiffs with legitimate claims are seeking—even many of those who experience real economic harm—and would provide that relief fully rather than only partially and symbolically, as at present. Plaintiff lawyers, who now appear to subsidize a large proportion of plaintiff claims, would more likely be compensated for their representation, as the absence of damages would make contingency arrangements unfeasible.

The defendants would also find substantial incentives in an alternative non-litigation process for resolving libel claims. The absence of money damages would remove the spectre of oppressive financial loss—something that only rarely happens but still seems to dominate the press' attitudes. Libel insurance premiums, which have increased, could be dramatically reduced. Perhaps most significantly, the elimination of privileges and simplification of fact-finding could substantially reduce the libel defendants' heavy commitment of resources to the litigation process.

The incentives for attorneys representing libel defendants are less clear. This may be the only group with no incentive other than the interests of the client, for their libel work could be substantially reduced. The amount of libel litigation involved in representation of a media client, however, is with rare exceptions exceedingly small, and the legal consultation prior to publication and in the more limited dispute resolution process would likely remain. Few defense lawyers, therefore, are likely to have a significant financial stake in the continuation of the present libel litigation system.

Finally, the judicial system, which devotes vast resources to libel claims, would be well served by non-judicial processes for the resolution of libel disputes. Because few libel cases are settled (relative to most other forms of civil litigation), and because the typical case will involve more than one level of formal judicial determination in advance of resolution or trial, the very small number of libel cases employ judicial resources that are vastly out of proportion to the resources devoted to most other forms of civil litigation.

For these reasons, the libel suit appears to be a particularly apt candidate for efficient and effective resolution through non-judicial processes, notwithstanding the presence of certain psychological and ideological preconceptions of plaintiffs and defendants that must be overcome. It should be observed, however, that legal reform directed toward determining falsity rather than fault would also likely result in more informal resolutions occurring within the confines of the litigation process. A relatively prompt and, more importantly, straightforward process leading to adjudication of falsity, without financial penalty other than costs of publication and reasonable lawyers' fees, will very probably induce both plaintiffs and defendants to attempt an agreeable resolution prior to formal adjudication. If, for example, the press' error cannot be predictably established, the plaintiff will have a substantial incentive to settle or drop the claim prior to adjudication. If, on the other hand, the error, upon investigation by the media defendant, is clear, it is likely that the defendant will prefer to admit and correct of its own volition (or at least with that appearance) rather than to have a third party adjudicate that error. In short, not only is there room for development of formal non-litigation alternatives; it is likely that with legal reform non-litigation processes implicit in the dynamics of pre-trial litigation will function in a larger proportion of the cases.

While the libel dispute appears to be an apt subject for a simplified, less expensive, and straightforward non-judicial process which induces voluntary resolution and, when called into play, reaches a prompt conclusion, the practical workability of non-judicial resolution can only be determined after further study and actual testing. Whatever the results of this undertaking, the judicial system will undoubtedly continue to play a role in at least some, and probably many, libel disputes. The need for reform in the law of libel and its judicial treatment, therefore, remains the most immediate and pressing objective. Whether change takes the form of an action to set the record straight or follows another path, it is our conviction that the time-tested process of common law evolution is needed. It is our hope that we have contributed to a clearer understanding of the libel dispute, and that a clearer understanding will facilitate and encourage much-needed reform.

Appendix A

METHODOLOGY AND DATA

The application of social science research techniques to the study of libel litigation creates a number of problems for the social scientist. This appendix discusses how the Iowa Libel Research Project attempted to solve these problems, and discusses the procedures used to gather the data for this study.

SOCIAL SCIENCE AND THE LAW

The use of social science research techniques to study problems of litigation and law is not new, but these techniques have been used infrequently to study the legal process.[1] Rather than focusing on individual cases, social science research techniques permit researchers to identify broad trends in litigation. These techniques can be valuable in ascertaining the reasons why plaintiffs sue, the chances of winning certain types of suits, the amount and type of damages awarded, the type of advice offered by attorneys, and the attitudes of plaintiffs and defendants toward the legal process.

The most ambitious attempt to use social science research techniques to study litigation was undertaken by the Wisconsin Civil Litigation Research Project.[2] Data for this study were gathered through hour-long interviews with over 1,300 attorneys in five federal judicial districts. In addition, data were gathered from over 3,800 individuals involved in about 2,000 civil disputes that were randomly selected from the five federal judicial districts and from a survey of households.[3] The main focus of the Wisconsin Civil Litigation Research Project was to study attorneys who were involved in civil litigation. The two central research questions that guided the study were: "(i) what determines the amount of time and money invested in a case; and (ii) how 'productive' are the investments which clients make in litigation; in other words, does the litigation investment 'pay.'"[4]

The Wisconsin Civil Litigation Research Project found that most civil cases in the United States involved disputes over money, usually amounts of less than $10,000. On the average, attorneys spent about 30 hours on a case, mostly on gathering facts and negotiating a settlement with opposing counsel. The average plaintiff did recover some money in the dispute, usually a sum larger than the cost of the litigation. Much to their surprise, the Wisconsin researchers found that attorneys who were on contingency spent more time on a case than did attorneys who were paid hourly.[5] The results of the Wisconsin study challenge many of the assumptions about civil litigation held by attorneys and the general public. Instead of finding a glut of cases in the courts, the Wisconsin researchers found that civil disputes rarely result in a judicial decision: in about 90 percent of all disputes attorneys successfully negotiate settlements.[6] According to the Wisconsin researchers, their study raises questions about the need for proposals to reform the legal system to deal more efficiently with civil disputes.[7]

It was only through the use of social science research techniques that the Wisconsin researchers were able systematically to examine civil litigation. Social science research techniques also have been used to study specific types of torts. Marc A. Franklin has relied on social science research techniques in two studies he has undertaken of libel cases. His first study was an examination of the case records of 534 defamation cases decided between 1976 and mid-1979.[8] Franklin had two research assistants read and code each case on a number of variables such as type of plaintiff, type of defendant, case outcome, and amount of damages awarded. The major research question that Franklin attempted to answer was: Are there any significant differences in defamation cases involving media and non-media defendants? Franklin's major finding is that media defendants win more cases before trial than do non-media defendants, with nearly half of the media cases being decided on motions for summary judgment. But plaintiffs win very few defamation cases regardless of the type of defendant. Only in 5 percent of the media cases and in 12 percent of the non-media cases did plaintiffs ultimately prevail. Among media defendants, newspapers accounted for nearly 60 percent of all the libel cases, with television accounting for 16 percent. Franklin found that the largest groups of plaintiffs were government employees, professionals, non-supervisory business employees, and owners and managers of businesses. Professionals and owners and managers of businesses won slightly more of their libel cases than did plaintiffs in the other employment categories. Franklin concluded his study by raising a perplexing question: Since so few plaintiffs win defamation suits and since the legal problems facing plaintiffs seem so insurmountable, why would anyone sue for libel? Much of the work of the Iowa Libel Research Project can be seen as answering this question.

In his second study of libel litigation, Franklin concentrated on 291 defamation cases involving media defendants that were decided between 1977 and 1980.[9] All of the cases were drawn from *Media Law Reporter* and *West* regional reporters. The results of this study tend to support the results of Franklin's initial study: media lose very few libel cases. In fact, plaintiffs ultimately prevailed in only 5 percent of the defamation cases when the defendant was a member of the mass media. Plaintiffs won a large number of cases at the trial level, especially if the case was heard by a jury, but most of these cases were reversed on appeal. Newspapers were the defendants in 62 percent of the cases studied, and broadcasters were the defendants in 15 percent of the cases. Interestingly, Franklin found that not a single broadcaster lost a defamation case. Plaintiffs who brought defamation suits were owners or managers of businesses (19 percent), professionals (12 percent) and government employees other than law enforcement personnel (12 percent). The types of stories that led to the filing of a libel suit usually dealt with plaintiffs' criminal activity (30 percent), moral failing (33 percent) or incompetence in trade or profession (17 percent).

The Wisconsin and Franklin studies make important contributions to our understanding of the litigation process. The information could have been obtained only through the use of social science research techniques. Still, the use of such research techniques to study litigation raises a number of methodological and operational problems. The first issue that confronts the researcher who studies litigation is how to identify the universe of cases from which to draw a sample for study. Social scientists interested in studying populations of people can obtain a sample by using such procedures as random-digit dialing or the random selection of names from voter registration lists or telephone directories. But none of these traditional sampling techniques can be readily adapted to the study of litigation. The first problem encountered by a researcher studying litigation is that there is no readily available list of *all* court cases from which to draw a sample of cases.

If the researcher samples cases in which a reported decision is available, the researcher would be dealing with a universe composed mainly of appellate-level cases. Most trial-level cases are not included in court reporters or in the various citation services that list reported decisions, and the researcher would not have any cases in which out-of-court settlements had been reached. For some studies, selecting cases from only reported decisions may not pose a problem, but for a study such as the Wisconsin Civil Litigation Research Project, reliance on reported cases would be unacceptable. If the Wisconsin researchers had limited themselves to reported cases, they would have dealt with only a small percentage of civil disputes, since they found that 90 percent of all disputes never resulted, in a judicial decision. To avoid the problem, the Wisconsin researchers developed complex and expensive sampling techniques. [10]

One advantage the Wisconsin researchers had in their study was that they were interested in studying nearly all types of civil disputes. [11] This permitted the researchers to narrow their study by randomly selecting judicial districts prior to sampling cases and disputes. Since the number of civil disputes in each judicial district is large, there was no concern that the researchers would not have sufficient cases or disputes to work with. But how would a researcher draw a sample of cases to study certain types of civil disputes? Studies such as the two conducted by Franklin cannot rely on the case records of just a few randomly-selected judicial districts because there are not enough libel suits filed in each district to allow the researcher to employ the sampling techniques used in the Wisconsin study. In his study of 7,800 civil cases between 1965 and 1970, Craig Wanner did not find a single libel or slander case in courts in Baltimore, Cleveland, and Milwaukee. [12]

How, then, does a researcher select cases for study of libel litigation? In his study that compared defamation cases involving media and non-media defendants, Franklin drew his sample of cases from the *West* reporter system. In his study of libel cases involving only media defendants, Franklin drew his sample from *West* and *Media Law Reporter*. Franklin recognized that by relying on cases in which there was a reported decision he would be biasing his study in favor of appellate-level cases since both *West* and *Media Law Reporter* contain only *some* trial-level cases. [13] Franklin explained his method of case selection by noting that the media tend to appeal libel cases they lose, and therefore he argued that few defamation cases involving media defendants in which the defendant lost at the trial level were missed. Although it appears that the media customarily appeal libel cases in which they receive an adverse judgment, it does not follow that plaintiffs customarily appeal cases they lose. Also, Franklin's data do not contain cases that had been settled out of court. Evidence we have obtained from a major libel insurer and from a survey of newspapers indicates that between 10 percent and 15 percent of libel cases involve money settlements.

Nevertheless, prior to Franklin's studies there had been no systematically-obtained data about the outcome of libel cases. Franklin showed that the media ultimately lose very few libel cases and that it may be plaintiffs who ought to be more concerned about their showing in libel cases. Because of Franklin's pioneering studies, we have for the first time been able to get a picture of the outcomes of libel cases, and to identify the types of individuals who sue the media for libel.

The Iowa Libel Research Project

In the Iowa Libel Research Project, we were interested in studying the entire libel litigation process, from the appearance of the allegedly libelous story, through discussions between plaintiffs and attorneys, to the outcome of the case. We were particularly interested in finding out why plaintiffs sued and what, if anything, the media could have done to prevent the filing of the libel suit. In addition, we wanted to obtain information about the plaintiffs' attitudes toward the allegedly libelous story, the media, their attorney, and the litigation process.

In designing the Iowa study, we attempted to deal with some of the methodological problems encountered in the Wisconsin Civil Litigation Research Project and in Franklin's two studies. One major problem could not be dealt with directly: how to select libel cases for study so that the cases would be representative of libel cases in the United States. We were concerned that by relying on reported libel cases we would bias our data in favor of appellate-level cases, but it became clear that there is no adequate way to identify all trial-level cases, and that any procedure to include trial-level cases would cause more problems than it solved. We concluded, as did Franklin, that most trial-level cases which the media lose are appealed. By relying on reported decisions, therefore, we would miss few cases which the media lost. On the other hand, as with Franklin, we had no way to know with any precision how frequently plaintiffs who lose at the trial level appeal their libel cases; and, of course, we had no way to know how many cases were dropped by plaintiffs prior to completion of the trial, or how many were settled. Since there is no way to identify these plaintiffs, we attempted to fill these gaps with information obtained about complaints and filed suits, as well as settlements, from the media, from media attorneys, and from a major libel insurer. The libel insurer's files provided us with information about the cases, including settlements. Interviews were conducted with a group of these plaintiffs. These data provided us with important information about plaintiffs who drop their cases, and plaintiffs who do not appeal.

In all, four main data-sets make up the Iowa Libel Research Project:

1. an analysis of virtually all reported defamation and privacy cases decided between 1974 and 1984[14]

2. a survey of libel plaintiffs
3. a survey of libel defendants
4. interviews conducted at selected media organizations

The remainder of this appendix discusses these data-sets and provides an overview of the type of information contained in each set. In addition to these data-sets, important supplemental information was obtained from four other sources. These were: (1) an examination of over 1,300 claims on file at a major libel insurer, (2) a survey of over 170 newspapers to determine rates of suit, liability, and settlement,[15] (3) interviews with attorneys who represented plaintiffs, and (4) interviews with attorneys who represent media organizations. By employing these multiple sources of data, we have attempted to broaden the scope of data to minimize any bias arising from data based on reported cases alone, while avoiding the costly and (for libel disputes) largely impracticable techniques employed in the Wisconsin study.

Defamation and Privacy Cases

The first data-set is composed of virtually all reported defamation and privacy cases decided between the 1974 case of *Gertz v. Welch*[16] and mid-1984. All cases were included in which libel or invasion of privacy was a cause of action, and the universe of cases included both media and non-media defendants. *Shepard's* and *Autocite* were consulted to make certain that the most recent adjudications were briefed. Reported cases that were appealed were added to the data base, replacing the lower court decisions. Cases were selected from several sources: (1) a search through *Lexis*, which provided a comprehensive list of state and federal court cases, was coordinated with a search of cases listed in *West's Decennial Service;* (2) all cases listed in the Libel Defense Resource Center's *50-State Survey* that did not appear in the *Lexis* search were added to the data base; (3) all cases that appeared in *Media Law Reporter* were included; and (4) all cases cited in law review articles were included in the data. This last source of data was particularly important for privacy cases, many of which do not appear in the index listing of any service.

In all, 932 privacy and defamation cases were identified, read, coded, and entered into a computerized data base. Each case was read and coded by three advanced law students. If the law students disagreed about how a case was to be coded, the case was discussed. If consensus could not be reached, the variable was coded as "in dispute" and deleted from any analysis involving that variable. Table A-1 breaks down the cases according to their main legal theory.

TABLE A–1   Main Legal Theory for
Defamation and Privacy Cases,
1974–84

Main legal theory	Number	Percent
Defamation	718	77.0
Disclosure of private facts	60	6.4
Appropriation	53	5.7
False light	25	2.7
Intrusion	23	2.5
Public disclosure and intrusion	17	1.8
False light and public disclosure	10	1.1
False light and appropriation	8	.9
Public disclosure and appropriation	3	.3
Other	15	1.6
Total	932	

Defamation cases made up by far the largest category of cases in the data-set, accounting for 718 coded cases or 77 percent of the total. In 75.3 percent of the defamation cases, the defendant was a member of the media, while non-media defendants were sued in 24.7 percent of the cases.[17] In addition, the libelous statements that caused plaintiffs to sue usually appeared in news stories (specifically, in 70.7 percent of the defamation cases). The next largest category of publication of the alleged libel was literature, which accounted for 5.9 percent of the cases.[18]

Plaintiff Survey

In this data-set, we attempted to gather information from as many libel plaintiffs as possible. Rather than attempt to study libel plaintiffs by randomly selecting cases, our goal was to examine *all* libel cases involving media defendants that were decided between May 1980 and April 1984. The cases were selected from *Media Law Reporter* and from the Libel Defense Resource Center's *50-State Survey*. The beginning and ending dates of the study were determined by estimating the number of cases we could examine given the amount of funding that was available for this part of the project. Since we were interested in obtaining information about plaintiffs' attitudes, we selected only recent cases to minimize the problem of recollection. For a case to be included, it needed to be a defamation case and to have as defendant a member of the electronic or print media, including newsletters and trade journals. Settled cases were added to the data-set from the files of a major libel insurer.

In all, we identified 323 cases that met the two requirements for inclusion. Of the 323, nine plaintiffs had died, 88 plaintiffs could not be located and 62 declined to participate. Interviews were obtained from the remaining 164 plaintiffs (representing 50.8 percent of the 323 cases selected for study). All but one of the interviews were conducted by telephone and all took between 45 minutes and an hour and a half. All but one of the interviews were conducted by attorneys or third-year law students.

To test the representativeness of the cases, we compared the data obtained from the 164 plaintiffs with the data obtained from the study of reported defamation cases decided between 1974 and 1984. In addition, we compared the results of the plaintiff interviews with the data obtained by Franklin in his study of media defamation cases. Since we did not use the same survey or coding instruments as Franklin, comparisons between the data-sets can only be considered suggestive. And although the data-sets overlap, they do not include the same cases or cover the same time periods.

Franklin's study of libel cases involving media defendants is the closest in form and content to our survey of the 164 plaintiffs. Franklin's study identified a number of demographic variables that can be compared with the data we collected from the plaintiffs interviewed. For example, Table A-2 compares employment categories of the plaintiffs in Franklin's study with the employment categories of the plaintiffs interviewed. Franklin found that 11 percent of the plaintiffs he studied were elected officials or had been candidates for office. About 17 percent of the 164 plaintiffs we interviewed were elected officials or had been candidates for office. Nine percent of Franklin's plaintiffs were employed in law enforcement, while 6.7 percent of our 164 plaintiffs worked in law enforcement. In general, the employment data in Franklin's study and the data obtained from our plaintiff interviews are similar.

Franklin found that newspapers were the defendants in 62 percent of the cases he studied. In our survey of plaintiffs, we found that newspapers were sued in 69.5 percent of the cases.[19] Franklin reported that broadcasters were sued in 15 percent of the cases he studied, while we found they were sued in 18.3 percent of the cases. Periodicals were sued in 14 percent of the cases in Franklin's study, and they were sued in 11 percent of the cases brought by plaintiffs we interviewed.

TABLE A–2   Comparison of Plaintiff Employment Between Franklin's Study and the Iowa Libel Research Project's Survey of Plaintiffs

Employment Categories	Franklin's Data	Plaintiff Data
Elected officials and candidates for office	27 (11%)	27 (16.5%)
Law enforcement	23 (9%)	11 (6.7%)
Government employee	29 (12%)	30 (18.3%)
Professional	30 (12%)	26 (15.9%)
Business owner or manager	47 (19%)	23 (14.0%)
Media-related	15 (6%)	7 (4.3%)
Businesses	22 (9%)	15 (9.1%)
Total	193 (78%)*	139 (85%)*

*The percentages do not add up to 100 because not all of the plaintiffs' employment categories could be readily compared. This table reports the results of those employment categories that could.

The success rate of media defendants is similar between Franklin's study and the plaintiffs we interviewed.[20] Franklin reported that newspapers won 92.1 percent of the cases in which they were defendants; we found that newspapers won 90.6 percent of the cases. Franklin found that no broadcaster lost a defamation case, but in our study we found three that did. When the defendant was a periodical, Franklin found plaintiffs lost 87.5 percent of the cases, and we found plaintiffs lost 90 percent of the cases.

Based on the comparisons of key demographic variables between Franklin's study and our survey of 164 plaintiffs, there are no significant differences between the two data-sets. This lends support to our belief that the 164 plaintiffs we interviewed are representative of libel plaintiffs in litigated libel suits. However, it is possible to strengthen this claim by comparing the cases involving the plaintiffs interviewed with the results of the study of media defamation cases decided between 1974 and 1984. To ensure that we compared only like variables, we constructed a subset of cases within the larger data base composed of media defamation cases, and then compared that subset with all media defemation cases. The subset contained all of the cases brought by the plaintiffs interviewed for which there was a reported decision. One problem with making this type of comparison is that we assumed that the type of plaintiffs who sued for libel and the reasons they sued did not change through the years.

In all, there were 536 coded defamation cases between 1974 and 1984 in which the defendant was a member of the media. In Table A-3, we compare the main legal issues adjudicated in these cases with the legal issues in the cases of the plaintiffs we interviewed. In both sets of data, negligence or malice was the main legal issue in the largest percentage of libel suits. For all media defamation cases, negligence or malice was the main legal issue in 42 percent of the cases. For the plaintiffs we interviewed, negligence or malice was the main legal issue in 56.7 percent of the cases. If we combine all of the cases in which constitutional privileges were principally involved, we find that privilege issues were the main legal issue in 87 percent of the defamation cases involving media defendants, and in 90 percent of the cases involving the plaintiffs interviewed. It is interesting to note that truth was the main legal issue adjudicated in only 12.6 percent of the media libel cases decided between 1974 and 1984, and in 10 percent of the cases involving the plaintiffs interviewed. On the main legal issues adjudicated in the cases, there are no significant differences between the plaintiffs interviewed and defamation cases involving media defendants between 1974 and 1984.

Of all media defamation cases, 85.1 percent resulted from statements that appeared in news stories.[21] For the plaintiffs interviewed, 93.8 percent of the cases were the result of news stories. In both data-sets, entertainment stories accounted for about 5 percent of the cases.

In 52.2 percent of the cases involving the plaintiffs interviewed, the alleged libel dealt with the plaintiffs' business or professional activities.[22] In 53.6 percent of all media defamation cases, the focus of the alleged libel

TABLE A–3   Comparison of Legal Issues Adjudicated in Media Defamation Cases Between 1974 and 1984 with Legal Issues Adjudicated in the Iowa Libel Research Project's Survey of Plaintiffs

Main Legal Issue	All Media Defamation Cases	Plaintiff Cases
Plaintiffs' legal status	64 (15.2%)	12 (10.0%)
Negligence or malice	177 (42.0%)	68 (56.7%)
Plaintiffs' legal status and negligence or malice	127 (30.1%)	28 (23.3%)
Truth	53 (12.6%)	12 (10.0%)
Total	421	120

was the plaintiffs' business or professional activities. In about 17 percent of the cases in both data-sets, the alleged libel dealt with the plaintiffs' moral conduct.

The two data-sets are identical when outcomes of the cases are compared.[23] Between 1974 and 1984, media defendants won 89.3 percent of all libel cases, and media defendants won 89.3 percent of the cases brought by the plaintiffs we interviewed. Based on comparisons involving the focus of the alleged libel, the context in which the libel appeared, and the outcome of the cases, there are no significant differences between the two sets of data. This adds more evidence to support our belief that the plaintiffs we interviewed can be considered to be representative of libel plaintiffs in the United States who press their disputes in the judicial system.

However, when the plaintiffs' legal status as shown in the two data-sets is compared, some differences emerge (Table A-4). Private individuals were the plaintiffs in about a third of all media libel cases between 1974 and 1984, but private individuals accounted for about a quarter of the plaintiffs we interviewed.[24] For media defamation cases decided between 1974 and 1984, public officials were the plaintiffs in 23.9 percent of the cases, but 34.1 percent of the plaintiffs we interviewed were public officials. Public figures were the plaintiffs in 32.4 percent of defamation cases decided between 1974 and 1984, and in our study they accounted for 34.8 percent of the plaintiffs. If we combine public officials with public figures, we find that public plaintiffs accounted for 56.3 percent of all media defamation cases, but represented 68.9 percent of the plaintiffs we interviewed. This means that the plaintiffs interviewed are underrepresented in numbers of private plaintiffs and are overrepresented in numbers of public plaintiffs. Still, the overall trends in both data-sets are the same.

TABLE A-4   Comparison of Plaintiffs' Legal Status: Media Defamation Cases Between 1974 and 1984 and Iowa Libel Research Project's Survey of Plaintiffs

Plaintiffs' Legal Status	All Media Defamation Cases	Plaintiff Cases
Public figures	161 (32.4%)	46 (34.8%)
Public officials	119 (23.9%)	45 (34.1%)
Private individuals	164 (33.0%)	32 (24.2%)
Private-figure corporations	23 (4.6%)	3 (2.3%)
Public-figure corporations	30 (6.0%)	6 (4.5%)
Total	497	132

On the whole, the data acquired from the plaintiffs we interviewed do not differ greatly from the data obtained by Franklin or from the data obtained from our study of media defamation cases decided between 1974 and 1984. Moreover, we found that the information provided by plaintiffs in settled cases was fully consistent with that provided by all other plaintiffs who had pressed their suit to the point of formal and reported judicial decision. These comparisons add support to our belief that the 164 plaintiffs we interviewed can be considered to be representative of libel plaintiffs in the United States who seriously pursue their libel claim. Since we could not randomly sample libel cases for study, we believe that the methods we used to identify cases and our attempts to verify the representativeness of the cases we studied add a considerable degree of reliability to our findings.

Defendant Survey

It became clear from the data obtained from the interviews with the 164 plaintiffs that from the plaintiffs' perspective the media's treatment of them was a major factor in their decision to litigate. The interviews raised a number of questions about the way the media handle complaints about news coverage. To obtain answers to these questions, a questionnaire was designed and administered to media defendants. We limited our study to newspapers which had been sued by one of the 164 plaintiffs we had interviewed. A number of the defendants refused to participate in the study, and some of the defendants had been sued by more than one of the plaintiffs. In all, we were able to obtain completed interviews with 61 defendants. The questionnaire was administered by telephone, and in almost every case an editor was the person who responded to it. We were not interested in obtaining information about specific libel suits in which the defendants had been involved. Rather, we wanted to obtain information about how the various news organizations deal with complaints about news coverage, especially complaints that might lead to the filing of a libel suit.

The data acquired from the media defendants suggest that the internal structure of the media is not well organized to deal with complaints about news coverage. The data help explain why the media's treatment of complainants may be a factor in the decision to file a libel suit. The media's role in libel litigation is discussed in Chapter 4.

In-Depth Media Interviews

We concluded that interviews with editors may not produce a sufficiently-rounded picture of what happens to complainants. To obtain a broader picture, we undertook a series of in-depth studies at six Midwestern newspapers. Our goal was to find out about complaint procedures from the vantage point of different newspaper personnel. At each newspaper, we interviewed everyone who might have contact with a person making a complaint, from the switchboard operator and receptionist to top editors. Chapter 4 discusses the results of the in-depth interviews.

A Note on Statistical Analysis

Normally in social science research, a confidence level of .05 is used to reject the hypothesis that two variables are independent. This means that the likelihood of the results of a comparison involving two variables occurring by chance is less than 5 in 100. In this study, we have set the confidence level at .1. Since no one had undertaken a study of this magnitude involving libel litigation, we were concerned that by adhering to too high a confidence level we might be prevented from reporting relevant information.

Even so, most of the variables we employed represent but one of a series of variables that bear on a given subject. Many of the key variables exhibit internally-consistent and expected patterns, both within a data base and across data-sets. Most of the comparisons we discuss, and especially those most fundamental to our analysis, meet the .05 standard and are accompanied by consistent trends in related variables.

Since libel has received so much attention from attorneys, journalists, legislators, and the courts, we deemed it important to shed as much light as possible on the libel process. Lowering the confidence level conceivably can produce some misleading results, but we believe that our conclusions are based on careful analysis of the data and are supported by consistent trends in several variables. Moreover, the data collected from the plaintiffs we interviewed represent between 30 and 40 percent (possibly as high as 45 percent) of all libel cases involving the media that were decided between 1980 and 1984. Unless otherwise noted, all discussions in the text involving relationships between variables are significant at or below the .1 level.

Notes

1. For an interesting review of studies that have applied social science research techniques to the law, *see* Schroeder, *Studies of Courts and Court Operations: A Literature Review*, Civil Litigation Research Project Final Report, University of Wisconsin Law School: III–42–III–87.
2. David M. Trubek, Joel B. Grossman, William L. F. Felstiner, Herbert M. Kritzer and Austin Sarat, Civil Litigation Research Project Final Report, University of Wisconsin Law School, 1983 [hereinafter Wisconsin Study].
3. For a discussion of the research methods used in the Wisconsin study, *see* Kritzer, *Studying Disputes: Learning from the CLRP Experience*, 15 *Law and Society* 503–24 (1980–81).
4. Trubek, et al., Wisconsin Study S–4.
5. *Id.* at S–1 to S–90.
6. *See* Chapter 8 for a discussion of the Wisconsin study's findings of resolution of disputes and how they compare with libel litigation.
7. Trubek, *et al.*, Wisconsin Study S–1 to S–90.
8. Franklin, *Winners and Losers and Why: A Study of Defamation Litigation*, 1980 American Bar Foundation Research Journal 455–500.
9. Franklin, *Suing Media for Libel: A Litigation Study*, 1981 American Bar Foundation Research Journal 797–831.
10. To select completed cases, the researchers used a form of cluster sampling based on the profile of terminated cases. To identify disputes that had not resulted in a judicial decision, the researchers located them through a random-digit dialing telephone survey. In all, these procedures yielded a sample of 2,631 disputes. The next phase of the study was to gather data about the disputes. This meant contacting all of the parties—including attorneys—who had been involved in the disputes. Contacting these individuals and obtaining their cooperation posed additional problems for the researchers. Fewer than half of the individuals who had been involved in the disputes could be located. Of the parties that could be located, about a fifth of the attorneys refused to participate in the study and about a quarter of the disputants refused. Out of the sample of 2,631 disputes, the Wisconsin researchers were able to obtain at least one interview from persons involved in 2,011 of the disputes, but in only 5 percent of the disputes were the researchers successful in obtaining interviews from all of the parties involved. For a complete discussion of the sampling techniques used, see Kritzer, *supra* note 3.
11. The Wisconsin Civil Litigation Research Project did exclude certain types of cases. These included divorce cases, unless there was a dispute over property; cases in which the amount of money in dispute was less than $1,000; and complex law suits.
12. Wanner, *The Public Ordering of Private Relations: Part One: Initiating Civil Cases in Urban Trial Courts*, *Law and Society* 421–40 (1974).
13. In his first study, Franklin argued that it was unlikely that media defendants settled many cases out of court. Franklin had to qualify this claim in his second study after finding that one libel insurer reported settling about 25 percent of libel cases. It is not known with any certainty what percentage of all libel cases involving the media result in some type of settlement, but data we have obtained from a major libel insurer and from a survey of newspapers suggest that the percentage of case settlements involving money is probably between 10 and 15 percent. *See* Chapter 7.
14. Except cases involving a different principal theory or theories of recovery in which defamation or privacy were alleged, but that were not seriously pursued or were

dismissed as frivolous or facially insubstantial. Thus, we did not code every reported case with a defamation or privacy headnote.

15. The survey of newspapers was conducted by the editors of the *Iowa Law Review*, in consultation with the Iowa Libel Research Project. The results of the survey will be discussed in a forthcoming article in the review.

16. Gertz v. Robert Welch, Inc., 418 U.S. 323, 344–45 (1974).

17.

Type of defendant sued in
defamation cases, 1974–84

	Number of cases
Media defendant	537 (75.3%)
Non-media defendant	176 (24.7%)

18.

Context in which alleged libelous
statement appeared

	Number
News	490 (70.7%)
Literature	41 (5.9%)
Entertainment	33 (4.8%)
Other (non-media)	129 (18.6%)

NOTE: "News" is defined to include articles in newspapers, magazines and periodicals, including essays and editorials on current topics. "Entertainment" is the fictional presentation of characters or events in print or broadcasting. "Literature" includes print and broadcast material of serious literary, cultural, historical, scientific, or artistic character.

19.

Comparison of media defendants between
Franklin's study and the Iowa Libel Research
Project's survey of plaintiffs

Type of Media Defendant	Franklin's Data		Plaintiff Data	
Newspapers	179	(62%)	114	(69.5%)
Periodicals	40	(14%)	18	(11.0%)
Television	36	(12%)	26	(15.9%)
Radio	8	(3%)	4	(2.4%)
Total[*]	263	(91%)	162	(98.8%)

[*]Some categories of media could not be readily compared between the two sets of data and have been deleted from the table.

20.

Comparison of case outcome between Franklin's
study and the Iowa Libel Research Project's survey
of plaintiffs

Case Result	Franklin's Data[*]		Plaintiff Data[**]	
Newspapers				
Plaintiff won	7	(7.9%)	8	(9.4%)
Defendant won	82	(92.1%)	77	(90.6%)
Periodicals				
Plaintiff won	2	(12.5%)	1	(10%)
Defendant won	14	(87.5%)	9	(90%)
Broadcaster				
Plaintiff won	0		3	(14.3%)
Defendant won	20	(100%)	18	(85.7%)

[*]Franklin's data represent completed cases decided on appeal.
[**]Cases finally resolved by judicial decision.

21.

Comparison of the publishing context of the alleged
libelous story in media defamation cases between 1974
and 1984 with the publishing context of the alleged libel
for the plaintiffs interviewed in the Iowa Libel Research
Project

	All Media Defamation Cases		Plaintiff Cases	
News	452	(85.1%)	136	(93.8%)
Literature	39	(7.3%)	2	(1.4%)
Entertainment	31	(5.8%)	7	(4.8%)
Other (non-media)	9	(1.7%)	0	

22.

Comparison of the focus of the allegedly libelous story in
media defamation cases between 1974 and 1984 with the
focus of the alleged libel for the plaintiffs interviewed in the
Iowa Libel Research Project

	All Media Defamation Cases		Plaintiff Cases	
Plaintiffs' professional or business activities	275	(53.6%)	70	(52.2%)
Plaintiffs' moral activities	91	(17.7%)	23	(17.2%)
Plaintiffs' professional or business activities and moral activities	147	(28.7%)	41	(30.6%)

23.

Comparison of case outcome in media defamation cases decided between 1974 and 1984 with case outcome for the plaintiffs interviewed in the Iowa Libel Research Project

	All Media Defamation Cases	Plaintiff Cases
Plaintiff won	41 (10.7%)	13 (10.7%)
Defendant won	341 (89.3%)	108 (89.3%)

24. The difference is slight, but to the extent that it is not solely the product of different time periods in the two data-sets, we think it reflects a slightly greater difficulty in finding private plaintiffs and in obtaining their cooperation.

Appendix B

THE QUESTIONNAIRE

The questionnaire developed for the interviews conducted with the 164 libel plaintiffs was designed to provide as much information as possible. Therefore, most of the questions were open-ended. The interviewers were either lawyers or third-year law students, all of whom had studied libel law during their academic training. All interviewers underwent extensive training, which included a number of practice interviews.

PLAINTIFF QUESTIONNAIRE

Demographic Information

1. What is the plaintiff's sex or status?
   a. Male
   b. Female
   c. Business
   d. Business and individual
   e. Other _____
2. What is the plaintiff's (perceived) legal status?
   a. Public official
   b. Public figure
   c. Private figure
   d. Uncertain
3. If plaintiff is a business, what type of business?
4. If plaintiff is a business, how long has business existed?
5. If plaintiff is a business, what are its total assets?

252

6. If plaintiff is a business, how many people does it employ?
7. What is plaintiff's age?
   a. Under 35
   b. 35 to 50
   c. 51 to 65
   d. Over 65
8. What was plaintiff's job at time alleged libel occurred?
9. What was plaintiff's marital status at time alleged libel occurred?
   a. Single
   b. Married
   c. Divorced
   d. Other
10. Did plaintiff have any children living at home when alleged libel occurred? If so, how many?
11. What was plaintiff's estimated annual household income at the time the alleged libel occurred?
    a. Under $15,000
    b. $15–25,000
    c. $25–35,000
    d. $35–50,000
    e. Over $50,000
12. What was plaintiff's highest level of education when the alleged libel occurred?
    a. Some high school
    b. High school graduate
    c. Some college
    d. College graduate
    e. Some graduate or professional school
    f. Graduate or professional degree
    g. Other
13. How many years had the plaintiff lived in the community prior to the publication or broadcast of the alleged libel?
14. Did the plaintiff hold public office at the time the alleged libel occurred?
15. Had the plaintiff held public office prior to the publication or broadcast?
16. Was the plaintiff active in community affairs at the time the alleged libel occurred? If so, what activities was the plaintiff involved with?
17. How prominent or visible in the community was the plaintiff?
    a. Very high
    b. Above average
    c. Average
    d. Below average
    e. Very low

The Alleged Libel

18. When did the alleged libel appear?
19. Where did the alleged libel appear?

20. If it appeared in broadcast media, what was the broadcast area?
21. If it appeared in a newspaper, what was the paper's circulation area?
22. If it appeared in a magazine, what was its circulation area?
23. If the story appeared in a newspaper, where in the newspaper did it appear?
24. If the story appeared in a broadcast, in what type of program did it appear?
25. If the article appeared in a magazine, where in the magazine did it appear?
26. How often was the alleged libel published or broadcast?
27. Was the plaintiff the subject of the allegedly libelous story? If not, what was the subject of the story?
28. Was the plaintiff's name used in the allegedly libelous story?
29. What did the allegedly libelous story deal with?
30. What did the medium say about the plaintiff in the allegedly libelous story?
31. What upset the plaintiff most about the alleged libel?
32. How was the plaintiff harmed by the alleged libel?
33. Apart from suing for libel, did the plaintiff do anything else about the alleged libel? Did the plaintiff contact anyone? If so, whom was contacted and why?
34. Thinking back to the time right after the alleged libel appeared, what could the medium have done that would have satisfied the plaintiff?

Media Relations

35. Did the plaintiff contact the medium about the alleged libel?
36. If yes, when and how was the medium contacted?
37. If no, why not?
38. Did the plaintiff's lawyer contact the medium?
39. Who contacted the medium first, the plaintiff or his lawyer?
40. Whom did the plaintiff contact first after the alleged libel appeared, the medium or a lawyer?
41. If the medium was contacted, how long after the publication or broadcast was it contacted?
42. If the medium was contacted, whom at the medium was contacted? Were these the individuals the plaintiff wanted to talk to?
43. If the medium was contacted, what did the plaintiff ask the medium to do about the alleged libel? How did the medium respond? How did the plaintiff feel about the response? Was the medium's response a factor in the plaintiff's decision to sue? If so, explain.

Lawyer-plaintiff Relations

44. How long after the alleged libel appeared did the plaintiff contact a lawyer?
45. Why did the plaintiff contact a lawyer?
46. How did the plaintiff select his lawyer?

47. Did any other lawyers represent the plaintiff in the libel suit? If so, explain.
48. Had the plaintiff sued anyone before he sued for libel?
49. Has the plaintiff sued anyone since he sued for libel?
50. Has the plaintiff filed any other libel suits?
51. Has the plaintiff filed any invasion of privacy suits?
52. Did the plaintiff's lawyer discuss the problems of libel law?
53. Did the plaintiff's lawyer discuss invasion of privacy that could result from suing for libel?
54. Did the plaintiff's lawyer discuss the chances of winning the libel suit?
55. Did the plaintiff's lawyer discuss the chances of reaching a settlement?
56. Did the plaintiff's lawyer discuss how long the libel suit might take?
57. Did the plaintiff's lawyer discuss the possibility that the libel suit might result in publicity about the plaintiff's past?
58. Did the plaintiff's lawyer discuss the possibility that the libel suit might result in the re-publication of the alleged libel?
59. Did the plaintiff's lawyer discuss fees and other costs?
60. How important was the lawyer's advice in the plaintiff's decision to sue?
61. Did the plaintiff decide to sue before or after talking with the lawyer?
62. What actions did the plaintiff's lawyer recommend?

The Libel Suit

63. Thinking back to the time the plaintiff decided to sue, how eagerly did the plaintiff approach the suit?
64. Why did the plaintiff sue for libel?
65. Did the plaintiff know whether the defendant had libel insurance? If yes, did this affect the plaintiff's actions?
66. What was the final outcome of the suit?
67. If the plaintiff won, was it by verdict, judgment, or both? Explain.
68. If the plaintiff lost, did the plaintiff accomplish anything by the suit? Explain.
69. If the plaintiff settled, what was the settlement, and why did plaintiff agree to it?
70. How long did it take to complete the suit from the time the alleged libel appeared?
71. Did the suit take longer than the plaintiff expected?
72. How much did the suit cost the plaintiff?
73. What were the plaintiff's lawyer fees?
74. How did the total cost compare with the plaintiff's expectations?
75. If the case is completed, could the plaintiff have pursued it further? If no, why not?
76. Overall, how does the plaintiff feel about his experience with the libel suit? What events contributed to these feelings?
77. Now that the suit is over, if the plaintiff were faced with a similar situation what would plaintiff do differently, if anything?

Alternatives to Litigation

78. Did the plaintiff's lawyer discuss other ways of dealing with the dispute without going to court? If yes, what was discussed?
79. If the plaintiff could have obtained a quick, fair, public finding on the dispute without going to court, would the plaintiff have chosen this means rather than a lawsuit? Explain.

The Case Record

80. What was the court's finding as to the plaintiff's legal status?
81. Who was the defendant in the suit?
82. What were the main legal issues adjudicated in the case?
83. What was the focus of the alleged libel?
84. In what context was the alleged libel published?
85. What was the case result?

Appendix C

SELECTED TABLES

This appendix presents some of the key findings from the interviews conducted with the 164 libel plaintiffs. Additional data can be found in the text.

1. Libel plaintiffs' employment

	Number	Percentage
Elected official or candidate for office	27	19.6%
White-collar employee	14	10.2%
Non-elected public employee	41	29.7%
Business proprietor or business manager	23	16.7%
Professional	33	23.9%

2. Libel plaintiffs' visibility in the community?

	Number	Percentage
Very highly visible	59	40.7%
Above average visibility	52	35.9%
Average visibility	14	9.7%
Below average visibility	11	7.6%
Very low visibility	9	6.2%

3. Focus of the allegedly libelous story?

	Number	Percentage
Personal or private activity	15	9.3%
Business or professional activity	50	30.9%
Public or political activity	72	44.4%
Criminal activity	25	15.4%

4. What upset plaintiffs most about the alleged libel?

	Number	Percentage
Story was false	106	65.4%
Story violated privacy	7	4.3%
Damaged personal reputation	11	6.8%
Damaged business or professional reputation	33	20.4%
Other	5	3.1%

5. How were plaintiffs harmed by the alleged libel?

	Number	Percentage
Suffered emotional harm	42	27.1%
Suffered emotional and financial harm	34	21.9%
Suffered financial harm	22	14.2%
Damaged business or professional reputation	34	21.9%
Damaged political status	23	14.8%

6. What could the media have done after the alleged libel appeared that would have satisfied the plaintiffs?

	Number	Percentage
Apologize	3	1.9%
Retract or correct the story	110	71.0%
Pay money damages	6	3.9%
Nothing	31	20.0%
Other	5	3.2%

7. After the alleged libel appeared, whom did plaintiffs contact?

	Number	Percentage
Media	73	49.3%
Lawyer	75	50.7%

8. Who contacted the media?

	Number	Percentage
Plaintiff	53	37.1%
Plaintiff's lawyer	50	35.0%
Both plaintiff and lawyer	26	18.2%
Neither	14	9.8%

9. What were the media asked to do about the alleged libel?

	Number	Percentage
Retract, correct or apologize publicly	100	78.0%
Apologize in person	2	1.6%
Pay money damages	1	.8%
Give space to plaintiff to respond to alleged libel	4	3.1%

Stop publication	6	4.7%
Discuss story with plaintiff	7	5.5%
Other	8	6.3%

10. How did the media respond to the request?

	Number	Percentage
Retracted, corrected or apologized publicly	26	20.6%
Did not repeat story	3	2.4%
Refused request	79	62.7%
Repeated story	14	11.1%
Other	4	3.2%

11. How did the plaintiffs feel about the response?

	Number	Percentage
Angered	71	56.8%
Dissatisfied	46	36.8%
Satisfied	5	4.0%
Ambivalent	3	2.4%

12. Was the media's response a factor in the plaintiffs' decision to sue?

	Number	Percentage
Yes	115	90.6%
No	12	9.4%

13. Why did the plaintiffs contact a lawyer?

	Number	Percentage
For general advice	66	45.5%
To obtain a retraction	8	5.5%
To sue	50	34.5%
Other	21	14.5%

14. How important was lawyer's advice in the plaintiffs' decision to sue?

	Number	Percentage
Very important	56	39.7%
Somewhat important	25	17.7%
Of little or no importance	60	42.6%

15. Did the plaintiffs decide to sue before or after talking with the lawyer?

	Number	Percentage
Before	81	56.6%
After	62	43.4%

16. What actions did the lawyer recommend?

	Number	Percentage
Bring suit	98	76.6%
Negotiate before suing	16	12.5%
Do not sue	4	3.1%
Plaintiff's decision	8	6.3%
Other	2	1.6%

17. Did the lawyer discuss the chances of winning the libel suit?

	Number	Percentage
Very good chance of winning	19	14.4%
Good chance of winning	57	43.2%
50 percent chance of winning	12	9.1%
Slight chance of winning	34	25.8%
Other	10	7.6%

18. Did the lawyer discuss the chances of reaching a settlement?

	Number	Percentage
Good chance of settlement	23	18.9%
Slight chance of settlement	17	13.9%
No chance of settlement	18	14.8%
Not discussed	45	36.9%
No prediction offered	19	15.6%

19. Did the lawyer discuss how long the suit might take?

	Number	Percentage
Less than one year	6	5.2%
One to two years	21	18.3%
Two to five years	36	31.3%
Five years or more	16	13.9%
Other	36	31.3%

20. Did the lawyer discuss the possibility that the libel suit might result in publicity about the plaintiff's past?

	Number	Percentage
Yes	84	71.8%
No	33	28.2%

21. Did the lawyer discuss the possibility that the libel suit might result in re-publication of the alleged libel?

	Number	Percentage
Yes	80	70.8%
No	33	29.2%

22. Lawyer's fee arrangement?

	Number	Percentage
Contingency	92	73.0%
Hourly	18	14.3%
Other (largely a combination)	16	12.7%

23. How eagerly did the plaintiffs approach their libel suit?

	Number	Percentage
Eagerly	54	34.4%
Willingly	55	35.0%
Reluctantly	48	30.6%

24. Why did the plaintiffs sue for libel?

	Number	Percentage
To restore reputation	48	30.0%
To win money damages	35	21.9%
To stop further publication (deter)	30	18.7%
To punish and for vengeance	47	29.4%

25. What was final outcome of the suit?

	Number	Percentage
Defendant won	108	66.7%
Plaintiff won	13	8.0%
Case settled	9	5.6%
Case pending	32	19.8%

26. Despite losing, what did the plaintiffs accomplish by the suit?

	Number	Percentage
Reputation defended	24	41.4%
Support from friends	5	8.6%
Media punished	6	10.3%
Further publicity stopped	23	39.7%

27. How long did it take to complete the suit from the time the alleged libel appeared?

	Number	Percentage
Under one year	10	6.6%
One to three years	49	32.2%
Three to five years	42	27.6%
Five to eight years	36	23.7%
Eight years or more	6	3.9%
Other	9	5.9%

28. How much did the suit cost the plaintiffs?

	Number	Percentage
Nothing	20	15.7%
Under $1,000	18	14.2%
$1,000 to $5,000	44	34.6%
$5,000 to $20,000	30	23.6%
Over $20,000	15	11.8%

29. What were the plaintiffs' lawyer fees?

	Number	Percentage
Nothing	45	47.4%
Under $1,000	8	8.4%
$1,000 to $5,000	21	22.1%
$5,000 to $10,000	7	7.4%
Over $10,000	14	14.7%

30. How did the total cost compare with the plaintiffs' expectations?

	Number	Percentage
Less costly	8	9.6%
About as expected	44	53.0%
More costly	31	37.4%

31. Overall, how do the plaintiffs feel about their experience with the libel suit?

	Number	Percentage
Extremely satisfied	9	6.0%
Satisfied	43	28.5%
Dissatisfied	52	34.4%
Extremely dissatisfied	47	31.1%

32. Now that the suit is over, if the plaintiffs were faced with a similar situation what would the plaintiffs do differently, if anything?

	Number	Percentage
Nothing, bring suit	87	68.5%
Not sue	7	5.5%
Get a better lawyer	16	12.6%
Exert more control	7	5.5%
Pursue non-litigation options	10	7.9%

33. If the plaintiffs could have obtained a quick, fair, public finding on the dispute without going to court, would the plaintiffs have chosen this means rather than a lawsuit?

	Number	Percentage
Yes, if could avoid suit	32	21.2%
Yes, if reduce time and money	15	9.9%
Yes, if more just outcome	32	21.2%
Yes, if outcome publicized	36	23.8%
Yes, if money damages available	14	9.3%
Yes, other reasons	5	3.3%
No, need to have money damages	2	1.3%
No, lawsuit is effective	7	4.6%
No, need judicial process	7	4.6%
No, other reasons	1	0.7%

34. Plaintiffs' legal status?

	Number	Percentage
Public figure	46	34.8%
Public official	45	34.1%
Private individual	32	24.2%
Public-figure corporation	3	2.3%
Private-figure corporation	6	4.5%

NOTES

CHAPTER 1

1. *See* W. Prosser, The Law of Torts 797–99 (4th ed. 1971); R. Sack, Libel, Slander and Related Problems 40, 129–42 (P.L.I. 1980). For further discussion of the role of falsity in libel litigation, with reference particularly to the recent requirement that libel plaintiffs must prove falsity, *see* Philadelphia Newspapers Inc. v. Hepps, 106 S.Ct. 1558 (1986); text accompanying notes 37–80, Chapter 8, *infra*.
2. The privileges are examined in great detail in the Prosser and Sack texts, note 1 *supra*.
3. 376 U.S. 254 (1964).
4. *Id.* at 270.
5. *Id.*
6. In this book we will use the term "media" defendants (which include newspapers, periodicals, broadcast or cable communication, and any other forms of mass communication) as synonymous with application of the constitutional negligence privilege. The line drawn by the Supreme Court is not so clear, however, for it appears by its recent decision in *Dun & Bradstreet, Inc. v. Greenmoss Builders, Inc.*, 105 S.Ct. 2939, 2946 (1985), that the line between negligence and strict liability depends on the extent of circulation, the presence of special (largely commercial) purposes, and the extent to which general disclosure of information is anticipated. The cases we describe with the shorthand "media" term will be subject to privilege under this test. For a more extended discussion of the privilege boundary, see text accompanying notes 12–24, Chapter 6.
7. *See* Gertz v. Robert Welch, Inc., 418 U.S. 323 (1974). In most such cases—at least those involving media defendants—the plaintiff must also bear a burden of proof on the issue of falsity, although the exact nature of this burden is not entirely clear. *See* Philadelphia Newspapers, Inc. v. Hepps, 106 S.Ct. 1558, 1564–65 & n. 5 (1986); text accompanying notes 37–80, Chapter 8, *infra*.
8. *Id.*
9. New York Times Co. v. Sullivan, 376 U.S. 254, 279–80 (1964); St. Amant v. Thompson, 390 U.S. 719, 731 (1968).
10. In media libel cases involving general or unrestricted circulation, the plaintiff must also prove actual falsity. Philadelphia Newspapers Inc. v. Hepps, 106 S.Ct. 1558 (1986). The precise scope of this new constitutional rule, and the precise "proof" of falsity

plaintiffs must introduce, are unclear. In any event, the *Hepps* decision does not alter the point that actual malice and negligence—both point-in-time issues—are analytically distinct from actual falsity, which plaintiffs must also prove under *Hepps*. *See* R. Sack, Libel, Slander and Related Problems 129–46, 210–26 (P.L.I. 1980); Restatement (Second) of Torts 613 (1965); note 9 *supra*.

11. R. Sack, Libel, Slander and Related Problems xxvi (P.L.I. 1980).
12. Anderson, *Libel and Press Self-Censorship*, 53 Texas L. Rev. 422 (1975).
13. *See* Appendix A for a detailed discussion of methodology.

CHAPTER 2

1. Franklin, *Winners and Losers and Why: A Study of Defamation Litigation*, 1980 American Bar Foundation Research Journal 455–500; Franklin, *Suing Media for Libel: A Litigation Study*, 1981 American Bar Foundation Research Journal 797–831.
2. See Appendix A for a discussion of the data sets and methodology used in the Iowa Libel Research Project.
3. Wanner, *The Public Ordering of Private Relations Part One: Initiating Civil Cases in Urban Trial Courts*, 1974 Law and Society 421–440.
4. The Wisconsin Civil Litigation Research Project found that individuals were the plaintiffs in more civil cases than were organizations. Specifically, the Wisconsin researchers found that individuals were the plaintiffs in about 70 percent of the cases they studied. But the differences between Wanner's study and the Wisconsin study can be explained by the procedures used by the Wisconsin researchers to select cases, which tended to overlook cases that would have involved organizations. *See* Grossman, Kritzer, Bumiller, Surat, McDougal and Miller, *Dimensions of Institutional Participation: Who Uses the Courts and How?*, The Journal of Politics 86–114 (1982).
5.

Type of plaintiff in defamation cases decided between 1974 and 1984

	Type of Defendant	
	Media	Non-media
Individual	444 (89.3%)	150 (90.4%)
Organization	53 (10.7%)	16 (9.6%)

6. Franklin found that males were the plaintiffs in 88.8 percent of the cases brought by individuals and that females were the plaintiffs in 9.7 percent of the cases. He found two libel cases (1.5 percent of the cases brought by individuals) in which children were the plaintiffs. Franklin, *supra* note 1.
7. The remaining 12 percent of the cases were brought by more than one individual. Wanner, *supra* note 3, at 423–25.
8.

Libel plaintiffs' visibility in the community

Very high visibility	59 (40.7%)
Above-average visibility	52 (35.9%)
Average visibility	14 (9.7%)
Below-average visibility	11 (7.6%)
Very low visibility	9 (6.2%)

9.

Libel plaintiffs' employment

Elected official or candidate for office	27	(19.6%)
White-collar employee	14	(10.2%)
Public employee	41	(29.7%)
Business proprietor or business manager	23	(16.7%)
Professional	33	(23.9%)

10. For a discussion of the cases we characterize as "media," see Chapter 7.
11. Constitutional privileges and libel law are discussed in depth in Chapter 6.
12. For a thorough discussion of the legal issues involved in distinguishing between public officials and public figures, *see* Schauer, *Public Figures*, 25 William and Mary Law Review 905–35 (1984); Ashdown, *Of Public Figures and Public Interest—The Libel Law Conundrum*, 25 William and Mary Law Review 937–56 (1984); Daniels, *Public Figures Revisited*, 25 William and Mary Law Review 957–68 (1984).
13. Schauer, *supra* note 12, at 908.
14. Gertz v. Robert Welch, Inc., 418 U.S. 323, 344–45 (1974); see Chapter 6 for a detailed discussion of these categories and the impact of the *Gertz* case.
15.

Plaintiffs' legal status for reported defamation cases between 1974 and 1984 involving media defendants

Public figure	161	(32.4%)
Public official	119	(23.9%)
Private individual	164	(33.0%)
Public-figure corporation	23	(4.6%)
Private-figure corporation	30	(6.0%)

16.

Plaintiffs' legal status compared with plaintiffs' level of education

	Plaintiffs' Education				
	High School or Less	Some College	College Graduate	Some Graduate School	Graduate or Professional Degree
Public figure	6 (15.0%)	8 (20.0%)	8 (20.0%)	0	18 (45.0%)
Public official	8 (19.5%)	12 (29.3%)	5 (12.2%)	3 (7.3%)	13 (31.7%)
Private individual	12 (40.0%)	5 (16.7%)	3 (10.0%)	3 (10.0%)	7 (23.3%)

p. < .09

17.

Plaintiffs' employment compared with plaintiffs' level of education

	Plaintiffs' Education				
	High School or Less	Some College	College Graduate	Some Graduate School	Graduate or Professional Degree
Elected official or candidate for office	5 (19.2%)	8 (30.8%)	3 (11.5%)	0	10 (38.5%)
White-collar employee	5 (38.5%)	3 (23.1%)	3 (23.1%)	1 (7.7%)	1 (7.7%)
Public employee	5 (12.2%)	11 (26.8%)	6 (14.6%)	4 (9.8%)	15 (36.6%)
Business proprietor or manager	8 (38.1%)	4 (19%)	6 (28.6%)	0	3 (14.3%)
Professional	4 (12.5%)	4 (12.5%)	3 (9.4%)	2 (6.3%)	19 (59.4%)

$p. < .03$

18.

Plaintiffs' legal status compared with plaintiffs' employment

	Plaintiffs' Employment		
	Elected Official or Candidate	White-Collar Employee	Public Employee
Public figure	10 (45.5%)*	2 (20%)	13 (40.6%)
Public official	11 (50.0%)	2 (20%)	16 (50.0%)
Private individual	1 (4.5%)	6 (60%)	3 (9.4%)

	Business Proprietor or Manager	Professional
Public figure	6 (35.3%)	10 (38.5%)
Public official	4 (23.5%)	9 (34.6%)
Private individual	7 (41.2%)	7 (26.9%)

$p. < .02$

*Percentages are based on columns not rows

19.

Plaintiffs' legal status compared with plaintiffs' community visibility

	Plaintiffs' Community Visibility				
	Very High	Above Average	Average	Below Average	Very Low
Public figure	16 (40.0%)	18 (45.0%)	3 (7.5%)	3 (7.5%)	0
Public official	24 (57.1%)	13 (31.0%)	1 (2.4%)	1 (2.4%)	3 (7.1%)
Private individual	8 (26.7%)	10 (33.3%)	5 (16.7%)	4 (13.3%)	3 (10%)

$p. < .05$

20. The relationship between plaintiffs' employment and the degree of community visibility is just outside the .1 range of statistical significance. However, the data do indicate that most libel plaintiffs are very visible members of their communities.

21.

Plaintiffs' employment compared with plaintiffs' community visibility

	Plaintiffs' Community Visibility				
	Very High	Above Average	Average	Below Average	Very Low
Elected official or candidate for office	18 (66.7%)	9 (33.3%)	0	0	0
Public employee	19 (46.3%)	13 (31.7%)	4 (9.8%)	3 (7.3%)	2 (4.9%)
Professional	8 (25.8%)	15 (48.4%)	3 (9.7%)	3 (9.7%)	2 (6.5%)
Business owner or manager	8 (36.4%)	10 (45.5%)	3 (13.6%)	0	1 (4.5%)
White-collar employee	5 (38.5%)	2 (15.4%)	2 (15.4%)	2 (15.4%)	2 (15.4%)

p. < .12

22.

Plaintiffs who held public office before or during the time of alleged libel

	Plaintiff Hold Public Office	
	Yes	No
Elected official or candidate for office	20 (74.1%)	7 (25.9%)
White-collar employee	3 (23.1%)	10 (76.9%)
Public employee	14 (35.9%)	25 (64.1%)
Business proprietor or manager	4 (19%)	17 (81%)
Professional	10 (32.3%)	21 (67.7%)

p. < .001

23. See Chapter 6 for a more thorough discussion of the criteria applied and the relevant cases.

24. Franklin, *Suing Media for Libel: A Litigation Study, supra* note 1.

25. *Id.* at 810.

26. The remaining 21 percent of the cases Franklin studied involved a wide variety of charges, including sexual misbehavior, the plaintiff being a poor credit risk, and plaintiff's physical or intellectual failings. It is unclear from his study what Franklin means by moral failing and why he does not include charges such as sexual misbehavior in the category. *Id.* at 812.

27. Each decision was read and the focus of the alleged libel recorded by three research assistants, all of whom were law students. The assistants then compared their findings and if there was not unanimous agreement as to the focus of the alleged libel, the case decision was reread and discussed. If the assistants still could not agree on the focus of the alleged libel, the focus of the alleged libel was classified as being "indeterminate."

28.

Focus of alleged libel for defamation cases between 1974 and 1984

Focus of Alleged Libel	Number	Percentage
Plaintiffs' professional or trade activities	362	50.4%
Plaintiffs' moral activities	125	17.4%
Both moral and business or trade activities	202	28.1%
Could not be determined	29	4.0%

29.

Type of defendant compared with focus of alleged libel for defamation cases between 1974 and 1984

	Focus of Alleged Libel		
	Plaintiffs' Professional or Trade Activities	Plaintiffs' Moral Activities	Both Moral and Professional
Media defendant	275 (53.7%)	90 (17.6%)	147 (28.7%)
Non-media defendant	87 (50.6%)	34 (19.8%)	51 (29.7%)

30.

Plaintiffs' legal status compared with the focus of the alleged libel for media defendants

	Focus of Alleged Libel for Media Defendants		
	Plaintiffs' Professional or Trade Activities	Plaintiffs' Moral Conduct	Both Moral and Professional
Public figure	91 (58.0%)	22 (14.0%)	44 (28.0%)
Public official	70 (59.8%)	2 (1.7%)	45 (38.5%)
Private individual	63 (40.6%)	59 (38.1%)	33 (21.3%)
Public-figure corporation	17 (77.3%)	0	5 (22.7%)
Private-figure corporation	22 (73.3%)	1 (3.3%)	7 (23.3%)

31.

Plaintiffs' legal status compared with content of alleged libel for plaintiffs who held public office either before or during the time alleged libel occurred

	Focus of the Alleged Libel			
	Personal or Private Activities	Business or Professional Activities	Public or Political Activities	Criminal Activities
Public figure	0	0	15 (83.3%)	3 (16.7%)
Public official	0	2 (9.1%)	17 (77.3%)	3 (13.6%)
Private figure	0	0	5 (100%)	0

$p < .53$

32.

Plaintiffs' visibility in community compared with focus of alleged libel

	Focus of the Alleged Libel[*]			
	Personal or Private Activities	Business or Professional Activities	Public or Political Activities	Criminal Activities
Very high visibility	2 (3.4%)	8 (13.6%)	39 (66.1%)	10 (16.9%)
Above average visibility	4 (7.8%)	15 (29.4%)	26 (51.0%)	6 (11.8%)
Average visibility	1 (7.7%)	5 (38.5%)	2 (15.4%)	5 (38.5%)
Below average visibility	1 (9.1%)	5 (45.5%)	2 (18.2%)	3 (27.3%)
Very low visibility	5 (55.6%)	2 (22.2%)	1 (11.1%)	1 (11.1%)

p. < .001

[*]Plaintiffs who have an above-average degree of community visibility tended to sue over stories that dealt with their public or political activities, while plaintiffs who have an average or below-average degree of community visibility tended to sue over stories that focused on their business or professional activities or on their alleged criminal activities.

33.

Have plaintiffs sued before filing their libel suit?

Yes	51 (32.9%)
No	104 (67.1%)

34.

Have plaintiffs sued after filing their libel suit?

Yes	41 (27.5%)
No	108 (72.5%)

35.

Plaintiffs' litigation experience compared with whom did the plaintiff contact at the media

	Whom Did Plaintiff Contact in the Media About the Allegedly Libelous Story?			
	Reporter	Editor or News Director	Publisher or Station Manager	More Than One of These
Filed at least one other suit besides libel suit	1 (2.8%)	15 (41.7%)	16 (44.4%)	4 (11.1%)
Only civil suit was the libel suit	11 (25.0%)	20 (45.5%)	10 (22.7%)	3 (6.8%)

p. < .02

36.

Plaintiffs' litigation experience compared with attorneys' fee arrangement

	Attorneys' Fee Arrangement with Plaintiffs	
	Hourly	Contingency
Filed at least one other suit besides libel suit	15 (31.9%)	32 (68.1%)
Only civil suit was the libel suit	3 (5.5%)	52 (94.5%)
p. < .002		

37. The comparison between these two groups of libel plaintiffs on the cost of the libel cases is just outside the .1 range of statistical significance.

38.

Plaintiffs' litigation experience compared with cost of libel suit for cases lost by plaintiffs

	Cost of libel suit*				
	Nothing	Under $1,000	$1,000–$5,000	$5,000–$20,000	Over $20,000
Filed at least one other suit besides libel suit	5 (13.2%)	3 (7.9%)	14 (36.8%)	12 (31.6%)	4 (10.5%)
Only civil suit was the libel suit	10 (21.7%)	11 (23.9%)	15 (32.6%)	8 (17.4%)	2 (4.3%)
p. < .14					

*Since attorneys on contingency who win take a percentage of any award, plaintiffs who ultimately prevailed in their libel suit report large litigation expenses. To control for this, the table reports litigation expenses only for plaintiffs who lost their libel case.

Chapter 3

1. See Appendix A, note 17.
2. See Appendix A, note 18.
3. Franklin found that newspapers were sued in 62 percent of the cases he studied; television stations were sued in 12 percent of the cases; magazines in 14 percent of the cases; and radio stations in 3 percent of the cases. Marc Franklin *Suing Media for Libel: A Litigation Study,* 1981 American Bar Foundation Research Journal 797–831.
4.

Location of allegedly libelous story in newspaper

	Number	Percentage
Front page	43	45.7%
Inside news page	33	35.1%
Editorial page	18	19.1%

5.

Plaintiffs' employment compared with location of alleged libel in newspaper

	Location of Alleged Libel in Newspaper		
	Front Page	Inside Page	Editorial Page
Elected official or candidate for office	8 (44.4%)	3 (16.7%)	7 (38.9%)
White-collar employee	3 (27.3%)	5 (45.5%)	3 (27.3%)
Public employee	14 (48.3%)	10 (34.5%)	5 (17.2%)
Business owner or manager	4 (28.6%)	9 (64.3%)	1 (7.1%)
Professional	10 (71.4%)	2 (14.3%)	2 (14.3%)

$p. < .05$

6.

Location of alleged libel in newspaper compared with focus of alleged libel

	Focus of the Alleged Libel			
	Personal or Private Activities	Business or Professional Activities	Public or Political Activities	Criminal Activities
Front page of newspaper	4 (9.5%)	6 (14.3%)	23 (54.8%)	9 (21.4%)
Inside page of newspaper	5 (15.2%)	13 (39.4%)	9 (27.3%)	6 (18.2%)
Editorial page of newspaper	0	5 (27.8%)	13 (72.2%)	0

$p. < .02$

7.

Circulation area of newspaper

Circulation Area	Number	Percentage
Local	57	51.8%
Regional	25	22.7%
State	21	19.1%
Multi-state	2	1.8%
National	5	4.5%

8.

When was alleged libel broadcast?

Time	Number	Percentage
Prime time	21	95.5%
Not prime time	1	4.5%

9

How the alleged libel harmed the plaintiffs, compared with focus of alleged libel

	How Alleged Libel Harmed the Plaintiffs				
	Emotional Harm	*Emotional and Financial Harm*	*Financial Harm*	*Business or Professional Reputation Damaged*	*Political Status Damaged*
Personal or private activities	8 (53.3%)	4 (26.7%)	1 (6.7%)	2 (13.3%)	0
Business or professional activities	5 (10.4%)	15 (31.3%)	15 (31.3%)	13 (27.1%)	0
Public or political activities	18 (25.7%)	10 (14.3%)	5 (7.1%)	16 (22.9%)	21 (30.0%)
Criminal activities	11 (50.0%)	5 (22.7%)	1 (4.5%)	3 (13.6%)	2 (9.1%)

p. < .001

10.

After the alleged libel appeared whom did plaintiff contact?

	Number	Percent
Media	73	48.7%
Attorney	75	50.0%
Other	2	1.3%

11.

Who contacted media prior to suit?

Person Contacting Media	*Number*	*Percent*
Plaintiff only	53	37.1%
Lawyer only	50	35.0%
Plaintiff and lawyer	26	18.2%
Neither	14	9.8%

12.

How long after alleged libel appeared were media contacted?

	Number	*Percentage*
Before publication	6	7.0%
Within two days	63	73.3%
More than two days later	17	19.8%

13.

Whom at media was contacted?

	Number	Percentage
Reporter	12	14.5%
Editor or news director	38	45.8%
Publisher or station manager	26	31.3%
More than one person	7	8.4%

14.

How were media contacted?

	Number	Percentage
In person	21	24.7%
By telephone	39	45.9%
By letter	22	25.9%
By telephone and letter	3	3.5%

15.

How media responded to plaintiffs' request

	Number	Percentage
Issued retraction, correction, or apology	26	21.3%
Did not repeat alleged libel	3	2.5%
Refused plaintiffs' request	79	64.8%
Repeated story	14	11.5%

16.

How plaintiff felt about media's response

	Number	Percentage
Angered	71	56.8%
Dissatisfied	46	36.8%
Satisfied	5	4.0%
Ambivalent	3	2.4%

CHAPTER 4

1. See Appendix A. In-depth interviewing was done at six newspapers during the summer of 1984. The papers are: Chicago Tribune, Des Moines Register, Kansas City Star and

Times, Minneapolis Star and Tribune, Omaha World Herald and Quad City (Ia.) Times. Unless otherwise noted, all statements by personnel of these newspapers were made during these interviews.

2. Associated Press Managing Editors Association Credibility Committee Report, 1984, at 9.

3. *Welcome to the Star*, Kansas City Star, at 11.

4. H. Eugene Goodwin, Groping for Ethics in Journalism, Iowa State University Press, at 27.

5. Terry Francisco, unpublished report, *Today's Ombudsmen: Their Role in Answering Complaints*, Jan. 16, 1985.

6. See Chapter 5 *infra* for discussion of the role of plaintiff's attorney in achieving plaintiff goals.

7. David Shaw, Los Angeles Times, Aug. 18, 1983.

8. *Proceedings of the American Society of Newspaper Editors*, 1983, at 125.

9. Editor & Publisher, Feb. 9, 1985, at 7–8.

10. *See* note 7 *supra*.

11. *What Can a Reporter Do to Keep From Being Sued?*, Associated Press Managing Editors Association.

12. *See* note 2 *supra*.

13. *See* note 7 *supra*.

14. Richard Cunningham, *When Readers Talk Back*, report to the National News Council, Sept. 1982.

15. Joseph T. Francke, *Reporting at Risk: Recognizing and Avoiding Liability for Libel and Invasion of Privacy*, unpublished manuscript, 1985.

16. Sharon v. Time Magazine, trial transcript, at 3196.

17. Time Magazine, May 6, 1985, at 6.

18. *See* note 2 *supra*.

19. Tom Patterson, Nov. 20, 1984 column, distributed by Minnesota Newspaper Association.

20. *In the Public Interest—III: A Report by the National News Council, 1979–83*, at 551–552.

21. While at least half (between 13 and 16 of 27) of the plaintiffs sued in the face of an apparently adequate retraction, it should not be presumed that they did so for unjustified reasons. In three of the 27 cases studied, clear economic loss appears to have occurred, and the retraction either failed to remedy this, or was too late to do so. In six of the cases the disputed statements appear to have been so emotionally trying (and often highly offensive), that the retraction could not quell the plaintiffs' need to take action. Whether a more self-effacing apology would have sufficed is unknowable, of course. There remain, however, seven or eight cases in which no apparent reason exists for the plaintiff suing in the face of an adequate retraction (other than the quest for vengeance and windfall recoveries).

22. Kurt M. Luedtke, *An Ex-Newsman Hands Down His Indictment of the Press*, The Bulletin of the American Society of Newspaper Editors, May–June 1982, at 17.

23. David Lawrence Jr., *From the Harvard Business School, Lessons on Newspapers, Accuracy*, The Bulletin of the American Society of Newspaper Editors, March 1984, at 7.

24. Rogert Tatarian, *How Do You Teach Accuracy?* The Bulletin of the American Society of Newspaper Editors, Sept. 1982, at 21.

25. Phil J. Record, *Journalists Reach for Credibility*, 1984–85 Journalism Ethics Report of the National Ethics Committee, Society of Professional Journalists, Sigma Delta Chi, at 3.

26. Elie Abel, upon receiving the 1984 First Amendment Defender Award by the Institute for Communications Law Studies of the Catholic University School of Law.

27. *See* note 2 *supra*.
28. Richard Capen, *Proceedings of the American Society of Newspaper Editors*, 1985, at 84.
29. Time Magazine, Dec. 12, 1983, at 85.
30. David Johnston, *The Wrong Stuff*, Washington Journalism Review, June 1984, at 25.
31. *See* note 30 *supra*.
32. Gregory Favre, *My Escape from the Windy City to Cool California*, The Bulletin of the American Society of Newspaper Editors, August 1984, at 36.
33. *See* note 30 *supra*.
34. *Newspaper Credibility: Building Reader Trust*, American Society of Newspaper Editors, 1985, at 19.
35. Newsweek Magazine, Oct. 22, 1984, at 68.
36. Michael Singletary, *Accuracy in News Reporting: A Review of the Research*, ANPA News Research Report, no. 25 (Jan. 25, 1980). It should be noted that the studies reported on allegations of error as they were perceived by news sources.
37. *See* note 3 *supra*, at 10.
38. *See* note 2 *supra*.

CHAPTER 5

1. *See* Table 5–28 *infra*.
2. The lawyers were contacted in connection with the plaintiff survey. Not all of the plaintiff lawyers' clients were interviewed, nor was contact made with all plaintiff lawyers. The population of lawyers, therefore, may not be representative.
3. *See* Tables 5–16 and 5–17 and accompanying discussion, *infra*.
4. Wisconsin Study S–28.
5. *See* Table 5–15 and accompanying discussion, *infra*.
6. A review of the recorded comments made by the plaintiffs during the interviews suggests that lawyer-initiated changes occurred most commonly at the time of trial, when additional experience was deemed necessary by the initial lawyer. Change also occurred at the point of filing suit. Based upon interview notes, it is clear that some of the changes occurring for reasons of experience were client-initiated and based in part on client dissatisfaction.
7. Six responses coded "other" are not included in the table, but did involve lawyer change for such reasons as conflict of interest or death, according to interview notes. The proportion of unexplained changes that were client-initiated cannot, for obvious reasons, be determined, but it is noteworthy that such reasons as death of the lawyer, conflict of interest, and the like are included in the separate "other" category.
8. *See* Chapters 6 and 7.
9. *See* Table 5–13 and accompanying discussion, *infra*.
10. *See* Chapter 8, note 29 and accompanying text, *infra*.
11. *See* Table 6–10, Chapter 6, *infra*.
12. Based on our review of media libel cases between 1974 and 1984, the incidence of success is significantly different depending on whether the plaintiff is a "public" plaintiff or a "private" plaintiff. The prospect of greater difficulty in succeeding is likely to account for the higher incidence of suggestions that suit may be unnecessary. *See* Table 6–10, Chapter 6, *infra*.
13. *See* Chapter 6 *infra*.
14. *See* Wisconsin Study S–18–19.

15. *See* Tables 5–16 and 5–28 and accompanying discussions, *infra*.
16. *See* Chapter 6, *infra*.
17. *See* Table 6–15, *infra*.
18. *See* Wisconsin Study S–29.
19. Excluding responses coded "other," "uncertain," or "refused to answer," 95 plaintiffs responded, 42 (or 44.2 percent) of whom paid fees exceeding $1,000.00; 53 (or 55.8 percent) of whom paid no fees or fees less than $1,000.00.
20. Wisconsin Study S–26.
21. *See* Wisconsin Study S–54–55.
22. This comparison is significant at .0436.
23. *See* Table 6–15 and accompanying discussion, *infra*.
24. "Punishment" is distinct from the interest in obtaining money from the suit. *See* Chapter 7, Table 7–5 and accompanying discussion, *infra*.
25. *See* Tables 7–1 to 7–3, discussed in Chapter 7, *infra*.
26. It is notable, as well, that the plaintiffs who sue for vindication and consider the lawyers' advice less important appear to be the public plaintiffs represented by lawyers on contingency.
27. For a discussion of the process of litigation for libel claims, compared with general civil litigation, see Chapter 6.
28. *See* New York Times, Inc. v. Sullivan, 376 U.S. 254 (1964).
29. *See* New York Times, Inc. v. Sullivan, 376 U.S. 254, 283 (1964); Gertz v. Robert Welch, Inc., 418 U.S. 323, 351 (1974). A "public figure" in defamation law is one who has achieved pervasive fame or notoriety, or one who voluntarily injects himself or is drawn into a particular public controversy, thus becoming a public figure for purposes of alleged defamations arising out of that controversy. *Id.* at 351. To succeed in a libel suit, public figures must show that the publisher of an alleged defamation published with "actual malice"—knowledge of a factual statement's falsity or reckless disregard of its truth or falsity in light of subjective awareness of probable falsity. *See id.* at 343, 351; St. Amant v. Thompson, 390 U.S. 727, 731 (1968).
30. Potential damage awards and inhibition of "robust" expression were major reasons for the constitutional privileges of *Sullivan* and *Gertz. See* New York Times, Inc. v. Sullivan, 376 U.S. 254, 269–71, 280 (1964); Gertz v. Robert Welch, Inc., 418 U.S. 323, 347, 349–50 (1974) (limiting damages).
31. The *Gertz* public figure definition was predicated in substantial part on the capacity of such persons to reply to an alleged defamation through the press, on the assumption that they have effective channels of access for response or denial because of the public status. Gertz v. Robert Welch, Inc., 418 U.S. 323, 344–45 (1974).
32. The majority of the retractions studied (drawn from a case sample independent of the plaintiff interviews) seemed either to compound the libel, as in Nevada Broadcasting v. Allen, 9 M. L. Rptr. 1769 (Nev. 1983), or to have been inadequate to purge a highly offensive report, as in Oregon v. Employers Reinsurance Corp., 350 N.W.2d 725 (Wis. 1984).
33. *See* text accompanying notes 27–32 *supra*.
34. *See* text accompanying notes 31–32 *supra*.
35. *See* text accompanying notes 9–27 *supra*.
36. *See* text accompanying notes 9–13 *supra*.
37. As discussed in Chapter 2, 85 percent of the plaintiffs who had previously sued for libel contacted the media first.
38. The criminal category (excluding business crime and political crime, which are incorporated into those two categories, respectively), follows a similar pattern.

39. A similar pattern holds for persons with "very high" visibility in their communities, who tend to contact the media first, and for persons libeled in connection with social or political activities.

40. *See* the discussion of falsity and perceived harm in Chapter 3 *supra*.

41. For a most interesting analysis that yields analogous conclusions in the very different setting of minor criminal prosecutions, *see* M. Feeley, The Process Is The Punishment (1979).

CHAPTER 6

1. Information on the nature or composition of the legal claims was drawn from two sources. First, virtually all reported cases in which a colorable privacy or defamation claim was seriously pursued between 1974 and 1984 were surveyed and coded. The data base permits a general assessment of the composition of communicative torts, in general, and related and comparative assessment of defamation actions, in particular. Second, information concerning the legal claim, the legal theory, the media involved as defendant, the course of litigation, and the cost of litigation was collected from a sample of libel cases between 1974 and 1984, from cases included in the plaintiff survey population, and from selected media defendants in those cases. See Appendix A for a complete discussion of methodology.

2. A tort is a legally compensable wrong done by one person (entity) to another in breach of a duty of care. Communicative torts represent those legally compensable wrongs that occur by communication—speech, writing, and the like. Communicative torts include defamation, which consists of the disparagement of one's reputation by published factual statements which are spoken (slander) or written (libel). This traditional distinction retains figurative, but not literal, force in today's communication environment. Libel now generally encompasses media of mass communication by broadcast, partly because of its substantial impact, and partly because—like print— the words and images can be physically maintained after the initial communication. Communicative torts also include invasion of privacy, product disparagement, and unfair competition, to name a few. For detailed discussion of these and other communicative torts, *see* W. Prosser, The Law of Torts (4th ed. 1971).

3. The number of total cases was larger, but only those that could be coded meaningfully are included in this analysis. For example, cases in which the identity of the defendant could not reliably be ascertained were not coded. *See* disscussion in Appendix A.

4. *See* Restatement (Second) of Torts 652E (1977); W. Prosser, The Law of Torts § 117 (4th ed. 1971).

5. *See* Restatement (Second) of Torts 652A (1977); W. Prosser, The Law of Torts § 117 (4th ed. 1971).

6. *See* Restatement (Second) of Torts 652D (1977); W. Prosser, The Law of Torts § 117, at 809 (4th ed. 1971).

7. *See* Restatement (Second) of Torts 652A (1977); W. Prosser, The Law of Torts § 117 (4th ed. 1971).

8. *Id*.

9. For discussion of the definition of "media" employed in the study, *see* Appendix A.

10. An example would be Miller v. Charleston Gazette, 9 Media L. Rptr. 2540 (W. Va. Cir. 1983), involving portrayal of the plaintiff in a political cartoon as an animal trainer whipping an elephant—a reference to his efforts to influence the Republican

Party to appoint him U.S. Attorney. Plaintiff claimed that the caption—"But will he respect me in the morning"—implied that he engaged in strange sexual behavior. As with virtually all false light claims, this one failed.

11. Sixty-four percent of the public disclosure cases involved media defendants. The higher level of non-media cases is explainable by the private and personal character of the information, and its greater susceptibility to communication through rumor or other more limited communicative channels, as well as a significant proportion of cases arising out of the employment setting. Finally, only 39 percent of intrusion cases involved media defendants. The larger proportion of these trespass-like actions involved physical invasions outside the media publishing context. The higher proportion of non-media defendants in privacy cases as a whole corresponds to the higher incidence of plaintiff success in privacy cases and in non-media cases, discussed in the following sections. See Tables 6–5 and 6–9 infra.

12. The current categorization was established in Gertz v. Robert Welch, Inc., 418 U.S. 323, 351 (1974).

13. Constitutional privileges dictated by the First Amendment are distinct from "common law" privileges developed by state courts, although the effect of common law privileges—to give special protection to certain types of expression, such as opinion on public issues or communication with employers—is similar.

14. See Gertz v. Robert Welch, Inc., 418 U.S. 323, 351 (1974); New York Times Co. v. Sullivan, 376 U.S. 254, 283 (1964).

15. Gertz v. Robert Welch, Inc., 418 U.S. 323, 351 (1974). Generally speaking, the public figure formulation of Gertz embraces both those plaintiffs formerly classified as public officials, and those formerly classified as public figures in the 1967 decision in Curtis Pub. Co. v. Butts, 388 U.S. 130, 147, 154–55 (1967), although the precise definitions are not coterminous and, to the extent that the definitions yield different results, the Gertz formulation controls.

16. See Bose Corp. v. Consumers Union of United States, Inc., 80 L.Ed.2d 502 (1984). While the operative definition for public figure corporations is essentially the same as for individuals, its actual application in the cases has had a decidedly checkered history. See Fetzer, The Corporate Defamation Plaintiff as First Amendment "Public Figure": Nailing the Jellyfish, 68 Iowa L. Review 35 (1982).

17. Gertz v. Robert Welch, Inc., 418 U.S. 323, 351–52 (1974).

18. Id.; St. Amant v. Thompson, 390 U.S. 727, 731 (1968).

19. Gertz v. Robert Welch, Inc., 418 U.S. 323, 347 (1974).

20. Id. at 343; Dun & Bradstreet, Inc. v. Greenmoss Builders, Inc., 86 L.Ed.2d 593 (1985). The plurality opinion in the Greenmoss case left open whether a distinction between media and non-media defendants was relevant to the application of negligence or strict liability, respectively, in private defamation actions. A majority of the justices rejected the distinction, but a majority also suggested that strict liability could exist in defamation actions brought by private plaintiffs and not involving a matter of public concern or wide distribution to the public. It is doubtful whether this standard is any different, in practical effect, from a media/non-media standard. In any event, it seems clear that strictly private defamation actions are still controlled by the common law rule of strict liability. Moreover, whether one characterizes "media" cases as categorically subject to privilege—as we do—or as privileged only to the extent of intention to distribute broadly and without narrow restriction as to audience per Greenmoss, all of the cases we define as "media" will be privileged, with the level of privilege depending, under Gertz, on the plaintiff's status. For our purposes, the impact of the Greenmoss case, if any, will be with the private, non-media cases, where we have

suggested *and found* that strict liability may still govern liability. *See* Bezanson, *Fault, Falsity, and Reputation in Public Defamation Law*, 8 Hamline Law Review 105, 105–06 nn. 4 & 5 (1985), for a listing of cases and jurisdictions in which negligence applies.

21. In the recent case of *Philadelphia Newspapers, Inc. v. Hepps*, 106 S.Ct. 1558 (1986), the United States Supreme Court held that in libel actions against media defendants (or involving general or unrestricted distribution), plaintiffs bear the burden of proving the falsity of the challenged statement. The exact nature of this burden, and the ways it may be satisfied (i.e., the type of proof necessary) were left to future cases. The Court's decision follows decisions in a number of jurisdictions that have placed the burden of proving falsity on the plaintiff, and reverses the longstanding common law rule that truth was a defense, falsity being presumed by a well-pleaded complaint of defamation.

    The impact of the *Hepps* decision on the adjudication of media libel cases is uncertain. It is hoped that the decision will focus greater attention in the litigation of claims on the central issue of truth or falsity, especially at trial. However, the dominance of the fault privileges, with the issue of subjective falsehood, may continue to deflect attention from the *actual* falsity question. The fault privileges will also most likely continue to dominate adjudication, especially at the pre-trial stage, and therefore the dominance of fault rather than actual falsity will likely persist, although the situation will hopefully improve. For a full discussion of the dominance of fault, and its impact on the adjudication of libel claims, see Chapter 8.

22. 418 U.S. 323 (1974).

23. *Id.* at 351.

24. Non-media cases, in light of the recent but somewhat ambiguous decision in *Dun & Bradstreet, Inc. v. Greenmoss Builders, Inc.*, 86 L.Ed.2d 593 (1985), consist of cases not involving media defendants and not relating to matters of public concern, which the Court judged substantially by the breadth and means of the challenged statement's distribution, and whether it was intended for limited and private or broad and public dissemination. 86 L.Ed.2d, at 604–05.

25. *See* Wanner, *The Public Ordering of Private Relations Part I: Initiating Civil Cases in Urban Trial Courts*, Law and Society 421 (Spring 1974); Chapter 2 *supra*.

26. *See* W. Prosser, The Law of Torts § 111 (4th ed. 1971).

27. *Id.*

28. A second explanation for the low incidence of corporate plaintiffs in *public* libel cases is that corporate and other artificial entities suing as libel plaintiffs are likely to be classified as private, rather than public, plaintiffs. This is borne out when the composition of the private plaintiffs is examined, although the difference in the composition of individual and corporate plaintiffs between public and private actions is small, and the large variance in proportion of individual claims between libel actions and civil litigation in general makes uncertain any conclusions drawn from the marginal differences. Private plaintiffs filed 43 percent of all defamation cases surveyed between 1974 and 1984. Claims brought by individuals comprise 87 percent of all private claims, and 85 percent of all such claims in private plaintiff media cases, compared with 92 and 90 percent, respectively, in public cases; 90 percent of private plaintiff non-media claims were brought by individuals.

    These data permit two observations to be made, although conclusions should be drawn carefully, given the marginal differences between the public and private populations. First, 8 percent of public cases are brought by corporate plaintiffs, while 13 percent of private cases are brought by corporate plaintiffs. Because the libel plaintiff data indicate that no apparent differences exist between these groups in terms of the nature of the claims or the circumstances in which they are brought, it is possible that corporate plaintiffs are more likely to be classified as private for purposes of libel litigation. Second, while there is no difference in the individual or corporate composition of public plaintiffs in media and non-media cases, a difference does occur in private cases. Fifteen percent of private media cases involve corporate plaintiffs, while under 10 percent of private non-media cases involve corporate plaintiffs. This difference is to be expected, as the corporate reputational interest is more likely to be injured through broad publication involving media. The greater incidence of corporate claims in private media cases, however, tends to confirm the suggestion advanced above that corporate plaintiffs are more likely to be classified as private for purposes of constitutional privilege in the cases in which the privilege issues are pertinent.

29. Indeed, in light of this it is surprising that such a large proportion of private plaintiff claims brought by individuals are brought against media defendants, for media publication might be expected generally to connote a measure of general interest and a relationship to a general public topic. Analysis of case results tends to bear this out. As discussed in greater detail later in this chapter, private individuals succeed in 23 percent of the cases brought against non-media defendants and in only 13 percent of the cases brought against media defendants. This pattern does not hold for corporate plaintiffs, however, for it appears that private corporate plaintiffs are at least as successful, if not more successful, against media defendants as against non-media defendants. *See* Tables 6–8, 6–9, 6–10, *infra*.

30. "News" was defined to include articles in newspapers, magazines, periodicals, including essays and editorials on current topics, and other publications with significant (i.e. not highly limited and special purpose) circulation dealing with current events or issues.

31. "Entertainment" included print or broadcast publication of fictional character or for entertainment purposes alone, having no relation to current events or issues.

32. "Literature" included both print and broadcast material of serious literary, cultural, historical, or artistic character.

33. The correspondence between the news, entertainment, and literature categories, and the media classification, is very close, with over 98 percent of the media cases falling within one of these groupings.

34. W. Prosser, The Law of Torts §§ 111, 117 (4th ed. 1971); R. Sack, Libel, Slander, and Related Problems (P.L.I. 1980).

35. *See* note 34 *supra*.

36. 376 U.S. 254 (1964).

37. As a technical matter, this need not happen. A determination of no actionable defamation or reputational injury would, in an appropriate case, conclude the case without privilege questions having to be addressed. An admission of truth, or a preliminary showing of truth, would have the same effect. Similarly, cases litigated to trial could—as in the *Sharon* case—address all of the issues, common law and constitutional. However, based on our case survey (which included only cases with reported decisions, and therefore may overstate the situation), the common practice appears to be that defendants raise and address the privilege issues at the pre-trial level, and the decisions at this point only infrequently address the common law issues (although they could often do so even in this posture).

38. *See* Appendix A for an explanation of the use and meaning of the media/non-media distinction used in this book; *see also* note 20 *supra*.

39. *See* Gertz v. Robert Welch, Inc., 418 U.S. 323, 351 (1974).

40. *See* Gertz v. Robert Welch, Inc., 418 U.S. 323, 347 (1974).

41. *See* note 20 *supra*. As indicated in note 20, the operative distinction is not "media" status of the defendant, as such, but its substantive equivalent of public distribution of material of public concern.
42. St. Amant v. Thompson, 390 U.S. 727, 731 (1968).
43. *See* Restatement (Second) of Torts 580B, comment (h) (1977); Anderson, *Libel and Press Self-Censorship*, 53 Texas L. Rev. 422, 461–62 (1975); Note, *In Defense of Fault in Defamation Law*, 88 Yale L. J. 1735, 1738 n. 15 (1979).
44. *See* New York Times Co. v. Sullivan, 376 U.S. 254, 270, 280 (1964); Gertz v. Robert Welch, Inc., 418 U.S. 323, 344–46 (1974).
45. *See* Appendix A for a discussion of the methodology employed in coding this variable.
46. *See* Tables 6–12 to 6–14 and accompanying discussion, *infra*.
47. While the Supreme Court has only recently held that plaintiffs bear the burden of proof on falsity in most media libel cases, *see* note 21 *supra*, it is unlikely that this will alter the dominance of privilege issues, as the data indicate. Privilege issues are still likely to remain the principal and, as a practical matter, first line of defense. It should be noted, however, that the cases analyzed here all preceded the *Hepps* decision, 106 S. Ct. 1558 (1986).
48. Virtually all cases coded media—and all cases in which media status has been explicitly considered relevant, as such, by courts—will satisfy the *Greenmoss* standard. *See* note 20 *supra*.
49. *See* Table 6–13 and text accompanying notes 107–109, *infra*.
50. *See* Table 6–14 *infra*.
51. *See* Chapter 8 *infra*.
52. Two methodological points should be mentioned. Because we relied upon reported judicial decisions, the coding was limited to those cases in which the opinion provided sufficient factual material to make a judgment about likely material disparagement and harm. Because facts were sometimes incomplete or in dispute, no adversarial adjudication having taken place (most cases involved opinions on privilege issues), many cases were not coded, and in marginal cases unanimity among the three coders was required. Even in coded cases, the tentative nature of fact development often required judgments—but the judgments were consistently applied. Second, a coding of "petty" does *not* mean that the published material was true, nor that its publication, if false, could not legitimately cause emotional distress to the plaintiff. A number of "petty" claims did involve admitted or probable falsity and/or perceived reputational harm, although the materiality of these elements was deemed insufficient to warrant a conclusion that the claim was "equitably" strong by common law standards.
53. For a more complete discussion of the disjunction of privilege rules and the strength of defamation claims, with citation of illustrative cases, *see* Chapter 8 *infra*.
54. 394 F. Supp. 721 (S.D.N.Y. 1975).
55. *See* Table 6–8 *infra*.
56. *See* Table 6–8 *infra*.
57. While Table 6–3 represents a census of the population of defamation cases, and therefore significance measures are perhaps unnecessary, the significance is .0617.
58. *See* Chapter 5 *supra*.
59. The success rates of plaintiffs can be profitably considered in light of the article "The Selection of Disputes for Litigation" by George Priest and Benjamin Klien, XIII Journal of Legal Studies 1 (1984). Priest and Klien hypothesize that the results in litigation for "dollar maximizing" parties should approximate 50 percent; that equality of the parties' stakes in a dispute—which will tend toward an average rate of recovery in litigation of 50 percent—contributes to the decision to litigate rather than settle.

The article assesses the vast proportion of empirical studies on results of litigation, with results that generally confirm the hypothesis.

Obviously, even the most generous rate of plaintiff success in recovering money damages in litigated libel claims falls far short of 50 percent. This suggests, as we have suggested and as Priest and Klien discuss in somewhat different contexts, that two other factors are at work in libel cases: first, that the incidence of damage recovery is not a true reflection of the incidence of success; and, second, that differential stakes exist between the parties, with "dollar maximizing" *not* representing accurately the stakes of either party. In one respect, however, our findings run counter to those hypothesized by Priest and Klien, for they suggest that the party with differentially high stakes will win more often than 50 percent of the time. If we posit that the libel plaintiffs' reputational interest and emotional commitment to litigation represent a differential stake, we would expect (under the Priest and Klien hypothesis) them to win more than 50 percent of the cases, for they would choose not to settle cases in which they would win. The explanation seems to us to be twofold: (1) plaintiffs *in fact do* win a high proportion of the cases, as *they* define winning; and (2) the defendants also have a differential (ideological *and* reputational) stake, and therefore they persist when we might otherwise expect them to settle.

60. The definition of "pending" cases requires explanation. Cases coded "pending" include: (1) judicial decisions (not later supplanted by subsequent decision) which did not relate to the merits of the libel claim, but instead involved preliminary matters relating to discovery, jurisdiction, and the like; (2) judicial decisions that anticipate further litigation, such as decisions remanding a lower court decision or trial judgment; (3) decisions on questions of law (often constitutional privilege) where it appears from the status of the case that subsequent litigation (usually trial) will take place, the only issue addressed being, for example, the standard of proof. Cases in which the legal determination is likely to be final, however, were coded "final." Examples would be a decision on plaintiff legal status, where the status decision triggers the malice privilege and the plaintiff has acknowledged, or the court intimated, that such a showing cannot be made; or a decision applying the actual malice standard to the facts and concluding that actual malice does not exist, thereby ending the case (in the absence of further appellate review, which was not discovered through Shephards, Westlaw, or Lexis). Many such cases involved subsequent denials of certiorari, therefore finally concluding the case. (4) Other cases in which the presence of subsequent judicial activity was known (from plaintiffs, lawyers, or other sources).

The term "pending" seemed to be the most fitting label for this defined group of cases, but it should be recognized that the cases so coded are not necessarily pending as of 1984 in the pure sense of the word. For example, some "pending" cases will actually have been finalized by voluntary withdrawal or settlement. Likewise, some "final" cases will not be final because further appeal has been taken but no reported indication of that fact will have been available to us. While these two factors may largely offset each other, we do not employ the "pending" category as a reflection of cases still in progress as of 1984, but rather as a manifestation of the level of cases involving judicial activity that is probably interlocutory in character. We also use the coding to eliminate, as best possible, incompleted cases so as to get a relatively pure measure of plaintiff and defendant success rates in cases finally resolved by judicial decision.

61. *See* note 60 *supra.*
62. *See* note 28 *supra.*
63. *See* Table 6–8.

64. This is because some level of privilege will be applicable in all—or virtually all—media cases, even after the *Greenmoss* case, but strict liability will apply in some private, non-media, cases. *See* note 20 *supra*.

65. *See* Tables 6–8 and 6–10 *infra*.

66. *See* text accompanying notes 98–107 *infra*.

67. Dun & Bradstreet, Inc. v. Greenmoss Builders, Inc., 86 L.Ed.2d 593 (1985). As indicated in note 20, the Court's decision is limited to the questions of presumed damages and punitive damages, and applies a "public concern" rather than a "media" standard for application of constitutional privilege in the private libel setting. It is likely, however, that the Court's damage rule will apply also to privileges governing liability, and the formulation of the "public concern" standard appears substantially similar to the distinction which would be drawn under a "media" standard. *See* Bezanson, *The New Free Press Guarantee*, 63 Virginia Law Review 731, 781–85 (1977).

68. For the definition of these torts, *see* text accompanying notes 4–8 *supra*.

69. *See* note 60 *supra*.

70. *See* Tables 6–4 and 6–8.

71. *See* Cox Broadcasting Co. v. Cohn, 420 U.S. 469 (1975); Time, Inc. v. Hill, 385 U.S. 374 (1967); Haiman, Speech and Law in a Free Society 73 (1981). *Cf.* Philadelphia Newspapers Inc. v. Hepps, 106 S.Ct. 1558 (1986).

72. Offensiveness of the material communicated in a fictionalized manner rather than defamation of reputation is required in false light actions. Restatement (Second) of Torts 652E (1977).

73. *See* Tables 6–9 and 6–10 *infra*.

74. *See* note 60 *supra*.

75. *See* note 60 *supra*.

76. In a separate survey of editors of 175 responding newspapers conducted by the *Iowa Law Review*, it was reported that the newspapers had been found liable in 23 of the 471 reported libel cases over the 10-year period from 1975–1985. This represents a liability rate of 4.9 percent. When corrected for pending claims, assumed to represent 30 percent of the cases, the liability rate was 7 percent. In addition, a settlement rate of 8.7 percent and (correcting for pending cases) 12.4 percent was reported. These rates of liability and settlement may be underreported because the responding editors were not always in a position to know the details of litigation. In any event, they seem essentially equivalent to the rates reported in Table 6–10, which would include cases resolved against the media and subsequently settled.

The *Law Review* survey also broke down the incidence of suit, liability, and settlement by size of circulation, with expected, but interesting, results. The results are summarized in the following Table.

Libel Claims Against Newspapers, 1975–85: Rates of Suit, Liability, and Settlement[***]

	Circulation				
	100,000 and up	50,000–99,999	25,000–49,999	15,000–24,999	Total
Total Suits	111	46	147	87	391
Total Final (est. @ 70%)	78	32	103	61	274
Newspapers Responding	18	15	72	70	175
Rate of Suit per Newspaper (Total Suits)	6.2	3.1	2.0	1.2	2.2

(continued)

Libel Claims Against Newspapers, 1975–85: Rates of Suit, Liability, and Settlement[***]
(*Continued*)

	Circulation				
	100,000 and up	50,000– 99,999	25,000– 49,999	15,000– 24,999	*Total*
Newspaper Liability Total Cases	2	2	3	12	19
Liability Rate—Total Cases	1.8%	4.3%	2.0%	13.8%[*]	4.9%
Liability Rate—Final Cases (est.)	2.6%	6.3%	2.9%	19.7%[*]	6.9%
Newspaper Settlements Total Settlements[**]	9	0	16	9	34
Settlement Rate—Total Cases	8.1%	0.0%	10.9%	10.3%	8.7%
Settlement Rate—Final Cases (est.)	11.5%	0.0%	15.5%	14.8%	12.4%

[*]The rate appears distorted by one small paper that accounts for 7 instances of liability.

[**]Includes non-monetary settlements, such as a printed retraction following negotiation.

[***]Source: Iowa Law Review Contemporary Studies Project, *Standards Governing the News*, 72 Iowa L. Rev. (1986).

77. The recent requirement that plaintiffs bear the burden of proving actual falsity of the challenged statement in most media libel cases can also be viewed as a constitutional privilege, but it is of a different character, as it goes to proof of the underlying defamation claim rather than an independent showing bearing no necessary relationship to the strength of the underlying defamation claim. *See* Philadelphia Newspapers Inc. v. Hepps, 106 S.Ct. 1558 (1986); note 21 *supra*.

78. *See* note 20 *supra*. This assumes, in light of the recent *Greenmoss* case, that the material published by the media defendant was of concern to the public, and was not distributed only to a highly limited, special purpose clientele.

79. *See* Table 6–9.

80. *See* text accompanying notes 52–56 *supra*.

81. The case totals in Table 6–11, as well as the totals in notes 82 and 83 *infra*, do not reflect all media defamation decisions during the year, and can be compared only generally with case totals used, for example, in the Franklin studies. Variances from a population count from Media Law Reporter, Westlaw, and the other sources used would result principally for the following reasons. (1) Only "final" cases are included, and therefore judicial opinions that do not decide the merits of the case, or opinions from cases known to have been remanded or appealed, are "pending" and therefore not included. (2) Only "codable" cases were used, and therefore, for example, cases with both media and non-media defendants (with neither being the real party in interest) would not be included. (3) Because of the longitudinal nature of the case data, cases with a reported decision in a particular year (even though resolving the merits of the claim) would be withdrawn from the year if in a subsequent year another decision in the same case were published. (4) For cases with multiple claims (privacy and defamation, for example), the case was coded in terms of the principle claim if it could be discerned. (5) Only cases involving seriously litigated claims of defamation were included, thus eliminating many cases involving a defamation count that was not colorable or not treated as a significant theory of liability. (6) Additional cases that are not picked up in the reporter services are included in various years, because some

cases without reported decision were drawn from the LDRC listings, and a limited group of cases was drawn from insurance company files (with enough information about the judicial action to code). (7) Finally, although we tried to scour the various sources and services for every reported decision, we do not claim infallibility. We take comfort, however, in the general consistency of our case numbers and codings with Professor Franklin's able studies.

82.

The proportions are as follows over the period: Media and Non-Media Defendants, Defamation Cases**

Year*	Media		Non-Media	
	#	%	#	%
1975	25	67.6%	12	32.4%
1976	30	57.7%	22	42.3%
1977	33	67.3%	16	32.7%
1978	44	65.7%	23	34.3%
1979	32	71.1%	13	28.9%
1980	68	71.6%	27	28.4%
1981	74	74.0%	26	26.0%
1982	115	82.7%	24	17.3%
1983	63	94.0%	4	6.0%

*Only partial data were collected for 1974 and 1984, and they have accordingly been deleted from the table.
**See note 81.

83.

Rate of Plaintiff Success By Year: Privacy and Defamation Cases, 1975–83

Year**	Cases Finally Resolved*		
	Total	Pl. Wins	% Pl. Wins
1975	35	8	23%
1976	48	6	13%
1977	56	7	13%
1978	72	13	18%
1979	58	8	14%
1980	93	12	13%
1981	82	13	16%
1982	120	13	11%
1983	55	6	11%

*Cases with more than one reported judicial decision were coded only once, and were grouped for purposes of this table by the most recent reported decision or order.
**Only partial data were collected for 1974 and 1984, and they have accordingly been deleted from the table. See note 81.

84. *Id.*
85. E.g., Hutchinson v. Proxmire, 443 U.S. 111, 120 n. 9 (1979); Calder v. Jones, 79 L.Ed.2d 804, 813 (1984).
86. With the Supreme Court's recent decision requiring that plaintiffs in most media cases must prove actual falsity of the challenged statement, this pattern may shift—for the better—toward greater emphasis on truth or falsity rather than privilege, even in the pre-trial stages. The change, however, is likely to be marginal, as negligence and malice privilege issues are likely, as a practical matter, to remain the principal, and initial, focus. The impact of the new plaintiff burden will be felt more substantially at trial. *See* Philadelphia Newspapers Inc. v. Hepps, 106 S.Ct. 1558 (1986); note 21 *supra.* For a discussion of the pre-*Hepps* role of privileges in the trial of defamation cases, *see* Chapter 8 *infra.*
87. Table 6–10. See also Table 6–14; text accompanying notes 45–58, Chapter 8, *infra.* This is not to suggest that the underlying factual issues of falsity, reputational harm, or damage are not known in all such cases. In many cases, these issues—particularly the falsity issue—are not uncertain (for instance, falsity may in effect be admitted), but the contested issue of fault precludes the relevance of the issues at the pre-trial stage when the focus is on privilege.
88. In addition to the plaintiff's public or private status for purpose of privilege, the other issue of application of the (actual malice or negligence) privilege to the facts involves questions of the reporter's and editor's state of mind on the issue of known or probable falsity *at the time of publication*, and the steps taken before publication in light of that state of mind. *See* St. Amant v. Thompson, 390 U.S. 727, 731 (1968); Gertz v. Robert Welch, Inc., 418 U.S. 323, 347 (1974); note 34 *supra.* None of these issues bears on the plaintiff's reputation, the *actual* falsity of that which was published, or damage. *See* Bezanson, *supra* note 20.
89. *See* note 86 *supra.*
90. *See* Table 3–1 *supra.*
91. *See* text accompanying notes 52–58 *supra.*
92. Table 6–10, success rate for public plaintiffs (actual malice) and private plaintiffs (negligence), respectively.
93. *See* Table 6–9.
94. *See* Chapter 8 *infra.*
95. Indeed, for media cases involving individual plaintiffs, weak claims are more successful in cases involving actual malice than those involving negligence. When corporate plaintiffs are included, the trend reverses. Likewise, for non-media cases (largely because of strict liability), private plaintiffs are more successful than public plaintiffs on weak claims.
96. Seven of the settlement cases are included in the 14 cases drawn for plaintiff interviews from insurance company files.
97. *See* text accompanying notes 119–121 *infra.*
98. The number of cases used was a function of selecting every fifth case in the general data base of cases, plus all decided cases in the original plaintiff survey population (114 cases) not selected at random.
99. This includes only cases with a formal reported judicial order, 25 percent of which reach trial. Many cases, however, are filed but do not reach the point of a reported judicial order, *see* Table 6–15, *infra*, and therefore the true incidence of trial in filed media defamation cases is significantly lower than 25 percent.
100. *See* text accompanying notes 98–99 *supra.*

101. Table 6–13.
102. Table 6–14.
103. For general civil litigation, the level of pre-trial disposition by summary judgment or dismissal is about 22 percent, as reported in the Wisconsin Study, S–82 n. 17.
104. Table 6–13.
105. *See* Wisconsin Study S–23.
106. *See* note 76 *supra*.
107. *See* Wisconsin Study S–23.
108. For purposes of the following discussion and Figures 1A, 1B, and 2, the following terms and definitions apply:

    1. GRIEVANCE: A situation in which an individual has an opportunity to use the courts if he or she so chooses.
    2. CLAIM: When an individual with a grievance complains to the offending party.
    3. DISPUTE: When an individual with a grievance seeks redress and is at least initially rebuffed by the offending party.
    4. LAWYER: When an individual with a grievance contacts a lawyer.
    5. FILING: When an individual with a grievance files a complaint.
    6. COURT ACTION BEFORE PRE-TRIAL: Court action taken prior to the pre-trial conference.
    7. COURT ACTION PRIOR TO TRIAL: Court action taken at or after the pre-trial conference, but prior to the trial.
    8. COURT ACTION AT OR AFTER TRIAL: Court action taken at trial or during post-trial.

109. This group of cases includes also some cases involving settlement with no published order, and cases that are self-reported by attorneys although no reported order is published. Conclusions drawn from this population, however, are limited to cases with reported orders. *See* Appendix A for a discussion of methodology.
110. *See* note 59 *supra*.
111. *See* note 113 *infra*. It appears from the data we have evaluated, as well as the reported experience of attorneys involved in libel litigation, that many libel suits are filed and thereafter dropped or left dormant. We also believe that a number of potential, serious libel claims are resolved prior to formal initiation of suit, usually through settlement. *See* Table 6–15. It may not be meaningful, therefore, to compare the incidence of trial for all filed libel suits with that for all filed civil suits (where the same phenomena surely occur). Even if it were meaningful, however, we have not been able to obtain reliable data for the universe of filed suits. The insurance data reflected in Table 6–15, interpreted in light of the experience with those cases, are consistent with other, more ad hoc judgments, that between 5 and 10 percent of filed suits are tried—a range not at variance with civil litigation in general.

    The truth of the matter, however, is that no one really knows the incidence of trial for all filed libel suits, and therefore we can draw no specific conclusions on that issue when compared to civil litigation. Our approach, in contrast, is to compare the process of litigation for *reported* libel suits with that for civil litigation in general, and to suggest that, while these universes are dissimilar, the general pattern for reported libel cases is representative of (although not equal to) that for seriously litigated libel suits. As to this comparison, we have greater confidence based on insurance information and experience provided by certain media, that the trial rate for libel cases is 10 to 15 percent, and perhaps higher. We also believe that this rate is likely higher than for comparable civil suits. For example, in civil suits the incidence of trial for cases involving formal judicial activity before trial is about 10 percent; for libel cases the comparable figure, we believe, is between the 10 to 15 percent assumed rate for serious suits and the 20 to 25 percent rate for libel suits with reported judicial action.

112. The representation of general civil litigation after the filing of a lawsuit in Figure 1B is based on information provided by the Administrative Office of the United States Courts and the Wisconsin Civil Litigation Study.

113. Our conclusion that the trial rate for reported cases is indicative of (although, we expect, higher than) the trial rate for the larger population of filed suits that are seriously pursued is based on a number of factors. First, Table 6–15 indicates that the level of plaintiff success for all filed insurance claims is 27 percent. This overall rate of success is greater than that indicated for the more limited population of cases involving a published judicial order (18 percent; 11 percent judicial wins and 7 percent additional settlements). Because the incidence of success for filed but not reported cases is at least as great, if not greater, than for reported cases, these data are consistent with (although they do not prove) the hypothesis that the incidence of trial for all serious libel suits is not significantly different than the 20 to 25 percent incidence for filed cases with reported judicial decision. Second, this conclusion is bolstered by the incidence of liability and settlement in all filed cases reported by 175 randomly selected newspapers (19 percent plaintiff success; 12 percent settlement and 7 percent adverse judicial decision), which is virtually identical to the 18 percent rate for the more limited population of cases with reported judicial orders. *See* note 76 *supra.* This similarity suggests a common underlying pattern of trial for the newspaper cases, which include all cases filed, whether or not reported. Third, a comparison of the actions, objectives, and motivations of the subgroup of 14 plaintiffs drawn from insurance company files whose cases were not reported, with the 150 other plaintiffs whose cases were reported, disclosed that both plaintiff subgroups exhibited similar characteristics. Finally, the rate of pre-filing settlement appears to be low (*see* text accompanying notes 105–107 *supra*), and the incidence of settlement activity involving money appears to occur after some form of litigation activity has occurred, according to many people with whom we have spoken. In light of these factors, we believe that the rate of trial for seriously pursued libel suits is not substantially at variance with the 20 to 25 percent rate for cases with reported judicial activity. Unfortunately, the insurance cases reported in Table 6–15 were not coded in a manner that would permit the separate identification of those settled cases which had been tried, but an overall trial rate of 10 to 15 percent of filed suits that are seriously pursued seemed consistent with the experience reported by persons familiar with the insurance company's litigation. While lower than the 20 to 25 percent for reported cases, this rate is higher than the 4 percent rate for filed civil claims, and we would expect the incidence of settlements before trial to be higher in this population of insured claims than in the population as a whole.

114. Wisconsin Study S–23.

115. Wisconsin Study S–19, 20.

116. *See* Table 6–15 *infra.*

117. *See* text accompanying notes 52–58 *supra.*

118. This is partly, although not exclusively, a result of the burden of truth being placed on the defendant. It is also a result of the difficult distinction between actual falsity and subjective falsity—the latter being a privilege issue. The recent decision in *Philadelphia Newspapers Inc. v. Hepps,* 106 S. Ct. 1558 (1986), which requires most plaintiffs in media

libel cases to prove actual falsity, may place a much-needed emphasis on the actual falsity issue. *See* note 21 *supra*.

119. Some of these dropped insurance claims involved a legal filing as well, but the proportion involving a filed suit cannot be determined. In any event, none of the cases involving a filed suit was prosecuted beyond that initial stage.

120. Settlements as a percent of filed suits may be a misleading measure, given the interrelatedness of the decision to settle and the decision to sue, and given also some ambiguity in the coding system.

121. *See* note 76 *supra*.

122. *See* Table 5–4 *supra*.

123. *See* Tables 5–3 and 5–4 *supra*.

124. *See* Table 5–5 *supra*.

125. *See* Table 5–15 *supra*.

126. *See* text accompanying notes 18–22, Chapter 5, *supra*.

127. Stating an "average" cost of litigation for a group as diverse as our 164 libel plaintiffs is both hazardous and, almost by definition, incomplete. The $7,015 "average" was arrived at by a straightforward weighted calculation, using the midpoints of the cost ranges employed for the question. The reasonableness of the figure (which, it should be noted, was self-reported by the plaintiffs), however, was judgmentally tested by reference to the distribution of plaintiffs in the various ranges (reported in the text), and an analysis of the litigation costs for only plaintiffs who lost, using all such plaintiffs and also eliminating the two high-cost (over $100,000) cases. Average litigation cost for all losing plaintiffs (final resolution) was $9,954; excluding the two high-cost cases, the average litigation cost was $5,894. In light of these averages for losing plaintiffs, the calculated figure of $7,015 for all plaintiffs (with final cases) seemed generally reasonable. It is noted in the text and bears repeating here, however, that about two-thirds of the plaintiffs experienced costs below $5,000.

128. The recent requirement that plaintiffs in most media libel cases must prove actual falsity may alter this risk calculus somewhat, although the dominance of privilege questions at initial stages of litigation will likely still result in most cases being decided on grounds of privilege rather than truth or falsity, or reputational harm. *See* Philadelphia Newspapers Inc. v. Hepps, 106 S.Ct. 1558 (1986); note 21 *supra*.

129. *See* Table 7–3 *infra*.

130. Our conclusions about lawyer fees and advice are restricted to those who actually bring suit on the plaintiffs' behalf. Many lawyers, we expect, give different advice and demand different fee arrangements, and may as a result discourage many plaintiffs who would otherwise sue. The insurance information in Table 6–15 suggests that perhaps 50 percent of the lawyers resolve a potential claim prior to litigation either by discouraging suit or obtaining settlement. Because the insurance data are not statistically reliable, the proportion may be greater.

131. Based on a survey of 229 newspapers conducted by a committee of the American Society of Newspaper Editors, it has been reported that the average cost of defending a libel suit was $95,852, excluding staff time. The average cost for the largest papers (over 400,000 in circulation, 13 papers responding) was $541,967. For papers with circulation between 50,000 and 100,000, the average cost was $53,789, and for the smallest papers (under 20,000 circulation) the cost was $10,367. The possible effect of a few very expensive cases on the average cost was not reported. The extent to which such costs are borne by insurance carriers was also not reported. *ASNE Bulletin*, at 38–39 (January 1986).

132. This is not to suggest that the plaintiffs do not want to win in court. They clearly do want to win, and their persistence in the litigation demonstrates that fact. The plaintiff lawyers also wish to persist, partly, it seems, because of the contingency arrangements, and partially, perhaps, because of the visibility of the litigation. Moreover, the dynamics of the litigation force plaintiffs to persist, for media defendants almost always immediately move for summary judgment on privilege grounds, and dropping the suit at this stage would likely be viewed as an admission of truth by the plaintiff.

CHAPTER 7

1. As developed in Chapter 6, the plaintiff rate of success by judgment in *reported* cases was about 10 percent. The rate of plaintiff success by judgment (in court) is even lower when the universe of cases is broadened to include those cases that are not reported as well as disputes resulting in notification of the insurer, although the incidence of settlement grows with expansion of the universe.
2. Plaintiff "wins" include only those judgments that were final, i.e., not reversed on appeal or still pending on appeal. In the 13 instances of plaintiff judicial victory (out of the 164 surveyed plaintiffs) the awards were as follows:

Plaintiff 1 $ 15,000	Plaintiff 7 $75,000
Plaintiff 2 $ 30,000	Plaintiff 8 $30,000
Plaintiff 3 $ 45,000	Plaintiff 9 $50,000
Plaintiff 4 $ 3,000	Plaintiff 10 -0-
Plaintiff 5 $222,000	Plaintiff 11 -0-
Plaintiff 6 $490,000	Plaintiff 12 -0-
	Plaintiff 13 ?

Average award (excluding #13) $ 80,000

Zero awards represent judgments for plaintiffs, with costs assessed, but without money damage awards.
3. The settlement amounts ranged from $300 to $18,000.
4. It must be kept in mind when interpreting the plaintiff responses that the information solicited is both retrospective and attitudinal, and therefore uniquely subject to error or bias. This has been noted as well with other responses previously discussed. While caution in interpretation and generalization is therefore warranted, we believe that the information is, on the whole, important and reliable. We have reached this conclusion for two primary reasons. First, the plaintiffs' attitudinal responses are internally consistent with a wide variety of other attitudinal and factual information collected in the study. Second, plaintiff responses break down in consistent and expected ways, yielding internal patterns of consistency among plaintiff subgroups which make error or bias less likely.
5. When asked what was accomplished, 58 losing plaintiffs (in final cases) responded. The number is lower because of nonresponses or uncodable responses, but 58 of the 67 losing plaintiffs who felt something was accomplished provided a codable response. Even using this lower number, 58 out of 106 plaintiffs who lost, or 55 percent, could provide a specific, and largely reputation-related reason, for feeling that the unsuccessful lawsuit accomplished something. Adding the 22 plaintiffs who won or settled, the most conservative estimate would provide that 80 out of 130 or 62 percent of all

plaintiffs whose cases were completed, felt the suit accomplished something, although only 10 percent actually won.

6. Table 7–1 excludes all pending cases.

7. This does not include those whose responses were uncodable, or who did not specifically respond when asked what was accomplished, but it does include those who had indicated that, while the defendant won, the suit accomplished something. *See* note 5 *supra*. Reputation is likely to be a factor with some of these plaintiffs, as well.

8. Interestingly, a higher proportion (75 percent) of the private plaintiffs expressed bitterness toward the judicial process than did public plaintiffs (60 percent) [excluding corporate plaintiffs].

9. *See* the discussion of the incidence of probable and actual falsity in adjudicated cases in Chapter 8.

10. This risk may now be largely eliminated by the recent Supreme Court decision placing the burden of proving falsity on the plaintiff in most media libel cases. *See* Philadelphia Newspapers Inc. v. Hepps, 106 S.Ct. 1558 (1986); note 21, Chapter 6, *supra*.

11. The clear impact of the actual malice privilege is to discourage suits by public figures, the objective being to facilitate robust, and often false, speech on public issues. *See* New York Times Co. v. Sullivan, 376 U.S. 254 (1964). Public plaintiffs with legitimate claims of falsity and defamation are discouraged from suing unless *calculated* falsehood or *calculated* indifference to truth is involved. *Id.* Neither of these issues has any necessary bearing on the questions of falsity and reputational harm, and both issues foreclose many, if not most, legitimate plaintiff claims of falsity and damage. *See* note 21, Chapter 6, *supra*.

12. Twenty-three plaintiffs (31 percent) wanted the outcome publicized and 12 plaintiffs (16 percent) wanted money damages.

13. Six plaintiffs (26 percent) demanded that the outcome of the non-litigation alternative be publicized, and only one (4 percent) conditioned non-litigation on receiving money damages.

14. *See* Table 7–4 and accompanying text *supra*.

15. Another factor related to the plaintiff's receptivity to non-judicial processes is the plaintiff's education.

The Plaintiffs' Education and Interest in Non-Litigation Alternatives

	High School or Below	Some College or College Grad	Graduate or Professional Degree
Prompt, Fair, Inexpensive	18	30	20
% column	67%	71%	48%
Outcome Publicized	7	11	14
% column	26%	26%	33%
Money Damages Available	2	1	8
% column	7%	2%	19%
	p. < .005		

The largest group of the libel plaintiffs (42 of 111 plaintiffs or 38 percent) have graduate or professional degrees. Of these 42 plaintiffs, the majority (22 or 52 percent) condition their acceptance of non-litigation alternatives on some affirmative act (money or publication) by the defendant. These numbers reflect what we would expect to be the interests of well-to-do professionals who may have suffered dramatic economic losses as well as those well-educated public plaintiffs whose primary loss can be resolved by some public notice which would restore their reputations. At the other end of the education scale, those plaintiffs with only a high school diploma or less appear less inclined to condition non-litigation alternatives on a specific remedy of publication or damages. Seven plaintiffs (26 percent) would consider non-judicial processes if the outcome would have been publicized, while 2 (7 percent) would have done so if money damages had been available. Nearly two-thirds would require neither as a precondition. Those plaintiffs who have had some college or have graduated from college followed the same pattern, with the interesting exception of the precondition of money damages, discussed below.

Perhaps the most significant comparisons across the three education classifications are the availability of damages and the interest in reducing cost and time. Nineteen percent of the graduate or professional plaintiffs expect money, compared with only 7 percent of the high school plaintiffs and 2 percent of the college plaintiffs. The graduate and professional plaintiffs who would consider non-litigation alternatives were much more preoccupied with their economic losses than were the other two classes of plaintiffs. On the other hand, it would appear that the high school or college educated plaintiffs would have accepted non-litigation if it were cheaper. Eleven percent of the high school plaintiffs and 21 percent of the college plaintiffs, compared with only 2 percent of the graduate plaintiffs, mentioned reduced cost and time as the most important factor.

CHAPTER 8

1. *See* Restatement (Second) of Torts § 559 (1977); R. Sack, Libel, Slander, and Related Problems 74–75 (P.L.I. 1980); W. Prosser, The Law of Torts (4th ed. 1971). A variety of justifications, in the form of common law privileges, exist, W. Prosser, at 776–96, including truth, fair comment, and certain communications within the employment setting, for example.

2. Damages in defamation actions fall under two broad labels: those which are designed to compensate the victim for harm suffered, whether economic (actual or presumed damages) or psychological (general damages); and those which are designed to punish the offending publisher and deter the publisher and others from engaging in the activity in the future (punitive damages). *See* Restatement of Torts §§ 569–70 & Comments (1938); W. Prosser, The Law of Torts (4th ed. 1971). Damage rules were complex at common law; they are even more complex in light of constitutional privileges. *See* Gertz v. Robert Welch, Inc., 418 U.S. 323, 349–50 (1974); Dun & Bradstreet, Inc. v. Greenmoss Builders, Inc., 86 L.Ed.2d 593 (1985).

3. Gertz v. Robert Welch, Inc., 418 U.S. 323 (1974). For a discussion of public officials, public figures, and private persons, as well as the actual malice and negligence privileges, *see* Chapter 6 *supra*.

4. New York Times Co. v. Sullivan, 376 U.S. 254, 269–71, 280 (1964); Gertz v. Robert Welch, Inc., 418 U.S. 323, 347, 350 (1974).

5. *See* Appendix C, Table 6.

6. *See* Chapter 5 *supra*; Appendix C, Table 8.

7. For all responding plaintiffs, 49 percent contacted the media first.

8. *See* Chapter 5 *supra*.

9. *See* Chapter 5 *supra;* Appendix C, Table 9.
10. *See* Chapter 5 *supra;* Appendix C, Table 10.
11. *See* Chapter 5 *supra;* Appendix C, Table 11.
12. *See* Chapter 5 *supra;* Appendix C, Table 12.
13. *See* Chapter 5 *supra;* Appendix C, Table 15.
14. *See* Chapter 5 *supra;* Appendix C, Table 24.
15. *See* Chapter 5 *supra;* Appendix C, Tables 4–6.
16. *See* Chapter 5 *supra;* Appendix C, Table 24.
17. *See* Appendix C, Table 4.
18. *See* Appendix C, Table 5.
19. In effect, many of these plaintiffs see the suit as a means of inhibiting *future* publication, rather than strictly as a remedy for prior statements.
20. *See* Appendix C, Table 33. With suitable conditions, 82 percent of the plaintiffs indicated that non-litigation alternatives would be considered. *See* Chapter 7 *supra.*
21. *See* Chapter 7 *supra.*
22. *See* Appendix C, Table 15.
23. *See* Chapter 5 *supra;* Appendix C, Table 14.
24. *See* Chapter 6 *supra;* Appendix C, Table 25.
25. *See* note 2, Chapter 7.
26. *See* Chapter 5 *supra;* Appendix C, Table 28.
27. This is derived from Table 5–13, where it is indicated that 73 percent of the plaintiffs engaged counsel on contingency fee.
28. Roughly 30 percent of the plaintiffs bore costs below $1,000. *See* Appendix C, Table 28.
29. *See* Appendix C, Table 27. The mid-point of each range was used as a multiplier in calculating the average, with 9 years being used for the "over 8" group. The average is 3.909.
30. *See* Table 6–13.
31. *See* Chapter 7 *supra;* Appendix C, Table 31.
32. *See* Chapter 7 *supra;* Appendix C, Table 26.
33. *See* Chapter 7 *supra;* Appendix C, Table 26.
34. *See* Chapter 7 *supra;* Appendix C, Table 32. The proportion of plaintiffs who lost and would sue again is similar, at 84 percent. All but one of the plaintiffs legally classified as public officials would sue again.
35. *See* Chapter 7 *supra;* Appendix C, Table 33.
36. One study reported that average libel defense costs for newspapers exceed $95,000. *See* note 131, Chapter 6, *supra.*
37. 376 U.S. 254 (1964).
38. 418 U.S. 323 (1974). For thorough and thoughtful discussion of the constitutionalization of libel law, *see* Eaton, *The American Law of Defamation Through* Gertz v. Robert Welch, Inc. *and Beyond: An Analytical Primer,* 61 Va. L. Rev. 1349 (1975); Anderson, *Libel and Press Self-Censorship,* 53 Texas L. Rev. 422 (1975); Robertson, *Defamation and the First Amendment: In Praise of* Gertz v. Robert Welch, Inc., 54 Texas L. Rev. 199 (1976); Note, *In Defense of Fault in Defamation Law,* 88 Yale L. J. 1735 (1979). Professor Marc Franklin has published two empirical analyses of defamation litigation. Franklin, *Winners and Losers and Why: A Study of Defamation Litigation,* 1980 A.B.F. Res. J. 455; Franklin, *Suing the Media for Libel: A Litigation Study,* 1981 A.B.F. Res. J. 795.
39. The actual malice standard is focused on the publisher's subjective awareness, or state of mind, in all applications. The question is whether the publisher actually knew of

falsity or entertained serious doubts about truth, publishing recklessly in light thereof. Innocent or ignorant mistake will not constitute actual malice. *See* St. Amant v. Thompson, 390 U.S. 727, 731 (1968). The negligence test judges the reasonableness of the publisher's action in light of what was known about truth or falsity. *See* Restatement (Second) of Torts 580B, comment (h) (1977). Whether a subjective element is part of all of its applications is the subject of differences of opinion among courts and commentators. *See* Anderson, *Libel and Press Self-Censorship*, 53 Texas L. Rev. 422, 461–62 (1975); Note, *In Defense of Fault in Defamation Law*, 88 Yale L. J. 1735, 1738 n. 15 (1979).

40. *See* R. Sack, Libel, Slander and Related Problems 129–42 (P.L.I. 1980); W. Prosser, The Law of Torts 797–99 (4th ed. 1971); Bezanson, *Fault, Falsity and Reputation in Public Defamation Law*, 8 Hamline L. Rev. 105–107 (1985).

41. Prior to Philadelphia Newspapers Inc. v. Hepps, 106 S.Ct. 1558 (1986), the requirement that plaintiffs prove falsity was the minority position, and many courts did not view such a rule as constitutionally required. *See* Bezanson, *supra*, note 40 at 106–107 n. 5. In light of the continued constitutionality of the public disclosure privacy tort, which rests liability on *truth*, a requirement that plaintiff prove falsity would be difficult to understand. *Id.*; Cox Broadcasting Co. v. Cohn, 420 U.S. 469 (1975). Even where falsity has been made a part of the plaintiff's case, this has most often taken the form only of a burden of pleading or prima facie proof, with the burden to rebut resting squarely on the defendant. *See* Bezanson at 106–107 n. 5. This is only slightly different from the common law rule, requiring only that the plaintiff deny truth formally. The impact of *Hepps* on these issues is unclear, given its limited scope and uncertain definition of required proof. *See* note 21, Chapter 6.

42. *E.g.*, Rinaldi v. Holt, Rinehart & Winston, Inc., 366 N.E.2d 1299, 1306 (Ct. App. N.Y. 1977); Steaks Unlimited, Inc. v. Deaner, 623 F.2d 264, 274–75 n. 49 (3d Cir. 1980); Nevada Indep. Broadcasting v. Allen, 664 P.2d 337, 343 (Nev. 1983).

43. *See* note 41 *supra*. Based on a review of the jurisdictions throughout the country, a requirement that plaintiff bear the burden of *proving* falsity—as distinguished from pleading it, presuming it from a well-pleaded complaint, or making out a prima facie showing through testimonial denial—existed in a distinct minority of the states prior to *Hepps*. *See* Bezanson, *supra* note 40, at 106–07 n. 5.

44. The exact scope of this rule's applicability, and the type of proof that will be required, is left largely unaddressed in the opinion. Philadelphia Newspapers Inc. v. Hepps, 106 S.Ct. 1558 (1986). *See* note 21, Chapter 6, for a fuller discussion of the case and its implications.

45. Philadelphia Newspapers Inc. v. Hepps, 106 S.Ct. 1558 (1986); *see* note 21, Chapter 6.

46. *See* Tables 6–13 and 6–14 *supra*.

47. Eighty-five percent of the pre-trial motions for summary judgment or dismissal were disposed of on constitutional privilege grounds.

48. *See* Tables 6–13 and 6–14 *supra*.

49. Eighty-five percent of post-trial appeals are disposed of on privilege-related grounds. For cases in which the media defendant prevails on post-trial appeal, 83 percent are decided on privilege grounds.

50. *See* Table 6–2 *supra*.

51. While these cases were decided prior to the Supreme Court's recent requirement that plaintiffs bear the burden of proof of falsity in most media libel cases, some of the surveyed cases came from jurisdictions that had adopted the requirement earlier, and

the predominant causes of failure to address truth or falsity are the constitutional malice and negligence privileges, not the burden of proof on falsity. Nevertheless, the *Hepps* decision should alter the situation to some degree. Philadelphia Newspapers Inc. v. Hepps, 106 S.Ct. 1558 (1986).

52. Ninety-two percent of the strong defamation claims won by defendants were based on privilege. Even with weak claims, 80 percent of defendant wins were based on privilege.

53. *See* note 49 *supra*.

54. *See* W. Prosser, The Law of Torts 797–99 (4th ed. 1971); R. Sack, Libel, Slander and Related Problems 40, 129–42 (P.L.I. 1980); H. Kaufman, LDRC 50-State Survey (1982).

55. *See* note 41 *supra*.

56. Philadelphia Newspapers Inc. v. Hepps, 106 S.Ct. 1558 (1986).

57. *See* note 39 *supra*. The extrinsic and intrinsic approaches to proof of actual malice are set out in St. Amant v. Thompson, 390 U.S. 727, 731 (1968). As noted in note 39, *supra*, the state-of-mind element of the negligence privilege is unclear, with various jurisdictions approaching the issue differently.

58. This result should be largely precluded by the recent decision in Philadelphia Newspapers Inc. v. Hepps, 106 S.Ct. 1558 (1986), requiring plaintiffs in most media libel cases to prove falsity.

59. 106 S.Ct. 1558 (1986).

60. *See* note 21, Chapter 6.

61. *See* note 69 *infra* and accompanying text.

62. *See* text accompanying notes 65–80 *infra*.

63. *See* Table 6–2 *supra*.

64. *See* Bezanson & Ingle, *Plato's Cave Revisited: The Epistemology of Perception in Contemporary Defamation Law*, in symposium, 90 Dickinson L. Rev. 585 (1986).

65. 394 F. Supp. 721 (1975), *remanded*, 538 F.2d 311 (1975).

66. Lawlor v. Gallagher Presidents' Report, Inc., 538 F.2d 311 (1975).

67. *See* 394 F. Supp., at 734–35.

68. *Id.*

69. *Lawlor* is illustrative of a number of successful media defamation cases involving both public and private plaintiffs in which the question of reputational harm or injury is simply not addressed, or in which the apparent injury appears, as in *Lawlor*, remote or immaterial in the circumstances. *See, e.g.*, Dixson v. Newsweek, 562 F.2d 626, 3 M.L.R. 1123 (1977); Catalano v. Pechous, 419 N.E.2d 350, 6 M.L.R. 2511 (1980); Embry v. Holly, 441 A.2d 966, 8 M.L.R. 1409 (Md. Ct. App. 1982); Miller v. Lear Siegler, Inc., 525 F. Supp. 46 (1981); Carson v. Allied News Co., 482 F. Supp. 406, 5 M.L.R. 2646 (1979); Buckley v. Littell, 539 F.2d 882, 1 M.L.R. 1762 (1976), *cert. denied*, 97 S.Ct. 786 (1977); Freeman v. Cooper, 414 S.2d 355 (1982); Bose Corp. v. Consumers Union, 104 S.Ct. 1949 (1984); Scripps Co. v. Cholmondelay, 569 S.W.2d 700 (1978); Retail Credit v. Russell, 218 S.E.2d 54 (1975); Sears v. Moten, 27 Ariz. App. 759 (Ariz. Ct. App. 1976); Vegod Corp. v. A.B.C., 25 Cal. 3d 763, 603 P.2d 14, *cert. denied*, A.B.C. v. Vegod, 449 U.S. 886 (1979); Gaeta v. N.Y. News, Inc., 454 N.Y.S.2d 179 (1982); Levita Mills v. Kingsport Times-News, 475 F. Supp. 1005 (1979); Sean McManns v. Doubleday & Co., Inc., 513 F. Supp. 1383 (1981).

70. *See* Gertz v. Robert Welch, Inc., 418 U.S. 323 (1974); Chapter 6 *supra*. A likely exception to this is an action brought by a private plaintiff against a non-media

publisher for a statement which, by virtue of its subject matter and the circumstances surrounding its publication, does not involve a matter of public concern. Dunn & Bradstreet, Inc. v. Greenmoss Builders, Inc., 86 L.Ed.2d 593 (1985).

71. *See, e.g.,* Anderson, *Libel and Press Self-Censorship,* 53 Texas L. Rev. 422 (1975); Robertson, *Defamation and the First Amendment: In Praise of* Gertz v. Robert Welch, Inc., 54 Texas L. Rev. 199 (1976); Note, *In Defense of Fault in Defamation Law,* 88 Yale L. J. 1735 (1979); Barron, *Access to the Press—A New First Amendment Right,* 80 Harv. L. Rev. 1641 (1967); Lange, *The Speech and Press Clauses,* 23 U.C.L.A. L. Rev. 77 (1975); Bezanson, *The New Free Press Guarantee,* 63 Virginia L. Rev. 731 (1977); M. Nimmer, Freedom of Speech (1984). *See also,* Bezanson, Herbert v. Lando, *Editorial Judgment and Freedom of the Press: An Essay,* 1978 U. Ill. L. F. 605, 618–23, for a discussion of the actual malice standard as a principled limitation on, or definitional boundary for, a guarantee of editorial freedom.

72. *See* Restatement (Second) of Torts § 559 (1977); W. Prosser, The Law of Torts § 117 (4th ed. 1971); R. Sack, Libel, Slander and Related Problems (P.L.I. 1980).

73. *See* W. Prosser, The Law of Torts 776–96 (4th ed. 1971).

74. Various formulations of fault or "cause" had to be established when certain common law privileges applied, or when punitive damages were sought. These standards of cause generally involved unreasonable conduct leading to publication, inaccuracy in quoting statements by others, or common law malice—defined as ill-will, as opposed to knowledge of falsity or reckless disregard of truth in the actual malice sense. *Id.; see* R. Sack, Libel, Slander and Related Problems (P.L.I. 1980), for an exceedingly careful and thorough discussion of these and related privilege issues.

75. *See* Gertz v. Robert Welch, Inc., 418 U.S. 323 (1974); Anderson, *Libel and Press Self-Censorship,* 53 Texas L. Rev. 422 (1975).

76. This conclusion is based on our extensive discussions with newspaper editors and lawyers for media companies. The *Iowa Law Review* has conducted an empirical study relating to these questions which confirms our conclusions. The study will be published as *Standards Governing the News,* 72 Iowa Law Review (1986).

77. New York Times Co. v. Sullivan, 376 U.S. 254 (1964).

78. Inadequate or non-specific consideration of reputational harm and injury may also be a function of libel doctrine and the various rules governing damages. For an interesting discussion of these questions, *see* Anderson, *Reputation, Compensation, and Proof,* 25 Wm. & Mary Law Review 747 (1984), and the comments by Professors LeBel and Van Alstyne that follow (pp. 779–824).

79. R. Sack, Libel, Slander and Related Problems (P.L.I. 1980).

80. For illustrative cases in which liability was based on actual malice or negligence in the absence of proof of reputational injury, *see* note 69 *supra.*

81. Numerous cases have imposed liability in the absence of proof of falsity. In many of the cases, falsity was required to be pleaded or proved under the law of the jurisdiction, but proof of negligence or reckless disregard for truth at the time of publication substituted for the absence of clear evidence of actual falsity. *E.g.,* Kuhn v. Tribune-Republican, 637 P.2d 315 (Colo. 1981); Cape Publications v. Adams, 336 So.2d 1197 (Fla. 1976); Stevens v. Sun Publications, 240 S.E.2d 812 (1978); Cianci v. New Times Pub. Co., 639 F.2d 54 (1980); Cantrell v. American Broad. Co., Inc., 529 F. Supp. 746 (1981); Marcone v. Penthouse, Ltd., 533 F. Supp. 353 (1982); Phillips v. Evening Star Newspaper, 424 A.2d 78 (D.C. Ct. App. 1980), *cert. denied,* 451 U.S. 989 (1981); Gaeta v. N.Y. News, Inc., 454 N.Y.S.2d 179 (1982); Peisner v. Detroit Free Press, Inc., 304 N.W.2d 814, 7 M.L.R. 1601 (Mich. App. 1981); Hansen v.

Stoll, 8 Med. L. Rptr. 1204 (1981); Rebozo v. Washington Post Co., 515 F.2d 1208 (5th Cir. 1975). In addition, there are cases in which the published fact was technically false, but in which the readers' or viewers' *perception* of falsity or its materiality is ignored. *E.g.*, Bose Corp. v. Consumers Union, 104 S.Ct. 1949 (1984); McManus v. Doubleday & Co., Inc., 513 F. Supp. 1383 (1981); Jenoff v. The Hearst Corp., 644 F.2d 1004 (1981); Vegod Corp. v. A.B.C., 25 Cal.3d 763, 603 P.2d 14, *cert. denied*, A.B.C. v. Vegod, 449 U.S. 886 (1979); Sears v. Moten, 27 Ariz. App. 759 (Ct. App. 1976). The recent Supreme Court decision in Philadelphia Newspapers Inc. v. Hepps, 106 S.Ct. 1558 (1986), represents an effort to limit the possibility of recovery for libel in the absence of falsity. The extent to which it succeeds will depend on the exact requirements of proof, the materiality of falsity which must be proved, and the scope of the proof burden's application, all of which remain unclear.

82. *See* note 20, Chapter 6, *supra*, for the impact of the *Dun & Bradstreet v. Greenmoss Builders, Inc.* decision, 86 L.Ed.2d 593 (1985), on the media/non-media distinction in defamation actions brought by private plaintiffs.

83. *E.g.*, Cianci v. New Times Publishing Co., 639 F.2d 54 (2d Cir. 1980) (fact v. opinion); Herbert v. Lando, 441 U.S. 153 (1979) (discovery); Seattle Times v. Rhinehart, 104 S.Ct. 2199 (1984).

84. Two sources are particularly helpful and able. Eaton, *The American Law of Defamation through* Gertz v. Robert Welch, Inc., *and Beyond: An Analytical Primer*, 61 Va. L. Rev. 1349 (1975); R. Sack, Libel, Slander and Related Problems (P.L.I. 1980).

85. St. Amant v. Thompson, 390 U.S. 727, 731 (1968).

86. Gertz v. Robert Welch, Inc., 418 U.S. 323, 343 (1974). As discussed previously, the media/non-media distinction has been acknowledged, although in modified form. *See* Dun & Bradstreet v. Greenmoss Builders, Inc., 86 L.Ed. 2d 593 (1985); note 20, Chapter 6, *supra*.

87. *E.g.*, Beneficial Mgt. Corp. of Am. v. Evans, 421 So.2d 92 (Ala. 1982); Jacron Sales Co. v. Sindorf, 276 Md. 580, 350 A.2d 688 (1976); Ramacciatti v. Zinn, 550 S.W.2d 217, 224 (Mo. App. 1977); Poorbaugh v. Mullen, 99 N.M. 11, 653 P.2d 511, 520 (Ct. App.), *cert denied*, 99 N.M. 47, 653 P.2d 878 (N.M. 1982); Bender v. City of Seattle, 99 W.2d 982, 664 P.2d 492 (Wash. 1983).

88. *See* Restatement (Second) of Torts 580B, comment (h) (1977); Anderson, *Libel and Press Self-Censorship*, 53 Tex. L. Rev. 422, 461–62 (1975); Note, *In Defense of Fault in Defamation Law*, 88 Yale L. J. 1735, 1738 n. 15 (1979).

89. For finally resolved cases, 66 percent (75 of 113 cases) of the appeals were taken prior to trial. These figures exclude pre-trial appeals in cases tried and appealed after trial (roughly two-thirds). *See* Table 6–13, *supra*.

90. *See* Table 6–2, *supra*.

91. *See* Table 6–8, *supra*.

92. *See* Tables 6–9 and 6–10, *supra*.

93. *See* Table 6–14, *supra*.

94. Roughly 85 percent of cases resolved prior to trial but including formal judicial decision were decided on contested issues of privilege (as opposed to issues of fact, reputation, falsity, strict liability, and the like).

95. *See* Tables 6–13 and 6–14, *supra*.

96. Illustrative of the difficulties are the following cases and academic writings. Gertz v. Robert Welch, Inc., 418 U.S. 323 (1974); Time, Inc. v. Firestone, 424 U.S. 448 (1976); Wolston v. Readers Digest Ass'n., 443 U.S. 157 (1979); Hutchinson v. Proxmire, 443 U.S. 111 (1979); Tavoulareas v. Washington Post, 8 Med. L. R. 2262

(D.D.C. 1982); Briag v. Field Commun., 9 Med. L. R. 1057 (Pa. Sup. Ct. 1983); Waldbaum v. Fairchild Publications, Inc., 627 F.2d 1287 (D.C. Cir. 1980); Steaks Unlimited, Inc. v. Deaner, 623 F.2d 264 (3d Cir. 1980); Ashdown, Gertz *and Fire-stone: A Study in Constitutional Policy-Making*, 61 Minn. L. Rev. 645 (1977); Christie, *Injuries to Reputation and the Constitution: Confusion Amid Conflicting Approaches*, 75 Mich. L. Rev. 43 (1976); authorities cited note 38 *supra*.

97. Rosenbloom v. Metromedia, Inc., 403 U.S. 29 (1971). The *Rosenbloom* approach, as it has come to be called, invoked constitutional privilege in defamation cases involving a public issue, irrespective of the identity or private character of the plaintiff bringing the action.

98. The chief concerns with the *Rosenbloom* public issue test of constitutional privilege were the lack of clear standards governing its application, and that the test involved the judicial branch in deciding what issues were of public importance for purposes of first amendment protection. *See* Gertz v. Robert Welch, Inc., 418 U.S. 323, 346 (1974). This same difficulty, however, may have been reintroduced by the Court's recent decision in Dun and Bradstreet, Inc. v. Greenmoss Builders, Inc., 86 L.Ed.2d 593 (1985). *See* note 20, Chapter 6, *supra*.

99. *See* Bezanson, *The New Free Press Guarantee*, 63 Va. L. Rev. 731, 740–50 (1977); note 20, Chapter 6, *supra*.

100. *See* note 96 *supra*.

101. 443 U.S. 111 (1979).

102. *E.g.*, Newson v. Henry, 443 So.2d 817, 10 M.L.R. 1421 (Miss. 1984); Schermerhorn v. Rosenberg, 426 N.Y.S.2d 274 (1980); Catalano v. Pechous, 419 N.E.2d 350, 6 Med. L. Rptr. 2511 (1980).

103. *See* note 81 *supra*; notes 112–115 *infra* and accompanying text.

104. *See* note 81 *supra*. The cases cited all precede Philadelphia Newspapers Inc. v. Hepps, 106 S.Ct. 1558 (1986). It is unclear to what extent *Hepps*, when applicable, will avoid this possibility.

105. *See* Herbert v. Lando, 441 U.S. 153 (1979).

106. The cases are legion. *E.g.*, Carey v. Hume, 492 F.2d 631 (D.C. Cir.), *cert. denied*, 417 U.S. 938 (1974); Gagnon v. Fremont Dist. Court, 632 P.2d 567 (Colo. 1981); Bruno & Stillman v. Globe Newspaper, 633 F.2d 583 (1st Cir. 1980); Miller v. Trans-America Press, Inc., 621 F.2d 721 (5th Cir.), *modified*, 628 F.2d 932 (5th Cir. 1980), *cert. denied*, 450 U.S. 1041 (1981); Lauterbeck v. ABC, 8 Med. L. R. 2407 (N.D. Iowa 1982); Seattle Times v. Rhinehart, 104 S.Ct. 2199 (1984); Nat'l Enquirer, Inc. v. California Sup. Court, 2d Civ. No. 67772 (Cal. App.), *cert. denied*, 103 S.Ct. 3128 (1983); Westmoreland v. CBS, 8 Med. L. R. 2493 (D.C. So. Car. 1982), 9 Med. L. R.1521 (1983), 9 Med. L. R. 2316 (1983), 10 Med. L. R. 1215 (S.D.N.Y. 1984); Rebozo v. Washington Post Co., 515 F.2d 1208, 1214 (5th Cir. 1975); Church of Scientology of California v. Adams, 584 F.2d 893, 899 (9th Cir. 1978); Keeton v. Hustler, 10 Med. L. R. 1405 (U.S. Sup. Ct. 1984); Calder v. Jones, 10 Med. L. R. 1401 (U.S. Sup. Ct. 1984); Arbitron v. E. W. Scripps, 9 Med. L. R. 1507 (S.D.N.Y. 1983); Flanders v. Assoc. Newspapers, 9 Med. L. R. 1669 (D.C. Minn. 1983); Edwards v. Assoc. Press, Inc., 512 F.2d 258 (5th Cir. 1982); Viking Penguin v. Janklow, 9 Med. L. R. 2219 (S.D.N.Y. 1983); Note, *First Amendment Interests in Trade Secrets, Private Materials, and Confidential Information: The Use of Protective Orders in Defamation Litigation*, 69 Iowa L. Rev. 1011 (1984); R. Sack, Libel, Slander and Related Problems 505–532 (P.L.I. 1980); Shumandine and Esinhart, *Litigation: The Pleading Phase, in* New York Times v. Sullivan: *The Next Twenty Years* 131, 206 (P.L.I. 1984).

107. *See* Note, *Structuring Defamation Law to Eliminate the Fact-Opinion Determination: A Critique of Ollman v. Evans,* 71 Iowa L. Rev. 913 (1986).

108. It bears repeating that 60 percent of the losing plaintiffs felt that the lawsuit accomplished something, and 90 percent of the losing plaintiffs (100 percent of the public officials) who lost would nevertheless sue again if faced with the same situation. *See* Chapter 7, *supra.*

109. Writings on the theory and function of freedom of expression are legion. At the risk of excluding many that deserve mention, some of the best include Nimmer, Freedom of Speech (1984); Z. Chafee, Free Speech in the United States (1941); J. S. Mill, On Liberty; A. Meiklejohn, Free Speech and Its Relation to Self-Government (1948); T. Emerson, The System of Freedom of Expression (1970); A. Bickel, The Morality of Consent (1975); Blasi, *The Checking Value in First Amendment Theory,* 1977 A.B.F. Res. J. 523; Bollinger, *Tolerance and the First Amendment,* monograph published by the Institute of Bill of Rights Law, College of William and Mary (1986); Kalven, *The New York Times Case: A Note on "The Central Meaning of the First Amendment,"* 1964 Sup. Ct. Rev. 191; Stone, *Content Regulation and the First Amendment,* 25 Wm & Mary L. Rev. 189 (1983); Whitney v. California, 274 U.S. 357, 375 (1927) (Brandeis, J., concurring); Abrams v. United States, 250 U.S. 616, 630 (1919) (Holmes, J., dissenting); New York Times Co. v. Sullivan, 376 U.S. 254 (1964).

110. Gertz v. Robert Welch, Inc., 418 U.S. 323, 340 (1974); Keeton v. Hustler Magazine, Inc., 104 S.Ct. 1473, 1479 (1984).

111. *See* note 81 *supra.*

112. Perhaps the classic example of this is the accusation made about a candidate during the course of an election campaign. If a material false statement about the background or character of a candidate is made in this setting, its "importance" under the First Amendment, if any, is completely dependent on the opportunity for *effective* rebuttal and, also, disclosure of its source; whose character, if the opposing candidate, may be more effectively disclosed by this than by any other means. The false statement, *itself,* however, has no appreciable value; the value lies in disclosing its falsity. A particularly compelling instance of apparent political slander is the case of *Schermerhorn v. Rosenberg,* 426 N.Y.S.2d 274 (1980).

113. Rebozo v. Washington Post Co., 515 F.2d 1208 (5th Cir. 1975).

114. The successful cases are remarkable because of their infrequency, *e.g.,* Davis v. Schuchat, 510 F.2d 731 (1975); Sprouse v. Clay Commun., 211 S.E.2d 674 (1975); Montandon v. Triangle Pub., 45 Cal. App.3d 938 (1975); Schermerhorn v. Rosenberg, 426 N.Y.S.2d 274 (1980); Phoenix Newspapers v. Church, 103 Ariz. 582 (1968); and even more so because most either involve doubtful reputational harm, *e.g.,* Blessum v. Howard County Bd. of Supervisors, 295 N.W.2d 836 (Iowa 1980); Hansen v. Stoll, 8 Med. L. R. 1204 (Az. 1981); Embry v. Holly, 441 A.2d 966 (Md. Ct. App. 1982); Buckley v. Littell, 539 F.2d 882 (1976); Carson v. Allied News, 482 F. Supp. 406 (1979); or are unsatisfying, as the truth or falsity of the challenged statement remains uncertain even after the litigation is complete, *e.g.,* Kuhn v. Tribune-Republican, 637 P.2d 315 (Colo. 1981); Appleyard v. TransAm. Press, 539 F.2d 1026 (1976); Cape Pub. v. Adams, 336 So.2d 1197 (Fla. 1976); Stevens v. Sun Pub. Co., 240 S.E.2d 812 (1978).

115. For other examples of cases in which the interest in truth or falsity of an apparently material and important public statement is submerged by privileges, *see, e.g.,* Newson v. Henry, 443 So.2d 817 (S.Ct. Miss. 1984); Schermerhorn v. Rosenberg, 426 N.Y.S.2d 274 (1980); Greenberg v. CBS, 419 N.Y.S.2d 988 (1979); Peisner v.

Detroit Free Press, 304 N.W. 2d 814 (Mich. App. 1981); Coronado Credit Union v. KOAT T.V., Inc., 656 P. 2d 896 (1982); Kuhn v. Tribune-Republican, 637 P. 2d 315 (1981); Alioto v. Cowes Commun., Inc., 623 F. 2d 616 (1980); Jenoff v. The Hearst Corp., 644 F. 2d 1004 (1981); Stevens v. The Sun Pub. Co., 240 S.E. 2d 812, *cert. denied*, 434 U.S. 945 (1978); Levita Mills v. Kingsport Times-News, 475 F. Supp. 1005 (1979); Cantrell v. ABC, 529 F. Supp. 746 (1981). Other cases involve private, rather than public interests, but are of the same character. *E.g.*, Gaeta v. N.Y. News, 454 N.Y.S. 2d 179 (1982); Phillips v. Eve. Star Newspapers, 424 A. 2d 78 (D.C. Ct. App. 1980), *cert. denied*, 451 U.S. 989 (1981); E. W. Scripps Co. v. Cholmondelay, 569 S.W. 2d 700 (1978).

116. *See* notes 105–106 *supra*.
117. 423 A. 2d 311 (1980).
118. *See* New York Times Co. v. Sullivan, 376 U.S. 254 (1964).
119. *See* Miami Herald Pub. Co. v. Tornillo, 418 U.S. 241, 256 (1974); Columbia Broadcasting System, Inc. v. Democratic National Committee, 412 U.S. 94, 124–25 (1973); Bezanson, Herbert v. Lando, *Editorial Judgment, and Freedom of the Press: An Essay*, 1978 U. Ill. L. F. 605; Bezanson, *The New Free Press Guarantee*, 63 Virginia L. Rev. 731 (1977).
120. *See, e.g.*, Philadelphia Newspapers Inc. v. Hepps, 106 S.Ct. 1558 (1986); Jacron Sales v. Sindorf, 350 A. 2d 688 (Md. 1976); Church of Scientology of Minnesota v. Minnesota State Medical Ass'n. Found., 264 N.W. 2d 152, 156 (Minn. 1978); Chase v. Daily Record, Inc., 515 P. 2d 154, 157 (Wash. 1973); Cianci v. New Times Pub. Co., 639 F. 2d 54, 59 (2d Cir. 1980); Meiners v. Moriarty, 563 F. 2d 343, 351 (7th Cir. 1977); Fitzgerald v. Penthouse Int'l, Ltd., 639 F. 2d 1076, 1079 (4th Cir. 1981). *See* notes 114–115 *supra* and accompanying text.
121. Philadelphia Newspapers Inc. v. Hepps, 106 S.Ct. 1558 (1986).
122. This, of course, is precisely what current public defamation law permits. Current law also permits imposition of liability on negligent publication, and imposition of punitive and presumed damages in the absence of a showing of actual malice or negligence, depending on the circumstances. *See* Gertz v. Robert Welch, Inc., 418 U.S. 323 (1974); Dun & Bradstreet v. Greenmoss Builders, Inc., 86 L.Ed. 2d 593 (1985).
123. Prior to *Hepps* this was true in defamation actions by virtue of the actual malice standard and the failure to require that the plaintiff bear the burden of proof on falsity. It is even clearer that such a result is constitutionally permissible in areas other than defamation. *See* Cox Broadcasting Co. v. Cohn, 420 U.S. 469, 489–90 (1975); Zacchini v. Scripps-Howard Broadcasting Co., 443 U.S. 562 (1977); New York Times Co. v. United States, 403 U.S. 713 (1971). Mr. Justice Brennan has suggested that mandated rights of reply or retraction would likely be constitutional. *See* Gertz v. Robert Welch, Inc., 418 U.S. 323, 330 n. 3 (1974) (Brennan, J., dissenting).
124. *See* Schaefer, *Defamation and the First Amendment*, 52 Colo. L. Rev. 1 (1980); Hulme, *Vindicating Reputation: An Alternative to Damages as a Remedy for Defamation*, 30 Am. U. L. Rev. 375 (1981); Note, *Vindication of the Reputation of a Public Official*, 80 Harv. L. Rev. 1730, 1739–47 (1967).
125. New York Times Co. v. Sullivan, 376 U.S. 254, 270 (1964).
126. *Id.*
127. *See* New York Times Co. v. Sullivan, 376 U.S. 254, 273 (1964); L. Levy, Judgments 146 (1972); L. Levy, Freedom of the Press (1984); Anderson, *The Historical Origins of the Press Clause*, 30 U.C.L.A. L. Rev. 455 (1983).

128. *See* New York Times Co. v. United States, 403 U.S. 713 (1971).

129. The concept of protected editorial judgment has been employed by the Supreme Court in many institutional speech settings. *See* New York Times Co. v. Sullivan, 376 U.S. 254 (1964); Miami Herald Pub. Co. v. Tornillo, 418 U.S. 241 (1974); Columbia Broadcasting System v. Democratic National Committee, 412 U.S. 94 (1973); Bezanson, Herbert v. Lando, *Editorial Judgment, and Freedom of the Press*, 1978 U. Ill. L. F. 605. The concept also seems to underlie the Court's decision in *Dun & Bradstreet, Inc. v. Greenmoss Builders, Inc.*, 86 L. Ed. 2d 593 (1985).

130. There is no doubt that libel litigation can be—and often is—prolonged, that substantial damage awards have been ordered, and that plaintiff claims for information during discovery are intrusive, although often necessarily so in light of the privilege hurdle that must be surmounted. *See* notes 105, 106 *supra*; Gertz v. Robert Welch, Inc., 680 F.2d 527 (7th Cir. 1982). On the other hand, the incidence of libel litigation is small, both in relation to civil litigation in general and, it seems, in relation to the number of media. *See* note 76, Chapter 6 *supra*. Likewise, the frequency of damage awards— much less large ones—is exceedingly rare. In our survey group, there were only 3 awards over $50,000, with the highest being $490,000. *See supra*, Chapter 7. The largest cost to media is the insurance premium, and these seem largely related to the cost of defending in litigation, rather than the cost of damage awards.

131. Ironically, while the legal system has moved toward libel criteria based upon standards of conduct by the press, the press has also been influenced by potential liability to minimize written standards for fear of their use in litigation. *See* Contemporary Studies Project, *Standards Governing the News*, 72 Iowa Law Review (1986); Chapter 4.

132. *See* Herbert v. Lando, 441 U.S. 153 (1979); Miller v. TransAmerican Press, Inc., 621 F.2d 721, *reh. denied*, 628 F.2d 932 (5th Cir. 1980); Downing v. Monitor Pub. Co., 120 N.H. 383, 415 A.2d 683 (1980).

133. *See* New York Times Co. v. United States, 403 U.S. 713 (1971); Nebraska Press Ass'n. v. Stuart, 427 U.S. 539 (1976); Near v. Minnesota, 283 U.S. 697 (1931).

134. New York Times Co. v. Sullivan, 376 U.S. 254 (1964).

135. *Id.*; Gertz v. Robert Welch, Inc., 418 U.S. 323, 340 (1974). For a thoughtful discussion of the value of false fact in the defamation context, as well as other settings, *see* M. Nimmer, Freedom of Speech § 3.03 (1984).

136. A. Bickel, The Morality of Consent (1975).

137. *See* Blasi, *The Checking Value in First Amendment Theory*, 1977 Am. B. Found. Res. J. 521; Stewart, *"Or of the Press,"* 26 Hastings L. J. 631 (1975); Van Alstyne, *The Hazards to the Press of Claiming a "Preferred Position,"* 28 Hastings L. J. 761 (1977); Bezanson, *The New Free Press Guarantee*, 63 Va. L. Rev. 731 (1977); Bezanson, Herbert v. Lando, *Editorial Judgment, and Freedom of the Press: An Essay*, 1978 U. Ill. L. F. 605.

138. 418 U.S. 241, 256 (1974).

139. *See* Bezanson, 1978 U. Ill. L. F. at 623–31.

140. *See* Abrams v. United States, 250 U.S. 616, 630 (Holmes, J., dissenting).

CHAPTER 9

1. Wisconsin Study, S–75, S–76.
2. *Id.*

INDEX